Sir Edward Reed

Japan 1879

Its history, traditions and religions

Sir Edward Reed

Japan 1879
Its history, traditions and religions

ISBN/EAN: 9783742840523

Manufactured in Europe, USA, Canada, Australia, Japa

Cover: Foto ©Andreas Hilbeck / pixelio.de

Manufactured and distributed by brebook publishing software
(www.brebook.com)

Sir Edward Reed

Japan 1879

THE TEMPLE OF MIYAJIMA, INLAND SEA.

Frontispiece to Vol. I.

JAPAN:

ITS HISTORY, TRADITIONS, AND RELIGIONS.

WITH THE

NARRATIVE OF A VISIT IN 1879.

BY SIR EDWARD J. REED, K.C.B., F.R.S., M.P.,

VICE-PRESIDENT OF THE INSTITUTION OF NAVAL ARCHITECTS;
MEMBER OF THE INSTITUTIONS OF CIVIL ENGINEERS AND MECHANICAL ENGINEERS;
KNIGHT OF THE IMPERIAL RUSSIAN ORDER OF ST. STANISLAUS, OF THE
AUSTRIAN ORDER OF FRANCIS JOSEPH, AND OF THE
TURKISH ORDER OF THE MEDJIDIÉ, ETC.

IN TWO VOLUMES.—VOL. I.

WITH MAP AND ILLUSTRATIONS.

LONDON:
JOHN MURRAY, ALBEMARLE STREET.
1880.

[The Right of Translation is reserved.]

LONDON:
PRINTED BY WILLIAM CLOWES AND SONS, LIMITED,
STAMFORD STREET AND CHARING CROSS.

PREFACE.

On arriving in Japan on the 10th of January 1879, in pursuance of an invitation which he had received and accepted from his Excellency Admiral Kawamura, the minister of marine, and from some of his colleagues, the author had no intention whatever of writing even a magazine account of his visit, much less of producing a volume upon Japan. He purposed addressing a letter or two to the leading journal upon such matters of interest as might present themselves, and for more than a month after his arrival in Tokio he formed no intention of doing more than this.

Early in March, however, on leaving the capital for the Inland Sea and the interior cities, it appeared desirable to take brief notes of the more interesting places and objects visited, and as these notes began to accumulate the author began to reflect upon the improbability of their ever becoming more than mere notes unless they were at once roughly developed into a narrative form during such leisure as could be secured. He soon decided to outline the story of his travels as he proceeded with them, and this was done, as far as possible, in the form in which that story here appears. The reader will be good enough to remember, in noting the crude familiarities and inequalities of style, and the many other defects which will doubtless be found in this book, that much of it was written during those alternations of excitement and weariness which attend rapid travelling in a strange land. Many and many a time, and day after day, during the journeys to Nara, the shrines of Isé, and the inland towns and cities, after rising before six in the morning, and travelling in *jinriki-shas* (hand-carriages) over jolting roads till the evening,* and then dining, the author had to find between 8 and 12 P.M. the only leisure which could possibly be obtained for recording his impressions of what he was seeing.

Another difficulty opposed itself to the author of this work. The cities, the towns, the battle-fields, the temples, the shrines, the castles, and the other memorable places visited, all were memorable because of persons, events, and incidents, which, if the author might judge of others by himself, were almost entirely unknown to English readers. What significance or interest, for example, would be conveyed to an English reader unacquainted with Japan and with its history by the mention of the personal names of Nintoku, Kobodaishi, Yoritomo, Nobunaga, or the Taiko ; or of the names of such places as Nara, Yamada, Uji, Kamakura, or even Nikko ; or of such events as the battles of Dan-no-ura or of Sekigahara, the revolts of Taka-Uji, or the siege of Odawara ? Even if all the existing books upon Japan ever published in England had been read, many such names would still have remained meaningless to the reader; but as it is, although so many books have been written upon Japan and upon Japanese affairs, the author knew of none which would have conveyed to English readers even a general idea of the early history of the country; certainly of none with which the public had become familiar. Hence he inferred that some account of the history of Japan was essential to the understanding of the records of his travels, and hence also the proportions to which this work has extended.

To write an outline of the history of Japan would have been an undertaking of some difficulty even to one conversant with the language and enjoying free access to the literature of the country; to one unacquainted with the language, and having access only to its translated literature,

---

* With brief intervals, of course, for luncheon and many tea-takings, after the fashion of the country.

the task was of necessity one of much greater difficulty. It appeared to the author, however, that the difficulties were not insuperable, especially as he had many unusual facilities for the work afforded him, and he trusts that the result, which appears in the following pages, will at least furnish the general reader with that information which the author himself would gladly have received from other hands had they applied themselves to the task.

It is obvious that the historical portions of this work must be mainly the results of compilation. Writers do not create history, but simply record it, the merit of their work consisting mainly in the fidelity of their statements, and in the judgment with which they are selected, grouped, and recorded. It is very desirable, however, that the reader should know on whose authority the records rest, and for this reason the author has been scrupulously careful to cite his authorities, and to give exact quotations where that could be done consistently with the immediate object in view. He has freely used the 'Transactions' of the Asiatic Society of Japan, which embody extremely valuable but of course detached masses of information, the principal contributors being, or having been, officers of the British Legation in Tokio, the chief of them all, estimated by the extent and value of his work, being Mr. Ernest Satow. The author has likewise made free use of the works composed by officers of the imperial Japanese government for presentation at the various foreign exhibitions of Japanese arts and manufactures, most notably that on Japanese Education which formed part of the exhibit of Japan at Philadelphia in 1876, and that published in France by his friend Mr. Matsugata, the vice-minister of finance, for use at the Exposition Universelle of 1878. Both of these (of which the latter is in French) are extremely valuable compilations of historic and other facts, and reflect great credit alike upon their authors and upon the administration of the public departments under the existing government of Japan. To the author and translator of the 'Kinsé Shiriaku' are elsewhere offered the acknowledgments so largely due. The author is much

indebted likewise to Mr. W. G. Aston, M A. (the assistant of
Mr. Ernest Satow at the British Legation, Tokio), whose
writings, especially those on the Japanese language, are
standard works. From Mr. Griffis's American work, entitled
'The Mikado's Empire,' have been made several quotations,
for which the author would express his best thanks. The
first perusal of this work created so favourable an impression upon the mind of the present author that another
work seemed almost unnecessary; but a further acquaintance
with the American volume tended to greatly weaken this
impression, partly on account of the book appearing in
considerable part to be composed of detached essays or
articles so brought together as to be wanting in historic
sequence, and partly, and still more, on account of insufficient
acknowledgment of the sources whence the work is derived.*
The key in which Mr. Griffis has pitched his work is likewise
somewhat too high for pleasant perusal in our country. But
notwithstanding these drawbacks, 'The Mikado's Empire' is
a highly interesting and instructive book, and one from
which the present author has, as will be seen, frequently
derived advantage. Since the author's return to England he
has received from Captain Pfoundes the 'Budget of Notes'
just referred to in a footnote, from which he has occasionally
taken interesting facts and illustration.

* I find, for example, that an ambitious passage of 'The Mikado's
Empire,' on the casting of Nitta's
sword into the sea, is taken without
acknowledgment, almost literally,
from a guide-book ('The Yokohama
Guide'), published three years before
—an appropriation so flagrant as to
be only excusable in any degree, and
in no degree justifiable, upon the
assumption that Mr. Griffis was himself the writer of the guide-book.
But even if that were so, it is most
inconvenient, and in a literary sense
wrong, for the passage to appear
without notice of quotation in two
such totally separate books. Since
reaching England, Capt. Pfoundes
has favoured the author with a copy
of parts of his 'Fu so Mimi Bukuro'
(or 'Budget of Japanese Notes'), re-
printed in 1875 from the Japan
Mail, and in this are several passages which appear in the text of
Mr. Griffis, published two years later,
with no acknowledgment that can be
traced except in an appendix, where
other passages are avowedly quoted
from Capt. Pfoundes's work. These
circumstances, however explained,
greatly detract from the merit and
value of Mr. Griffis's brilliant book
as an original work.

PREFACE.

The appearance since the author's return of Mr. Mounsey's able and engaging volume on the Satsuma rebellion has made it unnecessary for the present author to re-write the full story of that tragic revolt, or to do more with reference to it than briefly summarise the facts which Mr. Mounsey has so well recorded in detail.

For valuable notes upon the arts of Japan the author is much indebted to his friend Professor Anderson, of the Imperial Naval Medical College, Tokio;* for others, upon the language of the country, to Captain Brinkley, R.A., of that city, whose mastery of the Japanese tongue, both theoretical and practical, is said by those who are judges of the matter to be very great; and likewise to Mr. Hyde Clarke, whose valuable and suggestive notes upon Japanese ethnology and language are given in the text.

It affords the author much pleasure to acknowledge the aid which he has received from Mr. R. Stuart Lane, the accomplished English Secretary of the Japanese Legation in London, whose connection with that Legation has been, within the author's knowledge, of very marked value to both Governments. In Japan the author was much assisted by his learned friend Mr. Kondo Makoto, and by Mr. Murakami.

The thanks and acknowledgments of the author are most respectfully tendered, in the largest sense and in the highest degree, to His Imperial Majesty the Emperor of Japan, and to his ministers, for the opportunity the author had of visiting their country under the highest auspices, and for the uniform and unwearying kindness shown to him and to his son throughout a stay which lasted three months. Similar thanks and acknowledgments, differing only in degree, are due to many others in the country from whom great kindness and many valued presents were received, among whom should be mentioned the governors and vice-governors of the Kens passed through, the chief priests of the great Shinshu sections (eastern and western) of the Buddhist faith,

---

* The author is likewise indebted to Professor Anderson for the voluntary performance of a lengthened and troublesome surgical operation, in a manner which even the sufferer could not fail to admire.

and the leading native merchants of Osaka, Kioto, Nagoya, Tokio, and Yokohama.

The author would repeat here what he has elsewhere said, and express his conviction that the unbounded kindness shown to himself and son were due in no small degree to the fact that the Emperor, the ministers, and the people of Japan are heartily desirous of promoting friendly intercourse, courtesy, and good feeling with the Western nations, and with none so much as with ourselves. That their sentiments may be warmly and generously reciprocated by us, from our own gracious Queen and her ministers downwards, is the earnest desire of the author.

Most of the illustrations of this work have been engraved by that accomplished artist Mr. Josiah J. Whymper, chiefly from photographs, but in several instances from pencil sketches by the author's son, E. Tenn Reed. Eight of the full-page blocks were engraved in Japan, by native engravers, from the works of Hokusai.

A list of the Emperors of Japan, and of the year-periods, are given among the appendices at the end of the second volume.

E. J. R.

NOTE ON THE SPELLING AND PRONUNCIATION OF JAPANESE NAMES.

In translating Japanese words into English, the system usually followed by English scholars has been that of representing consonant-sounds by corresponding English consonants, and vowel-sounds by the vowels, taking their Italian pronunciation, as follows:—

A resembles the *a* in *father*, but is shorter.
E resembles the *ey* in *they*, but is shorter. In a syllable terminated by a consonant,* it is like *e* in *pen*.
I is like *i* in *machine*. In a syllable terminated by a consonant, it is like *i* in *pin*.
O is like *o* in *so*, or, before a terminatory consonant, like *o* in *on*.
U, as in *put*, or in *rural*.
Ai is like *ai* in our *aisle*.
Ae is properly *a-e*, but is often pronounced as *ai*.
Au is like *ow* in *cow*.

I have adopted the above system in the text of this work.

In studying Japanese it is necessary to carefully discriminate between short and long vowels, as the meaning often depends upon the difference, and they are consequently usually distinguished by marks or lines above them. Having to employ proper names only or mainly, I have myself taken little or no notice of these differences, for two reasons: first, because, while being undoubtedly troublesome to the general reader, these marks appear to me to furnish very imperfect

---

* In their 'English-Japanese Dictionary' (which with Mr. Aston's and other works I have consulted in preparing this Note) Mr. Satow and Mr. Masakata give the following footnote: "A single consonant in the body of a Japanese word belongs to the succeeding vowel, and forms with it a syllable, as in *tabeta*, etc. Here the *t* belongs to *a*, and consequently *be* is not said to be terminated by a consonant. When two consonants come together in the body of a word, the first belongs to the vowel which precedes it, as in *bekkó*, tortoise-shell. Here the first *k* belongs to *e*, and consequently *bek* is said to terminate by a consonant. Cases like *ten*, heaven, require no explanation."

indications of the true Japanese pronunciation of the words affected by them; and, secondly, because the whole system of rendering Japanese words into English is undergoing a great change, at least under the hands of some industrious English scholars in Japan: *au* is being written for the long *o*; *shiya* for *sha*; *chiyo* for *cho*; and so forth. Thus the title which I have written simply as *Shogun*, and which has usually been written *Shōgun* by the English in Japan, is now being written *Shiyaugun*, and *Kioto* as *Kiyauto*. It was obviously impossible for me to undertake to bring all the Japanese names which I have had occasion to employ into conformity with this new system, whatever may be its merits; and on the whole I have considered it best to adopt the simplest forms. By attending to the indications given in the earlier part of this note, the reader will have no difficulty in giving approximate pronunciations to the Japanese proper names, etc. The final *e* is generally more or less accented, but I have omitted the accent from it where the form of the word seemed sufficient of itself to suggest as much accentuation as is necessary.

CONTENTS.

(VOL. I.)

INTRODUCTION . . . . *Page* xxiii

CHAPTER I.

THE LAND AND ITS INHABITANTS.

Japan consists of four great, and many small, islands—Its nearness to Russia, China, and Korea—Its extent and area—The Kurile, Loo-choo, and Yaeyama islands—The mountains of Japan—Its harbours, rivers, and lakes—Its climate—The winters less rigorous than was anticipated; the hot season short—Effects of the *Kuro-shiwo*, or "black current," and of the *Oya-shiwo*, or "cold current"—The Japanese Mediterranean, or Inland Sea—This is shallow, and therefore variable in temperature—Dr. Rein's favourable description of the climate—Our own experiences of it—The geology of Japan—Volcanic disturbances—A summary record of its chief earthquakes—The god Daibutsu of Nara decapitated—The summit of the sacred mountain, Fuji, shaken in—The wreck of the frigate *Diana* by an earthquake—Typhoons—Dr. Maget's recommendation of Japan as a sanatarium—The measure of its heat and humidity—The origin of the Japanese people—Extraordinary ages of their god-ancestors—The first emperor's father, aged 836,042 years—Dr. Kaempfer's theory of a Japanese migration from Babel—The theory of an Aino origin—The Japanese a Tungusic race—Their route from Mantchuria, by Korea—The mixture of races—The men not usually of small stature—The women small but pleasing, and often beautiful in appearance—Defacing customs dying out—Improving condition of the people . . . . *Pages* 1-18

CHAPTER II.

THE GOD-PERIOD.

Japanese mythology abundant and varied—The sacred books *Kojiki* and *Nihonki*—Their origin and authorship—Their alleged errors—"In the beginning"—The Lord of the Centre of Heaven—The Lofty and

Divine Producers—The Japanese account of the Creation—The Male- and Female-who-Invite—The production of land and sea—Amaterasu, the sun-goddess—Origin of the Divine Insignia of the Imperial Power —Ninigi-no-mikoto, the "Sovran Grandchild"—His descent by the Floating Bridge of Heaven—The brother of the sun-goddess—His misbehaviour and its consequence—The winning of the sun-goddess from the cave—The origin of the religious symbols of Japan—Legends of the gods—The divine descent of the Mikados—Jimmu-Tenno, the first emperor—The Mikados themselves gods—Newer views—The old views said to be reconcilable with science . . *Pages* 19–38

CHAPTER III.

THE SHINTO RELIGION.

The early religion of the Japanese—Probably a natural and independent religious system—The *kami*, or gods of the country—The *Kami-no-michi*, "or way of the gods," must be learnt by studying the sacred writings—Its primal principle obedience to the god-Mikado—Good gods to be worshipped, and bad gods propitiated—Prayer of the Mikado —The worship of ancestors enjoined—Prayer to the god and goddess of wind—Other prayers—The gods of the sun and moon—The Rough Spirit and Gentle Spirit—The *kami-dana*, or Penates—The rituals of the Shinto religion—The harvest prayers and ceremonies—The divine descent of the priestly houses—Mr. Satow's translation of a very ancient ritual or *norito*—The necessity of distinguishing the ancient religion from its modern forms—Tendency of modern Japanese commentaries— Shinto a religious system in a true sense—Its influence upon the early Mikados—Their efforts at improvement, and devotion to their people —"Sujin the Civiliser"—The belief of the early Japanese in the help- fulness of their gods—Simplicity of their forms of worship—Shinto ceremonials contrasted with those of Buddhism and Roman Catholicism —The practice of purification—Respect for life—Simple demeanour of Shinto priests—Temples and votive offerings . . . 39–63

CHAPTER IV.

BUDDHISM IN JAPAN.

The primitive religions of India—Vedism—Brahmanism—Reactions against the doctrine of sacrifice—Shakyamuni Gautama, the founder of Buddhism—His life and teachings—The doctrine of Nirvāna—Extinc- tion or tranquillity ?—The Buddhistic use of idols—Spread of Buddhism —Curious analogies with Christianity—Buddhistic cosmogony—The elevated morality and purity of Buddhism—The doctrine of transmi- gration—Introduction of Buddhism to China, 250 B.C.—Its progress there, and spread to Korea—Its introduction thence into Japan—Its slow progress there—Its prince-patron, Shotoku Taishi—Story of his life—The first intercourse between Japan and China—Revival of Shinto under the Nara empresses—Subsequent revival of Buddhism—Its spread under the empress Shotoku—The temples of Hiyei-san—Kobo-daishi, the founder of the Shingon sect—Buddhism powerful in the state—Its priests resort to armed force—Later Buddhist sects in Japan—Shinran Shonin, the founder of Shin-shu—Its doctrines of salvation by faith in Amita Buddha—Original account thereof by a Shin-shu priest of Kioto—The Protestant Buddhists of Japan—Nichiren and his sect—The "Ranters of Buddhism"—Obstacles to the spread of Christianity in Japan—Kwannon, the goddess of a thousand hands—List of principal Buddhist sects—The influence of European civilisation upon them—A recent discourse on Infinite Vision, with a debate thereon . . . . *Pages* 64–99

CHAPTER V.

THE DESCENT OF THE CROWN.

The dynasty of Japan the oldest in the world—Commencement of the historic period—The first emperor, Jimmu—The Japanese year 1—Comparison of Christian and Japanese chronology—An interregnum—Descent of the crown by nomination—The successor of Jimmu-Tenno—A dozen successive emperors—The quasi-empress Jingu-Kogo—Her invasion of Korea—Ojin, the god of war—Generous contention of two brothers—Romantic suicide of one, and accession of the other to the throne—Nintoku, the self-denying emperor—His successors—Assassination of Anko-Tenno—Another generous contention of brothers—The consequent regency of their sister—Descent of the crown by election of the nobles—The system of concubinage—The rise of Buddhism—Its influence upon the occupancy of the throne—The first empress ascends the throne—Prince Shotoku-Taishi—His successor—Another empress, who abdicates, and after ten years resumes the crown—A plot frustrated, and an emperor slain—The thrones of Nara—A Twice-empress again—Attempt of a favourite priest to change the dynasty—The god consulted and the priest exiled—Assumption of the governing power by the Fujiwara regents—Dethronement of an emperor by a regent—Another attempt to subvert the dynasty—The "revolt of Shohei and Tenkei"—The "new emperor"—Other revolts—Numerous abdications of the throne—Troublous times—The power of the Taira family—Boy-emperors—The overthrow of the Taira—Four contemporary ex-emperors—Disputed successions—Alternate successions—The house of Hojo—An emperor exiled by a subject—Wars and troubles—The fall of the Hojo—The rise of the Ashikaga Shoguns—Taka-Uji—The dynasty divided—Northern and southern emperors—The alternate succession restored—The power of the Ashikagas—Further disputes—Orderly succession since the fifteenth century—Other empresses—The present emperor—The future succession   100–118

CHAPTER VI.

EARLY HISTORY, ENDING 1000 A.D.

The Japanese Pantheon—The first emperor, Jimmu, accepted as historic—His conquests and subsequent career—The emperor Sujin—Commencement of relations between Japan and Korea—Revolts in the west, east, and north—Yamato-Daké, "the Warlike"—His romantic career—Disguised as a dancing-girl he beguiles and slays the arch-rebel—The sacred sword "Grass-mower"— Yamato-Daké's wife offers herself to the sea god—Further relation with Korea—Naval architecture and navigation—Introduction of written characters and writing; and afterwards of Chinese literature—Simplicity of life of the early emperors—The influx of skilled persons from Korea and China—The emperor Tenji: administrator, inventor, and reformer—The offices of Dai-jo-Dai-jin and Nai-Dai-jin created—The reforming empress Jito: an advocate of "woman's rights"—Progress of education and art—The imperial residence becomes more settled—The city of Nara—The Nara empresses; the glory of their reigns—The founding of Miako, or Kioto—The "Château of Peace," a Château of Contention and War—Commencement of the struggles of the middle ages—The house of Fujiwara: its rise and eminence—The Sugawara family: its literary fame—Contests between Fujiwara-Tokihira and Sugawara Michisané—Exile and death of Michisané—His deification as the god Tenjin—The coming greatness of the Taira and Minamoto—A conspiracy discovered—The power of the Fujiwara culminates—The arts of peace still pursued . . . . *Pages* 119–136

CHAPTER VII.

THE TAIRA AND THE MINAMOTO—THE WARS OF THE RED AND WHITE FLAGS, 1000–1200 A.D.

The Taira red flag, and the Minamoto white flag—Indications of the struggles to come—Oppressive power of the Fujiwara house—Military tendencies of the Buddhists—Revolts of the Ainos—Yoshi-ye, afterwards Hachiman-Toro—Rising military power of the Taira and Minamoto—Their first contest at Kioto—The famous archer Tametomo—The great power of Taira-Kiyomori—A "cloistered emperor" immoral and conspiring—The Minamoto depress the Taira—The Taira revenge themselves: their ascendency—A conspiracy—The peasant girl Tokiwa becomes the mother of the renowned Yositsuné, the Bayard of Japan—His brother Yoritomo the founder of Kamakura—Yoritomo marries Masago, of the house of Hojo—Hatred of the Taira, and affection for the Minamoto—The city of Kamakura—Yoshinaka, the "Morning Sun General"—Overthrow and pursuit of the Taira: a prose epic thereon—Ascendency of the Minamoto—A review of the character and acts of Yoritomo—He becomes Sei-i-Shogun, "Barbarian Subjugating Great General"—His system of government—His royal court at Kamakura—His sceptre was his sword—Decay of his dynasty—His grave visited—What native historians say of him.

Pages 137–155

CHAPTER VIII.

THE HOJO DOMINATION.

Family struggles of the Minamoto and the Hojo—Masago imprisons her father—Efforts of the emperor Go-Toba to assert the imperial rights—Contest between the emperor and his minister—Two brothers become Mikado and Shogun—Good and patriotic services of the Hojo house—Invasion of Japan by the Mongol Tartars—Fall of the Hojo—Masashigé, or "Nanko," whose temple is at Hiogo—Undertakes to restore the emperor—Escape of the emperor from Oki—Nitta Yosisada—His desertion from the Hojo to the imperial cause—His military success—The eastern provinces support him—His attack upon Kamakura—His appeal to the god of the sea—His victory, and overthrow of the Hojo—Taka-Uji, the first of the Ashikagas—Restoration of the emperor Go-Daigo 156–166

CHAPTER IX.

THE SIMULTANEOUS DYNASTIES.

Ambition of successful generals—Distribution of confiscated fiefs unsatisfactory—Discontent of Ashikaga-Taka-Uji—His abrupt departure from the court—His letter of accusations against Nitta—His capture of, expulsion from, and efforts to regain Kioto—The emperor consults Kusunoki (Nanko)—His wise advice rejected—His memorable address to his son—The great battle of Minatogawa—Kusunoki commits *hara-kiri*—His fame as a patriot—His son Masatsura defeats Taka-Uji's general—His interview with the emperor—His gallant death—Taka-Uji again enters the capital—Retreat of the emperor—Enthronement of Komio—Two emperors and two courts—Kioto and Yoshino—The northern and southern dynasties—Defeat and heroic death of Nitta—Ashikaga-Taka-Uji reigns at Kamakura—He makes the Shogunate hereditary in his family—Diversified views of his character—The murder of Prince Morinaga—The wars of the rival dynasties—The southern emperors—The legitimate sovereigns . . 167–177

CHAPTER X.

THE ASHIKAGA SHOGUNS.

Supreme power of the Ashikagas—Rivalries and contests—Capture and recapture of Kamakura—Assassination of Mochi-Uji—Assassination of Shogun Yoshinori—The imperial insignia carried off—Their recovery—Terrible contests in Kioto in the fifteenth century—Rebellion of Katsumoto—Partisan contests—Two large armies meet in the capital—Flight of the court—The city fired—The Mikado taken to the palace of the Shogun—The war of brothers—The Shogun Yoshimasa—Progress of the arts—The Shogun Yoshitane imprisoned, restored, and again deposed—Further battles in Kioto—The introduction of muskets and cannon—Decline of the Ashikagas, and rise of Nobunaga—Disturbed state of the country in the sixteenth century—Nobunaga's victory in 1560 A.D.—He is commissioned by the emperor to pacificate the country—He overthrows the false Shogun—Appearance of Tokugawa Iyéyasu—The battle of Anagawa—Conspiracy and overthrow of the last Ashikaga Shogun—Review of the Ashikaga period . . . . *Pages* 178–187

CHAPTER XI.

NOBUNAGA AND HIDEYOSHI.

Ota Nobunaga the son of a warrior—He adopts his father's profession—Fuller display of his character—Return of the pursuits and pleasures of peace—Public acts of Nobunaga—He is made "Great Minister of the Right"—Hideyoshi, afterwards the Taiko—Originally a *betto*, or groom—Was patronised by Nobunaga—He becomes a great general—Takes rank with Iyéyasu—The three greatest generals of Japan—Buddhists and Christians—Nobunaga protects Christianity and attacks Buddhism—Padre Organtin's interview with Nobunaga—The Jesuit church, or "Temple of the Southern Savages"—Persecution of the Buddhists—Luxurious priests—Splendid rituals and unseemly lives—The gorgeous temples of Mount Hiyei destroyed—Butchery and conflagration—Fortified temple of the Shin Buddhists in Osaka—Its siege and ultimate surrender—Its priests scattered—Nobunaga, attacked by rebels, slays himself—The "Later Hojo" of Odawara—Hideyoshi appoints a child-successor to Nobunaga—Himself takes the real power—Defeat of Shibata—The "Seven Spearmen of Sedsagataké"—Romantic deaths—Shibata slays his wife by her desire—Fighting in the Kuanto—The later Hojo overthrown—Other rebels subdued—Hideyoshi declares war against Korea—Invades Korea and threatens China—Christians burnt at Nagasaki—The Jesuit priesthood—Ambition of Hideyoshi—He becomes the Taiko—His character reviewed—Anecdotes concerning him 188–203

CHAPTER XII.

IYÉYASU, THE FIRST TOKUGAWA SHOGUN.

The founder of the Tokugawa dynasty—His birth and native district—His castle in Suruga—He establishes himself in the Kuanto and founds

Yedo—He becomes sole regent—Governs well, and is conspired against—A western army brought against him—The famous battle of Sekigahara—Iyéyasu's victory—Is created Shogun in 1603—Revolt of Hideyori, a son of the Taiko—Osaka attacked and its castle besieged—Peace concluded—Second revolt of Hideyori—Osaka again attacked and carried—The fate of Hideyori—The Tokugawa family firmly seated in the Shogunate—Multiplication of Jesuit missionaries—The edict of expulsion against them—Apprehensions in Japan of foreign conquest—Consequent persecution of the Christians—The extirpation of Roman Catholicism from Japan attempted—The Spanish Inquisition imitated—Crucifixion, strangling, drowning, and worse—Revival of learning—Iyéyasu takes education and literature under his care—He takes control of the mines—Peaceful relations with Korea renewed—Foreign commerce encouraged—Public roads and highways improved—Death of Iyéyasu—His " Legacy "—His feudal system of administration—Daimios, Samurai, Hatamoto, and Gokenin—Yedo and its castle—Origin of the famous Tokugawa temples of Shiba, Tokio—Story of Son-o the priest . . . . . . *Pages* 204–223

CHAPTER XIII.

THE TOKUGAWA PERIOD (1603–1868).

Iyéyasu's successor, Hidetada—He sends a subject to Europe to study its religions—Decides against Roman Catholicism—Founding of the Wooyeno temples—Another empress reigns—Iyemitsu, the ablest of the Tokugawas—Foreign intercourse forbidden—The construction of sea-going vessels prohibited—The Christian revolt of Shimabara—Their castle seized and afterwards besieged and captured—Massacre of the Christians—An army of " martyrs "—The fatal rock of Pappenberg—" Christ " becomes a name of terror throughout Japan—Evil effects of foreign intercourse—Home enterprise of Shogun Iyemitsu—A prince-priest at Nikko—The emperor Go-Komio—Yedo ravaged by fire—Shogun Iyetsuna—His encouragement of literature—Maritime commerce of the country—A literary Shogun (Tsunayoshi)—His lectures at his court—The Dutch traveller Kaempfer—Tsunayoshi's defective finance—Changes in the coinage—Suppression of smuggling—A scientific Shogun (Yoshimune)—The observatory of Kanda—The calendar reformed—Prosperity of the country in the eighteenth century—The " Rice Shogun "—A census taken in 1744—Art and industry developed—Spread of public instruction—Russian demands upon Japan—Attack upon a garrison in Yezo—Spread of the Dutch language—Decline of the Tokugawa power—The long peace engenders luxury and decay—Violent opposition to foreign intercourse—Review of the Tokugawa period—List of the Tokugawa Shoguns . . 224–240

CHAPTER XIV.

THE REVIVAL OF THE IMPERIAL POWER.

Long-standing grievances of the princes of Choshiu and Satsuma—Their projects for restoring power to the emperor—Literary influences of like nature—American demands for commercial intercourse—Defensive preparations—Commodore Perry presses the American demands—Russian demands—Renewed visit of Commodore Perry—The Shogun yields—The imperial court resists—Arrival of the English—An English treaty—The tremendous earthquakes of 1855—Wreck of the *Diana*—Further defensive preparations—The Shogun resolves to abolish the law against foreign intercourse—Continued resistance of the court—The Daimio Ii created chief minister of the Shogun—He concludes treaties with foreign governments—Death of the Shogun—The "Swaggering Prime Minister" is murdered—Agitation for the expulsion of foreigners—Despatch of Japanese envoys to Europe—The Mikado orders the Shogun to court—The emperor again free to assert his power.
Pages 241-262

CHAPTER XV.

THE FALL OF THE SHOGUN.

The Mikado commands the Shogun to expel the "barbarian"—The Ashikaga images beheaded and pilloried—A day fixed for the expulsion—Assassination of Mr. Richardson—The English revenges—Bombardment of Kagoshima—Indemnities paid—The closing of the ports urged—Choshiu fires upon foreign ships—Bombardment of Shimonoséki—Internal difficulties of the country—Dismissal of the Choshiu clan from Kioto—Rebellion of the *ronins*—Choshiu attacks a Satsuma ship—Troubles in the north—Fighting in Kioto—Return and disgrace of the envoys to Europe—Hostile parties—Choshiu repels the attacks of the Shogun's forces—Death of the Shogun—The foreign squadrons go to Hiogo—The Mikado yields and approves the treaties—Reconciliation of Choshiu and Satsuma—The last Shogun, Keiki—Death of the Mikado—Abdication of Keiki 263-275

CHAPTER XVI.

THE IMPERIAL RESTORATION COMPLETED.

Shogun Keiki attempts to regain his power—He marches to Osaka—Goes with armed forces towards Kioto—The battles of Fushimi—Victory of the imperial troops—Honours granted to Choshiu and Satsuma—The foreign representatives received by the "Heaven-King"—The emperor's oath to further representative government—The ex-Shogun submits—His friends remain in rebellion—The warfare with the rebels—Preservation of the Nikko shrines—Fighting at Wooyeno, in Kioto—Destruction of the Tokugawa temples—The *Shogitai* and the "Shreds of Brocade"—Further military contests—The victories of Generals Yamagata and Kuroda—The "Wicked Party" and the "Righteous Party"—The Okubo memorandum—Reforms of the new empire—Suppression of the naval revolt—Admiral Enomoto—Rewards to the victors . . . . Pages 276–287

CHAPTER XVII.

FOREIGN RELATIONS OF JAPAN.

The early foreign relations of Japan with Korea and China—Attempted invasion of Japan—The Armada of the Mongol Tartars—Naval battles—Bravery of the Japanese—A miraculous storm aids them—Total destruction of the invaders—An ex-Shogun accepts from China the title "King of Japan"—Indignation of his countrymen—Beginning of intercourse with Portugal, Spain, England, and Holland—Foreign jealousies and treacheries—The Jesuit missionaries—They attack the Buddhist priests—Consequent reaction against Christianity—Fears of foreign invasion and domination—Interdict against the "Kirishitan" religion—An extraordinary proclamation—Japanese views of our religion—Other edicts against Christianity—Persecutions—Hideyoshi's invasion of Korea—Capture of the capital—Korea overrun—A singular parley—China helps Korea—The army of Japan triumphant—Its navy sustains a defeat—Japan contends for six years against both Korea and China—Withdraws on the death of Hideyoshi—The Island-kingdom of Loo-choo—Japan's recent war against Formosa—Her recent relation with Korea and China—Disputes with Russia—Surrender to Russia of Saghalin—Acquisition of the Kuriles and of the Bonin Islands.
288–318

CHAPTER XVIII.

THE REFORMS OF THE LAST TEN YEARS.

Surrender of the principalities—Abrogation of the clan system—Division of the country into Fu, Ken, and Han—A new army created—An imperial navy established—Japanese commercial steamships—The police force—Revision of the laws—The codes of 1871 and 1873—Repeal of barbarous laws—Abolition of torture—The central convict establishment—Gold and silver equally esteemed formerly—A new monetary system—A national paper currency—Diminished gold reserves—The *yen*, or dollar—The Japanese "trade dollar"—New postal system—Land telegraphs—Improved educational system—The university of Tokio—Despatch of students abroad—An education department created—Female schools—Interest taken by the emperor and empress in education—The Tokio female normal school—Other reforms and improvements . . . . . Pages 319–331

CHAPTER XIX.

THE SATSUMA REBELLION.

Mr. Mounsey's book—Seething state of Japan politically in the early days of the new empire—Saigo of Satsuma—The Shimadzu family—Shimadzu Saburo again—Saigo's hatred of the Tokugawas—Romantic story of Saigo and the priest Gassho—Recall of Saigo to Satsuma—Dissatisfaction of Saburo—An embassy sent to Kagoshima—Supposed political manifesto of Saigo — He takes office in Tokio—Becomes commander-in-chief—Takes offence and withdraws to his province — Saburo remonstrates with the imperial government—Satsuma remains independent—Its *samurai* disaffected — The first outbreak crushed—The removal of stores and arms from Kagoshima resisted—Admiral Kawamura's mission of peace—The rebel army constituted—Prince Arisugawa appointed to the chief command of the imperial forces—Investment of the castle of Kumamoto—Repeated contests—Kiushiu placed under martial law—Admiral Kawamura's attempted mediation—The rebels driven into Hiuga—Their repeated efforts to capture Kagoshima—They are forced into the open—Surrounded—Escape of Saigo—He captures Kagoshima—Is forced to withdraw—The lions in the lair—Taken in the imperial toils—The death and burial of Saigo—A speech by the emperor . 332–348

CHAPTER XX.

THE EMPEROR AND THE EXISTING GOVERNMENT.

The reigning emperor—The distracted empire to which he succeeded—His suppression of successive rebellions—Simplicity of his court—Reception by his majesty—The troubles of his reign—Its peaceful triumphs—The constitutional objects of the emperor—The new form of government—List of the cabinet—The prime minister Sanjo—The vice-minister Iwakura—Attack upon his life—Mr. Terashimi, late foreign minister—Mr. Ito, the home minister—Mr. Okuma, the finance minister—His financial reforms—A Japanese Gladstone—General Saigo, minister at war—Admiral Kawamura, minister of marine—Enouye Kawori, the new foreign minister—Attack upon him—His mission to Korea—Oki Takato, minister of justice—The conduct of business in Japan—General Kuroda Kiyotaku, the minister of agriculture and the colonies—His administration of Yezo—The senate—Progress of free institutions.
349–365

LIST OF ILLUSTRATIONS.

(VOL. I.)

Full-Page Engravings.

		PAGE
THE TEMPLE OF MIYAJIMA, INLAND SEA . . *Frontispiece.*		
THE GODDESS UZUMÉ . . . . . . *Facing*		34
A BUDDHIST "NIO," OR TEMPLE GUARD . . . "		92
KUSUNOKI MASASHIGÉ . . . . . . "		172
A COUNTRY SCENE . . . . "		235
COOLIES QUARRELLING . . . . . . "		272
A BRIDGE AT KINTAI, PROVINCE OF SUWO . . . "		336
TWO WARRIORS, RETAINERS OF YORITOMO . . . "		348

Minor Engravings.

IMAGE OF SEKI-SAN	xxii
OUR FIRST VIEW OF JAPAN	18
THE SACRED SHRINES OF ISÉ	38
A SHINTO PRIEST	63
THE EMPEROR'S COAT-OF-ARMS	118
ANCIENT STYLE OF JAPANESE ARCHITECTURE (A SHINTO SHRINE AT YOSHIDA, KIOTO)	136
GRAVE OF YORITOMO AT KAMAKURA	155
SIX-SIDED TEMPLE OF KIOTO	166
KOREAN DOGS	177
TENTO: HEAVENLY LANTERN	187
A BUDDHIST PRIEST	203
MIKADO'S PALACE, KIOTO	223
CUTTING RICE	262
HANDWRITING OF THE EMPEROR AT NARA . . .	275
FARM IMPLEMENTS	287
STONE IDOL OF RENRETZU	318
IMAGE OF KUYA SHONIN	331

Map.

JAPAN . . . . *Facing* 1

IMAGE OF SEKI-SAN.

INTRODUCTION.

The form which this work has assumed has been accounted for in the Preface, where it has been shown that the historical portion was an essential preliminary to the narrative of our visit. Never perhaps was it more necessary than in the present case to pass the past of a country under review before undertaking either to describe its present or to consider its future.

It was not upon a wild, barbarous, and untutored people that the fleets of America and Europe broke with menace and violence a few years ago, but upon an unique nation, which had developed within itself arts, letters, and religions in large part unknown elsewhere, and which now present to the scholar and the philosopher many novel and intensely interesting fields for research. Notwithstanding some adverse events, it is we English who are most earnestly invited to concern ourselves with this wonderful country, and to concern ourselves with it, not merely as traders and seafarers, but as men of intelligence and of progress, able to bear the banners of science and faith into the midst of a people in every way qualified to hail them with welcome, and to bring beneath them forces and ambitions not less worthy than our own.

Happily the time is fast fleeting away, if it be not already gone, when differences of language, of social usage, and of religion debar nations from establishing common interests and sympathies with each other. The large and liberating influence which Christianity has exerted upon Western peoples is eluding the narrow purposes, and still narrower forms, of its own priests and professors, and is spreading throughout mankind, giving force and efficacy to the words spoken at Athens by its greatest apostle, " God hath made of one blood all nations of men to dwell on all the face of the earth." Some of the greatest minds of the present age not only venture but delight to trace elements which we esteem as excellent among peoples who not long ago would have been spurned by us as uncivilised, idolatrous, and worthless. The growth of knowledge has helped in no small degree to bring about this noble development of modern times; and of all knowledge, that which, perhaps, has most contributed to the result has come out of our researches into the origin of races, languages, and religions. Worthiest of the labourers in this rich and fruitful field has been Professor Max Müller, who, better than any one, has shown us by what ancient and inseverable bonds the nations of mankind are bound together.

To this region of investigation Japan is manifestly destined to make many valuable contributions. Thus far she has lain almost entirely outside of it, her race, religion, and language having been but rarely studied, save by those members of our own and of other foreign legations resident there who have had leisure and faculty for the task. In the body of this work I have noted the principal results, in so far as Japan is concerned, of such investigations up to the present time, but I cannot refrain from adverting briefly here to the extraordinary conditions presented by her.

So completely is the language of Japan isolated from all others that it has remained without a place even in the fullest collections of languages of which the genealogy has been traced.* There are, it is true, some who speak with confidence as to its origin; but even those who have boldly classed it with the Tungusic branch of the Turanian tongues have done so because of its forms and characteristics, and not from any positive and considerable identification of its words. In the last-named respect it appears to have stood alone, or classed only with its own descendant, the Loo-chooan

---

* For example, in Max Müller's tables. See vol. ii. p. 52.

tongue. But this state of things is not destined to last much longer; and just as some scholars have traced in the Polynesian and also in the South African languages intimate relations with the Aryan groups, so others are beginning to identify Japanese with African roots, and to trace a close family connection between the Japanese and other tongues. The most notable example of this is to be found in the researches of Mr. Hyde Clarke, who has been good enough to furnish me with a brief statement of the results to which he has been led, and with a comparative table of word-roots common to the Japanese, the West African, and some other tongues. Strange as such relationships of language may seem, they are not more strange in the present than in other cases which may now be said to have been taken within the boundaries of settled science; such, for example, as the accepted relationship between the modern dialects of India and the ancient dialects of Greece, as equally belonging to the Aryan family.

It appears to me that by the study of the Japanese language, and the efforts made to reconnect it with dispersed branches of the same family, larger and higher objects than any yet attained by comparative philologists are being furthered. There are many scattered indications, already visible in philological works, of remote relations between the great groups of languages which philosophers are for the most part at present content to treat as wholly separate and independent, viz. the Aryan, the Semitic, and the Turanian groups.* The theory that the Chinese language has remote relations with the Aryan has been put forward; Mr. Aston has pointed out similar relations between some Japanese and Aryan roots; and Mr. Hyde Clarke's investigations point significantly to a pre-Aryan tongue, spoken in an ancient Turano-African empire, the dissolution of which changed the condition of mankind.

---

* In this paragraph I am not unmindful of the fact that some of the greatest comparative philologists have more or less clearly written of the convergence of these three great streams of language towards a common source.

From these identifications and relations of language, more surely than from any other source, may be expected to follow the solution of the question of race in Japan. It is doubtless a grave error to readily infer identity of race from identity of language, for languages often become more or less common to persons, and even to nations, differing greatly in race; but if it be allowable to infer from philological discoveries alone that "the ancestors of the Homeric poets and of the poets of the Veda must have lived together as members of one and the same race, as speakers of one and the same idiom," it cannot be futile to anticipate that we shall succeed in determining from what race or races the Japanese have sprung, when we have settled the question of their speech. If, for example, a foundation for the comparative philology of their language be truly laid in Mr. Hyde Clarke's results, we shall have fixed the place of their ancestors among the pre-historic nations, and shall have already before us the elements for investigating their origin and primeval history. Any occupation of the Nipon (Japan) group of islands by populations coeval with the Babylonians and Etruscans must have existed very long ago, and it would be from that very ancient date that the language has descended. In the long period of its descent there must have been many vicissitudes, tending to greatly modify the Japanese people, and for this reason their actual descent would still have to be traced with caution. For example, white conquerors may have intermarried with the women of a short race, and after a time the white male immigrants may have been cut off. But whatever modifications may have happened, it cannot be doubted that great light would be thrown upon the origin of the Japanese if it should be established that the language of Japan has proceeded from the same source as that of the Ashantees and other tribes of Western Africa; the more so as the latter are thought to have had the same origin as the tribes which organised the early American civilisation, and constructed the monuments of Mexico and Peru.

The same lines of study will doubtless tend to the elucidation in some degree of the origin of the ancient and mysterious religion of Japan, known as Shinto. Its most remarkable feature perhaps, is the inclusion among its gods, or *kami*, not only of the sun, moon, stars, and other sublime natural objects, but also of rivers, trees, plants, animals, and of all things which possess any eminent or extraordinary character. It would not be right to infer from this, without reference to other considerations, that we are here in contact with the remains of a primeval religion, of a comparatively low form, for it is never possible to say with certainty how far such ideas are the consequences of ascent or of descent from a previous state. Or, as the case has been put, "some worship everything, while others worship nothing, and who shall say which of the two is the more truly religious?" Moreover, what is known as Fetishism is rejected as a primitive form of religion by our best thinkers; and reverence for the forms and forces and creatures of nature is best accounted for upon the principle that however vaguely, however crudely, yet somehow, these things are respected because of the power, or the good, or the beauty, as the case may be, which they appear to embody, and are so far taken as manifestations of the All-Powerful, the All-Good, or the All-Beautiful, whom the greatest and best of us can but vaguely and crudely comprehend. Still, the retention, in the religion of a people so highly cultivated as the Japanese for centuries past have been, of this worship of multitudinous objects of nature, is a most remarkable circumstance, and may materially assist in the discovery of the origin of their faith. It appears to plainly indicate the existence of a strong *religious* element in the Japanese, as separate from, and partly in contrast with, their mythological doctrines. Nor is this distinction of little importance, for while it is easy to conceive of the essence of a religion becoming so obscured by mythological extravagances as to lose all healthful influence, it is scarcely possible to conceive of the worship of nature, in any form, destroying all reverence and awe in man for the powers there manifested, and beyond this it is needless to carry the idea of religion in this connection.

It is possible that some who read my description of the ancient religion of the country, and of its curious mythology, may be disposed to draw inferences adverse to the intelligence of the Japanese. But history forbids this error. Who that remembers ancient Greece can commit it? What did not Athens do for literature, for eloquence, for art, for science, for moral freedom? Yet what a system of religion and what sort of deities were hers! Besides the many acts of his gods that are unmentionable, the Grecian father had to recount to his sons, when giving them religious instruction, such deeds as that of Apollo flaying Marsyas alive, Neptune insisting on the exposure of Andromeda to a sea-monster, Kronos swallowing his children, and so forth. Nor were these deeds to the young Greek the fables they have become to the boys of Eton and Harrow; they were to him the solemn acts of the divinities whom he worshipped. An allegorical interpretation of them, even when it could be found, was not allowed. For casting doubts upon their real existence Anaxagoras was exiled, and Socrates put to death. But in spite of such monstrous myths and legends, Demosthenes composed his splendid orations, Plato penned his profound dialogues, and Phidias carved his immortal sculptures. The mythology of Japan is much less repulsive than that of Greece, and it will be seen in the following chapters that, to say the least, there has been nothing in the operation of the Shinto faith that has made against good works. I have displayed in the history of its early Mikados, whose only religion was Shinto, lives and works in the main worthy of any Christian king or emperor. It would be idle, of course, to seek in ancient Japan for such intellectual greatness as that which exalted ancient Greece above the nations; but it would be equally idle to infer from its mythological vagaries any general intellectual inferiority. The example of Greece has demonstrated once and for ever the independence of the intellect, and its power of coexisting with the most extravagant of all mythological beliefs.

In the chapter on the God-period, and in later chapters, I have set forth some of the many legends to be found in the ancient records of Japan, and have stated in outline much of that which I have been able to trace of the rituals and modes of worship. It is possible that from these, and from the fuller accounts which are sure to follow from the labours of the English and German scholars now in Japan, men capable of pursuing the task may hope to ascertain from what origins, and in what manner, these Japanese myths came into existence. Those whose learning qualifies them for the work may be able in some degree to identify them with the myths of other nations and races, or to trace them back to either historical events or natural phenomena. A more pleasing task it would be difficult to find for those who enjoy the necessary capability and leisure. In the grand conception of the Great First Cause, the solitary Lord of the Centre of Heaven; in the silent entrance upon the scene of the Divine and Lofty Producers, and the production by them of the undefinable substance out of which creation slowly emerged; in the appearance of Izanagi and Izanami, the Male- and the Female-who-Invite, and the generation of the solid lands by the means of rotatory motion in the fluid mass of matter; in the dazzling legends of Amaterasu, the sun-goddess, who was won from her cave of darkness by the powers of eloquence, song, music, and dancing; in the wild and joyous chanting of the goddess Uzumé amidst the laughter of the surrounding gods, and in many other such legends of the deities of Japan, future scholars may trace the story of the universe with as much joyous ardour as Ruskin has manifested in deciphering from the mythic tales of Greece the powers and fascinations of the blue-eyed Athena, the "Queen of the Air."

There is one characteristic of the Shinto faith, and as a consequence one marked feature of Japanese history, which is well worthy of special note. I mean the reverence, carried to the lengths of deification and worship, of great or heroic ancestors. The worship of the mythologic deities has, it is true, been perpetuated with an admirable loyalty, and down to the present hour the pilgrims wearily toil over plains and mountains to bow for a moment at the shrine of the Divine

Mirror of Uji, or of the Sacred Sword of Miya; but the worship of ancestors is the great humanising element of the Shinto religion. And surely the reverent recognition of worth in others, and especially the lasting memory of those who have worthily lived or died in the service of their country, even when pushed to an excess, must command somewhat of our admiration. It was by an oversight that the great and gentle Buddha became a canonised saint of the Church of Rome; but the Japanese are not at all exclusive in their respect for the dead, failing at times rather on the side of deifying eminent personages without sufficient regard to the nature of their claims to eminence. This, however, is an error which Mr. Carlyle, at least, will forgive, and which most of us will be ready to extenuate.

The Buddhist religion has played so large a part in Japanese history for thirteen centuries, and came so much into contact with the Christianity conveyed there in the sixteenth century; it has, moreover, developed in Japan such exceptional forms and doctrines, that I have not hesitated to trace pretty fully its rise and progress there. I have taken pains to set forth also, for the convenience of the general reader, the origin and character of this religion, which the Christian nations are beginning to treat with respect and appreciation, owing to the many striking analogies that it undoubtedly bears to Christianity. It is unnecessary in this place to enlarge upon the subject, but it seems desirable to say that, however pure and elevating may be the abstract doctrines of Buddhism, the practice of some of the Buddhist sects is neither more nor less, to all appearance, than gross idolatry and superstition. This is not, however, true of all the sects of Buddhism, and there is ample room among them for the discrimination of the philosopher, the scholar, and the Christian.

> "Higher than Indra's ye may lift your lot,
> And sink it lower than the worm or gnat;
> The end of many myriad lives is this,
> The end of myriads that."

But the great interest in Japan which the majority of my

readers will feel will doubtless have relation to its political and international prospects. This is a subject of so much delicacy that in the body of this work I have avoided it almost entirely, giving but slight and occasional intimations of the views and feelings which my visit to the country suggested. I have as much as possible refrained from references to existing political questions, or to the results to be anticipated from their possible solutions. Such considerations would almost necessarily have led to personalities, which would have been out of place alike in the historic and in the narrative parts of the book. At the same time any work purporting to give a fair picture of Dai Nippon would be markedly incomplete if no allusion were made to the political position and aspirations of the country as regards its foreign relations, and it is in this Introduction that these matters can perhaps be best discussed. The sudden opening up of intercourse with other nations, and the extraordinary changes thus produced, have given to International questions a pre-eminence in Japan above all others. The effect of foreign influence is so manifest in every direction that it is apt to be exaggerated. Every change, whether good or bad, is traced to the action of foreigners; and as in all such cases those who complain are louder than those who praise, the predominant cry is that foreign trade and foreign ideas are ruining the country. The thinking classes are of a different opinion, and recognise the benefit conferred, while they deplore the injury which in many instances has accompanied it. Consequently, on the one hand, one hears that the foreigners have drained the country of gold and infected it with vice; and on the other, that against the impoverishment of the nation and other evils should be set the incalculable gain of Western civilisation. But there is one thing about which all classes agree—the Optimists as well as the Pessimists, the Conservative *samurai* equally with the republican student—viz., that the diplomacy of the European powers has been seriously detrimental to the true interests of Japan. It is accused of having enforced one-sided treaties, and of having fostered one-sided trade. This, if true, is not as it should be. Diplomatic action which only averts hostilities without engendering international good feeling but half fulfils its mission. If we may judge by the openly expressed sentiments of the Japanese, England is the greatest sinner in this particular. We are, justly or unjustly, accused of having headed the opposition to the progress of Japan; of having objected when we ought to have approved; and of having induced other nations to take the same line. In comparison, the Americans and the Russians are spoken of with affectionate esteem. It is we who are said to have delayed the revision of the treaties; to have objected to the laws of Japan having reasonable application to foreigners; to have attempted to force on the country an illegitimate trade in opium; to have objected to the closing of the foreign post offices, and to have secretly fomented the difficulties with China on the Loo-choo question. The members of the Japanese cabinet are not, so far as I know, the authors of these complaints; to me, at least, they were exceedingly reticent on all such matters, exhibiting a delicacy of sentiment in this respect which we can only admire. It is in no sense as their mouthpiece, therefore, that I am here speaking. I am recording what I often heard from others upon whom neither the etiquette of office nor personal feeling imposed the restraints which ministers of state must necessarily and naturally feel. The views that I have recited above are nevertheless the views of well-informed persons, and were corroborated by such of the ministers as I could induce to speak upon the subject.

It was in vain that I was profuse in assurances as to the good feeling which existed in England towards Japan. It was admitted that this might be true as regards the people, and also as regards the Queen, the Government, and the Foreign Office; but I was told that the action of our legation in Tokio must be taken as the real test of sincerity, and that, so judged, there could be no doubt that we opposed Japanese views and wishes on most occasions, often with bare civility, and generally on unsustainable grounds. As this was openly said to me, I judged that stronger language was used behind my back. What then are the true reasons for this evident pain and hostility? Are there any real grounds for them, and what are the views seriously entertained by the leading Japanese as to their international relations? Many favourable opportunities for inquiring into these and kindred questions were afforded me, and I believe that I may be doing a lasting good to both sides by repeating the result of my investigations.

The main aspiration of the Japanese is for their country to be treated by the other powers on terms of absolute equality—to have its so called sovereign rights fully recognised, and its liberty of action entirely unfettered. To this sentiment everything is made subservient; it is the form which the modern patriotism of the nation has assumed. To carry it out, temporary advantages would gladly be waived; more than that, serious disadvantages would be submitted to. And we cannot but admire this feeling, even when we recognise that among European nations the object sought is really but a shadow and a form. What are the sovereign rights of a country but an antiquated fiction, an unchallenged theory—a principle of international law everywhere overriden by national necessities? In the Old World the assertion of perfect equality among sovereign states is so indisputably admitted, and so universally ignored, that it is never alluded to except to round off a sentence in a despatch, or to assist the loud-sounding peroration of a speech. But in Japan it is very different; it is there the echo of a feeling which has bound the nation in undeviating loyalty to its Mikados for twenty centuries; it is the keynote of any sympathetic union with other countries. On terms of equality Japan is ready and desirous to join heartily the concert of civilised countries; on any other conditions it will always regret the loss of its past isolation.

It is important to bear this pardonable aspiration in mind in connection with all the external relations of Japan; and if diplomatists would more willingly recognise it, their tasks would be much easier. Japan is not, as I have said, a country of yesterday, though so recently known to us. Its civilisation, though so different from our own, long preceded it, and in some essential particulars still remains superior to it. In courteous demeanour, in cleanliness, in education, the ordinary Japanese peasant far excels the artisan of the Black Country, the tenant of the Irish shanty, or the Russian moujik : while the acquaintance of the native officials with jurisprudence, political economy, the science of government, and international law will, on an average, favourably compare with that of the Europeans with whom they are thrown into contact. But I fear it must be acknowledged that all this is unknown or systematically ignored by us. Treatment against which the smallest South American republic would rebel has been considered proper in the case of Japan, and complaints have been met by replies which have been sometimes ridiculous and sometimes insulting. 'Stet pro ratione voluntas' has been, and still is, the principle of action adopted by foreign powers, usually and honourably excepting the United States of America. It would be a great mistake to suppose that this line of conduct is not correctly appreciated. The Japanese officials smile—they cannot help being courteous; but they are not deceived, and they only bide their time. They are thoroughly well informed as to their rights. They obtain the minutest information from Europe on all important questions. Able foreign advisers are attached to most of their legations, and in case of doubt the opinions of the best jurists are unhesitatingly taken. I have reason to believe that if their diplomatic correspondence were made public, it would be found wanting neither in dignity nor in accuracy, and would show that justice has been grudgingly accorded to them after tedious refusals and disrespectful delays. Concessions which could not longer be denied have been accompanied by conditions which robbed them of half their beneficial effect. In short, I fear it must with regret be acknowledged that the external relations of foreign countries with Japan have been but little supervised in Europe, but have been too often left to the administration of autocrats, undistinguished by the courtesies, and undisturbed by the opinions, of the countries they represent.

But fortunately in every sense this state of things is not likely to continue. The *solidarité*, which at first was almost a necessity in the policy of the Treaty Powers, has been broken up, and special interests and views have from time to time asserted themselves. This is a healthier state of things. A combination of many countries against one was sure to lead to abuses, or to appear to do so. At any rate, it was certain to be galling. The British minister for the time being has naturally been the centre of this foreign combination, and has thus probably had more than a just proportion of obloquy attached to him. When, however, the United States was found to have divergent views on some questions, the Japanese were not slow to take advantage of the opportunity, and for some time both that country and Russia have been played off against the rest. France, Germany, and Italy still apparently follow the initiation of England, and address identical notes to the Gaimusho; but diplomatic *solidarité* no longer exists in its old sense, and every successive change among the foreign ministers will still further destroy it. At the present time, however, the questions of Japanese policy in connection with foreigners need only be considered as they affect the United States, and the group inspired by and acting with England, Russia apparently holding aloof with a keen eye to eventualities. The points at issue may be conveniently grouped under two heads:—

1. Those which refer to such mutual obligations of Japan and other countries as are not specially defined by treaties.

2. Those which are defined in treaties, and which it is proposed to amend now or at some future time.

Under the first head appear the various difficulties which have arisen in connection with Japanese laws and regulations sought to be made binding on foreigners, as regards the shooting and preservation of game, the postal administration, the enforcement of quarantine and sanitary measures, the payment of taxes, the general coasting trade, the right to arrest foreign misdemeanants and criminals, the opening of the interior, etc. It is not now necessary, nor would it be interesting, to examine separately into each of these questions. Some have already been settled or compromised, but all of them are more or less affected by the same arguments. The Japanese maintain that all foreigners residing in Japan are subject to the *lex loci* in the same way that they themselves would be if voluntarily, for the sake of trade or pleasure, they visited other countries; that it is absurd to suppose that each nationality can carry about with it a particular code of laws, some of which are necessarily not applicable to all countries, while more or less different in form from each other; that the right of consular *jurisdiction* accorded by treaty does not confer the right of consular *legislation*, and that Japanese police can only properly take cognisance of Japanese laws. On the other hand, the British and other European representatives urge that the exceptional state of affairs in Japan requires exceptional treatment; that it would not be wise or safe to recognise the applicability of Japanese laws to foreigners; that the fact defined by treaty that their subjects are to be judged by European courts implies that such courts are to recognise only their own laws; that Japanese laws or regulations might be contrary to European notions of justice, and that punishments for their infractions might not exist.

The Americans some time back conceded the justice of the above-named demands of Japan, and their consuls were ordered to enforce all Japanese regulations with proper strictness. The Russians apparently took up the same attitude, and to show their desire to accord equal rights, actually consented to the exercise of consular jurisdiction by the Japanese authorities in Russia.

Much no doubt may be advanced on both sides, but the Japanese have always ready one argument which it seems difficult to meet. They say that foreigners come to their country voluntarily, and that if the laws there do not suit them, and proper diplomatic intervention fails to afford a remedy, no one obliges them to stay. At any rate they positively declare that foreigners shall not enjoy greater privileges than natives, and that until this is recognised no further encouragement shall be granted them, nor shall the country be further opened up, to increase the field for difficulties. Speaking on this subject with me, a Japanese gentleman of high rank instanced a case which the contention of the European ministers might give rise to. "A foreigner," he said, "might visit one of our temples, insult, or even destroy, the sacred emblems, and claim exemption from punishment on the ground that no crime recognised by or punishable under the laws of his own country had been committed." But an instance of injustice towards Japan more palpable than this imaginary one has lately actually occurred. The *Hesperia*, a German vessel, coming from an infected port, was ordered by the authorities to go into quarantine, to prevent the risk of importing cholera into Yokohama and Tokio. The captain, seeing the justice of the demand, was ready to accede to it, but the German representative refused to permit the Japanese regulations to be recognised, and the vessel was brought into harbour, in spite of all protests; and, under the protection of the guns of a man-of-war, the passengers and cargo were landed. A more brutal disregard of the rights of humanity and of international amity was perhaps never exhibited, and unfortunately, if my information is correct—I can scarcely believe it—this high-handed proceeding was also sanctioned by the British minister, the despatches from the British and German ministers in reference to the Japanese quarantine regulations being almost identical. This matter has given rise to an animated diplomatic correspondence, and it is to be hoped that the home governments, at any rate our own, will not approve a course of action which *primâ facie* the strongest language can hardly characterise.*

---

* In a recent number of the *British Medical Journal* appears a quotation from a note sent by the Hon. W. M. Evarts, Secretary of State to the United States National Board of Health, upon the recent outbreak of cholera in Japan. After giving the number of cholera cases as 156,204, and the number of deaths as 89,702, the official note goes on to say: "Mr. Bingham (the minister of the United States to Japan) expresses the opinion that the number of deaths by the disease would have been much less if the government of Japan had been aided, instead of being resisted, by cer-

In this and in all similar cases the Japanese authorities believe that the opinion of international jurists would be with them, and they confidently expect that justice will eventually be done. But the bulk of the nation do not bear their yoke so patiently, and it would be deplorable if the government were forced by internal pressure to extreme measures. Writers in the native press openly discuss these questions, and face the consequences which a peremptory assertion of what they consider their rights might produce. They say that a rupture would be infinitely preferable to the present state of things, and that everything should be risked to defend the national rights. "Better," said a Japanese to me—"better cease to be a nation in name, if we are no longer one in fact—at least we can fight better than the Zulus or the Afghans, and if we are eventually overpowered, we can throw ourselves under the protection of Russia or the United States."

I think it a duty to state these things plainly. I have full confidence that sooner or later Japan will be fairly treated, and that if we are unable to concede what is demanded, we shall at any rate have the international position clearly defined. But there should be no delay in this, or we may any day find ourselves face to face with serious troubles, which proper and timely treatment would render unlikely, if not impossible. When it is necessary to refuse, there are ways of saying "no" which have a more conciliatory effect than other ways of saying "yes." But there seems reason to fear that some European representatives in Japan have lost the skill of either acceding to demands with grace or refusing them with courtesy. Stories which are too often repeated to be forgotten are in every one's mouth, of champagne glasses dashed to the ground by an eminent

---

tain foreign powers in its endeavours to prevent the spread of the contagion by land and maritime regulations, and says that it affords him gratification to know that the efforts of the government of Japan to save the people of that empire from the pestilence were seconded by this government." The reader can imagine the indignation and shame of the Japanese at seeing the lives of their countrymen sacrificed in this manner by foreign interference with their own laws and regulations.

minister with the rudest comparison between their fragility and that of Japan, and of serious diplomatic correspondence demanding satisfaction for the loss of a chicken, or the unwarrantable intrusion of a dungheap on a road. If these stories have even a shadow of foundation, there should be an end put at once to such behaviour. I should long have hesitated to believe that there was any good ground for such strictures if an incident had not happened while I was in Japan which seemed in no small degree to justify them. I happened to learn that a strong remonstrance had one afternoon been made by one of the foreign ministers (in kindness I withhold his name) on the subject of an insult which he said had been inflicted on himself and the nation he represented by certain Japanese innkeepers, who had committed no less an offence than that of mistaking a foreigner travelling in the interior of the country for the minister himself! I believe an apology was demanded. At any rate the great diplomatist insisted that the matter should be seriously inquired into, and the minister appealed to undertook, with all the gravity he could command, to have the solemn request complied with. I did not hear the sequel, and as the new Japanese Code probably does not include any mention of the crime of *léze*-minister, I presume the remonstrance could not possibly have had any other result than to excite the merriment of the fun-loving Japanese. I do not attribute the recent retirement of Mr. Terashima from the post of minister for foreign affairs which has lately occurred to any complications arising from this deplorable incident of mistaken identity!

As regards the difficulties in connection with the postal question, I am glad to be able to say that they have at last been satisfactorily arranged by our present Government. A convention was signed on the 10th of October last under which the British post offices in Japan are to be closed, and reciprocal rights are secured in both countries for the due delivery of official despatches. The United States had made a similar arrangement some years back, but the Japanese declare that this is the first instance in which any

European power has made a bargain granting as much as it received, and they rejoice over it as a presage of future success in carrying out their favourite doctrine of national equality. Our Government deserve much credit for this wise and timely concession. France will no doubt follow the example of England in this matter.

Of the other questions, that respecting quarantine is still under discussion, and—as well as the enforcement of taxes on foreigners, the regulation of the coasting trade, and many others—will in all probability remain more or less in abeyance until the vital point is settled as to whether the right to legislate in such matters remains with Japan or belongs to foreigners. There appears little doubt that the latter will have to give up their pretensions if Japan is firm, but it will be highly disagreeable for some of the present foreign ministers to acknowledge such a defeat, and considerable changes in the *corps diplomatique* may be looked for.

There remains one more question of the highest importance, on which the hands of Japan are not tied by treaty. This relates to the general opening up of the country to foreign trade and residence. It is evident that much depends on the treatment of this matter. At present, whatever may be the real grievances inflicted on the Japanese by foreigners, they are confined to a very small portion of the country. Except for a short distance round the treaty ports, the Japanese are masters of the position, in special virtue of the clauses in the treaties which recognise their right to exclude all foreigners (except the diplomatic agents) from residing in, and if so desired from even visiting, the interior. Now, if it be true that other conditions of the treaties weigh unjustly on the country, there can be no doubt as to the wisdom of the policy which confines their direct action to certain specified and limited localities. But I did not hesitate to point out to my friends in Japan that there are two sides to the question, and that absolute equality with other nations could not even theoretically be fairly demanded if their own country were virtually closed to foreigners, who on the other hand opened theirs to all comers. It indeed appears indisputable that the territory of any country claiming, in the fullest sense, to form part of the concert of civilised states, must, as a concurrent condition, be not only accessible, but safely accessible, to all the world. While this was generally admitted, I was met by the statement that the country was not closed from any wish of the Japanese themselves; that the present state of things was entirely attributable to the unjust pretensions of the treaty powers, who claimed from Japan rights and privileges which they never themselves accorded to other nations; and that on terms of real equality and fair treatment the Japanese government would be ready at once to open up the whole country. They said that to have the country overrun by hordes of overbearing strangers, who refused to be bound by any laws but their own, which evidently could not be justly administered under the present system, was a state of things which should not be willingly consented to. They further argued that as long as it was contended that the control of the foreign trade no longer remained to them, the country might be still further impoverished. In reply, while recognising that it could not be expected that they would willingly increase their difficulties, or without adequate compensation surrender the vantage-ground they possessed in negotiating a settlement of these difficulties, I pointed out that the position which they assumed in dealing with the subject was not appreciated in Europe, and that on every ground they should make it perfectly clear by defining the conditions under which full freedom of trade and residence would be permitted. I was led to believe that on a fitting occasion the government would be quite prepared to take a decided step in this direction, and that in reality all they would insist on would be that foreigners in Japan should resign absolutely all pretensions to rights and privileges which they would not be permitted to enjoy in European countries other than their own in which they might reside. They all said that on lower grounds than this they would not wish to negotiate, but that there were further concessions which, if only of a temporary kind, might be yielded to bring about a proper settlement. The chief difficulties in the way are of course connected with the question of consular jurisdiction, to which I shall have occasion to refer later.

I own that I was much pleased to observe this disposition among enlightened Japanese. It points to a grand future for their country at no distant period, if judicious diplomacy is exercised. But the *rôle* of schoolmaster has been "played out" by the diplomatists of Europe, and the Japanese have become nervously impatient of officious control. Our representatives should leave off scolding, and not even proffer advice till it is asked for, and such advice should be sound and honest, and bearing at any rate the guise of being disinterested. This should be an easy and intelligible position for any well-trained diplomatist to assume, for nothing is more evidently short-sighted than a line of conduct which is confined to the mere backing up of the narrow interests of a small body of resident traders at the expense of all the instincts and feelings of the country to which a minister is accredited, and in disregard of the fact that in the long-run the true interests of both exporters and importers are identical. A short-lived advantage may be gained by craft or hectoring, and a few individuals may be enriched; but a lasting and valuable intercourse between two nations can only be secured by mutually advantageous arrangements.

It is now time to turn to the second class of difficulties between Japan and other countries, arising in connection with points defined, or assumed to be defined, in treaty arrangements, which are open to revision.

To understand the questions at issue, it will be necessary to refer briefly to the treaties themselves, and to the circumstances under which they were made; but inasmuch as Japan bound herself in almost identical terms to all the powers, it will be sufficient to confine ourselves to the British treaties. The first of these was made in October 1854, Admiral Sterling acting on our side. This treaty was of a very preliminary character, and at present is chiefly interesting as containing clauses in which it was stipulated that the British should conform to the laws of Japan, and that no high officer coming to Japan should alter this condition.*

The next and still valid treaty was signed at Yedo on the 26th of August 1858.† It is almost identical with the one signed a few months previously between the United States and Japan. It is important to notice this fact in consideration of the views held about it by Mr. Townsend Harris, who drafted and executed it.

Lord Elgin's treaty contained a stipulation‡ that subsequently the import and export duties should be subject to revision, and on the 25th of June 1866 a tariff convention was signed, which altered the customs duties, and also contained other regulations as to foreign trade. There can be no doubt that both in 1858 and in 1866 great pressure was used to induce the Japanese authorities to sign, and that they were entirely or nearly ignorant of the bearings of the engagements entered into. This is openly admitted by the Americans, and has never indeed been disputed by any intelligent writer. The treaty is also almost ridiculously one-sided, all appearance of mutual advantage having been rigorously excluded. In fact, beyond the right to send diplomatic agents and consuls to England,§ it is difficult to find a single benefit secured by it to Japan. But while the Japanese have hitherto scrupulously admitted their liability to respect this treaty, they now as persistently claim to modify it on two grounds. First, they point to a clause which confers the right of revision, on twelve months' notice, on

---

* "British ships in Japanese ports shall conform to the laws of Japan. If high officers or commanders of ships shall break any such laws, it will lead to the ports being closed. Should inferior persons break them, they are to be delivered over to the commanders of their ships for punishment." Convention at Nagasaki, 14th of October 1854. Sir E. Herbert, C.B., Treaties, British Foreign Office, thus explains this clause: "British ships and subjects in Japanese ports shall conform to the laws of Japan."

† See copy of treaty, Appendix, vol. ii.

‡ "Five years after the opening of Kanagawa, the import and export duties shall be subject to revision, if either the British or Japanese Government desire it."

§ Clause II. Appendix, vol. ii.

or after July 1, 1872,* and secondly, they contend that the treaty almost amounts to an abnegation of national existence, and as such could not be intended, and shall not be construed to be perpetual.

In 1872 the special Japanese embassy which visited America and Europe exhibited a desire that the treaties should be revised, but from one cause or another no progress was made, and all negotiations on the subject dropped for a time. No active steps were subsequently taken till 1877, the European powers wishing to leave things as they were as long as possible, the Japanese feeling that time was strengthening their position. In that year, however, formal notice was given by Japan of a wish to revise the treaties, and an outline of the changes proposed was submitted. That country claimed to reoccupy, as regards the right to fix her own tariffs, the position she held before the treaties were signed, and justified her demand chiefly on grounds of fiscal necessity. In return she offered to abolish export duties, and to open two more ports to foreign trade. This hardly seems a strong position to have taken up. If her claims were well founded, no bartering was required. If these could only be purchased by adequate concessions, it was useless to talk of national rights. The result of this application was not encouraging. Some of the powers returned vague answers; some, England among them, tried for further delay, on the ground that twelve months' formal notice was required before the question could be entertained. The United States alone consented to the demands, but even they deprived their friendly action of much of its value by stipulating that the new treaty conditions should only become operative after the adhesion to them of the other signatory powers. Issue was not anywhere joined on the main points, and much diplomatic fencing led to no result. It was then proposed that a conference to discuss the revision should be held in Europe. The place of meeting was subsequently changed to Japan, and so the matter now

---

* Clause XXII. See Appendix, vol. ii.

stands. Japan has not publicly defined her position, and the powers are apparently satisfied to allow things to drag on. At the same time, the question is unofficially discussed by all classes in Japan, with great interest, and in some quarters with much bitterness, and it is a moot point whether that country will now be satisfied with conditions which a few years ago would have been thought highly favourable.

The treaty of 1858, it will be seen, contained two principal concessions in favour of foreigners: first, a stipulated tariff on all imports, which though nominally fixed at 5 per cent., as now modified hardly secures an average of 3 per cent.; second, the right of so-called consular jurisdiction, which exempts foreigners from the operation of all Japanese courts of law, civil or criminal, except in such civil cases as the defendant may be a native.

To both these concessions the Japanese, as represented by their press, loudly object, but their government, wisely in my opinion, considered that the time had not come to demand the entire cessation of consular jurisdiction, and that by asking too much they might only be raising greater difficulties. They therefore confined their demands for the moment to the tariff questions—which are certainly of extreme importance to Japan, in respect of her revenues—and to such minor alterations in the treaty as experience might have shown to be desirable. The question of extra-territoriality deserves, however, some notice, as, even if shelved for the time, its consideration cannot be long delayed, and things move quickly in Japan. Its bearing also on the opening of the whole country is all-important.

There can be no question, and it is conceded by all intelligent Japanese, that at the time of the signing of the treaties it was absolutely essential, for the security of the persons and property of foreigners, that these should not be subject to the action of native courts. Torture, since happily entirely abolished, then existed in grim reality, and justice of all kinds was administered in a fashion utterly unsuited to foreigners. But a great change has taken place. Codes of laws, both civil and criminal, have been framed on the best models; while the procedure in the courts of justice would compare favourably with that in use in many European countries. But while codes may be made more or less speedily, the means of administering them rightly are not so readily procured. A judge *fit non nascitur*, and to be efficient requires the advantages of long experience as well as of great intelligence. To this it might with some show of reason be retorted that the objection applies with equal if not greater strength to the employment of such untrained administrators as are found frequently in consular courts, for the consuls and vice-consuls of some nationalities are now and again half-educated hucksters. But, even allowing this, it remains certain that, if miscarriage of justice must sometimes take place, it is better, at any rate for the Japanese, that it should occur through the ignorance of foreign, rather than of native, judges.

But all things considered, there can be no doubt that consular jurisdiction is at best but a makeshift, and, except in barbarous countries, should be looked on only as a temporary expedient, to be got rid of as soon as the native administration of justice becomes such as to justify its abolition. In this light only can it be justified, and by openly showing the desire to limit its continuance, not only would by far the loudest outcry against it be silenced, but a lasting benefit would be conferred on Eastern countries by affording them an effective encouragement to bring their system of justice as speedily as possible into harmony with Western ideas. But in the meantime no care or expense should be spared in making our consular jurisdiction as perfect as circumstances permit. Proper judges should be appointed in sufficient numbers to hear all important cases. Amateur lawyers should not be permitted to deliver elaborate judgments on matters utterly beyond their ken; and as soon as just and sensible codes exist in any country, these should be at once adopted by common consent among all foreign nationalities, so as to recognise the rights of the country, and do away with the anomaly of having different laws in each different court. It also seems eminently desirable that the diplomatic representative of a country should not even nominally have any control over judicial matters. Being specially removed from all contentious proceedings, he would be able to intervene with at least a semblance of impartiality in case of need. The system of mixing up the services by appointing consuls or consuls-general to be ministers, while still retaining their former posts, is also objectionable. It lowers the dignity of the minister, and is looked on as a bad compliment to the country to which he is accredited. To have men in such responsible positions exposed, possibly with much injustice, to be designated as "good enough for the East," is a mistake in many ways, and being altogether a late innovation, as well as contrary to the principles of international law, may soon, it is to be hoped, be put an end to. These remarks refer to other countries as well as, and in some respects even more pointedly than, to England. A Dutch vice-consul, leaving a potato-store to administer Dutch law, of the rudiments of which he is profoundly ignorant, in a case involving, for instance, the tenure of land held under lease from the Japanese government, is a pitiable sight, and one affording grounds for serious reflection.

In the case of Japan, then, it appears certain that consular jurisdiction will shortly have to be seriously dealt with. There is little doubt that either with or without the adhesion of the foreign powers the right of the country to make its own administrative laws binding equally upon its own subjects and foreigners will be practically exercised; but as regards general jurisdiction over foreigners, it seems probable that the final result will have to be reached by stages. At present foreigners plaintiff in civil cases, except between themselves, have to apply for redress to the Japanese courts. It will not involve any great change if this system is extended to cases in which they are defendants. As regards criminal charges against foreigners, I think the Japanese, if well advised, will be happy to leave them, for some time at least, to be dealt with in foreign courts; but if the interior is opened, they might reasonably insist that offences committed out of the immediate reach of a foreign court should, in the first instance, if the charge is a grave one, and without appeal if trivial, be taken before their own courts. The next step might probably be the appointment of foreign judges by the government to administer Japanese law throughout the country in cases involving the persons or property of foreigners. I believe that this system would work satisfactorily until Japanese judges had themselves gained sufficient experience; and I not only believe that the government would be ready to incur the necessary outlay in order to secure one uniform system of justice throughout Japan, but would under such conditions seriously entertain the question of opening the whole of the country to foreign enterprise—always, however, assuming that the important point as to the tariff being properly under their control had been satisfactorily settled by a revision of the treaties. To this point I shall now allude as briefly as possible.

At first sight it seems impossible that any foreign country should pretend to regulate indefinitely the tariff of another independent country. But further examination shows that the case is not altogether free from difficulty. The treaties were essentially treaties for trade, and for as long as they could be said fairly to last, might be held to forbid anything which seriously interfered with it. If then it were contended that on a revision the Japanese could insist on fixing their own scale of import duties, these might be so raised as to be prohibitory, and all trade might then be destroyed. It is also urged that a revision implies that the alterations in the treaty should be made by consent of all the signataries, and should only embrace such as experience had shown to all parties to be desirable; that vested interests are at stake, and that all countries (including Japan) would be injured by measures aiming only at one-sided advantages. The attitude of the United States is also generally considered of small value in the argument, as that country has scarcely any import trade with Japan, and would evidently be much benefited by the proposed abolition of the export duties.

On the Japanese side, the arguments seem to be at least as strong. They say that to contend that a revision is limited to alterations mutually consented to is practically to declare the treaty perpetual in its present form, as continual objections might be made on one side to any changes; that if this were all which was intended to be stipulated for in the revision clause, it was an unnecessary and useless addition to the treaty, as changes *mutually* agreed on could always be made; and that such a contention would, in fact, if valid, prevent both Japan and any of the powers from making any modifications unless and until all the signataries of the treaties unanimously consented to them, inasmuch as under the most-favoured-nation clause any country might claim the benefit which might thus attach to another one objecting, for instance, to modify the tariff to its supposed disadvantage; and in this way, following out the argument to its logical conclusion, any country, however small, if having a similar treaty with Japan, might for ever prevent alterations in the customs tariff, desirable as these might appear to the rest of the world.

This *reductio ad absurdum* seems fairly conclusive, as far as it goes; but it is to be hoped that Japan will not forget that theoretical positions are not always maintainable; that a nation joining the circle of civilised states must a little give and take, and exercise its sovereign rights with some regard for others; and that it would not be unreasonable to expect that proper safeguards for commerce should be afforded. The best solution of the difficulty would probably be a new and fair commercial treaty, drafted on European precedents, to last for a definite time. I believe that Japan is willing to agree to this, and if it were offered to the powers, accepted as it is in principle beforehand by the United States, public opinion would everywhere be on the side of Japan, and any treaty power objecting to consent to it, under cover of the unrighteous bargains previously made, would find no support. But beyond all this, and apart from all technical arguments, Japan is fully entitled to very great modifications in her treaty arrangements. At present her hands are absolutely tied. She can increase her revenue neither by higher import duties nor by excise taxes. Her customs duties, even including those chargeable on exports, which it is properly proposed to abolish, barely amount to 4 per cent. of the national income, which has in consequence to be almost entirely collected from direct taxation on land. And this state of things exists at a time when, consequent upon the revolutions of 1867-68, a long series of abnormal expenditures—the last of which, connected with the Satsuma rebellion, amounted alone to several millions sterling—have pressed severely upon the national exchequer.

Besides this, the country has by the action of foreign trade been almost drained of the precious metals, the great balance in the value of the imports and exports having to be made up by the export of bullion; while any efforts to establish native manufactories, even if entirely suitable to the country, are paralysed by virtually unrestrained importations by foreigners before fair competition has become possible.

It will thus be seen that it is not by any means a sentimental grievance under which Japan labours, and no consolation is afforded by the assurances proffered to her by British merchants that the present state of things will evidently work out to her advantage; and that even to a young country unrestricted free trade must be beneficial. The Japanese say that such advice, coming from a country interested in finding a market for her manufactures, is open to suspicion, and that before trying to force the system on an independent nation it should at least insist on its adoption by its own colonies; and that if in some cases fiscal necessities produce the same results as protection, they are willing for the time to be branded as unsound economists, in company with those directing the affairs of all the more important nations of the world, excepting England.

It is expected that the question of the revision of the Japanese treaties will shortly be seriously taken up. I earnestly trust that moderate counsels will prevail on all sides. Bullying and blustering will certainly not influence the Japanese as they formerly did. They know as well as we do that the days of forcing on trade by gunboats are quickly dying out, and that public opinion is now king in most countries. On the other hand they should not forget that this new monarch is not favourable to unpractical pretensions, and that extreme measures are not likely to promote either commercial prosperity or national greatness.

I would also, with the sincerest wish for the advancement of Japan, venture to impress upon the rulers of that country the desirability of placing a due value on the trump card which they undoubtedly hold in the present important game, viz. the control of the opening up of the country. They should take care not heedlessly to throw away such an advantage, nor unduly to keep it back. To other nations it is an important feature; to them, the key-stone of national progress. If the country can be safely opened, the future prosperity of Japan is to a large extent assured. It is not always remembered that internal commerce has generally a greater, though sometimes not so apparent an, effect on national prosperity as foreign trade. A country might thrive without foreign intercourse; it could not live without internal commerce. That is what is most needed in Japan. If the country were well provided with railways, its common roads multiplied, its mines well opened, and its agricultural resources largely developed, its wealth would soon be doubled and quadrupled; its exporting power would increase proportionately; the value of its paper money would quickly approximate to that of coin, and increased vitality would be apparent in every direction. All this can only be done, or at least can only speedily be done, by the introduction of foreign capital and foreign experience. This is, then, in my opinion, the point to be kept chiefly in view, both by the European diplomatists and the Japanese government. Japan, in order that she may assume her proper position, must have national freedom of action, limited only by practical necessities. But to be qualified to assume this position she must, after acquiring proper safeguards, welcome as other countries do the full co-operation of the outside world. Let her boldly take her stand on the platform of absolute equality and freedom for herself and others. She will then be able to defy safely all hostile criticisms and threats. She will have no necessity to contemplate checking the excess of foreign trade by passing sumptuary laws interdicting or taxing highly the use of articles of foreign manufacture; the difficulties of bringing foreigners under proper legislative control will quickly disappear, and international equality in its highest sense will produce its ripest fruit; for if, after availing herself of every opportunity of making a fair settlement of her difficulties, she were even to take the extreme step of denouncing the existing treaties, there would be no question of bombardments or blockades. Public opinion would protect her, and would insist on fair treatment for a country nobly struggling for free intercourse and fair trade.

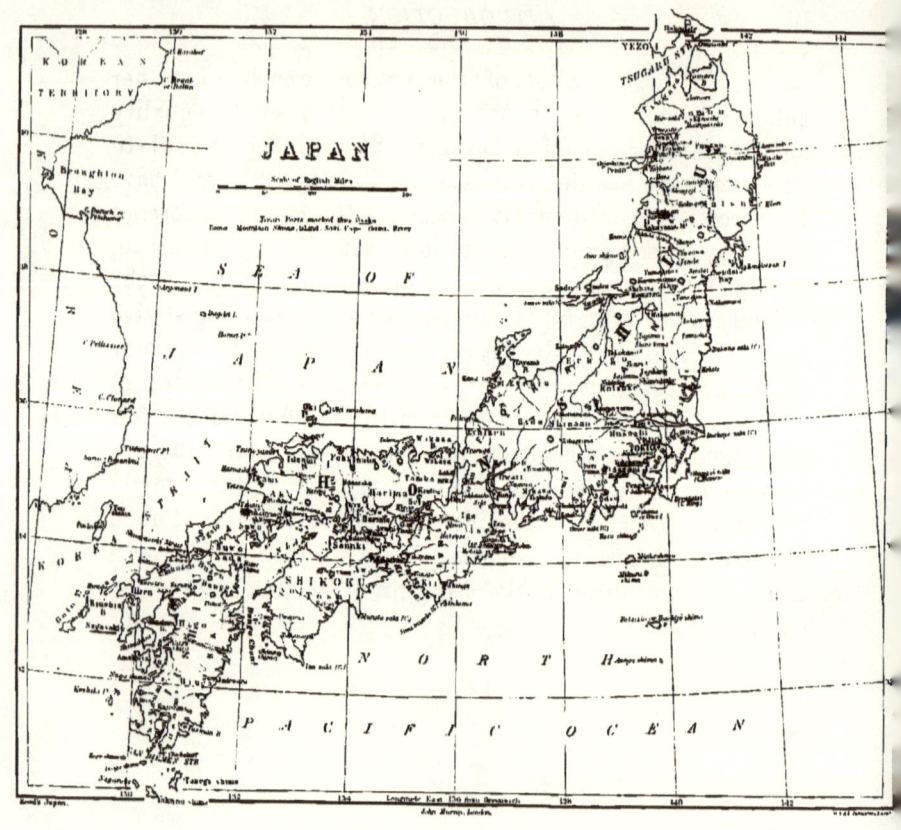

JAPAN:

ITS HISTORY, TRADITIONS, AND RELIGIONS.

CHAPTER I.

THE LAND AND ITS INHABITANTS.

Japan consists of four great, and many small, islands—Its nearness to Russia, China, and Korea—Its extent and area—The Kurile, Loo-choo, and Yaeyama islands—The mountains of Japan—Its harbours, rivers, and lakes—Its climate—The winters less rigorous than was anticipated; the hot season short—Effects of the *Kuro-shiwo*, or "black current," and of the *Oya-shiwo*, or "cold current"—The Japanese Mediterranean, or Inland Sea—This is shallow, and therefore variable in temperature—Dr. Rein's favourable description of the climate—Our own experiences of it—The geology of Japan—Volcanic disturbances—A summary record of its chief earthquakes—The god Daibutsu of Nara decapitated—The summit of the sacred mountain, Fuji, shaken in—The wreck of the frigate *Diana* by an earthquake—Typhoons—Dr. Maget's recommendation of Japan as a sanatarium—The measure of its heat and humidity—The origin of the Japanese people—Extraordinary ages of their god-ancestors—The first emperor's father, aged 836,042 years—Dr. Kaempfer's theory of a Japanese migration from Babel—The theory of an Aino origin—The Japanese a Tungusic race—Their route from Mantchuria, by Korea—The mixture of races—The men not usually of small stature—The women small but pleasing, and often beautiful in appearance—Defacing customs dying out—Improving condition of the people.

THE beautiful land of Japan consists of four great islands, which may be regarded as Japan proper, and of many smaller islands, some lying near their shores, and others stretching away into far-distant seas—the Kuriles all but touching the icy coast of Kamschatka, and the Loo-choos*

---

* Called Liukiu by the Chinese, and Riukiu by the Japanese.

reaching far down towards the tropic seas. The native name of the whole country is Nippon, or Dai Nippon (or Nihon),* and the four main islands are called Honshiu, Shikoku, Kiushiu, and Yezo.† Shikoku and Kiushiu may almost be regarded as continuous with the main island Honshiu, the straits between them being but narrow, and more easy to cross than are many rivers. The distance of the fourth island, Yezo, from the mainland is more considerable, but is not much greater than that of the Isle of Wight from Portsmouth, or than that of Kent from Essex at the Nore. In the case of Yezo and Honshiu, however, they are but the extremities which approach each other, the land of each stretching away in opposite directions.

Japan, while washed on its eastern and southern shores by the vast Pacific Ocean, is situated much nearer to other countries than many people suppose. Its mainland is within about 100 miles of the great continent of Asia at Korea, and between the two lies the large Japanese island of Tsushima, which is within 25 miles of Korea, and about 35 of Japan.‡ The island of Saghalin, lately taken over from Japan by Russia, is within about 20 miles of Yezo, and is very much closer still to the mainland of Asia, being

---

* The name is often written Niphon, or Nifon. Japan has many other native designations, mostly of an historical, poetical, and colloquial nature. One of these signifies "Country of the Great Islands," with reference to the legendary origin of the country; another signifies "Outspread Islands," from the fact of their being spread out over the sea like Japanese garden stepping-stones; another, "Cliff-Fortress Island"; others signifying "Country of the Sun," and "Nest of the Sun." Mr. Pfoundes, in his Japanese Notes, gives the following also: "Consolidated Drop," "Between Heaven and Earth," "Southern Country of Brave Warriors," "Country of Peaceful Shores," "Country ruled by the Slender Sword," "Princesses Country" (from its belonging to the sungoddess), "Land of Great Gentleness," and "Honourable Country." The word "Nihon," which I have given in brackets in the text, is an abbreviation of *Dai Nihon Koku*, or "Great Sun Source Country."

† Most geographies and schoolbooks erroneously limit the name Nippon, or Niphon, to the main island, Honshiu.

‡ In estimating these distances, in spelling the names of places, and in similar matters, I shall conform usually to the very valuable map of Japan compiled by Mr. R. H. Brunton, C.E., a highly competent authority, and published by Trübner & Co., of London.

distant only about 5 or 6 miles. The distance between Japan (Yezo) and that mainland (Russian Tartary), on the south side of Saghalin, is considerably less than 200 miles. This proximity of Japan to Korea, China, and the Russian possessions may prove of the greatest possible importance to her future, and is well worth bearing in mind by every one interested in her.

Taking the four great islands of Japan as one, the length of the country, measured north and south, is roughly nearly 900 miles; and its breadth, east and west, about 800. These dimensions would give, however, a very exaggerated idea of its size, unless qualified by the facts, that the actual width at the broadest part (neglecting minor protuberances) is below 200 miles, the average breadth being much less, while between the main islands is inclosed much inland water, including the beautiful Inland Sea. The approximate area of Japan is given by its present government as 148,700 square miles, that of the island of Great Britain being about 90,000, and that of the United Kingdom about 121,000 square miles. The southern extremity of Japan proper (Kiushiu) is in latitude 31° north, its northern extremity (Yezo) being in latitude 45½° north. The whole country lies, therefore, much farther south than England, the latitude of the south of Cornwall being 50° north.

The Kurile Islands, which have come into the recognised possession of Japan since the surrender to Russia of the much more important island of Saghalin, extend in a long line in a north-western direction, from Yezo to Kamschatka, over a distance of 600 miles. The Loo-choo and Yayeyama islands extend in an opposite, or south-western, direction, a distance of about 500 miles. A third group, or rather chain, of islands stretches away from the south-east part of Japan, beginning with the long volcanic island of Vries—which is still in volcanic activity, and was surmounted with a banner of smoke when we left Japan in April 1879—and ending with the Bonin group, which are nearly 500 miles from Japan proper. It will be unnecessary for the purposes of this work to do more than make slight mention of these far-reaching island dependencies of Japan, although the nearer islands will occasionally claim fuller notice.

The general appearance of Japan itself, and of these long chains of islands rising at intervals from the sea, conveys the idea that they all are the summits of mountain ranges, which in the course of ages have had their bases submerged by the rising of the sea, or else have gradually settled down beneath the sea's surface. The islands are for the most part steep and lofty in proportion to their area, and Japan proper is an exceedingly hilly country, the eminences often towering up into mountains of Alpine height. Fuji-san is 13,000 feet high; Mount Mitaké, 9000 feet; Asama, 8500; Chokai, 6000; Odai, 5400; and several others 5000 feet high: many of them are active, and some quiescent, volcanoes, the designation of "extinct volcano" being sometimes prematurely applied. The coasts are deeply indented by the sea, and the sea as deeply indented by high promontories, with many islands emerging, both off the coasts and from the inland waters. There are said to be more than three thousand islands in the Japanese group, some of them as large as our large counties, and others too small to deserve separate mention. There are fifty-six harbours and trading ports, many of which are, however, of too little depth to admit European ocean-going vessels. Nagasaki is a splendid deep-water harbour, sheltered on all sides by lofty and picturesque hills. The inland sea has many excellent anchorages for the largest ships.

The main island of Japan (Honshiu) being both narrow and mountainous, and the other three comparatively small, there are no great rivers navigable for hundreds of miles as in many European countries. The principal rivers, taken in the order of the approximate lengths of their main channels, are the Shinana-gawa, of which the main channel is 180 miles long; the Toné-gawa, 170 miles; the Kita-kami-gawa, 140; the Ishikari-gawa, in Yezo, 130; the Tenriu-gawa, 120; the Kiso-gawa, 115; the Sakata-gawa and the Okuma-gawa, each 110; and the Noshiro-gawa, 100 miles. Some of the shorter rivers are nevertheless formidable streams at times, spreading over beds a mile and more in width, and running with all the speed and violence of huge mountain torrents.* But few of the rivers bear the same name from source to mouth, the name often being changed more than once on its way to the sea.

As a mountainous country Japan has, naturally, numerous lakes, but owing to the narrowness of the mainland, and to the irregularity in its level, but few of them are of any considerable extent. The largest, Lake Biwa, near the centre of the main island of Honshiu, has an area of 190 square miles, and is a highly picturesque and beautiful sheet of inland water. Lake Kasumiga-Ura is 80 square miles in extent, and there are others of 35, 25, and 20 square miles, with several very much smaller. Hakoné Lake, which is best known to Europeans from its situation on the great high-road between Tokio and Kioto, and from its accessibility from Yokohama, is beautifully situated, but is 3½ square miles only in extent.

The climate of Japan is very different from that which some authors had led me to expect. The winter, in particular, was not nearly so rigorous as I had anticipated. Snow fell occasionally, and lay for several days, in Tokio, and occasionally cold winds blew. But the cold was relieved by so much bright sunshine that its chilling effects were the exception rather than the rule. It is true that the winter of 1878–79 in Japan was said to be as exceptionally mild as that in England was severe, and due allowance must be made, of course, for this fact; but those who have resided for several years in the country give a good account of its winters. Professor W. Anderson,† of Tokio, for example, in a scientific paper, states that from November to March inclusive the weather is exceptionally fine; "the

---

* "The Oi-gawa rises in the south-west of Kai, and traverses the province of Totomi, intersecting the Tokaido between Kanaya and Shimada. It is more remarkable for the breadth of its bed, which near the mouth is two and a half miles wide, and for the swiftness of its current, than for the length of its course."—*Satow*.

† Professor of Surgery and Anatomy in the Imperial Naval Medical College, and Medical Officer to the British Legation, L.R.C.P. Lond., and F.R.C.S. Eng.—a highly scientific and accomplished observer.

days are mostly warm and sunny, the sky clear and cloudless, and the air is dry and bracing." He adds, however, that there are sudden and great variations of temperature, which appear to occasion as much catarrh, bronchitis, pleurisy, pneumonia, and sub-acute rheumatism affections as in our own country. But these diseases are not caused by climate only, the construction of the houses and the dress of the people having very much to do with them, and in Japan both houses and dresses are such, in my opinion, as to tend greatly to multiply such complaints. In the months of April and May the weather is very changeable, "but it will compare very favourably," says the same authority, "with the corresponding period in England." From the middle of June to the middle of September there are heavy falls of rain, and these, combined with a high temperature, saturate the atmosphere with moisture, and produce great lassitude and debility. People have to keep indoors as much as possible during the heat of the day. About the middle of September the weather begins to improve, and October, although occasionally subject to heavy rains, is usually a healthy and pleasant month.

The climate of a mountainous country like Japan, with an extremely irregular contour, and extending over 11° of latitude, is of course very different in different places. It is further influenced on part of the coast by the well-known warm ocean stream known as the "black current" (*Kuro-shiwo*), which sweeps up from the warm south, past Shikoku and the south-eastern shores, and then onward across the Pacific to the coast of America, where it flows southward past California.* It has a marked effect upon the temperature of the land by which it flows, producing greater warmth than is experienced in the same latitudes on the opposite side of Japan, although a branch of the Kuro-shiwo flows northward into the sea of Japan. The island of Yezo, one would expect, is much colder than the southern parts of the empire,

---

* Or, as some authorities say, turns earlier eastward and south-eastward, and loses itself in the drift current of the Pacific, without reaching the American shores.

but the difference is greater than is due to difference of latitude alone. This is caused by a stream setting down past the eastern side of Yezo from the cold sea of Okhotsk. It is not a stream of great breadth or volume, but it produces a notable effect upon the neighbouring land. "The south of Kiushiu is washed by the strength of the Kuroshiwo, and in consequence has almost a tropical climate during the whole year; while the Oya-shiwo runs along the east coast of Yezo, which coast is fast bound in ice for twenty miles off the land during the whole winter."* Moreover, Japan has, as we know, its Mediterranean, and this exercises some influence upon its climate. It is comparatively shallow, and is consequently influenced in some degree by the river water flowing into it, and still more by the direct effect of the seasons. It is colder in winter and warmer in summer than the Pacific and Japan seas, with which it communicates, falling to 50° (Fahr.) in winter and rising to 77° in summer. The character of the climate is well stated summarily as follows, by Dr. Rein, Professor of Geography at the University of Marburg, in Germany, who has given great attention to the subject: "The climate of Japan reflects the characteristics of that of the neighbouring continent, and exhibits, like that, two great annual contrasts, a hot, damp summer, and a cold, relatively dry winter; these two seasons lie under the sway of the monsoons, but the neighbouring seas weaken the effects of these winds and mitigate their extremes, in such a manner that neither the summer heat nor the cold of winter attain the same height in Japan as in China at the same latitudes. Spring and autumn are extremely agreeable seasons, the oppressive summer heat does not last long, and in winter the contrast between the nightly frosts and the midday heat, produced by considerable insulation, but still more by the raw northerly winds, causes frequent chills, though the prevailing bright sky makes the season of the year much more endurable

---

* Capt. A. R. Brown, in an able paper on "Winds and Currents in the Vicinity of the Japanese Islands," read at the Asiatic Society of Japan, in 1874.

than in many other regions where the winter cold is equal. As a fact, the climate of Japan agrees very well with most Europeans, so that people have already begun to look upon certain localities as climatic watering-places, where the inhabitant of Hong Kong and Shanghai can find refuge from the oppressive heat of summer, and invigorate his health." * This appears to me to be one of the best, as well as one of the latest, statements of those who have given attention to the subject. We certainly experienced in Japan many lovely summer-like days, in Tokio, on the shores and islands of the Pacific coast, at Nagasaki, in the interior, at Nara, at Kioto, and on the Tokaido, and our visit was from the 10th of January to the 10th of April. Early in the last-named month the park of Wooyeno was alight with cherry and plum-blossoms, and crowded with people drawn forth from the city by the irresistible charm of springtime. On a moonlight evening spent at the river-side residence of Prince Hachisuka, we remained out of doors in evening dress and without hats long after the maiden splendours of the moon had turned the gardens into fairyland, and converted the blossom-strewn lake into a floor for Titania and her court. On the opposite side of the river Sumida the famous bloom-groves of Mukojima stretched apparently for miles in silver whiteness, and in a night almost as fair and mild as we English ever linger in at home. A little longer stay was necessary, however, in order to realise in its fulness the beautiful outbreak of a Japanese summer. "When the fields are sown with summer grains, and the flute-like song of the *uguisu* or Japanese nightingale is heard from out the young foliage of the bushes, summer is already present, and the vegetation now begins to develop under a powerful insolation, accompanied by plentiful and frequent showers of rain, a variety and fulness such as we seek in vain in the Mediterranean region. Japan owes these blessings to the south-west monsoon and to the Kuroshiwo, namely, its fertilising summer rain, its astonishingly

---

* Asiatic Society of Japan, 1878.

rich flora, and the possibility of reaping two harvests in the year off the same field" (Rein).

The conformation of Japan and of its outlying islands, considered in connection with its neighbouring islands and the adjacent continent, is a great temptation to writers, now that geology is a fashionable study, to speculate upon the great cosmic forces and methods by which this part of the world has been brought to its present form and conditions. A recent writer says, for example: "The Japanese islands form a link in that great chain of volcanic action which is carried on from Kamschatka through the Philippines, Sumbawa, and Java to Sumatra, and thence in a north-westerly direction to the Bay of Bengal."* Baron Richtofen, in a paper read before the Geological Society of Berlin,† states that the west and east portions of the Japanese islands, from Kiushiu eastwards through Suruga and Shinano, are the direct continuation of the mountain system of south and east China, and that this system is intersected at either end by another,‡ commencing on the west in Kiushiu, and extending southwards in the direction of the Loo-choos, and on the east constituting the northern branch of the main island, Honshiu, and with a slight deviation of direction continuing through the great islands of Yezo and Saghalin. The far-ranging Kurile Islands form a third system. The second of these systems is the scene of great volcanic disturbances, as are likewise the interferences or crossings of these several ranges, where indeed volcanoes most abound.

We had been but a very few days in Japan when we experienced our first rocking in that volcanic cradle in which Tokio (formerly Yedo) is nursed, and the experience was repeated during our stay in the capital nearly a dozen times. Sometimes the lateral vibration was quite violent, and sustained for many seconds, during most of which the house creaked and strained considerably. Those who have

---

* 'National Encyclopædia.' † Translated in Griffis's 'Mikado's Empire.'
‡ Running S.S.W. & N.N.E.

investigated the matter say that no trustworthy records exist of the earthquakes which doubtless occurred before the fifth century A.D., because prior to that date no system of writing existed in the country. But there are records of many destructive earthquakes since that period.* In 599 A.D. a severe shock destroyed all the buildings of Yamata, and prayer was offered, by command, to the god of earthquakes in all parts of the empire. In 642, 676, and 678, the same place was again severely shaken, the trembling lasting for three or four days on the first of these occasions. In 679 Tsukushi (now Chikuzen and Chikugo), in the great island of Kiushiu, was assailed by a tremendous shock, causing many fissures and chasms, one of which was four miles long. In 685, "innumerable lives were lost in many provinces," Shikoku suffering most, 2000 acres of land sinking down permanently into the sea on the coast of Tosa, in that island. In 715, a more eastern district, that of Totomi, was so shaken that enormous masses of earth fell from the hills, stopping the course of the Aratama River, and three counties (Fuchi, Chogé, and Ishida) were converted into a temporary lake. In 819, several of the more central and eastern provinces were so visited, that "mountains were rent asunder in several places, and innumerable lives were lost." Many calamitous earthquakes are recorded in the eighth and ninth centuries, mountains being rent, rivers dried up, castles thrown down, and many lives lost, one shock (in 855) even going the length of shaking the head off the famous colossal god (Daibutsu) of Nara, and rolling it down, over his golden lotus-seat, upon the temple floor; while in Mutsu, in 869, "the sky was illuminated, and the movement of the ground so violent that the people could not stand up, and many of them were crushed by falling houses, and others were swallowed up in fissures; soon afterwards the sea rolled in upon the coast with a tremendous noise, and washed away thousands of the people." In one of the Kioto temples,

---

* The following summary of earthquake shocks is abridged from Mr. J. Hattori's paper in the 'Transactions' of the Asiatic Society of Japan, 1878.

fifty priests were crushed in 976, this city being frequently subject to shocks about that time, and for some centuries afterwards. So also was Kamakura, after it became the eastern capital of the Shogun, all the houses there being overturned in 1257, the neighbouring hills being violently rent, and fissures, from which bluish flames streamed, opening. In 1293, during the tyrannical domination of the Hojo family at this city, an earthquake there is said to have destroyed more than 21,000 persons, and several temples. In 1331, the violence which nearly five hundred years earlier had decapitated the Daibutsu at Nara was greatly surpassed, for the head of the great and splendid mountain of Fuji was itself shaken off, or rather shaken in, its summit for a height (or depth) of 100 feet, disappearing, --an injury which the hands of man could not repair, as in the former case they did. The Daibutsu of Kioto was reduced to ruins by an earthquake in 1596. In 1707, the weather being hot and calm, a sudden and terrific earth-wave passed along the south-eastern provinces. Totomi, Kii, Setsu, Tosa, Iyo, and Idzu suffered most, and another great blow at the beauty of the still unrivalled Fuji was struck. "A frightful eruption of Fuji-san occurred, and a new peak on the side of the mountain, now called Hoyei-san, was produced." This peak it is which, from some points of view, is now a sad breach of the beautiful vast sweeping curve of the mountain's eastern side, although there are other points of view from which it lends an additional charm. During the present century some of the worst earthquakes of Japan have occurred. In 1854 the south-eastern provinces * were severely shaken. A gentleman of Tosa, who kept a journal, wrote: "At the hour of the monkey (about 3.30 P.M.) a great shock came from the north-west, with a noise like that of a typhoon. The ground heaved like waves of water for a long while. Afterwards enormous waves rushed up the rivers, and the city of Kochi caught fire. Seventy

---

* Suruga, Mikawa, Totomi, Isé, Iga, Setsu, Harima, and the island of Shikoku.

different shocks occurred in the night. . . . By the first great convulsion the earth opened, land-slips took place from the mountains, rivers were flooded, and all dwelling-houses and fireproof storehouses were either thrown down or severely wrenched. . . . At about eight o'clock a great noise was heard, and on inquiring its cause I was told that great sea-waves were rushing in upon the land. The confusion of the moment was indescribable, the people all rushed towards the high land." In this and the following year 817 shocks were experienced in Tosa in fourteen months. It was in the latter year (1855) that the Russian frigate *Diana* was wrecked at Shimoda by the disturbance of land and sea, and that a large part of the city of Yedo and a vast number of its inhabitants were destroyed.*

Japan is not subject to thunderstorms of great frequency or violence, but it is sometimes visited by typhoons of devastating power, which are usually accompanied by heavy rains. They have been spoken of as, "next to inundations, the greatest terrestrial plague in Japan." They are revolving storms, advancing along a curved (parabolic) path, and blowing round the storm centre in a more or less circular form, increasing in force in proportion to the distance from it. "July, August, September, are the months in which these revolving storms occur in Japan,† and they seldom make their appearance as early as June, or are delayed so late as October" (Rein). The close of the summer of 1874 was remarkable for the number of the typhoons which ravaged the western part of Japan, one of which did great

---

* Mr. Hattori gives the following as a verse well known among the people expressive of earthquake indications :—

"*Kuwa Yamai,*
Gohichi ga ameni
Yotsu Hideri,
Mutsu yatsu kosoica
Kaze to Koso shire."

or, in English :—

" These are things
An earthquake brings :
At nine of the bell they sickness foretell,
At five and seven betoken rain,
At four the sky is cleared thereby,
At six and eight comes wind again."

† Dr. G. Maget will be seen presently to speak of them as occurring at the end of April.

damage at Nagasaki, among the ships in harbour, in the Dutch quarter of the town (Deshima), and in the adjacent fields. Dr. Maget speaks of these typhoons as defying description, but they are only of brief duration.

The following is a summary of a paper in the *Archives de Médecine navale* by Dr. G. Maget, who has resided in the Japanese islands, and travelled through a large part of them:* "Collectively they present a surface nearly one-third larger than that of France, with a population of thirty-six millions. The vegetable productions are varied, abundant, and useful. The bamboo grows luxuriantly, rice is cultivated with the dwarf palm, the wax-tree, and the cotton-tree. The banana, the pomegranate, the orange, with the sugar-cane and the indigo plant, grow freely. The whole country is liable to monsoons; a cold monsoon from the north-east visiting it from October to February, its commencement being announced by deluges of rain and terrible tornadoes, and a hot monsoon blowing from the south-west, which lasts from May to August, also accompanied by copious rains. The great meridional length of the islands of Niphon and Yezo, which constitute the greater part of Japan, causes the climate and temperature to vary greatly in different parts, and M. Maget distinguishes six regions. The first is the most northern, and is named Saghalin, and is boreal; it is little known. The second is that of Yezo, also cold, and hitherto but slightly investigated. The third and fourth correspond to the northern and middle and southern parts of the Island of Niphon. The northern region of that island, comprised between the 42° and 37° N. lat., is comparable to the temperate climate of the north of England, though the extremes of heat and cold are much greater. The central region, in which Yokohama is situated, is similar to that of the south-west of France, but again with extremes of considerable variation. In the southern region the isothermic lines undergo a great declension, and the extremes are very wide. The fifth region, that of Shikoku,

---

* The *Lancet* of Feb. 17, 1877, summarised by Mr. Anderson.

in which is Nagasaki, resembles that of Provence in its northern, and that of Sicily in its southern, portions. The sixth climate is that of the islands making up the Southern Archipelago of the south of Japan, and is tropical in its character; it has not been studied. The typhoons occur at the end of April and commencement of September, and coincide with the equinoxes and the reversal of the monsoons." M. Maget recommends Japan as an admirable place for those who are debilitated by a long sojourn on the coasts of Asia. The best parts are near Kobé and Hiogo, where the temperature is tolerably equable, the soil sandy, and good water abundant.

The mean annual temperature of the eastern capital, Tokio, from 1860 to 1875, was registered as between 58° and 59°, but in 1876 the more perfect records at the Imperial Meteorological Observatory (by Mr. H. B. Joyner) showed a mean of 56·3°, and it is probable, says Mr. Anderson of Tokio, that had the same advantages for estimation previously existed the isothermal line of Yedo (Tokio) would be found between 56° and 57°, instead of 2° higher. The lowest temperature is in January or February, when it seldom descends below 25°; the greatest heat is in August, when the thermometer rises to 90°, 95°, and even 100° in the shade. The average for the month is about 82°. The average humidity is greatest from June to September inclusive, amounting to about 80 per cent.; it is least from November to March, being then about 70 per cent.

The origin of the Japanese people is a question which has been much discussed, but upon which no settled and generally accepted conclusion appears yet to have been formed. The solution of the question derived from the native histories and legends is that they have descended directly from the gods. I will be neither so rude nor so unphilosophical as to dispute this theory, not doubting that we all shall be able to lay claim to divine descent, when we are able to trace our ancestry back to a sufficient distance; but an origin of this kind is much too remote to satisfy the inquisitiveness of ethnologists. We shall see hereafter that

Ninigi-no-mikoto was the god who was sent down from the sun-goddess, or queen of the sun (whose grandchild he was), to take possession of the land, and it was his offspring, and the offspring of his suite, that peopled Japan. Now Ninigi himself lived, according to some accounts, to the age of 310,000 years; his son Hohodemi is said to have lived to the still riper age of 637,892 years; and a grandchild of his, Ugaya, died at what all must admit to be the very remarkable age of 836,042 years. This gentleman was the father of the first historic emperor, Jimmu. It is not, therefore, without cause that I speak of this divine derivation of the Japanese as a remote one, if we have to get back many such generations as these in order to trace it. It is fair to say, however, that these immense periods have probably been imported into Japanese chronology since it came under the influence of Chinese scholarship.

Dr. Kaempfer, whose great work on Japan was published in London in 1727,* recounts legends which go to show that the Japanese are of Chinese origin, but these stories he himself rejects, grounding his disbelief upon the dissimilarity of the early languages, religions, and modes of life of the two countries. He takes it for granted that it is needless to show that the descent of the Japanese is not Korean. Dr. Kaempfer propounded a theory of his own, which is to the effect that they have descended from the inhabitants of Babylon, and suggests that "the Japanese language is one of those which sacred writ mentions that the all-wise Providence thought fit to infuse into the minds of the vain builders of the Babylonian Tower." The Japanese themselves, according to him, passed through Persia, then along the shore of the Caspian, and by the bank of the Oxus to its source. Thence they crossed China, descended the Amoor, and found their way southward to Korea, and across to Japan. Dr. Kaempfer being himself a great and enterprising traveller, evidently

---

* A fine copy of this somewhat rare work exists in the library of the House of Commons. General Balfour, M.P., has favoured me with the loan of another fine copy.

gave the early Japanese credit for better travelling powers than others may be willing to acknowledge, especially as he accounts for their picking up none of the languages that lay along their route by assuming that their journey was made with remarkable rapidity. He grants that the Japanese stock thus established in the country may have been supplemented by Chinese immigrants and shipwrecked people. It is needless to discuss the main theory of Kaempfer.

Another theory, and a favourite one, is that the Japanese have descended from the Ainos, a hirsute race now inhabiting the northern island of Yezo. This theory is based upon the fact that these Ainos appear to have at one time occupied a large part of the main island of Honshiu, and that the languages of the Ainos and the Japanese have many resemblances and relationships. Further, "the evidences of an aboriginal race are still to be found in the relics of the stone age in Japan. Flint arrow and spear heads, hammers, chisels, scrapers, kitchen refuse, and various other trophies are frequently excavated, or may be found in the museum or in homes of private persons. Though covered with the soil for centuries, they seem as though freshly brought from an Aino hut in Yezo. In scores of striking instances, the very peculiar ideas, customs, and superstitions of both Japanese and Aino are the same, or but slightly modified" (Griffis). Many of those who have studied this subject are of opinion that the greater part of the nobility have an origin distinct from that of the bulk of the people.

Another authority, and one of whom Mr. Griffis speaks as "one of the most accomplished linguists in Japan," states that "the short round skull, the oblique eyes, the prominent cheek-bones, the dark-brown hair, and the scant beard, all proclaim the Mantchus and Koreans as their nearest congeners."[*] He considers it certain that the Japanese are a Tungusic race, and their own traditions and the whole course of their history "are incompatible with any other

---

[*] A learned writer in the *Japan Mail*—probably Mr. W. J. Aston, M.A.

conclusion than that the Korea is the route by which the immigrant tribes made their passage into Kiushiu from their ancestral Mantchurian seats."

In a later chapter of this work (Chap. III., Vol. II.) I have made reference to a new theory of Japanese descent by Mr. Hyde Clarke, whose investigations have led him to trace the origin of the Japanese people to an ancient Turano-African empire.

It can hardly be doubted, I think, that whatever may have been the origin of the early inhabitants of Japan, there is at present a considerable mixture of races there. I noticed in several places remarkably different types of head and face, some striking characteristics being apparently restricted to single villages. It is only reasonable to presume that many natives of the neighbouring continent of Asia and of the numerous islands south of Japan have in the course of ages been driven by stress of weather from the sea to the shores of Japan, as is often the case now, and have there settled, and mixed, and intermarried with the natives.

The men of Japan are not in the main, I found, the small race which might be inferred from the frequency with which Japanese of low stature and slight structure are seen in this country. How to account for so many of the student class who have been sent to Europe being so remarkably small I know not; but in travelling through the interior of the country one may pass through village after village, and town after town, in which large men are the rule, and small the exception. The *jinriki-sha* coolies, fishermen, and other outdoor labourers appear to range above the average height and size, the *jinriki-sha* men in particular giving evidences of great speed and endurance, as I shall have occasion to mention in the record of our travels. The women are as a rule small, and often very small; but they are frequently of pleasing, and in many cases of beautiful, appearance. "When young they are usually attractive, notwithstanding the unclassical outline of their features; the neck especially is nearly always beautifully modelled. . . . The skin is usually sallow, but in young girls may be as fair as that of a European" (Anderson). The hair of both men and women is always black, and usually straight. Both men and women acquire an aged look comparatively early—a fact which may be partly accounted for in the case of the women by the length of time for which the weaning of children is postponed, viz. three or four years, or even more. The custom which has prevailed among the women of Japan until lately (but is now becoming neglected) of blackening the teeth and shaving off the eyebrows after marriage detracts notably from both their beauty and their youthful appearance. In Japan there appear to be very few young and pretty married women, although the streets abound with young and pretty girls, and with women who seem to be middle-aged and more or less careworn. This state of things will improve with the abolition of the defacing customs just mentioned, and with the improvement in the condition of the people which is resulting under the new government of the country from the spread of comfort, education, freedom, and respect for the sex.

OUR FIRST VIEW OF JAPAN.

CHAPTER II.

THE GOD-PERIOD.

Japanese mythology abundant and varied—The sacred books Kojiki and Nihonki—Their origin and authorship—Their alleged errors—" In the beginning"—The Lord of the Centre of Heaven—The Lofty and Divine Producers—The Japanese account of the creation—The Male- and Female-who-Invite—The production of land and sea—Amaterasu, the sun-goddess—Origin of the Divine Insignia of the Imperial Power—Ninigi-no-mikoto, the "Sovran Grandchild"—His descent by the Floating Bridge of Heaven—The brother of the sun-goddess—His misbehaviour and its consequence—The winning of the sun-goddess from the cave—The origin of the religious symbols of Japan—Legends of the gods—The divine descent of the Mikados—Jimmu-Tenno, the first emperor—The Mikados themselves gods—Newer views—The old views said to be reconcilable with science.

JAPAN possesses a mythology almost as abundant and varied as that of Greece, and it is proper to pay to the Japanese nation the compliment of assuming that it at one time signified something, that there were at least a few clever persons who understood it, and that those who understood it agreed about it. I regret to say that it does not seem possible now to find anybody who understands it, and if there be a few, they certainly do not agree among themselves. But this is only saying what is equally true of the mythology of Greece; and even with regard to our own much humbler mythologies at home, derived from the East, there appears at times to be some want of understanding and agreement among those who profess to know most about them. I should be very glad if I could let the matter alone, as regards Japan, for two reasons: first, I know but very little about it; and secondly, the immortals gave themselves such tremendously long-breathed names (although they are not really very hard to deal with when one sees how their parts have been put together) that I am afraid the mere writing of them down will alarm my readers, and alarm them so much that they may fail to settle again even upon the simpler pages which follow. But it is quite impossible here to let the matter alone, for the simple reason that so many of these early gods and goddesses of Japan are worshipped still at the shrines and temples which we have visited, and about which I have to speak to the reader, that some previous mention of them is absolutely necessary. I have therefore read what Mr. Ernest Satow says concerning them in his various writings so far as I have seen them; I have studied carefully what Mr. Griffis and several others have written; and I have got some learned Japanese friends of mine to tell me independently what they could about the god-history, and to translate for me some of the most essential parts of the original sacred writings, the *Kojiki* and the *Nihonki*. Besides this, I have made many specific inquiries of the principal Shinto priests, at the sacred shrines of Isé and elsewhere; and I have gathered up such additional information as exceptional opportunities have afforded. I find the authorities cited not agreeing on several points, but I shall do my best to outline the subject with as much accuracy as the case admits of, observing that in Mr. Satow's writings one has the advantage of seeing the modifications of view held by some of the greatest writers who have commented upon the Shinto religion during the last century or two.*

I have already mentioned the two most sacred books of Japan—the *Kojiki* and the *Nihonki*: the former dates from 711 of our era, and the latter was completed eleven years later, 720 A.D. The *Kojiki* is a record of the ancient history of the country, the first part of which relates to the mythologic period. It is written in Japanese, but, according to

---

* The writings of Mr. Ernest Satow which I shall chiefly make use of in this chapter are his papers in the 'Transactions' of the Royal Asiatic Society, on 'The Revival of Pure Shinto' (vol. iii. pt. 1, 1875), and on 'Ancient Japanese Ritual' (vol. vii. pt. 2, 1879).

Mr. Aston, almost entirely in the Chinese characters known as "mana,"* while, according to the Japanese Education Department, Chinese characters were used only as phonetics of the Japanese sounds. It was presented by the minister Futo Yasumaro to the empress Gemmei, at Nara, prefaced by an address in pure Chinese.† Mr. Aston (in his work quoted in a footnote) states that the value of the *Kojiki* to the student of the Japanese language is much lessened by the employment of the Chinese characters in its composition, and a careful attempt was made by the great Japanese writer Motoöri (born in 1730, whom we shall have occasion to notice when we visit his birthplace) to restore, as he called it, the entire text in what he conceived to be the original Japanese form; but this attempt is considered unsatisfactory by Mr. Aston, who says that parts of Motoöri's version cannot be correct, "and it is impossible to accept it as genuine Japanese of the period when the *Kojiki* was written." ‡

It is not an uncommon thing to hear it said that the *Kojiki* was written by a woman. But those who read the following accounts of the matter will observe that this mode of putting the case is scarcely a correct one. In a dis-

---

* "Mana" means "true name," implying that this is the true use of a character, while "kana" means "borrowed name," as in this case the mere sound of a character is borrowed in order to express the whole, or more frequently only part of a word unconnected with it in meaning. See Aston, 'Grammar of the Japanese Written Language' (Trübner & Co.).

† Chinese composition had been introduced into Japan four hundred years earlier, during the reign of the emperor Ojin (270-312 A.D.), but the style of the composition at that time is unknown. In the fourth year of the reign of the empress Suiko (596 A.D.), at Dogo, in the province of Iyo, a stone monument was erected, the inscription upon it being preserved in the *Nihonki*. Thirty-one years after this an image of Buddha was made, which still exists in the famous temples of Hori-uji, in Yamato (where it was shown to us), and on the back of which is engraved an inscription which cannot be now read, owing partly to the effects of time, and partly also to the Japanese not having obtained perfection in Chinese composition. See official 'Outline History of Japanese Education.' Mr. Satow questions the introduction of the Chinese classics so early as the third century.

‡ In a later chapter I will give (in Roman letters) a verse of poetry from this ancient book, one of the oldest specimens extant of the Japanese language.

cussion at the Royal Asiatic Society in Tokio, the Rev. Dr. Brown stated that the *Kojiki* is acknowledged to be the work of a female peasant, who was possessed of so extraordinary a memory that she could repeat all the traditions she had ever heard, *verbatim et literatim*, and who, when in 712 A.D. the dynastic records had ceased to be worthy of credence, reproduced the ancient traditions from the beginning of all things down to her own times. On the same occasion another gentleman (Mr. von Brandt, late Minister of the German Empire in Japan) gave a fuller account of· the matter, and put it upon a sounder basis. He said : " As to the historical records of Japan, it is first mentioned that under the twentieth emperor, in 415 A.D., officials were sent into the country to verify and describe the names of all the families. Later a transcription of these records (originally written, in all probability, in the old Japanese letters, 'the gods' letters') in Chinese characters took place, and in 644 an historical account of the emperors, the country, the officials, and the people is said to have existed, which was destroyed when Iruka was murdered, and his father's palace, in which these records were kept, was burnt. Only the history of the country was saved. From this work, as well as from what the old men of the whole empire remembered, a new compilation was made under the emperor Temmu (672-686) ; and in order that it might not be lost again, it was read to a peasant girl, of the name of Aré, said never to forget anything she had once heard. From this record, and from what Aré still remembered, the first historical record of Japan known to us, the *Kojiki*, was compiled about thirty years later." According to this, the *Kojiki* has a much better and broader basis than would be indicated by saying that it was written by a woman, or by putting the case as the Rev. Dr. Brown puts it. Remembering how little is known of the origin of many of the " sacred books " of the world, one may fairly say that the *Kojiki*, if resting even upon this ground, would take quite a high place among them. I observe further, however, that Mr. Satow (who is probably a better authority than either of the other gentlemen), in a paper published the year following this discussion, pointed out that the preface to the *Kojiki* is the only authority for the accepted account of its origin, and recites from that source a statement somewhat similar to that just cited from Mr. von Brandt, but giving the full name of Aré as Hiyeda-no-Aré, and although in a footnote he remarks that Hirata has stated reasons for supposing this to be a woman, he himself speaks of Aré as of a man who had a marvellous memory, and says that the emperor Temmu caused him to be so practised in reciting from memory the genuine traditions and the "old language of former ages" that he came to know the whole by heart. In a work published by the authority of the present Government of Japan is the following reference to the same person: "There is no doubt that in the remotest periods events were transmitted from mouth to mouth, without being reduced to writing, as is seen in the case of a History of Japan, in three volumes, by Hiyetano Aré, the contents of which, it appears, were recited and learnt by heart before being reduced to writing." *

The *Nihonki* was compiled, as we have seen, but very little later than the *Kojiki*, and deals largely with the mythological period. Another name for the *Nihonki* is *Nihon-shoki*, and it is said that it also was presented to the empress by Futo Yusumaro, being written in Chinese. The unlettered could not, therefore, understand this and similar works which followed, and consequently there existed in the middle ages rules for the interpretation of the *Nihonki*, and gradually it came to be regarded as a religious work on Shintoism.†

I am afraid that when I come to notice the contents of these works they will be found to comprise much about the origin of gods and men, and of worlds likewise, that some

---

* See the later chapter of this work, on Language and Literature, in the early part of which I have more particularly referred to the Oriental practice of committing sacred books to memory.

† 'Outline History of Education in Japan.'

of my readers will find it very hard to accept without liberal reservation. The scholars of the present day appear to bear hardly upon both of these sacred treasuries of Japanese truth, in spite of all the labours of Motoöri, Hirata, and the rest of the scholars of the past. I have read a good deal of critical, and some hypercritical, writing about our own sacred books ; but I do not remember seeing them so roundly and trenchantly assailed as these Japanese Bibles, so to call them, are by American and English scholars in Japan. Fortunately I have not met any native gentleman or lady who is likely to become heartbroken on account of such criticisms : nor have I known any rise into ecstasies of ill-temper, as some people unhappily do, when defending their sacred books. Still, it is always a little touching to see a clear-headed, cold-blooded critic turned loose among the old, delicate, and fragile porcelain, so to speak, of a people's beliefs. Mr. Griffis, for example, speaking of both these books (the *Kojiki* and the *Nihonki*), says : " These are the oldest books in the language. Numerous and very valuable commentaries upon them have been written. They contain " (and here one almost hopes that something favourable is coming, but no) " so much that is fabulous, mythical, or exaggerated, that their statements, especially in respect of dates, cannot be accepted as true history." Mr. Satow is no milder in his treatment of the *Nihonki*. He shows that its dates are almost certainly wrong ; he will not allow that the emperors Suinin and Keiko were over a hundred and forty years old when they died, or that the famous Takeuchi-no-Sukune lived to be three hundred and fifty before he left us—although we all know perfectly well from our own records that Adam lived to be nine hundred and thirty years old ; that Seth died only eighteen years younger ; that Enos was over nine hundred when he died, Methuselah nine hundred and sixty-nine, and so forth. Even Noah himself, with all his anxieties and troubles (among others those of ship-building, which I have found to be very considerable), lived to the age of nine hundred and fifty ! With these records (which we are not permitted by our friends to question) in our own sacred history, it will seem to some hard to deny to the direct descendants of the gods themselves—which the Mikados of Japan always have been—the privilege of living for a paltry century and a half or so! But Mr. Satow goes further than this; for he shows that the *Nihonki* contains abundant indications of Chinese influence, and that some of the speeches attributed in it to the ancient Mikados contain passages that are wholly Chinese, both in their meaning and their form, and therefore are necessarily fictitious. In view of all which, I would simply observe that it really does not much matter how the *Nihonki* was got together. The great questions with reference to sacred books, in all countries, are—first, How long have they been reverenced? Secondly, How long are they likely to be? It is not so much the amount of divine inspiration put into them, as the amount of human reverence that has surrounded them, for which most people care, and in this respect the *Nihonki* is quite authoritative enough for our present purpose.

Coming a little closer to our subject, I would next remark that what I find so troublesome in mythologies—and in theologies, too, very often—is not their want of ancient authority, but their lamentable facility in contradicting themselves. Parts of them are so perplexingly inconsistent with other parts. In these sacred books of Japan, for example, a god does not always remain a god, but sometimes becomes a goddess; and goddesses become gods in like manner. Worse than this: two or three gods very often make their appearance as only one god; or, what is probably the case, one god gets two or three names given to him, and under each of these names gets idolised. I may instance "the gods of the gate," of which the *Kojiki* says that the three are but one; whereas, at the Mikado's court, two gods of the gate were separately worshipped.

As to the manner in which creation goes on in these mythologies—I mean creations of gods as well as of material objects —it is really impossible to avoid regretting that a different system was not adopted. We all remember in what a very unpleasant and unsatisfactory manner many of the divinities of Greece originated, and the mythology of Japan is no great improvement upon the European. One would think that people, having all the beautiful earth and heavens spread out before them, and being entirely free to account for their origin as they please, would invent none but really beautiful myths and divine stories by way of explaining them all: and this, in spite of gales and thunders and earthquakes, and all the other violent incidents of earthly life. And no doubt some of the myths of all countries are beautiful and natural; and, I suppose, those that are otherwise must be attributed to the weakness and impurity of the imagination of early peoples. Parts of these Japanese accounts of the beginning of things are pretty enough in spite of some extravagances, and the story of the winning of the sun-goddess from the cave is as fascinating as one could desire. Nor must I forget to add that the divine age is continually reflected in the present one, and the life of the Japanese people, both religious and secular, at the present hour abounds with emblems and reminiscences of the gods.

The account of the origin of things in the Hebrew Bible is in some respects an admirable one, and not the least part of its merit consists in the total avoidance of an extremely obscure question, viz. In the beginning did void space exist, or had space something in it? "In the beginning God created the heaven and the earth;" that is what we are told, and that is all we are told, and those who wish to conceive the original space filled with matter can do so if they please, while those who wish to disport their imaginations in an absolute void are equally at liberty to suppose the original abyss empty. It is just possible that the *Kojiki* may leave us equal freedom; but unfortunately those who are able to read it give us precisely opposite interpretations. Mr. Griffis, for instance, tells us that in the Japanese beginning there was a chaos, and that "the idea of space apart from matter is foreign to the Japanese philosophical system." Mr. Satow, on the contrary, says that in the beginning there was infinite space: " neither heaven, nor earth, nor the sun, nor moon, *nor anything else* existed." It may seem very presumptuous for me to say so, but my opinion is that both these accomplished gentlemen are wrong, and that I shall do the *Kojiki* and the Shinto religion and Japanese philosophy strict justice by saying that, according to them, there existed in the beginning one god, and nobody and nothing besides.

"Far in the deep infinitudes of space,
Upon a throne of silence,"
sat the god
Ame-no-mi-naka-nushi-no-kami,
whose name signifies

The Lord of the Centre of Heaven;

and next, and before anybody or anything else entered upon the scene, appeared these two gods, viz.—

Taka-mi-musubi-no-kami,
and
Kamu-mi-musubi-no-kami;

these names respectively signifying

Lofty Producer, and
Divine Producer.

This, then, defines the condition from which we are to start, viz. that of pure infinite space, inhabited only by the three deities just named, the Lord of the Centre of Heaven, and the Lofty and Divine Producers. By the power of these last-named gods there was brought into existence something which words cannot define. It appeared in the midst of space, not exactly floating there, for there was nothing for it to float in; but the Producers created something there, and we may imagine it almost as we please— either diffused uniformly throughout a vast space, or set in the midst of space, and occupying a small amount of it. Newton found that a spherical inch of air removed four thousand miles from the earth would be so much relieved from pressure that it would expand into a sphere more than filling the orbit of Saturn; so that a very little matter will go a long way if required, and there need be no difficulty in imagining enough matter to fill any portion of the infinite space which we are able to conceive. Mr. Herbert Spencer, in his Essay on the Nebular Hypothesis, imagines " a rare and widely diffused mass of nebulous matter," and proceeds to consider what are the successive changes that will naturally take place in it. He shows that such a mass will in course of time resolve itself into flocculi of precipitated denser matter; that a rotatory motion will be afterwards set up, both in the flocculi and in the medium in which they float; that the flocculi will form into groups—and, in short, that you will get the universe formed as we now see it. I am sorry to have to correct so clear and profound a thinker—perhaps the clearest and profoundest at present alive—but he is certainly wrong in his reasoning as to what *would* happen in the beginning, because what really *did* happen was this: From the mass of nebulous matter produced by the two gods there went forth upwards a sort of horn or sprout, which widened out into the heaven, or the high plain of heaven, and from which were produced two additional gods,* and afterwards the sun. The nebulous matter also sprouted downwards, and from this downward development was afterwards produced the moon. The *five* gods already mentioned existed separately, and were known as the gods of heaven.

During the upward and downward outspreadings of the substances developed from the nebulous mass, there were produced fourteen additional gods and goddesses, with the last pair of whom alone we need concern ourselves: these were Izanagi-no-kami, the Male-who-Invites, and Izanami-no-kami, the Female-who-Invites. This pair produced the land, the sea, the elements, and the eight islands of Japan, now called Awaji, Shikoku, Oki, Kiushiu, Iki, Tsushima, Sado, and the main island. They are likewise the parents of the deities of the sun and of the moon (not of the sun and moon themselves, as we have already noted their origin); and they are also the progenitors of all the later gods. In this illustrious couple we may doubtless see the first pair of

---

* Umashi-ashi-kabi-hiko-ji-no-kami, and Ame-no-toko-tachi-no-kami.

lovers, and the primal embodiment of the art and exercise of love.* Among their many children were Amaterasu-oho-mi-kami, the From-Heaven-Shining-Great-Deity—otherwise Ten-Sho Dai-jin †—the immortal goddess of the sun; and her younger brother, Susanoö-no-mikoto, who was afterwards appointed the god of the sea. Some accounts say that on returning to the earth from the nether region, to which he descended in search of his wife (who had gone thither in consequence of his looking upon her when she had enjoined him not to do so), Izanagi washed himself in the sea, and produced certain gods by blowing as he plunged among the shoals; and that afterwards by the washing of his left eye Amaterasu was produced, and by the washing of his right eye, Susanoö.

Amaterasu, on account of her bright beauty, was by her father made queen of the sun, and shared with the two creator-gods the government of the world. In sending her to her dominion Izanagi gave her the necklace of precious stones from his neck, and told her to go up by way of the floating bridge to be hereafter referred to. As the sun was then near, she ascended without difficulty. Desiring afterwards to give the government of the earth to her grandson, Ninigi-no-mikoto, after considerable trouble in getting the god in possession to make way for him, she was able to carry out her purpose, and despatch him to his post. She proclaimed him sovereign of Japan for ever and ever, and appointed his descendants to rule it as long as the heavens and the earth endure. Before starting—and here let the reader note carefully the history—he received from his grandmother, the sun-goddess, the Three Divine Insignia of the Imperial Power of Japan, viz. the Sacred Mirror, which is still worshipped at the Naiku Shrine in Isé as the goddess's representative; the Sacred Sword, which is still

---

* The *Nihonki* philosophises, Chinese fashion, about the Producer Gods, as we call them, representing respectively the positive or negative principles. But Motoöri repudiates these ideas, and says that they would lead one to look upon Izanagi and Izanami as mere abstract principles, whereas they are really "living powers."

† "Great Goddess of the Shining Heaven."

enshrined at the Temple of Atsuta, near Nagoya, at the head of the bay of Owari; and the Sacred Stone, or "Magatama," which is always in possession of the emperor of Japan. Possessed of these divine symbols, and accompanied by a number of inferior gods, Ninigi-no-mikoto descended upon the Floating Bridge of Heaven, or the "Ama-no-uki-hashi." Grains of rice were thrown broadcast in the air to dispel the darkness of the sky. The Ama-no-uki-hashi was expressly intended for facilitating communication between heaven and earth in those days, and, although it is sometimes spoken of as a bridge, it is at other times called a boat; and if it happened to be, as it really was, a mountain-top, the propriety of both terms would be admirable. Everybody has seen a mountain-top standing so high up in a clear sky as to enable the gods to descend upon it with ease, just as if it were a bridge, the very same mountain-top at other times, being cut off by clouds from the land below it, seeming to float like a boat upon the surface of them. In this instance, however, Ninigi-no-mikoto and his staff of gods do not appear to have descended directly upon the bridge or boat, but passed to it by means of *hashidates*, or eminences.

My readers will be much interested to learn that the conspicuous mountain of Kirishima, near the south-western extremity of Japan, 5000 feet high, is the very floating bridge of heaven itself of which we have been speaking; that the rice thrown about at the time of the god's descent grows wild upon it to this day; and that the very mounds (*hashidates*) over which the god advanced to it are still traceable in the provinces of Harima and Tango. I ought to state, however, that after the descent of the "Sovran Grandchild" (as Ninigi is called in the rituals, as translated by Mr. Satow), the sun and the earth receded much farther from each other, communication by means of the bridge ceased, and the *hashidates* fell down, and have since lain on their longest side. That near Miyadzu in Tango measures 22,290 feet in length.

Now that we know all about the bridge of heaven, I must

pause to mention that although I have correctly stated that Izanagi and Izanami produced the land, I have not yet pointed out a circumstance of great interest in connection with this proceeding. The land generally, and most of the islands of Japan, were produced by the god and goddess as usual, but before this could be done an island for them to rest upon was of course necessary, and this was created in an exceptional manner. The two deities, standing on the bridge of heaven, pushed down a spear into the green plain of the sea, and stirred it round and round. When they drew it up, the drops which fell from its end consolidated, and became an island, which was that of Onogorojima, which has been identified with a small island at the northwest corner of Awaji, on the eastern part of the inland sea, called Ye-shima. The sun-born pair descended on to the island, and, planting the spear in the ground point downwards, built a palace round it, taking that for the central roof pillar. The spear became the axis of the earth, which had been caused to revolve by the stirring round. The island must then of course have been situated at the pole of the earth, but for some reason or other (probably on account of the climate) it has been brought where it now is, and where Sir G. Nares would have no difficulty in finding it. I have seen it there myself.

It is painful to have next to refer to the misconduct of the younger brother of the sun-goddess, whom we have noted as Susanoö-no-mikoto. I shall record the nature of his misconduct on an important occasion more fully when we get to the shrines of Isé; suffice it here to say that he so seriously offended his bright and beautiful sister that she went away and concealed herself in the cave of Ameno Tuaya, closing the entrance with a large piece of rock. From this time the country was dark all over, and given up to the noise and disturbances of all sorts of inferior gods. This state of things was so distressing that all the gods assembled * at

---

* Mr. Griffis says 800,000 in number, but I believe I am correct in saying that there were eight millions. There certainly is said to be that number now, as we shall see by-and-by, when we visit the Kioto temples.

the cave's mouth, on the bank of the Yasukawa River, and deliberated upon the means to be adopted for inducing the petulant goddess to reappear—for be it understood that after the birth of the sun-goddess no light could be obtained except from her brightness, as she had been appointed to illuminate the space between earth and heaven, and it was the brightness of her body that shone through the sun. At the council of the gods it was decided to entice the goddess forth by means of an image of herself; and one of the gods (Ishi-keri-dome-no-mikoto) and a blacksmith made mirrors in the shape of the sun with iron from heaven. The first two mirrors produced were small and unsatisfactory, but the third was large and beautiful, and is now the deity of the inner shrine of Isé. The gods also planted hemp and *kodzu*, and with their fibre and bark respectively wove clothing for the goddess. They also cut down timber and built a palace. Magatama jewels (carved and polished pieces of stone), such as were worn in those days as ornaments, were also produced; and wands were made from sakaki branches and bamboo. One of the gods then pulled up a sakaki-tree by the roots, and on its upper branches hung the necklace of jewels; at the middle he hung the sacred mirror, and to the lower branches he attached coarse and fine cloth. "This formed," says Mr. Satow, "a large *mitegura* (or *gohei*), which was held by Ama-no-futo-dama-no-mikoto, while he pronounced an address in honour of the goddess." And *goheis* like this, with jewels, mirrors, and strips of cloth (cut zigzag), we shall see hereafter in the hands of the young priestesses at the shrine of the goddess herself, and the simpler *gohei*, or wands, with strips of cloth or paper attached, are now to be seen, as they have for ages been, all over Japan, at every Shinto temple or shrine, and in thousands of other places.

But we must proceed with the story. A number of cocks were next collected, and set to crow in concert; a strong god was concealed by the door of the cavern, to wrest it open at the favourable moment; and a very renowned goddess, Uzumé (in full, Amé-no-uzumé-no-mikoto), was set to dance divinely, blowing music out of a bamboo tube pierced with holes, while the gods kept time to her by striking two pieces of hard wood together. A sort of harp was made by placing six bows together, with the strings upward, and this was played by the drawing of grass and rushes across it. Uzumé, who appears to have entered upon her task with great spirit, bound her sleeves close up to the arm-pits, and grasped in her hand a bundle of twigs, and a spear wound round with grass, with small bells attached to it. Bonfires were lighted, and a circular box or drum was placed for her to dance upon. Then this young goddess commenced to tread with measure upon the hollow box and cause it to resound; sang a six-syllable song or charm of numbers; and, gradually quickening her dance, wrought herself up to such a pitch of excitement, or rather "such a spirit descended on the goddess," that she loosened her dress, revealing more and more of her loveliness, and at last, to the intense amazement and delight of the gods, appears to have neglected her dress altogether.* With the laughter of the gods the heavens shook. The address in her honour (which, by-the-by, pleased the goddess more than anything she had heard before), the stirring sounds of the music and dancing, and the loud and joyous laughter of the gods were too much for Amaterasu, and, slightly opening the door, she softly said from inside, "I fancied that because of my retirement both heaven and Japan were in darkness! Why has Uzumé danced, and why do the gods laugh?" Uzumé replied, "I dance, and they laugh because there is an honourable deity here" (pointing to the mirror) "who surpasses you in glory;" and as she said this the mirror was pushed forward, and shown to the sun-goddess, reflecting her own radiant loveliness, of course, and her astonishment was greater even than before. As she peeped out of the door to look round, the strong god pulled the rock-door open, and drew the bright goddess forth. Then a rice-straw rope was passed behind her, and one of

---

* For the song sung by her, see the chapter on Language and Literature.

the gods said, "Go not back behind this." As they were putting the mirror into the cave it was struck against the door, and received a flaw which remains to this day. They then removed the goddess to her new palace, and put a straw rope round it to keep off evil gods.

I have already observed that the *gohei* is still in universal use throughout Japan; so, too, are the two pieces of hard wood struck together. You see and hear them in every theatre, and at every sort of public performance, and unpleasant they are, with their harsh sharp sound, to our ears. The instrument formed of bamboo tubes, pierced at the joints, is likewise very common, especially in temple music, and few things are more common than the drum-like instrument like that on which Uzumé danced. Masks and pictures of Uzumé herself—with small forehead and large out-blown cheeks—are also to be seen to-day in the shops of every town and village in Japan. The straw rope is still stretched across the Shinto *toriis* and shrines throughout the country. The "mirror" is seen throughout the temples of Japan, but that is usually a Buddhist and not a Shinto symbol, the one true Shinto mirror being itself concealed from sight at the shrine of Uji in Isé.

There are endless varying legends about this god-period of Japan which it might amuse the reader to cite, but I need not for my present purpose add much here to what has already been said, the less so as I shall have frequent occasion hereafter to refer to it. When we visit Isé, for example, we shall have to speak of the deities of its sacred and ancient shrines; when we come to Nagoya, we shall tell more of the sacred sword treasured in the neighbouring temple of Atsuta; and on other occasions additional explanations will have to be given. All that we need now further say in the way of reciting the legends of the gods has relation to the descent of the mikados of Japan from the deities of whom we have been speaking. It was the misconduct of Susanoö that drove the sun-goddess into the cave, and for this misconduct he was banished. Some say that, instead of proceeding to his place of banishment, he

THE GODDESS UZUMÉ.

From Hokusai.   Reproduced for this Work by a Japanese Engraver.

To face page 34, Vol. I.

descended, with his son Idakiso-no-mikoto, upon Shiraga (in Korea), but not liking the place went back by a vessel to the bank of the Hinokawa River, in Idzumo, Japan. At the time of their descent, Idakiso had many plants or seeds of trees with him, but he planted none in Shiraga, but took them across with him, and scattered them from Kiushiu all over Japan, so that the whole country became green with trees. It is said that Idakiso is respected as the god of merit, and is worshipped in Kinokuni. His two sisters also took care of the plantation. One of the gods who reigned over the country in the prehistoric period was Ohonamuchi, who is said by some to be the son of Susanoö, and by others to be one of his later descendants; "and which is right, it is more than we can say," remarked one of my scholarly friends. However, during his reign he was anxious about the people, and, consulting with Sukunahikona-no-mikoto, applied "his whole heart," we are told, to their good government, and they all became loyal to him. One time he said to his friend just named, "Do you think we are governing the people well?" and his friend answered, "In some respects well, and in some not," so that they were frank and honest with each other in those days. When Sukunahikona went away, Ohonamuchi said, "It is I who should govern this country. Is there any who will assist me?" Then there appeared over the sea a divine light, and there came a god floating and floating, and said, "You cannot govern the country without me, and you can do great good with me." And this proved to be the god Ohomiwa-no-kami, who built a palace at Mimuro, in Yamato, and dwelt therein. He affords a direct link with the Mikado family, for his daughter became the empress of the first historic emperor, Jimmu. Her name was Himétatara Izudsu himé. All the descendants of her father are named, like him, Ohomiwa-no-kami, and it is said that the present empress of Japan is probably a descendant of this god.

As regards the descent of the emperor Jimmu himself, we already know that Ninigi-no-mikoto, the "sovran grandchild" of the sun-goddess, was sent down with the sacred symbols of empire, given to him in the sun, by the sun-goddess herself, before he started for the earth. Now Ninigi married (reader, forgive me for quoting the lady's name and her father's) Konohaneno-sakuya-himé, the daughter of Ohoyamazumino-kami, and the pair had three sons, of whom the last, named Howori-no-mikoto, succeeded to the throne. He is sometimes called by the following simple (and possibly endearing) name, Amatsuhitakahikohohodemi-no-mikoto. He married Toyatama-himé, the daughter of the sea-god, and they had a son, Ugaya-fuki-ayedsu-no-mikoto, born, it is said, under an unfinished roof of cormorants' wings, who succeeded the father, and who married Tamayori-himé, also a daughter of the sea-god. This illustrious couple had four sons, of whom the last succeeded to the throne in the year 660 B.C. He was named Kamu-yamato iwarehiko-no-mikoto, but posterity has fortunately simplified his designation to the now familiar Jimmu-Tenno, the first historic emperor of Japan, and the ancestor of the present emperor.

Some important consequences follow from the above record, in the opinions of the great Japanese writers who flourished before the recent revolution. The chief of these have been thus summarised from Motoöri. Japan being the country which gave birth to Amaterasu, the sun-goddess, is superior to all the other countries which enjoy her favours. The goddess, having endowed the "sovran grandchild," Ninigi-no-mikoto, with the three sacred treasures, proclaimed him sovereign of Japan for ever and ever, and his descendants shall continue to rule it so long as the heavens and earth endure. He being invested with this complete authority, all the gods under heaven, and all mankind, submitted to him, with the exception of a few wretches who were quickly subdued. To the end of time each Mikado is the son of the goddess. His mind is in perfect harmony of thought and feeling with hers. He does not seek out new devices, but rules in accordance with precedents which date from the god-period. The age of the gods and the present age are, therefore, not two ages but one, for not only the Mikado, but his ministers and subjects also, act upon the traditions of the divine age. Every event in the universe is an act of the gods: good events are acts of the gods that are good, and evil events the acts of evil gods. The Mikado, being appointed by the deities who created the country (Izanagi and Izanami), is its immovable ruler, who must endure as long as the sun and moon continue to shine. In ancient language he was called a god, and that is his real character. He must, therefore, be implicitly and without question obeyed. Human beings, having been produced by the spirit of the two creative deities, are naturally endowed with the knowledge of what they ought to do and ought to refrain from. It is unnecessary for them to trouble themselves with systems of morals, for if that were necessary men would be inferior to animals, who know what they ought to do, only in an inferior degree to man. Just as the Mikado himself worshipped the gods of heaven and earth, so his people prayed to the good gods in order to obtain blessings, and performed rites in honour of the bad gods to avert their displeasure.

But here we stop, as the Shinto religion will form the subject of a later chapter. Let it be remembered that the theory just quoted from Motoöri was propounded in the last century, and that after the changes which have taken place in Japan during the last few years much of what was then thought and written would be no more readily accepted by educated Japanese of the present day than it would be by ourselves. Indeed, as Motoöri attacked the Chinese philosophy severely in defence of the early Shinto faith, he was long ago severely attacked in return, and the faith likewise. It would be going beyond the limits laid down for this chapter were we to enter at all upon these discussions, but it is worthy of remark that some of the controversialists of Japan have shown no little dexterity and courage in claiming for their sacred books the corroboration and authority of modern science, so far as they allow that to be accurate. "When we come," says one of them, Hatori, "to compare our ancient traditions as to the origination of a thing in the midst of space, and its subsequent development, with what has been ascertained to be the actual shape of the earth, we find that there is not the slightest error, and the result confirms the truth of our ancient traditions." We have noticed something very like this in our own country before now, English theologians being remarkable even among theologians for the courage with which they will in one age claim for their views the support of that very scientific truth which in the preceding age they vehemently denounced as flagrant heresy and impiety.

THE SACRED SHRINES OF ISÉ.

CHAPTER III.

THE SHINTO RELIGION.

The early religion of the Japanese—Probably a natural and independent religious system—The *kami*, or gods of the country—The *Kami-no-michi*, or "way of the gods," must be learnt by studying the sacred writings—Its primal principle obedience to the god-Mikado—Good gods to be worshipped, and bad gods propitiated—Prayer of the Mikado—The worship of ancestors enjoined—Prayer to the god and goddess of wind—Other prayers—The gods of the sun and moon—The Rough Spirit and Gentle Spirit—The *kami-dana*, or Penates—The rituals of the Shinto religion—The harvest prayers and ceremonies—The divine descent of the priestly houses—Mr. Satow's translation of a very ancient ritual or *norito*—The necessity of distinguishing the ancient religion from its modern forms—Tendency of modern Japanese commentaries—Shinto a religious system in a true sense—Its influence upon the early Mikados—Their efforts at improvement, and devotion to their people—"Sujin the Civiliser"—The belief of the early Japanese in the helpfulness of their gods—Simplicity of their forms of worship—Shinto ceremonials contrasted with those of Buddhism and Roman Catholicism—The practice of purification—Respect for life—Simple demeanour of Shinto priests—Temples and votive offerings.

WE have seen that the historic dynasty and government of Japan profess to date from 660 B.C., and it was not until the sixth century A.D. that Buddhism obtained a hold upon the country. If by our refusal to the early emperors of the long lives claimed for a few of them we have to strike off, say, two hundred years from this interval, we shall still have an historic period of nearly a thousand years, during which the Shinto was the only religious faith of the Japanese nation. And the question then arises, Was this an indigenous system, or was it imported from Korea, China, or elsewhere? Mr. Griffis says: "After all the research of foreign scholars who have examined the claims of Shinto on the soil, and by the aid of the language and the sacred books and commentators, many hesitate to decide whether Shinto is a genuine product of the Japanese soil, or whether it is not closely allied with the ancient religion of China, which existed before the period of Confucius. The weight of opinion inclines to the latter belief." But in his paper on "Ancient Japanese Rituals," which is of later date than the work of Mr. Griffis, Mr. Satow, speaking of the Shinto of the primitive Japanese, says: "If we can separate it from the spurious counterfeits and adulterations which are presented to us as Shinto, we shall probably arrive at a natural religion in a very early stage of development, which perhaps originated quite independently of any other natural religion known to us, and that certainly would be of value as showing one way in which a natural religion may spring up."

Shinto is itself a Chinese term, and one the use of which has occasionally been complained of by vindicators of the ancient religion. The native designation of that religion is *Kami-no-michi*, or way of the gods. In order to get, if we can, at the meaning of this, we will first inquire what is the true signification of the word *kami*. It will be found a very broad one. The word is applied first to all the gods of heaven and earth who are mentioned in the ancient records, and to their spirits which reside in the temples where they are worshipped. The *kami* of the divine age were mostly human beings, and amongst human beings who are at the same time *kami* are all the mikados (who in the ancient writings are called *tôtsu-kami*, "distant gods," on account of their being far removed from common men); and besides the mikados many other men, some of whom are revered as *kami* by the whole empire, while others are limited to a single province, department, town, village, or even family. Further, birds, beasts, plants and trees, seas and mountains, and all other things whatsoever which possess powers of an extraordinary and eminent character, or deserve to be revered or dreaded, are called *kami*—observing that "eminent" does not here mean solely worthy of honour, but is applied also to those who are to be dreaded on account of their evil character or miraculous nature. The thunder is also called the *naru-kami*, or the " sounding god." Dragons, goblins (*tengu*), and the fox are also *kami*, for they are likewise eminently miraculous and dreadful creatures. The tiger and wolf are spoken of in some of the sacred books as *kami*. Izanagi gave sacred names to the fruit of the peach-tree, and to the jewels which he wore on his neck. Rocks, stumps of trees, leaves of plants even, are said to have spoken in the divine age, and to be *kami*.* There are many cases of the term being applied to seas and mountains. " It was not a spirit that was meant, but the term was used directly of the particular sea or mountain: of the sea on account of its depth and the difficulty of crossing it; of the mountain on account of its loftiness " (Satow). The mirror in the Naiku at Isé is itself spoken of as a deity by some persons; others speak of it as a mere image of the goddess.†

The meaning of the word *kami* does not much assist us, evidently, in understanding the " way of the gods." We must therefore seek assistance elsewhere. But before looking into the narrower interpretations of the native religion, it may be well just to say, in fairness to it, that however much even Japanese writers may limit its scope, it can hardly be questioned, I presume, that it was originally based upon a belief in a divinity prevalent throughout the realm of nature. " The religion of the Japanese," says General Le Gendre in his 'Progressive Japan,' "consists in the belief that the

---

* In his 'Ethnology and Philology of the Hidatsa Indians,' Mr. Washington Matthews says of this race, found on the Missouri: "If we use the term worship in its most extended sense, it may be said that besides 'the Old Man Immortal' or 'the Great Spirit, the Great Mystery,' they worship everything in nature. Not man alone, but the sun, the moon, the stars, all the lower animals, all trees and plants, rivers and lakes, many boulders and other separated rocks, even some hills and *buttes* which stand alone—in short, everything not made by human hands, which has an independent being, or can be individualised, possesses a spirit, or, more properly, a shade. To these shades some respect or consideration is due, but not equally to all. . . . The sun is held in great veneration, and many valuable sacrifices are made to it."

† "The appearance of anything unusual at a particular spot is held to be a sure sign of the presence of the divinity."—*Le Gendre*.

productive ethereal spirit being expanded through the whole universe, every part is in some degree impregnated with it, and therefore every part is in some measure the seat of the deity; whence local gods and goddesses are everywhere worshipped, and consequently multiplied without end. Like the ancient Romans and the Greeks, they acknowledge a Supreme Being, the first, the supreme, the intellectual, by which men have been reclaimed from rudeness and barbarism to elegance and refinement, and been taught through privileged men and women, not only to live with more comfort, but to die with better hopes."

But we must look into what the native writers say on the subject. According to Motoöri, the way of the gods essentially consists in implicit obedience to the god-mikado, without question of his acts. This "way" was, according to him, established by Izanagi and Izanami, delivered by them to the sun-goddess, who handed it down by Ninigi-no-mikoto, and that is why it is called the "way of the gods." The nature of the *way* is only to be learnt by studying the sacred Japanese writings. One of its chief characteristics was the celebration of rites in honour of the gods, upon whose will everything depends. Not only are the good gods to be worshipped with a view to increase of good, but the gods who work mischief and evil must likewise be propitiated in order that they may not inflict injury upon us. There were no elaborate creeds or doctrines in this system, for there was no need of any; the duty of the mikado being merely to rule, and that of the people to obey. Government was reduced to mere worshipping, and worship was ordinarily a very simple matter. The early sovereigns, we are told, worshipped the gods in person, and prayed that their people might enjoy a sufficiency of food, clothing, and shelter; and twice a year, on the sixth and twelfth months, they celebrated the festival of the General Purification, by which the whole nation was purged of calamities, offences, and pollutions. The liturgy employed in celebrating it is used to this day.

The religious rites of Shinto always occupied the first place in books wherein are recorded the rules and ceremonies of the court. After the introduction and adoption of Buddhism, the national rites got neglected; but the emperor Jintoku (who reigned from 1211 to 1222 A.D.) endeavoured to reform the court practice, and said, "The rule of the Forbidden Precinct is that the worship of the gods comes first, and other matters afterwards. At morning and evening the wise resolve to do honour to the gods is carried out with diligence. Even in the slightest matters the *Jingu* [the Temples of Isé] and the *Naishi-Dokoro* are not to be placed after the emperor. According as all things arrive at maturity, they shall be offered up first [to the gods]; but things presented by Buddhist monks and nuns, and from all persons who are under an interdict, these shall not be presented."* The following is quoted as a prayer used by the Mikado:—

"O God, that dwellest in the high plain of heaven, who art divine in substance and in intellect, and able to give protection from guilt and its penalties, to banish impurity, and to cleanse us from uncleanness—Hosts of Gods, give ear and listen to these our petitions!"

As it was the duty of the subjects to imitate the practice of the incarnate god who was their sovereign, the necessity of worshipping his ancestors, and the gods from whom they sprang, was enjoined on every one. Hirata, writing in the early part of the present century, said that as the number of gods who possess different functions is so great, it will be convenient to worship by name only the most important, and to include the rest in a general petition. Those whose daily affairs are so multitudinous that they have not time to go through the whole of the prescribed morning prayers, may content themselves with adoring the residence of the emperor, the domestic *kami-dana*, the spirits of their ancestors, their local patron god, and the deity of their particular calling in life. In praying to the gods, the blessings which each has to bestow are to be mentioned in a few words; and they are not to be annoyed by greedy petitions, for the Mikado in his palace offers up petitions daily on behalf of his people,

---

* Satow's translation.

"which are far more effectual than those of most of his subjects." He goes on to give instructions: "Rising early in the morning, wash your face and hands, rinse out the mouth, and cleanse the body. Then turn towards the province of Yamato, strike the palms of the hands together twice, and worship, bowing the head to the ground." The prayer given by Hirata, translated by Mr. Satow, is as follows:—

"From a distance I reverently worship with awe before Ame-no-Mi-hashira and Kuni-no-Mi-hashira [the god and goddess of wind], also called Shinatsu-hiko-no-kami and Shinatsu-himé-no-kami, to whom is consecrated the palace built with stout pillars at Tatsuta no Tachinu, in the department of Heguri, in the province of Yamato. I say with awe, deign to bless me by correcting the unwitting faults which, seen and heard by you, I have committed, by blowing off and clearing away the calamities which evil gods might inflict, by causing me to live long like the hard and lasting rock, and by repeating to the gods of heavenly origin and to the gods of earthly origin the petitions which I present every day, along with your breath, that they may hear with the sharp-earedness of the forth-galloping colt."

Hirata proceeds to enumerate other prayers: the second is addressed to Amaterasu and the other gods and goddesses who dwell in the sun, and simply consists in calling on them by name. In this connection, Mr. Satow remarks that the common belief of the lower classes appears to be that the sun is actually a god, and they may often be seen to worship on rising in the morning by turning towards it, placing their hands together, and reciting prayers. The third prayer is addressed to the gods who dwell in the moon, which it was considered unlucky to admire generally, as "man grows old by accumulating moons," but to which it was customary to make offerings on the fifteenth day of the eighth month, because of her great brilliancy at that season. The fourth prayer is addressed to the gods of Isé, with a number of subordinate deities. The worshipper is directed next to turn towards the province of Hitachi, wherein is Kagushima, and bowing as before, but towards the three temples of Adzuma, to deliver a short prayer to the gods Take-mika-dzuchi and Futsu-nushi, who descended from heaven to conquer the country for Ninigi-no-mikoto. After persuading the ruling god to surrender the sovereignty of Japan, these gods "slew or expelled all the evil gods who glittered like fireflies, or were disorderly as May-flies; banished to foreign countries all the demons who made rocks, stumps of trees, leaves of plants, and the foam of the green waters to speak;" and then ascended to heaven from Hitachi on a white cloud, leaving their parted spirits behind in the temples built to their honour. The sixth prayer is addressed to the god and goddess of the Unseen, who ordain all those supernatural events which cannot be ascribed to a definite author. "Never mind the praise or blame of fellow-men," says Hirata, "but act so that you need not be ashamed before the gods of the Unseen. If you desire to practise true virtue, learn to stand in awe of the Unseen, and that will prevent you from doing wrong. Make a vow to the god who rules over the Unseen, and cultivate the conscience implanted in you, and then you will never wander from the way. You cannot hope to live more than a hundred years under the most favourable circumstances, but as you will go to the unseen realm of Oho-kuni-nushi after death, and be subject to his rule, learn betimes to bow down before him." Other prayers are addressed to the "Rough Spirit" of the last-named god, and also to his "Gentle Spirit," and to his son the God of Truth (Kotoshiro-nushi); also to the Goddess of Long Life; to the *ichi no miya*, or chief temple of the province in which the worshipper lives; to the *Uji-gami*, or ancestral god; and to the *kami-dana*, or shrine of the Penates, of which there is one in every Japanese household. The following prayer is to be addressed to the *kami-dana*:—

"Reverently adoring the great god of the two palaces of Isé in the first place, the eight hundred myriads of celestial gods, the eight hundred myriads of terrestrial gods, all the fifteen hundred myriads [figurative expressions all these] of gods to whom are consecrated the great and small temples in all provinces, all islands, and all places of the Great Land of Eight Islands [Japan], the fifteen hundreds of myriads of gods whom they cause to serve them, and the gods of branch palaces and branch temples, and *Sohodo-no-kami*, whom I have invited to the shrine set up on this divine shelf, and to whom I offer praises day by day, I pray with awe that they will deign to correct the unwitting faults which, heard and seen by them, I have committed, and, blessing and favouring me according to the Powers which they severally wield, cause me to follow the divine example, and to perform good works in the Way."

From the previous remarks, and from the prayers quoted, it is easy to gather indications of the ideas which predominate in Shinto worship, and to these we shall presently be able to add others derived from the practice of the worshippers. But before attempting this it will be well to avail ourselves of the light which has been quite lately thrown upon the subject by Mr. Satow's publication of the further results of his painstaking examination of the ceremonials and rituals of the religion* of which so little exact and specific knowledge has hitherto been available to English readers. The author explains that an important part of every performance of Shinto rites is the reading of a sort of liturgy or ritual addressed for the most part to the object of worship, in which the grounds of the worship are stated and the offerings presented are enumerated. It will be seen afterwards that, by the courtesy of the Government, we were so privileged as to witness the performance of this ceremony, together with the formal presentation of offerings, accompanied by music and chanting, at the sacred shrine of Isé itself on the occasion of our visit.

The Japanese name for this ritual or liturgy is *norito*. Such *norito* often are composed for special occasions, and it is stated that the Government gazettes of the years immediately succeeding what may be called the Mikado's

---

* In the paper on " Ancient Japanese Ritual " in the 'Transactions' of the Asiatic Society of Japan, 1879.

restoration in 1868 contain many of them—amongst them rituals recited to add greater solemnity to the oath by which the sovereign bound himself to govern in accordance with liberal ideas; to celebrate his removal to the eastern metropolis; to promote military success over his enemies; to give sanctity to the institution of an order of lay preachers, who were intended to spread abroad the teachings of Shinto; to honour the gods of war, and to confirm the bestowal of posthumous titles on certain predecessors of the mikado, who had hitherto not been recognised as legitimate sovereigns. The *norito* which Mr. Satow has just published, and which I shall presently quote, is an ancient one, and full of interest on account of its containing copious allusions to the original gods, so to speak. The scholar Mabuchi considers it was written in the reign of Kuwammu-Tenno (770-782 A.D.), basing this opinion chiefly upon certain peculiarities in the use of the Chinese characters employed to represent Japanese words; but Mr. Satow considers, for reasons given, this opinion invalid, and thinks it more likely that these *norito* were transmitted orally without any material alteration for many generations before they came to be written down. It is the ritual or form employed at the praying for harvest on the fourth day of the second month of each year, at the capital, in the office for the worship of the Shinto gods, and in the provinces by the chiefs of the local administration. At the celebration in the capital were assembled the ministers of state and their functionaries, and the priests and priestesses of 573 temples, containing 737 shrines, kept up at the expense of the Mikado's treasury; while in the provincial celebrations, rites were performed in honour of nearly 3000 other shrines, comprised in a catalogue, besides "a large number of unenumerated shrines in temples scattered all over the country, in every village or hamlet, of which it was impossible to take every account." The offerings consisted of coarse woven silk; thin coloured silks; cloth of bark or leaf, and small quantities of the raw materials of the same; a pair of tables or altars; a shield, a spear-head, a bow, a quiver, a pair of stag's horns, a hoe, a measure of *saké* (rice-beer or rice-spirit), edible sea-weed, salt, etc.; also a *saké* jar, and a few feet of matting for packing. To each of the Isé temples was presented in addition a horse; to the temple of the harvest-god, a white horse, cock, and pig: and a horse to each of nineteen other temples. "The final preparations being complete, the ministers of state, the virgin priestesses, and the priests of the temples to which offerings were sent by the Mikado, entered in succession, and took the places severally assigned to them. The horses which formed a part of the offerings were next brought in from the Mikado's stable, and all the congregation drew near while the reader recited or read the *norito*. This reader was a member of the priestly family or tribe of Nakatomi, who traced their descent back to Amenekoyane, one of the principal advisers attached to the sun-goddess's grandchild when he first descended on earth." It is "a remarkable evidence of the persistence of certain ideas," continues Mr. Satow, "that up to the year 1868 the nominal prime minister of the Mikado, after he came of age, and the regent during his minority, if he had succeeded young to the throne, always belonged to this tribe, which changed its name from Nakatomi to Fujiwara in the seventh century, and was subsequently split up into the five Setsuké, or governing families." At the end of each clause the priests all responded "O!" the equivalent of "Yes!" in those days. When the reading was over, the offerings were distributed to the priests for conveyance and presentation to their gods. A special messenger was despatched with the offerings to the Isé temples. The assembly then broke up.

In reading the following ritual the reader must bear in mind that it dates from a very remote period of antiquity, and that the translator has endeavoured to be as literal as possible, using English words which exactly express in their original and etymological meaning the sense of the Japanese characters. The "He" with which the clauses commence is the reader of the ritual, of the ancient consecrated tribe, and the word rendered by "says" signifies that the speaker is supposed to be speaking the words of the Mikado.

RITUAL.*

He says: "Hear all of you, asembled kannushi and hafuri."†

He says: "I declare in the presence of the sovran gods, whose praises, by the WORD‡ of the sovran's dear progenitor's augustness and progenitrix, who divinely remain in the plain of high heaven, are fulfilled as heavenly temples, and country temples: I fulfil your praises by setting up the Great Offerings of the sovran GRANDCHILD'S augustness, made with the intention of deigning to begin the HARVEST in the second month of this year, as the morning-sun rises in Glory."

He says: "I declare in the presence of the sovran gods of the HARVEST: If the sovran gods will bestow in many-bundled ears and in luxuriant ears the late-ripening harvest which they will bestow, the late-ripening harvest which will be produced by the dropping of foam from the arms, and by drawing the mud together between the opposing thighs, then I will fulfil their praises by setting up the first-fruits in a thousand ears, and many hundred ears, raising high the beer-jars, filling and ranging in rows the bellies of the beer-jars, I will present the first-fruits in juice and in ear. As to things which grow in the great field plain—sweet herbs and bitter herbs: as to things which dwell in the blue sea-plain—things wide of fin and things narrow of fin, down to the weeds of the offing and weeds of the shore: and as to CLOTHES—with bright cloth, glittering cloth, soft cloth, and coarse cloth will I fulfil praises. And having furnished a white horse, a white boar, and a white cock, and the various kinds of things in the presence of the sovran god of the HARVEST, I fulfil his praises by setting up the great OFFERINGS of the sovran GRANDCHILD'S augustness."

He says: "I declare in the presence of the sovran gods whose praises the chief PRIESTESS fulfils: I fulfil your praises, declaring your NAMES—Divine PRODUCER, Lofty PRODUCER, Vivifying Producer, Fulfilling Producer, Soul-lodging Producer, woman of the great HOUSE, great goddess of FOOD, and Events-symbol Lord, thus:

---

* I have made a few slight and unimportant but convenient modifications of the text, which chiefly consist in not italicising the words supplied to complete the sense, and in avoiding a bracketed expression.

† Chief and inferior priests.

‡ Words printed in capitals are those which in the original carry the honorific prefix *mi*, signifying descent from the gods, from the Mikado, or from the imperial princes. It is equivalent to our "august." Its frequent repetition is avoided by the use of the capitals.

Because you praise the age of the sovran GRANDCHILD'S augustness as a long AGE eternally and unchangingly, and bless it as a luxuriant AGE, I fulfil your praises as our sovran's dear progenitor's augustness and progenitrix's augustness by setting up the great OFFERINGS of the sovran GRANDCHILD'S augustness."

He says: " I declare in the presence of the sovran gods whose praises the PRIESTESS of Wigasuri* fulfils : I fulfil your praises, declaring your names, Vivifying Well, Blessing Well, Long-rope Well, Footplace and Entrance-limit, thus : Because the builders have made stout the HOUSE pillars on the bottommost rocks, which the sovran gods command, have made high the cross beams to the plain of high heaven, and have constructed the fresh ABODE of the sovran GRAND-CHILD'S augustness, and he hiding therein as a SHADE from the heavens and as a SHADE from the sun, tranquilly possesses the countries of the four quarters as a peaceful country, I fulfil your praises by setting up the great OFFERINGS of the sovran GRAND-CHILD'S augustness."

He says: "I declare in the presence of the sovran gods whose praises the PRIESTESS of the GATE fulfils : I fulfil your praises, declaring your NAMES, Wonderful Rock-Gate's Augustness, and Powerful Rock-gate's Augustness, thus : Because you obstruct like innumerable piles of rock in the GATE of the four quarters, in the morning open the GATES, in the evening shut the GATES, guard the bottom if unfriendly things come from the bottom, guard the top if they come from the top, and guard by nightly guarding and daily guarding, I fulfil your praises by setting up the great OFFERINGS of the sovran GRANDCHILD'S augustness."

He says: "I declare in the presence of the sovran gods whose praises the PRIESTESS of Ikushima fulfils : I fulfil your praises, declaring your NAMES, Country Vivifier, thus : Because the sovran gods confer on him the many tens of islands which the sovran gods command, the many tens of islands, without any falling short, as far as the limits of the taniguku's† passing, as far as the bound where the salt foam stops making the narrow countries wide and the hilly countries plain, I fulfil your promises by setting up the great OFFERINGS of the sovran GRANDCHILD'S augustness."

He says: " Parting the words,‡ I declare in the presence of the From-Heaven-Shining-Great-Deity who sits in Isé : Because the sovran great DEITY bestows on him the countries of the four quarters

---

* Held to be a corruption of Wi-ga-shiri, "behind or by the well," and of the gods of the wells, and places afterwards named in the text, observing that "footplace" is the place where the foot is set down on leaving the house.
† A large kind of frog.
‡ Taking up a fresh and special theme.

over which her glance extends, as far as the limit where heaven stands up like a wall, as far as the bound where the blue clouds lie flat, as far as the bounds where the white clouds lie away fallen:—the blue sea-plain, as far as the limit whither come the prows of the ships without letting their poles or paddles be dry, and the ships which continuously crowd on the great sea-plain:—the road which men go by land, as far as the limit whither come the horses' hoofs, with the baggage-cords tied tightly, treading the uneven rocks and tree roots, and standing up continuously on a long path without a break:—making the narrow countries wide and the hilly countries plain, and as it were drawing together the distant countries by throwing many tons of ropes over them; because she does all this, he will pile up the first-fruits like a range of hills in the great presence of the sovran great DEITY, and will tranquilly take to himself the remainder."

"Again, because you praise the AGE of the sovran GRANDCHILD's augustness as a long AGE, eternally and unchangingly, and bless it as a luxuriant AGE, I plunge down the root of the neck cormorant-wise* before you as our sovran's dear progenitor and progenitrix's augustness, and fulfilling your praises by setting up the great OFFERINGS of the sovran GRANDCHILD's augustness."

He says: "I declare in the presence of the sovran gods who sit in the FARMS: Declaring your names, Takechi, Kadzuraki, Tohochi, Shiki, Yamanobe, and Sofu: Because the sweet herbs and the bitter herbs which grow in these six FARMS have been brought, and the sovran GRANDCHILD's augustness takes them as his long FOOD and distant FOOD, I fulfil your praises by setting up the great OFFERINGS of the sovran GRANDCHILD's augustness."

He says: "I declare in the presence of the sovran gods who sit in the mouths of the mountains: Declaring your NAMES, Asuka, Ihari, Osaka, Hatsuse, Unebi, and Miminashi: Because the builders, having cut the bases and ends of the big trees and little trees which have grown up in the distant mountains, and the near mountains, brought them and constructed the fresh ABODE of the sovran GRANDCHILD's augustness, and he, hiding therein as a SHADE from the heavens, and as a SHADE from the Sun, tranquilly possesses the countries of the four quarters as a peaceful country, I fulfil your praises by setting up the great OFFERINGS of the sovran GRANDCHILD's augustness."

He says: "I declare in the presence of the sovran gods who dwell in the partings of the waters: I fulfil your praises, declaring your NAMES, Yoshinu, Uda, Tsuge, and Kadzuraki, thus: if you will bestow in many-bundled ears and luxuriant ears the late-ripening

---

* A simile for bowing the head.

harvest which the sovran gods will bestow, I will fulfil your praises by setting up the first-fruits in ear and in juice, raising high the beer-jars, filling and ranging in rows the bellies of the beer-jars, and the remainder the sovran GRANDCHILD's augustness takes with ruddy countenance as the divine grains of morning FOOD and evening FOOD as his long FOOD and distant FOOD. Therefore, hear all of you, the fulfilling of praises by the setting up of the great OFFERINGS of the sovran GRANDCHILD's augustness."

He says: "Parting the words, let the kannushi and the hafuri receive the OFFERINGS, which the Imibe,* hanging thick sashes to their weak shoulders, have reverently prepared, and, lifting, bring and set them up without erring."

All who have seriously applied themselves to the study of Shinto have recognised the necessity of carefully distinguishing between the system as it existed in ancient times, and the form which it took under the hands of the writers of the last and present centuries, who nearly always were the *protégés* of either the Mikados' courts, or the mock courts of the Tokugawa Shoguns. The distinction appears to me to be as broad as that which should divide a religious from a political system. With the latter aspect of it we have but little here to do; Mr. Satow was no doubt justified in saying, as he once did, that, as expounded by Motoöri, Shintoism was an engine for reducing the people to a condition of mental slavery, although it certainly must be an error to connect this view of it with its resumption as the religion of the imperial court in 1868. It is simply impossible for a monarch or his ministers at the same time to seek to reduce a people to mental slavery and to crowd the schools of the country with English, American, and German professors, and to fill the public libraries with English, American, and German literature. Nothing was more natural, as it seems to me, after the setting free of the mikado from the unnatural restraints of the Shoguns, than

---

* A class of hereditary priests whose duties were to prepare the more durable articles offered to the gods at the principal services; to cut down the timber required for the building of the temples, and to construct the temples. They were allowed to read the liturgies at the two services of the Luck-wishing of the great palace and gates.

for the court to revert to the ancient religion of the country, under the prestige of which the imperial family had reigned for more than 2000 years, and from which the very insignia of its rule had been derived. Whatever changes may hereafter take place in the religion of Japan, and of its emperors—and it is hardly likely under existing circumstances that Japan will escape, or will long desire to escape, from that great and searching reform of all religions which science is rapidly working throughout the civilised world—those changes will be at least quite as well made from Shinto as a starting-ground as from one of the branches of the Buddhist faith. I view even the writings of Mabuchi, Motoöri, and Hirata (with which Mr. Satow's labours have made us in some degree acquainted) rather as efforts to break away from Buddhist restraints, and to profit by such gleams of scientific light as occasionally broke in upon Japan, than as attempts to enslave the minds of their countrymen.

The ancient religion appears to me—contrarily to what some have said—to have really partaken in a great degree of the elements and characteristics of a religious system. As regards its beliefs, it taught primarily the existence of gods, and in the division which it made of them into good and bad, recognised that fundamental and eternal distinction between right and wrong, the deep-rooting of which in the human soul has been man's safeguard against what is bad in religions and in everything else. The history of the country shows that one of its first-fruits, and one of its best fruits, was the tender anxiety of the Mikados for the well-being of the people. It was not alone the emperor Nintoku, among the early emperors, who manifested this disposition; the very first historical emperor, Jimmu, is said to have been a far-seeing and enlightened prince, solicitous for the real welfare of his subjects. After settling the country, he busily occupied himself with the development of agriculture, making the soldiers employ their spare time in cultivating the soil; he despatched commissions to bring fresh lands into cultivation, and had cereals largely planted in the neglected eastern provinces. He even composed several poems on subjects of this nature, and although it might be fairly said that these things were not necessarily the result of his religious views and sentiments, the fact of his performing these services to his people, while building temples to his ancestral gods, should be allowed to weigh in favour of the practical influence of his faith. In the case of his son, the emperor Suisei, there is reason to believe that his filial grief at Jimmu's death was so great as to unfit him for the duties of government for two or three years, which was at least a sign of great natural tenderness.

The emperor Sujin, whose reign ended thirty years before the advent of Jesus Christ, while distinguishing himself by the zeal with which he built, classified, regulated, and endowed Shinto temples, distinguished himself much more by his promotion of works tending to the well-being of his subjects. In the fourth year of his reign (94 B.C.) he issued the following edict to his officers: "It was not for themselves that our ancestors were set upon the throne of Japan, but to arrange the worship of the gods, and to govern the people well; therefore it was that they performed a great service, and did great good to the nation. Now that I have the opportunity of being emperor, I shall follow the example of my ancestors, be kind to my people, and continue their happiness for ever. Therefore you, officers, take care that my will is carried out, and that the people's well-being is promoted accordingly." He is renowned for his advancement of agriculture, for the benefit of which he created large reservoirs for irrigation, and cut canals on a scale of extraordinary magnitude. He also greatly advanced the art of naval architecture, for the improvement of maritime communication. Mr. Griffis speaks of this emperor in the highest terms, heading one of his chapters "Sujin the Civiliser," and declaring that his whole life was one long effort to civilise his half-savage subjects. Sujin was, he says, "according to the *Dai Nihon Shi*, a man of intense earnestness and piety. The traits of courage and energy which characterised his youth gave him in manhood signal fitness for his chosen task of elevating his people. He mourned over their wickedness, and called upon them to forsake their sins, and turn their minds to the worship of the gods. A great pestilence having broken out, and the people being still unrepentant, the pious monarch rose early in the morning, fasted, and purified his body with water, and called on the *kami* to stay the plague. After solemn public worship, the gods answered him, and the plague abated; a revival of religious feeling and worship followed. In his reign dates the building of special shrines for the adoration of the gods." And while thus devout and thus ardent in his faith as a Shinto emperor, he " may also be called," says Mr. Griffis, " the father of Japanese agriculture, since he encouraged it by edict and example, ordering canals to be dug, watercourses to be provided, and irrigation to be extensively carried on."

The next emperor, Suinin, pursued the humane work which his father thus nobly began. This emperor, who reigned throughout the life of Jesus Christ, issued in the sixth year of our era a proclamation ordering canals and watercourses to be constructed in more than eight hundred places; he also caused storehouses, for the preservation of rice, to be provided; and as a signal proof of his humanity and kindness of heart, he forbade, by a remarkable decree, the cruel system of servants causing themselves to be buried alive in the tombs of their masters, ordaining that earthern effigies should be substituted in the tomb for the living servants.* And it was this man, thus signalising himself

---

* In the *Nihonki* it is said that at the funeral of a prince all his retainers were buried alive round his grave, and lived for several days. Their cries were reported to the Mikado, who instructed his counsellors to devise some method of abolishing the ancient custom of sacrificing to the dead those whom they during life had loved. Later, when the Mikado's wife died, he again urged a change in the cruel system, and then one of his advisers, Nomo-no-Sukune, recommended that a hundred workmen who wrought in clay should be brought from Idzuno. This was done, and clay images of men, horses, &c., having been produced, it was ordered, by imperial decree, that such images should thenceforth be substituted for living persons at the burial ceremony.

to all time by his humane and wise regard for his people, who was so ardent a Shintoist that he was the founder of that renowned temple at Isé of which I have so often to speak, and which he made the shrine of shrines, by placing there for ever the awful mirrored-image of the radiant goddess of the sun. I shall elsewhere tell the story of the beautiful fraternal strife between the emperor Nintoku and his brother in the fourth century (A.D.), in which that brother gave up his own life in order to secure for his country the benefits of Nintoku's rule, esteeming his brother more highly than himself; and I shall also tell elsewhere how devoted to his people Nintoku proved. But I may as well mention here that this monarch allied with his pious reverence for his gods, and with his love for his subjects, a most vigorous administration of the country for the country's good, raising great embankments, cutting additional canals, forming new roads, building new rice-magazines, and promoting the culture of the silkworm and the weaving of silk fabrics.

The next emperor, Richiu, although his reign was short, enabled one of the briefest sketches of his country's history to record of him that "he caused the reservoir of Iware and the canal of Iso-no-kami to be constructed; he also named in each province a functionary charged with the registration of historic poets, and the preparation of detailed reports on the state of the country, and on its productions." Of the emperor Yuriaku (456–479 A.D.) we are told that he made great efforts to protect and encourage the silkworm culture; and that his empress herself, for example's sake, took part in the gathering of the mulberry-leaves. He ordered the mulberry-tree to be planted wherever the climate permitted its growth. He also caused potteries to be established, and organised workmen for their operation; he laid down new roads, built the first houses of more than one story ever known in the country, and so forth. History says: Yuriaku-Tenno having during his life taken the greatest interest in the affairs of his empire, felt as his death approached that the organisation of the country was not completed, and therefore made a testament, and charged the great dignitaries of his court to finish his work. His successor, whose reign was brief, signalised it by acts of consideration for his people, calling for reports on the condition and the morals of the country, and forbidding the sending of presents to himself as an unnecessary burden upon his subjects. We are told: "Seinei-Tenno, a very just man, oftentimes himself administered justice, and in other cases assisted personally at its administration." The next emperor was one, Kenso-Tenno, who in his early years had taken refuge among the common people, and who for a long time refused his brother's solicitations to assume the crown in his place; and we learn that, having, while living among them, seen the true situation of the people, he applied himself on mounting the throne to the amelioration of their condition, and made many useful reforms. His short reign was consequently one of great prosperity. Ninken-Tenno, who succeeded him, was endowed with great intelligence, and a great fund of generosity, and throughout his reign promoted the happiness of his people. The emperor Keitai fostered agriculture, and otherwise worked for his country's good.

Now all these emperors were Shinto worshippers; their religion was the only religion known in Japan in their day. It was during the reign of the last-named emperor, Keitai, that the Koreans conveyed statues of Buddha into Japan; but the new religion did not at once take root in the country, "the inhabitants refusing to adore the strange gods." In so far, therefore, as religion operated upon the early emperors, it was the Shinto religion that did so; and as, if our own religion were in question, we should doubtless include among its fruits these continual manifestations of love and care for the multitude which these first rulers of Japan exhibited, it is but fair to allow the Shinto religion like credit. Setting aside, therefore, the mere mythologic extravagances of the sacred books, which seldom have much to do with the practical religion of any country, and judging the Shinto faith by its first-fruits, we must acknowledge that it possessed the power of a real religion, and that its operation was for the advantage of the country.

The early Shinto religion likewise taught men, as we have seen, to recognise the operation of superior power and superior will in the exercise of the forces of nature. It is true that, in those old days, the attitude of the believer to these forces was that of one who had to propitiate by prayers and offerings somewhat arbitrary gods; and this is an attitude which is getting more and more discredited among us as time advances. It is also true that the machinations of the bad gods had to be guarded against by at least equal obsequiousness; whereas, we have ourselves fallen of late years very much out of the habit of accrediting evil gods and demons with a real existence, even the chief demon being expected to manifest himself nowadays more frequently under the guise of a wily political chieftain, or a fradulent bank director, than under that of a creature with hoofs and tail, or even that of the friend of Faust. Still, it is not so very long ago that evil-eyes and witches and possessing devils played lively parts in the life of our Christian country; and there are not a few who would even now be shocked to hear any sort of doubt cast upon the real existence of the beguiling serpent of paradise. But there is this very important thing to be said for the early Shintoists: they did not so believe in gods and demons as to leave everything to them; they put their own shoulders to the obstructed wheels of their own fortunes, and, as we have just seen, dug canals, raised embankments, bred silk-worms, and planted mulberry-trees on their own behalf. It was probably with them as it has in the main been with others, and as it will be to the end: when people discern what ought to be done for their own benefit, and are able to do it themselves, they usually attempt it; but when they find themselves helpless in the presence of want or of calamity, they cry to their gods. But few religions are good enough or bad enough to greatly interfere with the operation of this principle; but it is always to the credit of a religion if it leaves the natural ability and aptitude of men to help themselves fairly free; and this merit must be conceded, I think, to Shinto.

At the same time, it cannot be doubted that their belief in the helpfulness of the gods, when duly propitiated, was a very real one. In illustration of this I quote the following passage from the diary of an old court noble, of a thousand years ago. He was sailing towards Osaka, and was opposite to Sumiyoshi, when a gale sprang up, and in spite of all efforts the vessel fell gradually to leeward, and was in great danger of being wrecked. "'This god of Sumiyoshi,' said the captain, ' is like other gods. What he desires is not any fashionable article of the day. Give him *nusa* * for an offering.' The captain's advice was taken, and *nusa* were offered; but as the wind, instead of ceasing, only blew harder and harder, and the danger from the storm and sea became more and more imminent, the captain again said, ' Because the august heart of the god is not moved for *nusa*, neither does the august ship move. Offer to him something in which he will take greater pleasure.' In compliance with this advice, I thought what it would be best to offer. ' Of eyes I have a pair; then let me give to the god my mirror, of which I have only one.' The mirror was accordingly flung into the sea, to my very great regret. But no sooner had I done so, than the sea itself became as smooth as a mirror." †

The Shinto religion appears, further, to have possessed the merit of accustoming the people to extremely simple forms of worship, whereas there is probably nothing which so much tends to enslave a people to a priesthood as elaborate and splendid ceremonials: it is so hard for a simple, uneducated eye to "see through" emblazoned emblems and long-wrought rituals. In the account of our visit to the central shrine of the sun-goddess in Isé, I shall have occa-

---

* *Gohei*, or the irregular strips of cloth or paper seen in Shinto shrines and introduced, as we have seen, at the winning of the sun-goddess from the cave.

† 'Transactions' of the Asiatic Society of Japan, vol. iii. pt. 2, p. 128, by W. S. Aston, Esq.

sion to remark upon the stark simplicity of the worship, even at the end of long and laborious pilgrimages. The rinsing of hands and mouth, the gift of a coin, a stroke or two of the hands, a bend of the neck or body, and a few short words of prayer, are all that the brightest of the gods and goddesses exacts from her adorers. On great occasions, as we have seen, there was more ceremony and more state; but as the rule, the Shinto system of worship is one of marked innocence and simplicity; and this, perhaps, is why Buddhism, with its golden gods and brazen altars and monster bells, when it once obtained a footing, made such rapid way among the Japanese; and why, too, the Roman Catholic Church, with its still more striking parade of sights and sounds—scarcely distinguishable from the Buddhist save by its excessive display—in its turn made rapid way alike among Buddhists and Shintoists. Still, whatever may be the penalties attached to simplicity and purity of religious worship, honour must be given to those who do not lay upon men, under the guise of religious rites, burdens heavier than can well be borne.

Personal purification and cleanliness, which always have a certain merit when kept within reasonable limits, have played an important part in the exercise of the Shinto faith. All over Japan the bath is an institution which the people patronise and delight in. They use hotter water than seems good for us, and even nowadays (though this is rapidly giving way to European ideas) the ages and the sexes mix in the bathing-house and the bath more than we deem fitting; but in spite of these drawbacks, it is impossible not to appreciate the sanitary and even the higher advantages of national cleanliness. I have not myself seen or read evidence which would justify me in saying as much on the general subject of purification as Mr. Griffis says; but in a short chapter on "The Ancient Religion," he states that Shinto "expresses great detestation of all forms of uncleanness, and is remarkable for the fulness of its ceremonies for bodily purification. Births and deaths are especially polluting. Anciently, the corpse and the lying-in woman were assigned to buildings set apart, which were afterwards burned. The priest must bathe and don clean garments before officiating, and bind a slip of paper over his mouth lest his breath should pollute the offerings. Many special festivals were observed for purification, the ground dedicated to the purpose being first sprinkled with salt. . . . The ancient emperors and priests in the provinces performed the actual ablution of the people, or made public lustrations. Later on, twice a year, at the festival of purification, paper figures representing the people were thrown into the river, allegorical of the cleansing of the nation from the sins of the past six months. Still later, the mikado deputised the chief minister of religion, at Kioto, to perform the symbolical act for the people of the whole country."

Another feature, and a meritorious feature, of Shintoism is its respect for life. Unlike those of the ancient system described in our sacred books, and practised by the Jews, its altars did not stream with blood, nor its courts resound with suffering. The life of animals has always been held more or less sacred throughout Japan, neither Shintoism nor Buddhism requiring or justifying the taking of the life of any creature for sacrifice.* Even for food neither cattle nor sheep were killed until "civilisation" introduced the improvement. The offerings of Shintoism, even on the greatest occasions, were, as we have seen, the fruits of the earth, and articles made from the earth's produce, with a few living animals for the use or convenience of the gods.

The priests of the Shinto shrines, with many of whom I have conversed through interpreters, are men of great simplicity of demeanour. The highest of them are nobles of the court, and members of consecrated families. Those of all ranks are practically officers of the government, although a small number only of the temples are directly supported by the state. They are at full liberty to marry,

---

* How strange that in such a country the system of *hara-kiri*, or the taking of a man's life by his own hands, should have sprung up, and prevailed so long!

and often do so, and of course rear up families, not shaving their heads, and dressing when they are off duty in ordinary attire. When on duty they wear loose robes and long caps of different colours. The priestesses of the shrines are virgins, and in the frequent instances in which we saw them were always young. The shrine of Isé, containing the sacred mirror, has always (for two thousand years) been under the care of an imperial princess.

The temples are usually of very simple style, being constructed of wood and thatched. They contain no images or idols; but in the courtyards or approaches figures of real and imaginary animals are not at all uncommon, especially in the case of the large temples. The approach is spanned by a *torii* or *toriis*. The *torii*, it is now generally admitted, was originally a perch for the fowls offered to the gods, not as food, but to give warning of daybreak. "It was erected on any side indifferently. In later times, not improbably after the introduction of Buddhism, its original meaning was forgotten; it was placed in front only, and supposed to be a gateway. Tablets with inscriptions were placed on the *torii* with this belief, and one of the first things done after the restoration of the Mikado in 1868, in the course of the purification of the Shinto temples, was the removal of these tablets. The *torii* gradually assumed the character of a general symbol of Shinto, and the number which might be erected to the honour of a deity became practically unlimited. The Buddhists made it of stone or bronze, and frequently of red painted wood, and developed various forms. It is to the present day a favourite subject for *ex-voto*" (Satow). At the outer shrine of Isé, called the *gékû*, there is an immense number of votive *toriis* standing close to each other, in long rows. But the most common form of votive offering is a large lantern, standing several feet high from the ground, and formed either of wrought stone or bronze. These are sometimes of very large size, even ten or twelve feet high, and are often crowded thickly near the approaches alike of Shinto and Buddhist temples, as I shall have occasion to mention more than once hereafter. It should be said that the worshipper does not enter the temple to worship at a Shinto shrine. He stands in front of it, striking his hands together, and offers, bowed, and usually in silence, the short and simple prayer which his own necessities dictate.

A SHINTO PRIEST.

CHAPTER IV.

BUDDHISM IN JAPAN.

The primitive religions of India—Vedism—Brahmanism—Reactions against the doctrine of sacrifice—Shakyamuni Gautama, the founder of Buddhism—His life and teachings—The doctrine of Nirvāna—Extinction or tranquillity?—The Buddhistic use of idols—Spread of Buddhism—Curious analogies with Christianity—Buddhistic cosmogony—The elevated morality and purity of Buddhism—The doctrine of transmigration—Introduction of Buddhism to China, 250 B.C.—Its progress there, and spread to Korea—Its introduction thence into Japan—Its slow progress there—Its prince-patron, Shotoku-Taishi—Story of his life—The first intercourse between Japan and China—Revival of Shinto under the Nara empresses—Subsequent revival of Buddhism—Its spread under the empress Shotoku—The temples of Hiyei-san—Kobo-daishi, the founder of the Shingon sect—Buddhism powerful in the state—Its priests resort to armed force—Later Buddhist sects in Japan—Shinran Shonin, the founder of Shin-shu—Its doctrine of salvation by faith in Amita Buddha—Original account thereof by a Shin-shu priest of Kioto—The Protestant Buddhists of Japan—Nichiren and his sect—The "Ranters of Buddhism"—Obstacles to the spread of Christianity in Japan—Kwannon, the goddess of a thousand hands—List of principal Buddhist sects—The influence of European civilisation upon them—A recent discourse on Infinite Vision, with a debate thereon.

BUDDHISM, taking its rise in India, and travelling by way of China and Korea to Japan, is there essentially a foreign faith; but it has nevertheless been so important an element of Japanese life for a dozen centuries that some account of it must of necessity be given here. Out of consideration for those readers who, like myself, have chiefly taken an interest in the matter in the present connection, I will first offer the briefest possible statement of its origin and nature from authentic sources.

The primitive religion of India, known as Vedism, and

set forth in the collection of sacred songs, prayers, etc., called Veda, substantially consisted in the worship of sun, fire, wind, rain, and other substances and forces of nature conceived as deities—not so conceived vaguely and indefinitely, but imagined as bright and powerful beings, and sometimes as possessing the specific characteristics of kings, parents, and friends. Hymns and liturgies were composed in their honour, the family of the gods being by some regarded as descendants of a more ancient pair, of whom heaven was the father and earth the mother. Out of Vedism grew Brahmanism, which was framed in satisfaction of a craving for a belief in some one Supreme God. It embodied and expressed the doctrine that there existed an All-Pervading Spirit, manifested alike in the physical world and in the souls of men. It was a pure essence diffused everywhere, forming everything, growth and expansion being its fundamental characteristics. It derived its designation, "Brahma," from a word signifying those properties. "Sacrifice" became the most essential feature of its service, to which everything else was subordinate. A sacrifice in fire was offered at a man's birth; his body was burnt in sacrifice after his death. As in Japan, the gods had not only to be gratified but propitiated likewise; but in India animal life, and not the mere fruits of the earth, were offered for the purpose. Brahmanism developed besides this—and probably, it is thought, as a reaction from this system of sacrifice, with its consequent burdens of ritualism and sacerdotalism—a more mystic and spiritual system, of which the ultimate expression was a belief in a "way" by which the soul of man became delivered from the limitations and oppressions of individuality, and absorbed in the supreme and eternal soul. Buddhism, like this latter development of Brahmanism, is supposed to have been a reaction against the doctrine of sacrifice, and against the burdens which that drew with it. But the reactionary force in this case was stronger than in the other, and carried Buddhists further. Buddhism condemned altogether animal sacrifices, and the priests and priestcraft that attended them. In common with the other development, it embodied the principle of the soul's migration through various bodily forms and conditions of existence, as steps towards the attainment of the final result—absorption into Brahma and Buddha respectively.

The founder of Buddhism was an Indian prince, the son of a king, not in a remote or inferred sense like that in which Christ is called the Son of David, but in the ordinary sense of the phrase, his father being king of the Kapilavastu district, near the mountains of Nepaul, about one hundred and fifty miles north-east of Patna. He is known by the name of Shakyamuni Gautama Buddha, his proper name having been Gautama, his tribe that of Shakya, and Buddha ("the enlightened") being the name adopted by him on a certain day when his long wrestlings with the spirit of evil terminated in his triumph, and the light of truth burst full upon him. In Japan he was oftener, in my hearing, spoken of as Shakya, or Shaka, than as Buddha. By some he is regarded as the great originator and instigator of the Buddhist reaction against the sacrificial, sacerdotal, and caste systems of Brahmanism; others hold the opinion that he was probably the great apostle of a sect and a faith which existed long before him—an opinion to which the previous reactions within the limits of Brahmanism itself, already adverted to, lend countenance. The period at which Gautama lived is variously stated; most authorities concur, however, in fixing it at about five centuries before Christ; the Buddhists of Ceylon (where Buddhism has probably preserved more of its primitive characteristics than elsewhere) name the year 543 B.C.; while a Chinese account places it as far back as the year 949 B.C. His life is now enveloped in mythic and legendary inventions, but the most noteworthy points in it have thus been recently summarised by the greatest English authority on the subject: "That soon after his marriage and the birth of a son, he is said to have become impressed with the vanity of all human aims and occupations; that he decided on devoting himself to self-mortification and philosophy in the hope of acquiring perfect knowledge; that he tore himself away from his wife and child, and from all other domestic ties, and from all prospect of advancement in the world; that he withdrew to the forests, and continued practising severe bodily mortification for six years; that when wasted and debilitated by long fasting he sat down to meditate under a Peepul tree;* that there he was assailed by the great Spirit of Evil and by all the powers of darkness, who tempted him to renounce his fixed resolution, and held out to him the prospect of a complete deliverance from all suffering of mind and body if he would consent to return to the pleasures and glories of the world. The Buddha is said to have wrestled long and manfully in agonising conflict with his spiritual foe, and for a long time the issue of the struggle appeared to be doubtful. At length his strength seemed to be giving way. All was on the point of being lost. But at that supreme moment his indomitable will triumphed, and the light of true knowledge burst upon his mind. From that time forward he became a new man. Self-discipline had done its work. He had at last attained to perfect knowledge. He had grasped the four truths: that all existence involves suffering; that all suffering is caused by desire; that relief from desire and suffering is only effected by extinction of existence; and that extinction of existence is only effected by following the middle path, which consists in right mental vision, right thoughts, right words, right actions, right means of living, right application, right memory, right meditation.† . . . In the humility of mind, which was one of his chief characteristics, he always

---

* "This tree is familiarly called the Bo-tree (*fur bodhi-vriksha*), and is as sacred a symbol with the Buddhists as the Cross is with Christians." It is sometimes called the "jambu" tree.

† Dr. Eitel, while stating the first two of the "truths" in substantially the same way as our author, gives a different statement of the remaining two, which he expresses thus:

"That the extinction of passion is possible through fixed meditation; and that the path to this extreme meditation results in the absorption of existence which would be a state of unlimited happiness." Of course these truths have often been variously interpreted, but a closer agreement between modern scholars might now be looked for.

declared that Buddhahood had been attained by many others before himself, and would be attainable by many others after himself."* In all this there was no real antagonism to Brahmanism, the object in both cases being the same, viz. the attainment of perfect knowledge. But what a process for attaining knowledge, and what knowledge to attain, in comparison with the processes of modern science, and the knowledge thereby reached!

Buddha, however, did not limit himself to Brahmanistic teachings, nor did he by any means accept all of them. He denied the authority of the Veda, rejected the doctrine of the soul's immortality, and recognised no other deity than man himself, advanced to Buddhahood. The greatest doctrinal contrast between the two systems is to be seen in the fact that while in Brahmanism absorption of the individual being into the Supreme Being is the great end to be secured, in Buddhism the final aim is individual extinction. I must not omit to say, however, that the identity of Nirvâna with individual extinction or annihilation is not by any means universally admitted either by Buddhists or by European scholars. Some view it as the annihilation of desire, and the vacation of the soul, so to speak, by every disturbing influence, so that it remains in eternal unbroken tranquillity. Which of the two views was held by Buddha himself can never be known, as there are no manuscripts ancient enough to settle the point, and the Buddhist canon has been subjected to repeated amendments. All that can be said is that some Buddhist schools and sects teach the one doctrine, and others teach the other. I should myself be inclined to prefer tranquillity to extinction, although there can be no doubt that tranquillity is in itself the extinction of no small part of what we know and enjoy as "life." In his recently published 'Light of Asia,'† Mr. Edwin Arnold speaks of

"NIRVĀNA where the Silence lives;"

---

* Professor Monier Williams, in *Contemporary Review*, Dec. 1878.
† Trübner & Co., Ludgate Hill.

and he concludes his great and splendid, though unequal, poem thus:—

"The Dew is on the Lotus!—Rise, Great Sun!
And lift my leaf and mix me with the wave.
Om mani padme hum, the Sunrise comes!
The Dewdrops slip into the Shining Sea!"

It will be seen from the above that Buddhism was a religion of great scope, and suggestive of great toleration. It had no complex system of doctrine or dogma to force into adoption; no elaborate ritual or ceremonial to carry out; no violent antagonism to any other system, or to any parts of other systems, provided they left the Buddhist free to pursue his own course towards his own enlightenment, and his own ultimate attainment of *Nirvāna,* or the calm haven of tranquillity and silence. So far as I have been able to investigate the matter, there is no such idea as that of a Saviour in ancient Buddhism. Buddha himself is but an example and a guide. There is a hell, there are indeed many hells, for the wicked; but man is his own saviour, his own efforts are his sole dependence, his own acts fix his own fate. A Buddhist might have written the couplet:—

"Our acts our angels are, and good or ill,
Our fatal shadows that walk by us still."

The Buddhist employed idols and adored relics, but only as reminders either of Buddha himself, or of other great ones of the past; adoration of departed spirits he forebade. He presented flowers on the altars of his images, but only as symbols of his reverence for certain truths. He gave praise, but it was to the excellence of Buddha. He nevertheless was willing to recognise the Hindu gods as great and powerful beings, and Buddha himself showed no small worldly wisdom in preferring the popular gods to others, though he never gave to them a place equal to that of the enlightened man. The spread of his religion in Japan was immensely facilitated, after a delay of several centuries, by some of its leaders adopting the gods of Japan as manifestations of Buddha. The Buddhist never persecuted; religious persecution entered Japan with its so-called Christian priests.

Buddhism greatly flourished first in India, but partly by the influence exerted upon it by Brahmanism, and partly by the influence exerted upon Brahmanism by it, the distinctions between the two systems grew less and less, and at length Brahmanism, in appearance at least, overcame Buddhism. But this was in so far as India only, or rather parts of India only, were concerned. In other parts of Asia it has so far prevailed that, as has been said, "the history of Eastern Asia is the history of Buddhism." Nearly five hundred millions of people, or about a third of the human race, are said now to worship Buddha; and, according to some, the real conquests of the Buddhist faith are by no means confined to Asia.*

Curious analogies have been discovered between Buddhism and Christianity, more especially as regards the lives of their founders. Dr. Eitel sums some of them up thus: "Shakyamuni Buddha, we are told, came from heaven, was born of a virgin, welcomed by angels, received by an old saint who was endowed with prophetic vision, presented in a temple, baptised with water, and afterwards baptised with fire; he astonished the most learned doctors 'by his understanding and answers,' he was led by the spirit into the wilderness, and having been tempted by the devil he went about preaching and doing wonders. The friend of publicans

---

* "The Germans Feuerbach and Schoppenhauer, the Frenchman Comte, the Englishman Lewis, the American Emerson, with hosts of others, have all," according to Dr. Eitel, "drunk more or less of this sweet poison, and taken as kindly as any Asiatic to this Buddhistic opium pipe; but most of all that latest product of modern philosophy, the so-called system of positive religion, the school of Comte, with its religion of humanity, is but Buddhism adapted to modern civilisation, it is philosophic Buddhism in a slight disguise." I venture to think, however, that Dr. Eitel himself is probably as much of a Buddhist as any of the writers whom he names are, or ever were; and I fear it is rather as a delegate of the London Missionary Society than as a philosopher that this scholarly gentleman wrote as above. I am bound to acknowledge, however, that he is usually a most impartial recorder of the merits as well as of the shortcomings of Buddhism, and a safe guide in the discussion of the main question. I had the pleasure of meeting him at the cosmopolitan table of Governor Pope Hennessy at Hong Kong.

and sinners, he too is transfigured on a mount, descends to hell, ascends up to heaven; in short, with the single exception of Christ's crucifixion, almost every characteristic incident in Christ's life is also to be found narrated in the Buddhistic traditions of the life of Shakyamuni Gautama Buddha." This is accounted for, however, at least by Dr. Eitel, upon the supposition that, although Buddha preceded Christ by several centuries, the Christian history was the first to be circulated, and that it was from this that most of its legendary incidents, in so far as they resemble the Christian narrative, flowed into the history of Buddha. He states that, although many books claiming to be expositions of the orthodox (Buddhist) faith were in circulation at the time of Christ, and a number of them appear to have received the approval of the Œcumenic Council of Cashmere about that time, the earliest written compilation of the modern Buddhist canon, as a whole, dates from between the years 412 and 432 of our era.

It is said in the sacred books of Buddhism that the true theory of the cosmogony is this: Out of the chaos of waters rose a lotus-flower, and out of this flower rose the universe, unfolding successively its various spheres, terrestrial and celestial. This conception, although usually vulgarised into a mere prosaic statement, is really a poetic one, thoroughly oriental in the form taken by it, amounting to this: "That, as a lotus-flower, growing out of a hidden form beneath the water, rises up slowly, mysteriously, until it suddenly appears above the surface and unfolds its buds, leaves, and pistils, in marvellous richness of colour and chastest beauty of form; thus also, in the system of worlds, each single universe rises into being, growing up out of a germ, the first origin of which is veiled in mystery, and finally emerges out of the chaos, gradually unfolding itself, one kingdom of nature succeeding the other, all forming one compact whole, pervaded by one breath, but varied in beauty of form. Truly an idea that might be taken for an utterance of Darwin himself" (Eitel). Many of the teachings of Buddhism require this kind of extrication from the symbolism and imagery in which they have been orientally expressed, and which have led to their misconception and depreciation by many western writers and philosophers. At the same time the sacred books doubtless contain much which has to disappear before the sun of science, and which is as puerile as anything in the mythologies of other countries. The Buddhist faith does not, however, rest on matters of this sort. Like Christianity itself, it can afford to let many childish and many erroneous dogmas be swept from its surface, and will shine the brighter for the change.

It is in its elevated morality and in the purity of its precepts that lies the real strength of Buddhism, whatever that strength may be. Its primary principle is the suppression of self. It was by this that Buddha distinguished himself, and it is to this that his followers must most earnestly apply themselves. They must not for their own selfish ends kill that which has life; they must not take from another that which belongs to him; they must not permit themselves any form or degree of unchastity; they must not lie to others; they must not drink liquors that intoxicate. These are the first mandates of Buddha, and they are obviously aimed in each case at self-indulgence, and designed to lead men along the path of self-renunciation. "Its commandments are the dictates of the most refined morality. Besides the cardinal prohibitions against murder, stealing, adultery, lying, drunkenness, and unchastity, 'every shade of vice, hypocrisy, anger, pride, suspicion, greediness, gossiping, cruelty to animals, is guarded against by special precepts. Among the virtues recommended, we find not only reverence of parents, care of children, submission to authority, gratitude, moderation in times of prosperity, submission in time of trial, equanimity at all times,—but virtues such as the duty of forgiving insults, and not rewarding evil with evil'" (Griffis).

Buddhism may be said to have been rooted in the right of man to exercise perfect personal freedom from the interference of others in spiritual matters. Gautama himself went into the wilderness to meditate and to resolve alone, and the event, as well as the act itself, was an absolute revolt against the religious and social systems of his day, and as absolute a declaration of individual liberty. "One of the principal charges brought by the orthodox Brahmans against the followers of Buddha was that 'they went forth' (*pravrag*), that they shook off the fetters of the law before the appointed time, and without having observed the old rules enjoining a full course of previous discipline in traditional lore and ritualistic observances."* But that which was its strength was also its obstruction. A system which enjoins upon men as a duty the setting aside of property, social relations, and all that makes life worth having in the esteem of most men, inevitably tends in the opinion of many to monasticism, priestcraft, and the very evils the overthrow of which Gautama proposed to himself as the moving cause of all his labours and privations. And this has been a great hindrance, possibly, to the living acceptance of Christianity, in much more than name, by the civilised world. The story of the rich young man who was told that he must sell all that he had and give the proceeds to the poor; and the injunctions to men to take

---

* The sentence which I have here cited from the *Hibbert Lectures* is succeeded by a passage so thoughtful, so eloquent, and so characteristic of Max Müller that I cannot refrain from quoting it. "But though we need not," says the author, " mimic the ideal life of the ancient Aryans of India, though the circumstances of modern life do not allow us to retire into the forest, when we are tired of this busy life, nay, though in our state of society it may sometimes be honourable 'to die in harness,' as it is called, we can yet learn a lesson even from the old dwellers in Indian forests, not the lesson of cold indifference, but the lesson of viewing objectively, within it, yet above it, in the life which surrounds us in the marketplace; the lesson of toleration, of human sympathy, of pity as it was called in Sanskrit, of love as we call it in English, though seldom conscious of the unfathomable depths of that sacred word. Though living in the *forum*, and not in the forest, we may yet learn to agree to differ with our neighbour, to love those who hate us on account of our religious convictions, or at all events unlearn to hate and persecute those whose own convictions, whose hopes and fears, nay, even whose moral principles, differ from our own. That, too, is forest life, a life worthy of a true forest-sage, of a man who knows what man is, what life is, and who has learnt to keep silence in the presence of the Eternal and the Infinite."

no thought for the morrow, and to live in daily anticipation of vast changes in the world: these have been great stumbling-blocks to many, and probably to many of the best of those who otherwise would have leaped at the noble and generous and helpful sayings of the founder of Christianity. There are, however, many, as we well know, to whom they are no stumbling-blocks at all, and who apparently have no difficulty whatever in reconciling all such sayings, and the whole Christian code, with a great deal of thought about to-morrow, and with the constant enjoyment, on a liberal scale, of this world's good things.

I have not referred sufficiently thus far, I fear, to the important part which the transmigration of souls plays in the Buddhist system. Although he did not appear to know it himself at first, Buddha had undergone about 550 previous births before that after which he established his religion. The fundamental idea appears to be that the embodiment of the soul is in itself a form of bondage. "The soul, so united, commences acting, and all actions, good or bad, lead to consequences. Hence in order to accomplish the working out of consequences—the adequate reward or punishment of acts—it is necessary for the soul to be removed to temporary heavens or hells. Thence it must migrate into higher, intermediate, and lower corporeal forms, according to its various degrees of merit or demerit, till it attains the great end—entire emancipation from bodily existence" (Monier Williams). But while in Brahmanism this process was supposed to follow a natural law, drifting or setting the soul, so to speak, always towards Brahma; in Buddhism the soul is supposed, by its own actions, to exert a most important influence upon its own migrations. Vices will occasion re-birth in one of the hells; virtues will insure a new birth in one of the heavens. Transmigration, therefore, according to Buddhism, is a system for distributing rewards and punishments, and for lifting the soul, by virtue of its own merits, the more quickly to the eternal peace of Nirvāna.

Buddhism made its way into China as early as the year

250 B.C., and about the year 121 B.C. a gigantic golden statue of the god Buddha was carried among the spoils of its enemies to the Chinese court. It was not, however, until after the time of Christ that the new religion made its way there. In the year A.D. 61, the Chinese emperor Ming-ti is said to have had a dream in which he saw a gigantic image, gleaming like gold, and with a sun-bright halo, enter his palace. It was explained to him that this was a statue of Buddha, and that the vision amounted to a command from heaven for the imperial court to adopt Buddhism. The emperor accordingly sent to India an embassy which returned with a Hindoo priest, a sandalwood statue of the god, and a sacred book. Other Hindoos, other statues, and other books followed, and the new religion thus got well-grounded in China, whence doubtless it speedily travelled on to the neighbouring Korea. We shall see afterwards that the court of Japan was in frequent communication with the small kingdoms of Korea from before the time of Christ onwards; but it was not until the reign of Keitai-Tenno, in the beginning of the sixth century A.D., that statues of Buddha are said to have been taken across the sea. In the reign of the emperor Kimmei (540–571 A.D.) the king of Kudara (of Korea) sent to Japan statues of Buddha, altars, banners, etc., and wrote to the emperor a letter recommending the adoption of the worship of Buddha, the power of which he strongly asserted. The emperor, we are told, would probably have accepted the advice, but the dignitaries of his court formally opposed it. The emperor then gave the Buddhist emblems to one Sogano-Iname, recommending him to adopt the Buddhist faith. Iname took them home, obeyed the emperor's advice, and turned his house into a temple. About this time, however, Japan was ravaged by an epidemic; the court dignitaries attributed this to the presence of false gods, threw them into the water, and burnt the temple. But in spite of that it is said that from that moment Buddhism took root in the country. In the next reign (of Bitatsu-Tenno) two envoys, returning from Kudara, again brought two statues of Buddha into the country, which were given to Sogano-Umako, who

founded a temple and put them in it. Then broke out a new epidemic, and again those zealous conservatives, the court dignitaries, induced the emperor to put down the Buddhist religion and burn the temples and statues. Soon after, however, the emperor, and his most Protestant minister, were both smitten with illness, and the Buddhists did not fail to see in this phenomenon the chastisement of their impiety. Umako pressed the emperor to be converted, or rather to convert himself, but the emperor told him that he, Umako, could adore whomsoever he pleased, but that it was wrong of him to seek to convert others. Yomei, the successor of Bitatsu, falling ill, wished to adopt Buddhism, and thus gave rise to difficulties and jealousies, in the midst of which the Buddhist convert Umako had one of the ministers assassinated, as I shall have occasion to recount in the chapter on the Descent of the Crown. In that chapter I shall also make mention of Prince Toyoto-Mimi, afterwards known as Shotoku-Taishi ("Unusual Virtue"), who was heir to the throne, but died without succeeding to it; but to him I must nevertheless here more particularly refer.

The history of this prince is surrounded with legendary matter. I take the following from an account of him which a learned priest of the head church of the Western Shin-shu sect, in Kioto, was good enough to extract for me from a fuller history written in the Japanese language. He is there said to have been born with his right hand clenched, and his body giving forth a pleasant perfume. He could speak when but a few months old. When two years old he faced to the east, and saying Nambutsu ("Save us, O eternal Buddha"), opened for the first time his right hand, disclosing therein a relic of Buddha. When about five or six years old he was disputing with other princes in the palace. The emperor Bitatsu rose up with a stick in his hand, and all the princes excepting him ran away; he, who was bare to the waist, went towards the emperor. (What a glimpse, this, into the simple human life of these early mikados, gods though they were esteemed!) "Why do you remain when the others flee?" asked the emperor; and the boy replied,

"As I can neither rise to heaven by a ladder, nor hide myself by digging in the ground, I can only remain to be beaten." "The emperor," says the ancient story, "rejoiced, thinking him an excellent boy." When he became older he loved to read, and showed himself very clever and intelligent. On one occasion eight people appealed to him at once, and although he heard them all at the same time, he made no mistake. He was consequently called "Hachiji-no-Wanji" (*Hachi* meaning "eight," and *ji* "ears"). The emperor "loved him with his heart," and bade him live in the best house, which was south of the palace. Buddhism was not widely spread at this time, but the young prince loved it very much, and read many of its sacred books.

When Umako urged the emperor Bitatsu during the plague to adopt the Buddhist religion as already stated, the emperor consulted this boy-prince on the subject, so great was his confidence in him. Afterwards, when the emperor Yomei fell sick, as I have related, "the prince sitting near to the emperor always prayed for his recovery." The prince was fifteen years old only when Umako had the minister murdered. About this time he carved four warriors in wood, and putting them on his head followed the army. These very ancient and interesting images have been preserved, and were shown to us in a temple at Osaka. In this account it is stated that Umako murdered the emperor Sushun, and put the widow of Bitatsu, the prince's mother, on the throne, the prince himself thus becoming heir-apparent; he was made in some sense regent, so that "all power came into his hands." It was by his own desire, doubtless, that in the following year the empress urged the prince and Umako to encourage the Buddhist religion, and consequently people emulated each other in the building of temples and pagodas. In the following year a Korean priest named Eji arrived in Japan, and the prince-regent made him his tutor, and received from him the five Buddhist commandments, the substance of which I have already cited. The prince likewise published books or tracts upon the new religion, and the empress allowed him to expound them to others, and to be questioned upon them by a priest wearing Buddhist clothes, and handing incense. He so answered the questions that the empress was much gratified, and "gave him land, and increased his income." He gave all to the temples. In the fifth year of her reign she proposed to create him *Tai-ho-wan*, "highest priest," but he stoutly refused the title. He appears to have applied himself to the distinguishing of different ranks, to the improvement of Japanese ceremony, and to the composition of rules for regulating such matters.

In the year 604 he issued, with the sanction of the empress, seventeen edicts as the laws of the country. It was at his suggestion that the empress sent to China to procure a book which he wanted, her ambassador bearing a letter of his composition, and returning with a Chinese ambassador who brought the book, and also an autograph letter and presents from the Emperor of China (of the Zui dynasty) to the Empress of Japan. This was the commencement of intercourse between Japan and China. It is said that on the empress expressing her desire to see the people hunting, he remonstrated with her, telling her that one of the five commandments was against taking the life of anything, and asking her to issue an edict accordingly. My translation says: "From that time it was determined that the corresponding day in every year should be spent in getting medicines (medicinal herbs, probably), which was called *Yaku-rio*, or medicine-hunting." In 620 A.D. the Prince (alas! in conjunction with the murderer Umako, from whom neither he nor the empress appears to have been alienated, although he took the life of Shushun-Tenno, who was her brother and his uncle) published a Japanese history.

I have already adverted to the mission sent by the empress to China. This mission was accompanied by two students, Takamuku and Minamibushi, and by a priest named Bin, to be educated in China. These students remained there for ten years, until the Zui dynasty was superseded by that of To. Takamuku remained more than twenty years longer, but the priest and Minamibushi returned sooner. The latter gave instruction to Prince Nakano Oye (afterward the emperor Tenji), and to an historic character who afterwards became known as Fujiwara Kamatari. The emperor Kotoku, on coming to the throne in 645 A.D., made the Prince Oye heir-apparent, and Fujiwara Kamatari chief privy councillor. He also appointed Takamuku and Bin to professorships of the provincials schools, giving them shares in the administration of the government. This was the first instance of natives being appointed to professorships, Korean scholars having alone previously occupied those posts. In 621 the prince was attacked by a malady, and the empress sent Prince Tamura to condole with him, and to learn his wishes. His answer was, "I hope you will ask the empress to extend the new religion greatly." He died in his forty-ninth year, and was buried in the hill called Shinaga. "There was no person," says my narrative, with quaint and touching simplicity, "who did not mourn the death of him. At every place the voices of crying were heard, and did not cease after a month." The prince built nine temples, among which was the famous temple of Horinji (Tatsuta), in Yamato, which remains with little alteration to this day, and which we had the privilege of visiting on our way to Nara, as will be hereafter set forth. It contains portraits, etc., of the prince, the productions of his hand, and the most ancient works of Japanese art.

The great impulse which this remarkable prince gave to the Buddhist religion in Japan formed an era in its history. It is worthy of note that during his life the state of Koma (in Korea), learning that the empress had ordered the construction of a monumental statue of Buddha, sent a large sum in gold to assist in defraying the cost of it, and sent several Buddhist priests at the same time to Japan. The Buddhist system of burning the body was only introduced into Japan at the end of the seventh or beginning of the eighth century by a priest named Dosho.

In the reigns of the Nara empresses, the Shinto religion and the ancient history of the country occupied most of the imperial attention, and the famous *Kojiki* and *Nihonki* were written. In the succeeding reign of Shomu-Tenno, however, the intercourse with China increasing, and Chinese literature finding its way more freely into Japan, Buddhism appears to have received a new impulse. Orders were given for the erection of a Buddhist temple in each province, and the endowments of the clergy were increased. Soon after the middle of the eighth century the emperor Junjin authorised the construction of a convent for Buddhist nuns in each province of the empire. The empress Shotoku, who was a devoted Buddhist, soon afterwards had constructed a million of miniature three-storied pagodas, in each of which was placed a small collection of prayers printed by means of impression plates, such as are still used in Japan, but then employed for the first time. I have seen several of these miniature pagodas, which are circular and apparently lathe-turned, and about six inches long, many of them having been preserved to the present day.*

The emperor Kuwammu, who reigned at the close of the eighth century, was less of a devotee, and forbade private individuals to have chapels in their own houses, or to sell lands or houses to the priests. He laboured hard in other ways for the benefit of his people, and is justly considered, says one historian, one of the great emperors of Japan. It was in his reign, nevertheless, that the priest Saicho founded the great temples of Enriaku-ji, on Mount Hiyei (Hiyei-san), the priests of which became so powerful and troublesome in later reigns. It was shortly before Kuwammu's reign commenced that a Japanese priest and scholar who exerted great influence upon the fortunes of Buddhism in the country was born. This was the learned Kobo Daishi, who studied in China, and took a great interest in the progress of literature as well as of Buddhism, and who is perhaps best known to fame as the inventor of the *I-ro-ha* syllabary, from its first three letters, just as we know the "Alpha-bet" from the first two Greek letters. He was likewise the founder of the

---

* One shown to me by Mr. Fukusawa, of Tokio (the learned school-proprietor and reformer), contained the original small scroll of prayers. Another, which Prince Date showed me, was precisely similar, but the scroll was wanting.

Shingon ("True Words") sect of Buddhists in Japan. "The master-stroke of theological dexterity was made early in the ninth century, when Kobo . . . achieved the reconciliation of the native belief and the foreign religion, made patriotism and piety one, and laid the foundation of the permanent and universal success of Buddhism in Japan. This Japanese Philo taught that the Shinto deities or gods of Japan were manifestations, or transmigrations, of Buddha in that country, and by his scheme of dogmatic theology secured the ascendency of Buddhism over Shinto and Confucianism" (Griffis). This is putting the case very strongly, but it will serve to indicate the importance of the labours of the learned priest. The emperor Saga, who began to reign in 810, or three years before Kobo Daishi founded his new sect, nevertheless revived the Shinto religion, ordering the repair of its temples, and commanding the clergy "not to conduct themselves in an immoral manner, nor to abuse the public credulity" —a Carlylean king, evidently. The emperor Daigo, who lived nearly a century afterwards, seems to have had a dash of the same spirit in him, or one of his subjects would scarcely have addressed to him a memorial the eleventh clause of which was "to maintain in their posts *only* those members of the clergy who acquitted themselves worthily of their functions." The emperor Shirakawa, who was contemporary with our William the Conqueror, was a devoted Buddhist, and caused more than fifty thousand pagodas and statues of Buddha to be erected.

By this time Buddhism had become so powerful in the state, and the priests consequently so bold, that they took to settling the differences that arose between their several temples by force of arms. Numerous disturbances with bloodshed had in this way been organised in the capital city, Kioto. The priests of the great and splendid temples of Enriaku-ji (Hiyei-san), near the city, so far took advantage of the tolerance and favour of the government as even to raise troops of their own; and the use they made of them was, when they had some reclamation to make from the government, to take an armed force with them to the palace of the emperor when they went thither to address him. The emperor had the spirit to order the police to attack and disperse the clerical rebels, which I trust they did successfully. He is said, however, to have remarked (in a very different spirit from the Carlylean Saga), "There are three things over which I have no power: the waters of the river Kamogawa [which frequently overflowed], dice, and priests." During the next reign, that of Horikawa, a younger brother of the reigning emperor, named Kakugio, became a priest of the temple of Ninnaji; he was the first prince of the blood who took holy orders.

We have now arrived at a period from which, henceforth, the Buddhist religion must be considered as an integral part of the Japanese empire, the history of the two being practically one. This would hardly have been the case had Japan been constituted like European countries, where the people have exerted so strong and direct an influence upon the national religion, for as yet Buddhism, though adopted by the court and by the official and learned sections of the community, had not become the religion of the people; but it is only during the last few years that the people of Japan have been allowed to do much more than obey either imperial or military dictators, and the adoption of Buddhism by these practically settled the question for centuries to come. Other Buddhist sects were, however, about to be founded, and to have important results. "The thirteenth of the Christian era is the golden century of Japanese Buddhism; for then were developed those phases of thought which were peculiar to it, and sects were founded, most of them in Kioto, which are still the most flourishing in Japan. Among these were, in 1202, the Zen ('Contemplation'); in 1211, the Jodo ('Heavenly Road'); in 1262, the Shin ('New'); in 1282, the Nichiren. In various decades of the same century several other important sects originated, and the number of brilliant intellects that adorned the priesthood at this period is remarkable. . . . The adoption of Buddhism by all classes may be ascribed to the missionary labours of Shinran and Nichiren, whose banishment to the north and east made them itinerant apostles. Shinran travelled on foot through every one of the provinces north and east of Kioto, glorying in his exile, everywhere preaching and teaching and making new disciples" (Griffis).

The doctrine of Shinran Shonin, and of the very powerful section of Buddhism which he founded, occupies a remarkable place in the Buddhist system. I have before said, in speaking of the fundamental principles of this religion as it arose in India and flowed over through China to Japan, that there is in it no such idea as that of a Saviour; and others, who know much more about it, are of the same opinion. Dr Eitel says, for example: "Buddha is not a saviour. The only thing he can do for others is to show them that way of doing good and overcoming evil, to point out the path to Nirvāna by his example, and to encourage others by means of teaching and exhortation and warning to follow his footsteps. If any human being is to reach Nirvāna, it must be done by independent action. Do good and you will be saved; this is the long and the short of the Buddhist religion." And this view, it must be acknowledged, seems to be an inevitable inference from what we know of the origin, the antecedents, and the diffusion of Buddhism. But here, in the Shin-shu (Shin-sect), we not only have the doctrine of a saviour taught, but with it the old Christian doctrine of justification by faith likewise—but by faith, not in Jesus, but in Amita Buddha. The Buddhists of Nepaul worship by preference one of several ancient Buddhas, designated Adi-Buddha, endowing him with a sort of supremacy, and with the purest virtues. The majority of northern Buddhists assume the same attitude towards Amita Buddha. He is the god of the paradise of the west, and in reality, although seldom in as many words, they worship him as Almighty God is worshipped by others. It is this Amita Buddha in whom the Shin Buddhists especially put their trust; and although ancient Buddhism seems to know of no sin-atoning power, they do not admit this, but trust in him for eternal salvation. My opportunities for getting at the truth in this very important matter were, as will hereafter be seen, of an unusual character, as I had the advantage of being entertained by the heads, both of the eastern and the western Shin-shu, from both of whom we received much kindness while at Kioto. In the Nishi Honganji, in company with the archbishop of the western church, was a learned *bozu*, or priest, Mr. Akamatz; and it is not a little characteristic of the energy and enterprise of this great religious body, that this gentleman had lived several years in Europe, studying the Christian sects, and preparing the way for the conversion of Europe to the Shin faith. Mr. Akamatz was kind enough to favour me, at my request, with a short statement in English of the principles of that faith, and for many reasons it seems well that I should here reproduce it without alteration. It runs as follows:—

A BRIEF ACCOUNT OF "SHIN-SHU."

Buddhism teaches that all things, abstract and concrete, are produced and destroyed by causes and combinations of circumstances; therefore the state of our present life has its cause in what we have done in our previous existence up to now: and our present actions become the causes of our state of existence in the future life.

As our doings are good or bad, and of different degrees of excellence or evil, so they produce many effects, having many degrees of suffering or happiness. All men and other sentient beings have an interminable existence, dying in one form and being reborn in another; so that if men wish to escape from a miserable state of transmigration, they must cut off the causes, which are the passions, such for example as covetousness, anger, etc.

The principal object of Buddhism is that men should obtain salvation from misery, according to the doctrine of extinction of passion. This doctrine is the cause of salvation, and salvation is the effect of this doctrine; this salvation we call Nirvāṅa, which means eternal happiness, and is the state of Buddha.

It is, however, very difficult to cut off all the passions,

but Buddhism professes many ways of obtaining this object. Nagadjuna, the Indian saint, said that in Buddhism there are many ways, easy and difficult as in worldly roads, some painful like a mountainous journey, others pleasant like sailing on the sea. These ways may be classed in two divisions, one being called "self-power," or help through self; and the other called "the power of others," or help through another.

Our sect, called "Shin-shu," literally meaning "True Doctrine," which was founded by Shinran Shonin, teaches the doctrine of "help from another."

Now what is this "power of another"? It is the great power of Amita Buddha. "Amita" means boundless, and we believe that the life and light of Buddha are both boundless, and that his knowledge and mercy are both perfect; also that all other Buddhas obtained their state of Buddhaship by the help of Amita Buddha. Therefore Amita Buddha is called the chief of the Buddhas.

Amita Buddha always exercises his boundless mercy upon all creatures, and shows a great desire to help and influence all people who rely on him, to complete all merits and be reborn into paradise (Nirvāna).

Our sect pays no attention to the other Buddhas, and, putting faith only in the great desire of Amita Buddha, expects to escape from the miserable world and to enter into paradise for the next life. From the time of putting faith in the saving desire of Buddha we do not need any power of self-help, but need only keep his mercy in heart, and invoke his name in order to remember him. These doings we call thanksgiving for salvation.

In our sect we have no difference between priest and layman, as concerns their way of obtaining salvation, tho only difference being in their profession or business; and consequently the priest is allowed to marry, and to eat flesh and fish, which are prohibited to other Buddhist sects.

Again, our sect forbids all prayers or supplications for happiness in the present life to any of the Buddhas, even to Amita Buddha, because the events of the present life cannot be altered by the power of others; and teaches the followers of the sect to do their moral duty, loving each other, and keeping order and the laws of government.

We have many writings stating the principles inculcated by our sect, but I give only the translation of the following creed, which was written by Rennyo Shonin, who was the chief priest of the eighth generation from the founder.

Creed.

Rejecting all religious austerities and other actions, giving up all idea of self-power, rely upon Amita Buddha with the whole heart for our salvation, which is the most important thing; believing that at the moment of putting one's faith in Amita Buddha our salvation is settled.

From that moment invocation of his name is observed to express gratitude and thankfulness for Buddha's mercy. Moreover, being thankful for the reception of this doctrine from the founder and succeeding chief priests, whose teachings are as kind and welcome as the light in a dark night.

We must also keep the laws which are fixed for our duty during our whole life.

It is obvious from this statement, coming from a source so entirely unquestionable, that for six centuries and a half there has existed and flourished in Japan a section of Buddhists who believe in the doctrine of salvation by faith; who consider heaven attainable at the close of this life by means of that faith; who have swept aside many of the most prominent restrictions of what we have all supposed to be the ancient Buddhist faith—celibacy, penances, fastings, seclusions, pilgrimages, etc. They have justly been called the Protestants of Japan, building their temples in great thoroughfares, and in many other ways appealing directly to the people. At the same time their priests are highly educated, not by study only, but by travel—one of the present archbishops having himself been to France and other European countries. Of their hope of converting Europe I have elsewhere made mention. The followers of Shinran have, it is said by independent witnesses, wielded vast influence in the religious development of the people, and have always been characterised by singleness of purpose.

Of Nichiren, and the sect which he founded, Mr. Griffis has given a very full and good account, from which, as the most convenient source, and with thankful acknowledgments, I will condense the particulars to be given in this paragraph. Nichiren ("Sun-Lotus") was so named by his mother, who dreamed that the sun had entered her body—a not unfrequent occurrence with mothers of great Japanese men. Born in view of mountains and near the sea, in the southern province of Awa, he was a dreamy and meditative child. Although early put under the care of a holy *bozu* (priest), when grown to manhood he was dissatisfied with the existing sects and doctrines, and resolved to found one of his own. A profound student of Buddhist literature, both in Sanskrit and in Chinese, he set aside the usual prayer, "Hail, Amita Buddha!" or "Save us, Eternal Buddha!" and taught that the true invocation was, "Glory to the Salvation-bringing Book of the Law," or, literally, "Hail, True Way of Salvation, Blossom of Doctrine;" and this the Nichiren sect employ. He founded numerous temples, and was busy throughout his life in teaching, preaching, and spreading his views. In consequence of the bitterness with which he attacked other sects, he was banished to Cape Ito, in Idzu, for three years, and, being contumacious, was subsequently arrested a second time, confined in an underground prison, and condemned to death. The story of an attempt to behead him on the beach near Enroshima being frustrated by a beam from heaven blinding the executioner and splintering his sword, I shall narrate when I record our visit to the spot. He was afterwards released in a general amnesty, and died at Ikégami, near the Kawasaki station, on the short line of railway between Yokohama and Tokio, where are now, consequently, to be seen gorgeous temples, pagodas, and shrines, and solemn groves and cemeteries. The success and power of his followers are due to the directness and exclusiveness of his teachings. They are intolerant even of other Buddhist sects, protesting that in no case save that of the acceptance of their own tenets can they combine with them. The proscription of other sects, and the practice of abuse and reviling as a proselytising agency, was new to Japan when introduced by Nichiren, and stirred up persecution against him and his sect, which has nevertheless flourished greatly, and "produced a greater number of brilliant intellects, uncompromising zealots, unquailing martyrs, and relentless persecutors than any other in Japan. . . . In their view, all other sects than theirs are useless." According to their vocabulary, the adherents of Shingon are "not patriots"; those of Ritsu are "thieves and rascals"; those of Zen are "furies"; while those of certain other sects are sure and without doubt to go to hell. "Among the Nichirenites are more prayer-books, drums, and other noisy accompaniments of revivals than in any other sect. They excel in the number of pilgrims, and in the use of charms, spells, and amulets. Their priests are celibates, and must abstain from wine, fish, and all flesh. They are the Ranters of Buddhism. To this day a revival-meeting in one of their temples is a scene that beggars description, and may deafen weak ears. What with prayers incessantly repeated, drums beating unceasingly, the shouting of devotees, who work themselves into a state of excitement that often ends in insanity, and sometimes in death, and the frantic exhortation of the priests, the wildest excesses that seek the mantle of religion in other lands are by them equalled if not excelled. To this sect belonged Kato Kiyomasa, the bloody persecutor of the Christians in the sixteenth century, the '*vir ter* execrandus' of the Jesuits, but who is now a holy saint in the calendar of canonised Buddhists."

It is manifest that we have here, in Shin-shu and the Nichiren sect, Buddhism presented under a contrast of extremes, and a proof that there are Buddhists and Buddhists. It is no doubt the hope of many, and the object of some, that Japan may become Christianised, and it needs no great perspicacity to see that those two sects present to us remarkable examples of the class of obstacles to be overcome in the process. In Shin-shu, indeed, we have a religion closely allied to the best types of Christianity, not only in its spirit, but in the form of its leading doctrine. Salvation by faith in an all-powerful and all-willing Saviour is common to both these religions. A wise and temperate use of our life and faculties on earth is also sanctioned and encouraged by both, whatever there may appear to be to the contrary in the beginnings of both religions. A mutual desire to convert and embrace each other on the same basis of belief also exists. But when one remembers that in the one case the faith of the Church is centred in Jesus Christ, and in the other case in Amita Buddha, one is ready to ask, What miracle can bring about the desired conjunction and coalition? The Nichirens appear on the other hand to be animated by sentiments and accustomed to practices which spring from a spirit not by any means alien to some bodies of Christians, and in common with them appear to esteem a book, or bible, before and above everything, finding therein their "Way of Salvation" and "Blossom of Doctrine." But then how different the Book in each case!

Before proceeding further, I must make reference to that Goddess or God of a Thousand Hands who is so widely worshipped throughout Japan, and to whom I shall have occasion hereafter to make repeated references. This is the famous Kwannon, who usually is endowed with arms and hands to the large number just intimated, grasping in each some symbol of doctrine, or some weapon of defence. Kwannon has had numerous incarnations, and many are the temples of its worship in the cities, towns, and villages of the land of the slighted sun-goddess. This deity does not appear to have been associated either with Vedism or Brahmanism, or with the beginnings of Buddhism, but was largely worshipped in Northern and Central India a few centuries after Christ, appearing either as a man or a woman according to the requirements of the case—sometimes with three faces, the ideas embodied being those of great vigilance and great helpfulness, especially as regards those who experience the dangers of the deep. Sometimes, in the Indian records, this god was declared to be a spiritual reflex or son of Amita Buddha. Shivaism also had its influence, says Eitel, upon the formation of the dogma in question, and Avalôkitéshvara (her Indian name) is consequently often represented in India, as she is in Japan, with three eyes, with a crown of skulls on her head, or a necklace of skulls, or a rosary made of finger-bones. She is there viewed as a female deity, endowed with great powers of magic and sorcery, and her formula *om mani padme hum* is used by all northern Buddhists for exorcisms, and is inscribed on amulets, articles of common use, houses and public places, as a charm against calamities and evil influences of all kinds. A Japanese legend relates that during the civil wars of the middle ages a political refugee, called Morihsa, hid himself in the temple of the thousand-handed Kwannon at Kiyomidzu, Kioto (to which I shall have occasion again to refer in recording our visit to it), and implored this deity with ceaseless prayers for a thousand days. His enemies, however, discovered his retreat, and dragged him out to the sea-shore for execution. But the executioner found all his efforts foiled by the god Kwannon, for at every stroke he essayed the sword-blade split into a thousand pieces without injuring Morihsa. His enemy, who had previously slain all other members of Morihsa's clan, received also a warning through his own wife, to whom Kwannon had appeared in a dream, interceding on behalf of Morihsa. The latter was therefore set at liberty, and, being the acknowledged protégé of Kwannon, he rose to the highest power in the state.

In the reign of the emperor Go-Uda, during which the invasion of Japan by the Mongol Tartars was nobly repelled, it was ascertained that the Buddhist temples in Japan numbered 11,037, belonging to the following eight sects, viz.:—

1. The San-ron, founded by the Korean priest Ekuwan, in the reign of the empress Suiko.
2. The Hoso, or Isiki, founded by Prince Dosho, in the reign of Kotoku.

3. The Gusha, a branch of the Hoso, founded by the priests Gomei and Miozen, in the reign of Kuwammu.
4. The Djojutsu, founded by unknown priests, under the empress Suiko.
5. The Ritsu, introduced by the Chinese priest Kanshin, under the empress Koken.
6. The Kegon, or Kenshu, introduced by the Chinese priest Dozen, in the reign of Shomu.
7. The Tendai, founded by the priest Saicho, under Kuwammu.
8. The Shingon, by the priest Kukai (Kobo), under Saga.

To these may be added:—

9. The Jodo, founded by the priest Genku, under Takakura.
10. The Zen, by the priest Gisei, under Tsuchi-Mikado.

Later three new sects were formed:—

11. The Shin, or Ikko, by Hanyen, better known as Shinran, a disciple of Genku.
12. The Ji, by the priest Ippen.
13. Hokke, by Nichiren.

Mr. Griffis, writing of the present day, truly says that it is extremely difficult to get accurate statistics of Buddhism, and gives the table quoted below (abridged) in the footnote.* It was compiled for him by a learned priest of the Shin denomination, in the temple of Nishi Honganji, in Tsukiji, Tokio. Besides those given there are, he says, twenty-one other sects, which act apart from the others, and in some cases have no temples or monasteries.

Such further records of Buddhism, or Buddhists, as are needed for the purposes of this volume will be found in either the historical or the other chapters; but a few words on the present state of matters must be given before

---

* TABULAR LIST OF BUDDHISTS IN JAPAN.

Chief sects (Shiu, or Shu).	Total number of Temples.
I. Tendai	6,391
II. Shingon	15,503
III. Zen	21,547
IV. Jodo	9,809
V. Shin	13,708
VI. Nichiren	unknown.
VII. Ji	586

In the Census of 1875 there were returned 207,669 Buddhist *religieux*, of whom 148,807 were males, and 58,862 females.

closing this. Now that the ports of Japan have been opened to the importation, duty free, of that curious product of western manufacture known as "civilisation," the existing religions of the country are becoming subjected to the same scrutiny—often sceptical and unfriendly scrutiny—as western religions; and this, not by foreigners alone, but likewise by Japanese themselves. It is not for nothing that Japan has sent so many of its youths to the continents of Europe and America and to England, and has opened schools for foreign education in its great cities and towns. Already Buddhism is being very curiously inquired into, and Buddhist priests have to confront plain and sceptical speech and questioning within the limits guarded by their grim gate-keepers, beneath their gilded temple-roofs, and in the presence of their ancient and astonished gods. I could give several instances of this, but one will suffice.* It shall be one which will serve to illustrate some of the strange theories of Buddhism, as well as to exhibit the beginnings of the spirit of religious inquiry in Japan.

A learned Buddhist priest of some note in the Itsu-Ko sect, named Sata Kaiseki, attended at the temple of Shinkaiji, at Shinagawa, in the eastern capital, Tokio, in August 1878, to deliver an address on *Tengan*, "Infinite Vision," or that state of perfection to which Buddha attains. His discourse was interspersed with interruptions and arguments by objectors. No sooner was the subject announced than one of the audience rose and observed that it was the custom of the priests to relate wonderful events respecting the life of Buddha and his five hundred disciples, and to give graphic descriptions of the Buddhist hell and heaven, illustrating these by parables, or, when they fail to convince, by metaphysical reasonings which they did not themselves understand. He went on to ask for some clearer

---

* I abridge the account which follows in the text from a translation by Capt. J. M. James, of Tokio, an English gentleman and a Japanese scholar in the employment of the Japanese government. He considered it so interesting that he read the translation at the Asiatic Society of Japan in March 1879.

A Buddhist "Nio," or Temple Guard.

To face page 92, Vol. I.

account of hell and heaven, stating his own difficulties in believing in a hell buried ten thousand miles in the bowels of the earth, or in a heaven several hundreds of thousands of miles high. He bluntly added: "All that the priesthood affirms on the subject is a mere fabrication, an assertion the truth of which any man can plainly perceive without the aid of an eyeglass. If you explain the visible, which the eye can see and the understanding grasp, well and good : but as to the invisible, who can believe?" The priest answered, with great calm apparently, that everything which takes place in the world, from the least to the greatest, is comprehended under the operation of the two great constantly operating forces, cause and effect. To understand these a man must be educated, and the greater knowledge he possesses the more readily will his doubts be dispelled, and everything become clear to his reason; whereas the reasoning faculties of an uneducated man not having been developed, he cannot understand arguments, which serve only to confuse and perplex him. He went on to explain that before a person can attain to Tengan, or Infinite Vision, he must first possess the three Talents of Knowledge, viz.: 1, the faculty of forming correct conclusions from things presented to our organs of sight; 2, the faculty of drawing inferences—for instance, of learning that men must be near you when you hear the voices of men without seeing them; 3, the faculty of comprehending the impossible—which, being rather difficult of explanation, the priest left undefined till a later period of his address. "Therefore," said he (one scarcely sees why), "if Infinite Vision exists, and sees freely around and beyond endless mountains, thereto comparing our feeble knowledge, which sinks into comparative nothingness beside it, there can be no doubt as to the existence of hell and heaven." Here another of the audience asked the priest for a more particular description of the species of vision which he termed Infinite Vision,*

---

* "The faculty of comprehending in one instantaneous view or by intuition all beings in all the worlds."—Eitel's 'Handbook of Buddhism.'

predicating of it the power of seeing over the above-named vast distances. The priest replied that Infinite Vision was indeed inconceivable by ordinary human beings in their unenlightened state, but that he would try, by means of a series of doctrinal proofs, to explain the matter thoroughly, and should thereby probably convince them. He then defined the Five Spiritual Attributes of Infinite Permeating Power, which are, 1, the Infinite Vision; 2, the power of hearing and understanding all sounds produced in all universes; 3, the knowledge of the innermost thoughts of all mankind; 4, the knowledge of all that has transpired in all pre-existing ages; 5, the knowledge of all existing things, including the power of Transformation and Transmutation. The first, he said, was the order of vision which perceives the four extremes, viz.: *Hi*, the order which includes all things, even to infinity [of greatness, I presume]; *Shiyo*, the order which subdivides, and distinguishes between, all things to infinity; *Sai*, the order which perceives all things which are too minute for the human eye or intellect to take in, even with the aid of a microscope; and *Wen*, the order of infinite perception, which "perceives things that no human eye or intellect could grasp in their present unenlightened state, even though they should use a telescope a million times more powerful than any yet invented." Whatever hindrances may present themselves to our sight or reasoning powers, none are present, said the priest, to the Infinite Vision, permeating, as it does, everywhere and everything: "There can, therefore, be no doubt as to the existence of hell and heaven." Here again one of the congregation reminded the priest of his promise not to relate anything miraculous of which he could not bring forward proof positive, and reproached him for deviating considerably from this, by telling them incredible stories about different kinds of eyes, of which he, for one, could make nothing. So far as he knew there was but one kind of eye, viz. that common to all living beings possessed of sight. Upon this the priest narrated the following story, as an illustration of the existence of another and higher form of vision:—

"In ancient times, in China, during the reign of the Emperor Bun, there were doubts entertained among the literati of the day as to the existence of a certain plant called *Kuwa-Kuwan-Pu*, a herb which was said, on being burnt, to possess the virtue of cleansing, without consuming, any clothing material that might be placed on its fire; hence its name, which is equivalent to 'cleansing by fire.' After due deliberation, it was decided that no such plant, or substance, could possibly exist, as such a thing was without all reason; and to commemorate this decision, the emperor caused the same to be inscribed on a stone tablet, which was placed outside one of the principal gates of the city, for the edification of all who might pass by and care to read it. Some years subsequently, during the reign of the emperor Mei, son of the former emperor, Bun, an embassy bearing presents from the kingdom of Ko arrived in the capital, and presented, among other things, some specimens of the identical plant. They were brought as a special rarity, only indigenous to the envoy's country. The emperor, on learning that a plant possessing such wonderful virtues really did exist, felt deeply humiliated at the ignorance displayed by his late father and his father's ministers, and forthwith issued an edict for the stone tablet to be removed and destroyed."

This illustration the priest considered quite conclusive as to the existence in this world of things which, until demonstrated to exist, seem out of all reason: of such things there are many. He next endeavoured to explain the five different kinds of vision as described in the Buddhist Sutra, viz. Mortal Vision, Infinite Vision, the Vision of the Law, Enlightened Vision of a Benevolent Order, and Divine Vision.*

For want of time he expounded the nature of Mortal Vision only. This is of eight kinds: 1. Vision produced by the reflection of borrowed light (as of sun, moon, stars, or artificial light); to this human vision belongs. 2. Vision possessing innate power, needing no assistance from such borrowed lights: the vision of the cat, dog, rat, cow, and horse are of this order. 3. Vision obtained solely through the action of the light of the sun, such as that of pigeons, sparrows, and other birds, which can see only by day. "Cases have been known," said the priest, "of human beings

---

* *Niku-gan, Ten-gan, Hofu-gan, We-gan,* and *Butsu-gan;* collectively called *Mu-Riyo-Zhiyn.*

marked by the like characteristic." 4. Vision which dreads or shuns the overpowering rays of the sun, such as that of owls, bats, etc. 5. Vision such as is possessed by the eagle and other birds of prey: "the eagle, if soaring up aloft, can distinctly see the hunter as he sets his bait, thinking to entrap him, even though the hunter be ten miles distant." 6. Sleepless vision, which is possessed by the fish tribes: "the eye of the fish never closes, nor does it require rest." * 7. Vision of the order which dogs and monkeys possess, having the power of seeing fairies, hobgoblins, and elves in their true form, so that its possessor cannot in any way be bewitched, or led astray by such supernatural beings: "Human beings do not possess this faculty of supernatural vision, and consequently are often bewitched, beguiled, and led astray by foxes and racoon-faced dogs, who temporarily put on the form of some object which entrances the senses of the individual, and causes him or her to do whatever best pleases the beguiler." 8. Periodically changing vision, such as that of the cat, which changes at noon and at midnight. "I have now fully explained to you," continued the priest, "the eight different orders of sight variously possessed by human beings and by the animal tribes generally, each order differing considerably from the others. It, therefore, should neither astonish nor perplex you if I tell you of the existence of Infinite Vision." (The word "therefore" appears to possess some remarkable property in Japan, if we may judge by the use which Satai Kaiseki makes of it—a property quite unknown to Whately and Mill.)

Another perplexed and rather weak-kneed interrogator (speaking figuratively) now rose in the audience, and said that he could "almost believe" that other orders of vision than man's do exist; still, he should like to hear the order of Infinite Vision accounted for. There must, he thought, be some limit, probably not exceeding twenty miles; and

---

* The priest explained that when padlocks first came into use in ancient times the shape adopted was that of the fish's eye, emblematical of that which was supposed never to rest or sleep, but to be ever on the alert.

therefore he doubted the Infinite Vision which, the priest said, could see all things plainly at a distance of a million of miles. The wary priest was not surprised that this should be doubted at first, as there seems no evident reason why Infinite Vision should exist; but when we reflect more deeply, the reason appeared. He would show that Buddha alone attained such vision, and prove it by comparisons drawn from creatures known to possess a certain inferior order of it. One of the congregation asking what creatures these were, the priest explained that the fox, racoon faced dog, ourang-outang, and *ten-gu* (a Japanese hobgoblin of human shape with a long nose) were endowed with an inferior grade of the Infinite Vision, and " their sight consequently extends for hundreds and thousands of miles in all directions." In proof of this he related a story of a fox, who bewitched a man of Tsugaru, and showed to him places and persons over five hundred miles distant. If then his audience allowed that the fox possessed such visual powers, surely they could no longer doubt that Buddha possessed Infinite Vision, and that of the purest order!

Another staggerer on the path of faith here interposed, admitting that the fox and racoon-faced dog could see for hundreds and even thousands of miles, but Buddha being a mere man, like ourselves, although an Indian prince, why should he—he wanted to know—possess Infinite Vision and we not? Whereupon the priest, doubtless understanding his man and his audience generally pretty accurately, broke out into a rhapsody on the marvels of photography and electric telegraphy, for the prediction of which a hundred years ago a man's life would have been forfeited. But now, being enlightened, we know that these wonders do exist, and, once understanding them, even a child sees no great mystery in them. "It is the same with Infinite Vision "—and if the good priest had been candid enough, he might, with equal conclusiveness, have said that "it is the same" with anything else, whether a sublime truth or a piece of arrant nonsense, for electricity and photography do not necessarily illustrate the existence of "infinite vision" any more than they illustrate the existence of anything else which priests or others choose to contend for. "If," continued the priest, " we admit that the fox and racoon-faced dog possess some degree of Infinite Vision, as men are superior to them in intellect and reasoning powers it follows as a natural consequence that every human being must possess the seed of Infinite Vision."

He went on to explain that there are four different orders of this faculty, namely two of a cultivated, and two of instinctive, order. The latter is that belonging to the animals before-named; the former belongs to man, its two branches being Magic and Tranquil Abstraction. The Magic-power, and the art of obtaining it, has gradually been lost. For a human being to attain it, he should cleanse his heart from all worldly lusts and desires, and live an ascetic life in some remote mountain district, where, removed from all human society, existing for a lengthened time on the simplest diet, and breathing the pure mountain air, " his whole material and spiritual being is finally purified, and so changed from that of ordinary human beings that he is enabled to fly through the air at will, and to accomplish and perceive things which are beyond the ken of ordinary mortals." To become proficient in the second part, Tranquil Abstraction, unceasing effort is required on the part of the devotee to overcome the six principal sins— avarice, anger, ignorance, suspicion, pride, and lust. Among the branches or disciplinary paths leading to it is "fixed manifestation," which includes five different methods by which the light of reason is made manifest and fixed in the heart. The first of these, which may be taken as an illustration of them, is counting the number of breath-inspirations, " in which the believer concentrates his mind on his inspirations of breath, to the annihilation of all other thoughts, while reclining on the couch of Tranquil Abstraction." There are other methods or paths, the last of which is called Reciprocal Splendour, the nature of which, however, this curiously learned priest did not, to my judgment, make clear.

A member of the congregation again spoke, saying, "I understand, then, that Infinite Vision is only to be attained through the light of the manifestation of tranquillised splendour?" and the priest explained that the paths which the novice must tread with unswerving devotion, in his pursuit of Infinite Vision, "grow gradually brighter by the rays of manifested splendour falling, with ever-increasing power, on the inward spark of reason the further he proceeds, until it culminated in Tranquil Abstraction in its most perfect form as a light of the purest and most overwhelming brilliancy, the light, namely, of Infinite Vision." Finally, the preacher explained that the Instinctive Infinite Vision of animals can only see for a thousand miles, whereas the Cultivated Infinite Vision of man can, according to the development of its seed, see for ten thousand, a hundred thousand, or a million of miles, or even "a portion of paradise may be visible, or the *San-Zen-Gai* (three thousand worlds or spheres), or the *Jifu-Pau-Koi* (all surrounding worlds)." "Truly great," said he, "are the differences of endowment"; and that observation assuredly no one who peruses all this will for a moment question.

I can only say, in conclusion, that, whether my readers possess any form of Infinite Vision or not, I sincerely hope their cultivated finite vision will enable them to discover what the good priest really meant by his wonderful theories. I make bold to say for myself that I am too far removed from the ape and from the fox and from the racoon-faced dog to be able to make anything out of them. But while the priest's theories remain what they are, I hope he will never meet with any more formidable interrogators than the frequenters of the Shinkaiji temple. He would scarcely be let off so easily by Darwin, Huxley, Tyndall, or Herbert Spencer.

CHAPTER V.

THE DESCENT OF THE CROWN.

The dynasty of Japan the oldest in the world—Commencement of the historic period—The first emperor, Jimmu—The Japanese year 1—Comparison of Christian and Japanese chronology—An interregnum—Descent of the crown by nomination—The successor of Jimmu-Tenno—A dozen successive emperors—The quasi-empress Jingu-Kogo—Her invasion of Korea—Ojin, the god of war—Generous contention of two brothers—Romantic suicide of one, and accession of the other to the throne—Nintoku, the self-denying emperor—His successors—Assassination of Anko-Tenno—Another generous contention of brothers—The consequent regency of their sister—Descent of the crown by election of the nobles—The system of concubinage — The rise of Buddhism—Its influence upon the occupancy of the throne—The first empress ascends the throne—Prince Shotoku-Taishi—His successor—Another empress, who abdicates, and after ten years resumes the crown—A plot frustrated, and an emperor slain—The thrones of Nara—A Twice-empress again—Attempt of a favourite priest to change the dynasty—The god consulted and the priest exiled—Assumption of the governing power by the Fujiwara regents—Dethronement of an emperor by a regent—Another attempt to subvert the dynasty—The "revolt of Shohei and Tenkei"—The "new emperor"—Other revolts—Numerous abdications of the throne—Troublous times—The power of the Taira family—Boy-emperors—The overthrow of the Taira—Four contemporary ex-emperors—Disputed successions—Alternate successions—The house of Hojo—An emperor exiled by a subject—Wars and troubles — The fall of the Hojo—The rise of the Ashikaga Shoguns—Taka-Uji—The dynasty divided—Northern and southern emperors—The alternate succession restored—The power of the Ashikagas—Further disputes—Orderly succession since the fifteenth century—Other empresses—The present emperor—The future succession.

WHEN the Chinese dynasty of So succeeded at the end of the tenth century, after many years of wars and troubles, to the extinct dynasty of To, the new emperor gave audience to the Japanese priest Chonen, and, we are told, was struck with admiration on learning that Japan had been governed by the same dynasty from time immemorial. After the lapse of another nine hundred years, the same imperial family still reigns in Japan, and it was a descendant of its ancient emperors who gave me the honour of audience during our recent visit to his country. "The dynasty of the imperial rulers of Japan is the oldest in the world. No other family line extends so far back into the remote ages as the nameless family of mikados. Disclaiming to have a family name, claiming descent, not from mortals, but from the heavenly gods, the imperial house of the kingdom of the Rising Sun occupies a throne which no plebeian has ever attempted to usurp" (Griffis). There have nevertheless been, as we shall see, many vicissitudes in the descent of the crown, not a few of them of a character scarcely less romantic than if the throne had been a prize for which nobles had competed, politicians had schemed, and warriors had waged battle.

The histories of Japan, prepared under the sanction of the present Japanese government, date the commencement of the historic period from the first year of the reign of the first emperor, Jimmu-Tenno,* who is said to have ruled for seventy-six years, viz. from 660 to 585 B.C. Some persons consider that this reign, and a few reigns that succeeded it, probably or possibly belong to the legendary period; because while, on the one hand, the Emperor Jimmu is described as the founder of the present empire, and the ancestor of the present emperor, on the other, he is described as the fourth son of Ukaya Fukiaezu-no-mikoto, who was fifth in direct descent from the beautiful sun-goddess, Tensho-Daijin. But as no such thing as writing existed in Japan in those days, or for many centuries afterwards, it would not be surprising if a real monarch should have a mythical origin assigned to him; and as I have quite lately heard the guns firing at Nagasaki an imperial

---

* The word Tenno, signifying "Heaven-King" or "Heaven-Son," is usually affixed to the names of the emperors, even in lists and tables. I shall only repeat it after the name, however, when I find it convenient, as it often will be.

salute in honour of his coronation, and have seen the flags waving over the capital city, Tokio, in honour of his birthday, the Emperor Jimmu is quite historical enough for my present purpose. The commencement of his reign shall fix for us, as it does for others, the Japanese year 1, which was 660 years prior to our year 1, so that any date of the Christian era can be converted into one of the Japanese era by the addition of 660 years, and *vice versâ*. Some of the emperors will be found to have lived very long lives, no doubt; but as I have said elsewhere, none of them lived nearly so long as our Adam, Methuselah, and others, in whose longevity so many of us profess to believe; and besides, it is impossible for me to attempt to correct a chronology which Japanese scholars, and Englishmen versed in the Japanese language, have thus far left without specific correction. Deferring for after consideration the incidents of the successive imperial reigns, except in so far as they bear directly upon the descent of the crown, let us, then, first glance at the succession of emperors and empresses who have ruled the Morning Land.*

After the death of the Emperor Jimmu there appears to have been an interregnum for three years—although it is seldom taken account of—the second emperor, Suisei, who was the fifth son of the first emperor, having ascended the throne 581 B.C., and reigned till 549. The cause of the interregnum appears to have been the extreme grief which Suisei felt at the death of his father, in consequence of which he committed the administration of the empire, for a time, to one of his relatives—an unworthy fellow, as he proved, named Tagishi Mimi-no-mikoto, who tried to assassinate his master and seize the throne for himself, and who was put to death by Suisei for his pains. My readers will observe that the *fifth* son of the emperor Jimmu was nominated by him as his successor, and it is probable that older

---

* Japan is still literally the Morning Land to travellers across the Pacific, the day being changed on the voyage between San Francisco and Yokohama, and *vice versâ*, at the meridian of 180°—E. or W. as you please.

sons were living and passed over, and that the throne was inherited in part by nomination even in this its first transfer.

A dozen emperors followed Suisei, apparently in orderly succession, as I have not observed any intimation to the contrary in histories in which departures from direct succession are recorded; and although I have given elsewhere a complete list of the emperors, it will be well to record here the names of these twelve, so as to show at a glance what amount of historic ground we are covering. They were—

	Date from 1st year of Jimmu.	Date, Christian Era.	Age at death.
Annei	. 112.	B.C. 548	. 57
Itoku	. 150.	„ 510	. 77
Koshio	. 185.	„ 475	. 114
Koan	. 268.	„ 392	. 137
Korei	. 370.	„ 290	. 128
Kogen	. 446.	„ 214	. 116
Kaikua	. 503.	„ 157	. 115
Sujin	. 563.	„ 97	. 119
Suinin	. 629.	„ 29	. 141
Keiko	. 731.	A.D. 71	. 143
Seimu	. 791.	„ 131	. 108
Chuai	. 852.	„ 192	. 52

There will be a few words to say respecting some of these emperors in other chapters; but the good old age to which most of them appear to have contrived to live is the only circumstance calling for remark at present.

But now, at the death of Chuai, a remarkable suspension of the direct imperial rule took place, owing to the fact of that emperor having had a remarkable woman for his wife. This was no other than she who is famous beyond all women in Japanese history as the empress, or quasi-empress, Jingu-Kogo. Her husband, the emperor Chuai, dying suddenly at a critical time for the empire—when rebels were in arms at Kumaso (Kiushiu), and Korea required, in her opinion, punishment*—she concealed his death, despatched a general with the necessary force for crushing the rebellion, and,

---

* The people of Korea were believed by her to have instigated the revolt at Kumaso.

although herself in what has always been deemed an interesting condition, assumed the dress and arms of a warrior, and embarked with her troops for the shores of Korea. One after the other the kings of Shiraki, Koma, and Kudara (all parts of Korea), in consternation, laid down their arms, surrendered hostages, paid tribute, and promised good behaviour for the future, which for a long time afterwards they loyally observed. On her return to Japan, this formidable lady gave birth to her baby, subdued some other revolted princes, proclaimed herself regent, and governed the country till her husband had been dead seventy years, dying at the age of 100 years. I may have more to say about this renowned woman hereafter, for wonderful exploits of hers are recounted, and among the most wonderful, perhaps, is that of postponing for many months the birth of her boy. Moreover, she is worshipped in many a temple of Japan down to the present day, although not in so many as the babe referred to, for he grew to become the great emperor Ojin, known and worshipped everywhere as the Spirit and God of War. My present purpose is, however, only with the suspension of the imperial rule which ended with her death.

This son Ojin immediately succeeded her, and reigned forty years. Before his death he designated as his successor his favourite son, Prince Waki-Irako (or Uji Wakairatsuko). But this prince was a modest and generous gentleman, and considered that the country would be better governed by his elder brother, Nintoku, who had been passed over, but who was known for his intelligence and erudition. He accordingly besought Nintoku to accept the throne, which he desired to abdicate in his favour. Nintoku, however, stoutly refused this sacrifice. While the brothers were engaged in this friendly strife, another prince of the imperial family, Oyama-Mori, attempted to usurp the throne, but I am happy to say the brothers discovered his plot, and promptly put him for ever beyond the sphere of plotting. For three years Prince Waki-Irako did not cease to pray his brother to accept the crown, but Nintoku would not at all consent. In despair, the younger brother at length put himself to death, and in this romantic manner, after an interregnum of three years, constrained his brother to mount the throne, with what feelings let noble minds alone attempt to conceive. This was how the crown of Japan came to adorn the head of that emperor, Nintoku, who, before all others, is remembered for his self-denying love of the people. It is he of whom it is recorded that when residing at Naniwa, the modern Osaka, he ascended a hill (or the terrace of his palace, as some accounts say), and, observing the sadness and want of prosperity which the appearance of the city indicated, at once decreed the abolition of taxes for three years, and so reduced his household expenses that the imperial palace fell out of repair, letting the rain through the roof, and becoming scarcely habitable. Some years later, on again looking over the city in company with his empress, he was agreeably surprised to see it presenting a flourishing and joyous aspect. "Now," said he to the empress, "I have become rich!" "Rich?" said she. "How can you speak of riches with a palace like yours, which lets the rain through the roof, has its fences fallen down, and scarcely affords us shelter!" "The people," replied the emperor, "are the true substance of an empire; when the people become rich, the sovereign may consider himself rich." The people hearing of this wished to have the tax reimposed, and to be allowed to rebuild the palace; but the emperor refused, and some years elapsed before he yielded to their wishes. Nintoku reigned for eighty-six years, dying (notwithstanding the damps and draughts of his tumble-down old palace) at the ripe age of one hundred and ten, in the year 399 A.D.

After Nintoku came four emperors, respecting whose accession no irregularity appears to have occurred. They were—

	Date from Jimmu.	Christian Era.	Age.
Richiu	1060	400	77
Hansho	1065	405	60
Inkyo	1071	411	80
Anko	1113	453	56

The last-named emperor, Anko, was assassinated. He was succeeded by his younger brother, Yuriaku (in 457), who was the fifth son of the previous emperor, Inkyo. Before ascending the throne, Yuriaku put to death the assassins of his brother and their accomplices. He was himself succeeded by the emperor Seinei (in 480), who, having no children of his own, searched out the two sons of Prince Ichinobe-no-Oshiwa. This prince, having been executed by order of the emperor Yuriaku, his two sons—Prince Okeno-o and Prince Kenso—had taken flight, and lived in concealment among the people. The emperor Seinei, on tracing them out, named the elder, Prince Okeno-o, as his successor. On the death of Seinei, however, this prince desired to decline the crown in favour of his younger brother, Kenso, whom he believed to be more enlightened than himself. But Kenso refused, and the consequence was that their eldest sister, Princess Iitoyo-no Awo, was appointed regent. At the death of this princess, Prince Okeno-o renewed his solicitations to his brother, and, these being supported by those of his courtiers, Prince Kenso at last yielded. Prince Okeno-o has subsequently been dropped altogether out of his place among the emperors, but after the above explanations he will doubtless take a deservedly high position in the estimation and regard of my readers. The whole period covered by the reigns of these two brothers was, however, only a couple of years, after which Kenso was succeeded by another, and older, brother of his, named Ninken, who reigned ten years. He was succeeded by Buretsu-Tenno, in 499 A.D., who was himself succeeded by Ketai-Tenno (507), one of the descendants, in the fifth generation, of the Great Emperor Ojin, to whom, in the absence of issue of Buretsu, the crown was offered by the dignitaries of the court. In this case, therefore, as frequently afterwards, there was something very like an election to the crown, but the choice then, as always, was made of a member of the imperial family.

The supply of imperial princes was in all probability kept up sufficiently by the system of concubinage which has always existed in Japan, but not, so far as I have been able to trace the facts, by the system of adoption which in other cases has so greatly facilitated family succession, and which is very prevalent even to-day.

Ketai-Tenno was followed on the throne by three of his sons successively, viz., first, the emperor Ankan (532); next the emperor Senkuwa (536); and lastly, the emperor Kimmei (540). This last-named emperor, it is to be noted, was succeeded by Bitatsu-Tenno, the husband of Kimmei's daughter,* although he had sons, two of whom, Yomei and Sushun, subsequently reigned. Bitatsu reigned sixteen years, Yomei two, and Sushun five, bringing us down to the year 592 A.D.

We have here arrived at a period in the history of Japan when an alien religion, that of Buddhism, had taken root in the country, and begun to influence the occupancy of the throne. In the reign of Ketai-Tenno the Koreans began to send images of Buddha into Japan, and from time to time subsequently the Korean kings availed themselves of opportunities for seeking to spread the new faith in the land of the god-Mikados and of their ancestress the sun-goddess. In the reign of Bitatsu two statues of Buddha were brought from Kudara (in Korea), and were given to one Sogano-Umako, who founded a temple for their reception. The next emperor, Yomei, falling suddenly ill, wished to become a Buddhist, and this Umako secretly introduced Buddhist priests into the palace, and vowed eternal hatred against two high court dignitaries, Moria and Katsumi, who had done their utmost to oppose the emperor's conversion, and to keep the idols out of the palace. The emperor Yomei being dead, Moria wished the crown to pass to Prince Anahohe. Umako, on the contrary, wished it to pass to Sushun, the brother of Yomei. He therefore caused Prince Anahohe to be assassinated, and, in concert with his pretender, attacked

---

* It should be borne in mind, in connection with this incident, that although children of the same mother were forbidden to marry, this was not the case with children of different mothers by the same father—a common state of things in countries where polygamy is practised.

Moria in his house and killed him. Sushun then ascended the throne, and strongly supported Buddhism. He reigned but five years, as we have seen. After his death, an empress for the first time formally ascended the throne of Japan.

This was Suiko-Tenno, daughter of the emperor Kimmei, eldest sister of the emperor Sushun, and widow of the emperor Bitatsu. Sushun having died without issue, the dignitaries of the court offered her the crown, and she accepted it, and reigned by virtue of these acts. Here, therefore, is another example of the crown of Japan being disposed of by something very like election, the recipient again, however, being a member of the imperial family, but this time a woman. We shall presently see that the throne was on several subsequent occasions occupied by women.

The heir-presumptive of the empress Suiko was one of the most notable characters in the history of his country, as we have already seen, viz. the prince Shotoku-Taishi. As the empress survived him, he never succeeded to the throne. The part taken by him in connection with the introduction of Buddhism has been previously sketched. At his death the empress selected for her successor the grandson of Bitatsu-Tenno, who reigned for thirteen years as the emperor Yomei. Dying without issue, he was succeeded by his widow, who was also a descendant of Bitatsu-Tenno, and who reigned for three years as the empress Kokioku. During her reign an attempt was made to assassinate an imperial prince, to dethrone the empress, and to alter the succession; but the plot was discovered, and Prince Naka-no-oe, her son, took an active part in putting the conspirators to death. The empress, therefore, offered to abdicate in his favour; and he, refusing the crown for himself, offered it to the younger brother of the empress, who accepted it, and reigned for ten years as the emperor Kotoku. At his death, the ex-empress took back the crown for herself, reascended the throne, and reigned for seven years, becoming known to posterity as the empress Saimei (655-661 A.D.). The reader will, therefore, please to remember that the empresses Kokioku and Saimei were really one and the same lady. That she was a strong-willed and enterprising person there could be but little doubt, even if we knew no more of her; but, in point of fact, she was preparing to "personally conduct" a military enterprise to Kudara (in Korea) at the time of her death. Her son, Prince Naka-no-oe, then took the throne, and reigned for nine years as the emperor Tenji.

The crown next went in due course to the eldest son of Tenji, whose reign was, however, short and sad, especially in its termination. The cause can be easily explained. His father had designated as his successor, not his son, but his own brother, Prince Oshi-Ama; but at the emperor's death, this brother declined the crown, retired to Yoshino, and there became a *bozu*, or "shaven-crown." The son, Prince Otomo, thereupon mounted the throne, but, having some fear of his uncle, most improperly resolved to get him assassinated. The uncle, being advised of this, and very naturally disapproving of it, placed himself at the head of a body of troops, and went and attacked and killed his nephew; and that is how he came to reign for so short a time (viz. 671-72 only). He is known as the emperor Kobun. A modern Japanese historian, who tells this story, curiously adds: "Kobun-Tenno was a highly instructed and very good man. He was the author of several pieces of verse in the Chinese language which are highly esteemed." It is a pity that this good man and famous poet tried to murder his uncle.

Three additional monarchs bring us down to the thrones of Nara. The first and last of the three were the emperors Temmu and Mommu; the second was the empress Jito. Nara was made the capital city by the next empress, Gemmei (a daughter of Tenji-Tenno, and mother of the emperor Mommu), in the year 708. The empress Gemmei was succeeded by her daughter, the empress Gensho; and next to her came the emperor Shomu, who was followed by his daughter the empress Koken. And here we come to another "fault" (to speak geologically) in the succession. The son of the empress Koken would under ordinary circumstances have succeeded her; but as this young prince "thought only of his pleasures," she disinherited him, and named in his place the emperor Junjin, in whose favour she abdicated: but only for a time, for this empress, like Saimei-Tenno, took to the throne again when it once more became vacant. Nor, in this case, did she wait for it to become vacant in the ordinary course of events. The fact is, she had been persuaded to abdicate by one of her high officers, who was a sort of minister at war; and when after a while this gentleman revolted, and was put to death, she dethroned the emperor Junjin, and took back the reins of government as the empress Shotoku. A somewhat impudent attempt to deprive her prematurely of her throne a second time was made. A favourite priest of hers, named Dokio, who had great influence over her, conceived the idea of usurping the throne and changing the dynasty, divinely appointed as it was; and with this object he spread the rumour that the god Hachiman of Usa had said that the throne of Japan should be given to his favourite servant Dokio. The empress, doubtless taking better care of her rights than Dokio anticipated, despatched a civil functionary to interrogate the god at Usa; and he wisely and properly brought back the message that the imperial throne ought to remain in the same dynasty for ever, and that no one else ought to aspire to it. This gentleman's name not inappropriately began with the word "Wake" (Wake-no-Kyo-Maro was his full designation). I am sorry to say Dokio behaved as badly to him as if he had brought to the empress a message of his own instead of a message of the god, for he deprived him of everything, and exiled him to Kiushiu. The empress was so far in the hands of Dokio as to allow this; but after her death the tables were turned upon him, he being exiled, and Wake, or Kyo-Maro, was recalled.

"O what a tangled web we weave"

when we pretend to take messages from the gods to one another!

The empress Koken-Shotoku dying without issue, the court dignitaries (of whom the Fujiwara were the chief) chose as sovereign the grandson of the emperor Tenji, and son of

Prince Shiki, who reigned for twelve years as the emperor Konin. He was succeeded by his eldest son, the emperor Kuwammu, who reigned fourteen years. This prince but narrowly escaped the loss of the throne. As the heir-presumptive, he had been deprived in the previous reign of his rights, and when a successor had to be found the choice lay between the princess Sakabito and Prince Hieda. Fujiwara-no-Momokawa, however, knowing that the crown prince was an enlightened man, interposed, and persuaded the emperor to restore the succession to him. He, again, was succeeded by his first, second, and third sons, as follows:—

	Date from Jimmu.	Christian Era.	Age.
Heizei	1466	806	51
Saga	1470	810	57
Junna	1484	824	55

Followed by

Nimmio	1494	834	41
Montoku	1511	851	32
Seiwa	1519	859	31
Yozei	1537	877	82

Here I am obliged to pause to state that the last-named sovereign was dethroned by his regent, Fujiwara-Moto-Tsune, the reason assigned being that Yozei was not a just ruler. It was during the previous reign, when Seiwa was under age, that the chief of the house of Fujiwara assumed the governing powers in the shape of a regency, and they were retained almost hereditarily in that family for long afterwards. This dethronement of the emperor Yozei, "because he was not just," was a pretty strong exercise of them. The emperor Koko, who was set up in place of Yozei, reigned less than three years, and was succeeded by the emperor Uda, who after reigning ten years resigned in favour of his son the emperor Daigo. This emperor reigned thirty-three years. Then followed these:—

	Date from Jimmu.	Christian Era.	Age.
Shujaku	1591	931	30
Murakami	1607	947	42
Reizei	1628	968	62

	Date from Jimmu.	Christian Era.	Age.
Enyu	1630	970	33
Kuwazan	1645	985	41
Ichijo	1647	987	32
Sanjo	1672	1012	43
Go-Ichijo *	1677	1017	29
Go-Shujaku	1697	1038	37
Go-Reizei	1706	1046	44
Go-Sanjo	1729	1069	40
Shirakawa	1733	1073	77
Horikawa	1747	1087	29
Toba	1768	1108	55
Shutoku	1784	1124	46
Konoye	1802	1142	17

It is necessary to say but very little about the descent of the crown through the two centuries covered by the reigns of these sixteen monarchs, because it invariably went to a member of the imperial family either by direct descent or by nomination of the reigning sovereign.

In the reign of Shujaku, the first of the sixteen, a formidable attempt was made to interrupt the imperial dynasty, known as the revolt of Shohei and Tenkei.† Taira-Masakado rebelled in Shimosa, chose Sarushima as his capital, and set himself up as Shin-Wo, or "new emperor." He received the support of Fujiwara-Sumitomo, who raised an army in the province of Io to aid the rebel cause. The government, however, successfully attacked the leaders, and in the end the heads of the two chiefs, Masakado and Sumitomo, were sent to Kioto under the disadvantage of being severed from their bodies.

There were other revolts, and also numerous abdications, during the period, the emperors Enyu, Kuwazan, Ichijo, Sanjo, Go-Ichijo, Go-Shujaku, Go-Sanjo, and Konoye—or one half the number of these emperors—having each received the crown on the abdication of his predecessor. The last emperor on the list, Konoye, was but a young child when

---

* The prefix "Go" is equivalent to "the second," this emperor's name, therefore, being equivalent to Ichijo the Second; and so on with those that follow.

† The names of the years in which it existed.

he succeeded Shutoku, and although he reigned fourteen years, was considerably under age when he died. The last of the above group of abdicating emperors, Shutoku-Tenno, appears to have been dissatisfied with the results of his self-denial, for in the reign of Go-Shirakawa-Tenno, the elder brother and successor of the emperor Konoye, he desired to recover the crown, and commenced a series of troubles which have scarcely yet ceased to operate, and in following which my readers and myself must patiently take our humble part in later chapters.

The attack of ex-emperor Shutoku upon the throne of Go-Shirakawa was unsuccessful, his army was defeated, and he was exiled, as we shall see in more detail hereafter. But after a reign of only three years, Go-Shirakawa voluntarily abdicated the throne. He was succeeded by Nijo, a youth of sixteen, who reigned seven years, and who was himself succeeded by a much younger monarch; for this little fellow, the emperor Rokujio, was but two years old when he was lifted on to the throne, off which he was lifted, as involuntarily no doubt, at the age of five. Having got rid thus early of the cares of empire, he escaped the cares of life likewise eight years later, dying when he was thirteen. The next emperor, Takakura, was eight years old when he replaced the child Rokujio on the throne, and ruled for a dozen years, when, being nearly of age, he abdicated in favour of his son Antoku, who was already nearly three years old!

We are here in the midst of very troublous times, as we shall see hereafter, with Taira-Kyomori putting these imperial boys on and off the throne as best suited him, so that we need not be surprised at learning that this three-year-old emperor was off the throne again in the course of three or four years. But this time the boy-emperor abandoned the throne from the compulsion of others.

Kyomori was dead, and succeeded by his son Munomori; but even before the child Antoku was enthroned, the power, and the tyrannous use of power, of the Taira had engendered so much antagonism that a powerful combination was formed between the Minamoto family and some of the offended imperialists for the purpose of overthrowing, and even of slaying, Kyomori. The hostilities thus commenced were continued after Kyomori's death (which was a natural one), and with the result that in the third year of the nominal reign of young Antoku the Taira were driven by the Minamoto from Kioto, carrying him with them, the victors, or rather the ex-emperor Shirakawa, raising Antoku's brother, Go-Toba, to the abandoned throne as his successor.

Go-Toba was the fourth son of the former emperor, Takakura, and he reigned from 1184 to 1198 A.D. He was succeeded by his son Tsuchi-Mikado, who reigned twelve years, and was followed by his younger brother Juntoku, who reigned eleven years. All three of these last-named emperors — Go-Toba and his two sons Tsuchi-Mikado and Juntoku — became ex-emperors, and were exiled, the last of them, Juntoku, being deposed in 1221 A.D., as the result of the war of Shokiu, which we shall notice hereafter. Indeed, a couple of months before the crisis arrived Juntoku resigned and appointed his son Chukio, a youth of seventeen, to succeed him, and it was this young fellow who was really dethroned by Yoshitoki two months later, so that in point of fact there were four ex-emperors at this time.

The next emperor was Go-Horikawa (1221-1232 A.D.). He was a grandson of the emperor Takakura, and was succeeded by Shijo-Tenno, who reigned till 1242. After his death, the court party wished to nominate Prince Tadanari, a son of the ex-emperor Juntoku, to succeed him; but this the Shukken, or minister, Yasutoki opposed, and caused the crown to be given to the fourth son of the ex-emperor Tsuchi-Mikado, who ascended the throne as the emperor Go-Saga. He abdicated the throne after reigning three to four years, and was succeeded by his two sons—Go-Fukakusa, who reigned thirteen years, and Kame-Yama, in whose favour Go-Fukakusa then abdicated, and who also reigned thirteen years.

Kame-Yama abdicated the throne in the year 1274, and was succeeded by his own son, Go-Uda. This was displeasing to the ex-emperor Go-Fukakusa, and not unnaturally so, considering that he had himself worn the crown before his brother, and had sons of his own who were thus passed over. On the other hand, their father, the emperor Go-Saga, had in his will ordained that the sons of his favourite son, Kame-Yama, should succeed to the throne. After a reign of thirteen years, however, Go-Uda was forced by Go-Fukakusa to resign in favour of his (Go-Fukakusa's) eldest son, who reigned for eleven years as the emperor Fushimi.

The dispute about the succession was a very serious and prolonged one, however, and it was at length decided that the two branches of the family should in turn take the throne. In pursuance of this agreement, after a short reign (two years) of Go-Fushimi, the son of Fushimi, Go-Nijo assumed the crown. Go-Nijo was the eldest son of Go-Uda, and grandson of Kame-Yama, and his heir was to be Prince Tomihito, the grandson of Go-Fukakusa. After Go-Nijo had reigned six years, he abdicated the throne, and was duly succeeded in 1308 A.D. by Prince Tomihito, who reigned till 1318 as the emperor Hanazono. He then abdicated, and was succeeded by the emperor Go-Daigo, grandson of Kame-Yama, and second son of Go-Uda.

The house of Hojo had long been very domineering (as we shall see in our later sketch of the history of the country), and the emperor Go-Daigo determined to put it down if he could, and as a pretext for a rupture announced to the minister Hojo Takatoki that he intended to designate his own son, the prince imperial, Morinaga, as his successor. Takatoki pointed out that this was contrary to the convention made in a former reign, and subsequently conformed to, and insisted that the prince Kadzuhito, son of the emperor Go-Fushimi, should next occupy the throne. The emperor declared war against Takatoki, but the army of the latter defeated the imperial troops, and carried off Go-Daigo himself. Takatoki sent his imperial master into exile in the island of Oki, and sat prince Kadzuhito on the throne, under the title of Kuwoogon-Tenno. Other forces were raised, however, the Hojo troops were beaten, the Hojo

I 2

family practically annihilated, and Go-Daigo, returning from exile, re-entered Kioto, dethroned Kuwoogon, and remounted the throne himself. His troubles were not, however, over. In distributing the confiscated property of the Hojos he gave great dissatisfaction to the military caste, and when some of the aforetime vassals of the Hojo house revolted, the general who was sent against them, Ashikaga-Taku-Uji, turned against the emperor, marched upon Kioto, and carried it. He was, however, soon after driven out, and forced to fly to the west; but he there reorganised his army, again marched upon and besieged the capital, and caused the emperor Go-Daigo to fly to Yoshimo. Taka-Uji then proclaimed emperor Kuwoogon's brother, Yuta-Hito, who took the name of Komio-Tenno. From this time, for more than half a century (fifty-seven years) Japan had two emperors: one at Yoshino, called the Southern Emperor, and one at Kioto, called the Northern Emperor.

The southern emperor, Go-Daigo, was succeeded in 1339 by his son, Go-Murakami-Tenno, who reigned for thirty-five years, being succeeded in 1374 by Go-Kame-Yama-Tenno. In 1349 the northern emperor abdicated in favour of his nephew Shuko, who was displaced after a short time (three years) by Go-Kuwoogon-Tenno. In 1374 this emperor abdicated in favour of his son, afterwards known as the emperor Go-Enyu, who in 1383 in his turn abdicated in favour of his own son, Go-Komatsu-Tenno. In 1391 the Shogun Ashikaga-Yoshimutsu, observing that the power and the domains of the southern emperor were steadily diminishing, proposed to him to return to a single dynasty, upon the old basis of an alternate succession in the two branches of the family. To this the southern emperor assented, and, returning to Kioto, handed the insignia of empire to Go-Komatsu. The true power was in the hands of the Ashikaga Shoguns; but Go-Komatsu reigned till the year 1412. His successor ought evidently to have been the son of the ex-emperor, Go-Kame-Yama, but the Shogun Yoshimochi violated the compact, and gave the throne to Shoko-Tenno. Then followed more fighting, but Shoko retained the throne till his death in 1428, when, dying without issue, he was succeeded by the emperor Go-Hanazono, who was a descendant of the northern emperor, Shuko. In this reign, which lasted till 1464, there was more fighting on account of the violated convention as to the succession, one of the sons of the emperor Go-Kame-Yama, Prince Ogura-no-Miya, taking arms in defence of it, but without success.

Of the succession to the throne from the latter half of the fifteenth century onward to the present time there is little that need be said in this place. The succession appears to have been so far orderly as neither to have occasioned any great commotion nor to have been the result of any. There were wars enough, and many more than enough, from the reign of Shuko onwards till the year 1600, when the general Iyéyasu won a great battle at Sekigahara, and gave the country peace for two and a half centuries under the domination of the Tokugawa Shoguns; but the fighting was between rival Shoguns, Shoguns and their ministers, and would-be Shoguns, the crown taking but a comparatively minor part in the proceedings, and not itself again coming under serious question. It is worthy of remark, however, that in 1630 A.D., after a lapse of eight hundred and sixty years, another empress ascended the throne. This was Miosho-Tenno, daughter of her predecessor the emperor Go-Miwo by his wife Too-Fuku-no-in, who was herself a daughter of the Tokugawa Shogun Hidétada. She reigned fourteen years. At a late period another empress, who proved to be (so far as we know at present) the last of the governing empresses, occupied the throne for eight years. This was Go-Sakura-Machi-Tenno (1763–1770 A.D.), who was the daughter of one emperor and the eldest sister of another. She assumed the government in consequence of her brother's son being very young at the time of his father's death; when the boy grew up she abdicated in his favour.

The present emperor, Mutsu-Hito, succeeded to the throne in 1867 on the death of his father. In him, as at once the representative of the most ancient of the existing dynasties of the world, and one of the most enlightened and prudent men in Japan, the best hopes of peace and progress for his country are centred. Unhappily none of the children of the empress and himself are now alive. But they are both young, and may yet have surviving children. Failing these, there are other members of the imperial family whose title to the throne would be undisputed.

THE EMPEROR'S COAT-OF-ARMS.

CHAPTER VI.

EARLY HISTORY, ENDING 1000 A.D.

The Japanese Pantheon—The first emperor, Jimmu, accepted as historic—His conquests and subsequent career—The emperor Sujin—Commencement of relations between Japan and Korea—Revolts in the west, east, and north—Yamato-Daké, "the Warlike"—His romantic career—Disguised as a dancing-girl he beguiles and slays the arch-rebel—The sacred sword "Grass-mower" — Yamato-Daké's wife offers herself to the sea-god—Further relation with Korea—Naval architecture and navigation—Introduction of written characters and writing; and afterwards of Chinese literature—Simplicity of life of the early emperors—The influx of skilled persons from Korea and China—The emperor Tenji: administrator, inventor, and reformer—The offices of Dai-jo-Dai-jin and Nai-Dai-jin created—The reforming empress Jito: an advocate of "woman's rights"—Progress of education and art—The imperial residence becomes more settled—The city of Nara—The Nara empresses: the glory of their reigns—The founding of Miako, or Kioto —The "Château of Peace," a Château of Contention and War—Commencement of the struggles of the middle ages—The house of Fujiwara: its rise and eminence—The Sugawara family: its literary fame—Contests between Fujiwara-Tokihira and Sugawara Michisané—Exile and death of Michisané—His deification as the god Tenjin—The coming greatness of the Taira and Minamoto—A conspiracy discovered —The power of the Fujiwara culminates—The arts of peace still pursued.

SOME writers on Japanese history profess to see in the Pantheon of Japan, pictured in the *Kojiki* and *Nihonki*, nothing more than a collection of distinguished personages who lived and laboured and contended in the country before the historic period, thus bringing deified men and women down to earth again. Such persons accept the records of Jimmu-Tenno's origin as essentially accurate in so far as they state what is human and reasonable, rejecting them only when they set forth what is supernatural, and, to them, unbelievable. Others, on the contrary, consider, or profess to consider, the supernatural portions of these narratives as perfectly trustworthy, and discredit only those statements concerning the first of the sacred emperors which would seem in any way to detract from his divinity. I should be sorry to have to argue the case with either of these parties, but I must take the liberty of accepting as sufficiently accurate as much of the recorded lives of Jimmu and his successors as the modern prosaic histories in Japan are content to put forth, and no more.

Proceeding upon this basis, there is not much to be said of the reigns of the mikados who ruled before the Christian era, beyond what has been already stated in previous chapters. As regards the first emperor, his ancestor, Ninigi-no-mikoto—whether a god or not, or whether he came down from the sun by means of "the bridge of heaven" or not—appears to have established his residence at the ancient Himuka, now Hiuga; there it was that Jimmu-Tenno first resided, and thence it was that he started on his historic and memorable career. The central parts of Japan were militarily occupied by rebels (whose names are preserved), and it was to subdue them that he proceeded eastward. He stopped for three years at Takashima, constructing the necessary vessels for crossing the waters, and then, in the course of years, making his way victoriously as far as Naniwa, the modern Osaka, encountered his foes at Kawachi, and defeated them, the chief generals being left dead on the battle-field. Jimmu was now sole master of Japan, as then known, and in the following year he mounted the throne. The eastern and northern parts of the country were, however, still, and long afterwards, peopled by the Aino race, who were at a later period treated as troublesome savages, and conquered by a famous prince, Yamato-Daké, by help of the sacred sword, as we shall presently see. The spot selected by the emperor Jimmu for his capital was Kashiwabara, in the province of Yamato, not far from the present western capital of Kioto. He there did honour to the gods, married, built himself a palace, and deposited in the throne-room the sacred mirror, sword, and ball, the insignia of the imperial power handed down from the sun-goddess. He organised two imperial guards, one as a bodyguard to protect the interior of the palace, and the other to act as sentinels around the palace. What else there is to be said historically of the first emperor, and of his successors down to the time of Christ, has been recounted in the chapters on the Descent of the Crown, the Shinto Religion, and other parts of this work, with one important exception, however, viz. the beginning of intercourse between Korea and Japan.

It was in the reign of Sujin, which terminated thirty years before the birth of Christ, that were commenced those relations between Japan and its nearest neighbour which lasted for many centuries. The state which we now know as Korea—and which is a projection towards Japan of the great continent of Asia, adjoining, on the land side, the empire of China—was at that time divided into a number of small independent kingdoms, named Mimana, Shiraki, Kudara, Tokujiun, Koma, etc. The state of Mimana being menaced by the neighbouring state of Shiraki, with reference to a province named Sanbamon, of which both claimed the possession, Mimana applied to the Japanese government for assistance against Shiraki, and offered to pay tribute to Japan by way of recompense for this service. The government accepted this offer, and sent a long-named general (Shiotaritsu-Hiko-no-mikoto) to force Shiraki into submission. The object was accomplished, and Mimana, faithful to its promise, sent to Japan an ambassador named Sonaka-Shichi, bearing presents and tribute to the emperor. In the following reign, that of Suinin-Tenno (the contemporary of Jesus Christ), the prince royal of Shiraki, named Amano-Hiboko, proceeded to Japan, and was there naturalised.

The reign of the emperor Keiko, commencing in the year 71 A.D., and lasting for sixty years, was a memorable one for Japan—memorable chiefly for the romantic career of the emperor's son, Prince O-usu, better known by his later name, Yamato-Daké (" The Warlike "), given him in recognition of his valour. The brief prose history of the reign outlines the matter as follows: A tribe named Kumaso (in Kiushiu) having revolted, the emperor took command of the troops in person, and repressed the rebels, returning to his capital, however, only after a delay of six years. The same tribe again breaking out, the prince O-usu was sent against them. The prince was successful, the rebel chief was killed, and his partisans made their submission. After this, one of the dignitaries of the empire returned from the eastern and northern provinces, and reported that in the latter there was a province named Hitakami, inhabited by a savage race, with their hair growing wild and their bodies tattooed; that these people bore the name of Emishi (Ainos), that their province was large and fertile, and that it was desirable to annex it to the empire of Japan. Profiting by this advice, the emperor sent Prince O-usu against the Ainos, who reduced most of them to submission, and led back a large number of prisoners, who were distributed throughout the other provinces of the country. Some remaining tribes of Ainos were subdued, and the dignitary of the court who suggested this extension of the Japanese dominion received in recompense a title which signified Pillar of the Empire.

The career of this prince, thus prosaically and coldly sketched, has, as I have intimated, a romantic aspect when illuminated by the legendary light which has gathered about it. When in Kiushiu, putting down the second rebellion, for example, this handsome young prince disguised himself as a dancing-girl, and presented himself before the sentinel, " who, dazed by the beauty and voluptuous figure of the supposed damsel, and hoping for a rich reward from his chief, admitted her to the arch-rebel's tent. After dancing before him and his carousing guests, the delighted voluptuary drew his prize by the hand into his own tent. Instead of a yielding girl, he found more than his match in the heroic youth, who seized him, held him powerless, and took his life " (Griffis). This is why they called him "The Warlike."

Again, it is recorded that before starting to subdue the Ainos he went to the shrine of the sun-goddess in Isé, and, laying his own sword under a tree, obtained from the priestess the sacred sword that had been sent down from heaven. During the war, the prince's army was threatened with destruction by blazing brushwood to which the savages had set fire; when, at the suggestion of the sun-goddess herself, the sacred sword was drawn, the grass cleared with it, and the flames not only arrested, but driven back upon the foe, as I have elsewhere related.* Another story told of him, and one which perhaps more than any other has touched with tenderness his name and fame, is to the effect that, having encountered a severe storm in crossing the entrance of the Bay of Yedo from the coast near Uraga to the shore of Awa, in order to appease the sea-god his young wife leaped into the raging waters. Long afterwards, when on his way home he descried from a distant mountain height the Bay of Yedo, and the scene of his wife's sacrifice, he exclaimed, " *Adzuma, Adzuma!* "—" My wife, my wife!"† It appears to be a fact—both a prosaic and artistic one—that it is to this prince that the Japanese and the world owe the introduction of their beautiful lacquer-work; for we read: " Le prince O-usu ayant découvert l'urushi (*Rhus Vernicifera*), ordonna à Toko-Hiwa-no-Sukune de faire fabriquer des objets recouverts de la laque extraite de cet arbre, et lui donna le titre de Nuribe, directeur de la fabrique de laques."‡ Yamato-Daké was the grandfather of Ojin-Tenno, the " God and Spirit of War."

The story of the ad-interim-empress or regent, Jingu-Kogo, has already in the main been told in a previous chapter. It is important to remark, however, that it was during her exercise of the imperial power that diplomatic relations between Japan and China were commenced by the despatch to China of envoys charged to study the geographical situation and the manners of that country. Some time

---

* Hence the " Sacred Sword " of Japan derived its designation of " Grass-mower."

† 'The plain of Yedo is still, in poetry, called Adzuma. One of the princes of the blood uses Adzuma as his surname ; and the ex-Confederate ironclad ram *Stonewall*, now of the Japanese navy, is christened *Adzuma-Kan*."—*Griffis*.

‡ ' Le Japon à l'Exposition Universelle de 1878.'

afterwards, the state of Gi, in China, sent an envoy named Teshun to the court of Japan. During Jingu-Kogo's regency, and the reign of her son Ojin, the communications between Japan and Korea became very active, the warlike lady herself conducting a hostile expedition, as we have seen, to the latter country, under interesting conditions.

The building of ocean-crossing vessels became a matter of considerable importance to Japan in consequence of these communications with Korea, and especially of Jingu-Kogo's expedition. The art had previously received attention, as it was sure to do in a country so much intersected by the sea, the god Susanoö-no-mikoto having ordered trees to be planted with a view to shipbuilding timber being provided. In the reign of Sujin-Tenno, an imperial order drew attention to the importance of facilitating naval construction, "for the people suffer on account of the inconvenience of transportation." And now, during the reign of Ojin-Tenno, an order was issued to build a ship no less than one hundred feet long! When completed, it was tried at sea, and it was found to be "as quick as if a man were running, and the name *Karuno* (meaning a light one) was given to the ship." When the timbers of the *Karuno* decayed, and she was no more fit for use, it was ordered by the imperial government that her name should be made known to future times. A piece of her timber was, by the emperor's order, made into a *koto* (a stringed musical instrument); the remaining timbers were used as fuel for the production of sea-salt, the proceeds being applied to the building of new vessels. On one occasion there were five hundred vessels from different provinces stationed in the harbour of Muko. The tribute-bearer from Shiraki accidentally set these ships on fire, and in his anxiety to assist in repairing the mischief that was done the king of Shiraki sent over a clever naval architect. From that time the art of naval architecture became much improved and largely extended in Japan—although there is great room for both improvement and extension still, after the lapse of nearly two thousand years.

It was as long ago as this reign of Ojin (270-310 A.D.) that Japan began to profit largely by the learning of the Koreans—so, at least, history relates, although some doubt has been thrown by modern scholars upon the dates involved. There were no written characters whatever in use in Japan prior to the reign of the emperor Kaikua, and consequently all knowledge was until then transmitted solely by tradition. In the year 157 B.C., a native of Okara (in Korea) is said to have visited the country, and to have introduced such characters to the knowledge of the Japanese. Sixty years later another person from the same country aided in the adoption of a written language. The coming of the royal prince of the same country to Japan, as previously related,* tended to promote this object. From this time foreigners frequently visited Japan, and it is believed that the art of writing dates from this period, although the early histories are not at all clear on the point. On the return of the empress Jingu-Kogo from Korea, she brought with her all the books and writings found in the capital. Her successor, Ojin, was fond of literary pursuits, and during his reign Chinese composition was introduced into Japan. In the year 270 A.D., the youngest son of Ojin, when a mere boy, endeared himself to his father by his love of reading, and was nominated as his successor to the throne, with results which we have seen in the tragic story of his suicide.†

Early in Ojin's reign Kadara sent to Japan an envoy, named Anaki,‡ who took with him sempstresses,§ horses, arms, and mirrors. Anaki was skilled in the use of the Chinese language, and was made tutor to the favourite prince. On being asked by the emperor some time afterwards if he knew any one superior in learning to himself, he named

---

* Some accounts state that a Korean prince previously visited Japan, during the reign of Sujin, and entered the service of that emperor.

† Pages 104 and 105.

‡ Sometimes spoken of as Ajiki, and said to be a son of the king.

§ Chinese sempstresses also were sent to Japan from China during this reign, at the request of the emperor.

one, Wani, whom he considered the most learned man in his country. Wani was therefore sent for, and arrived in the following year, taking with him weavers and brewers, whom he placed at the disposal of Ojin. He also took and presented to the emperor the Chinese books known as the 'Confucian Analects' and the 'Thousand Character Classic.' This was the commencement of the study of Chinese literature in Japan. The prince imperial of Japan made great progress in his studies under the instruction of Wani, so that upon one occasion, when a letter was sent by the king of Koma, he detected in it uncivil terms, tore the letter up, and severely reproved the envoy who presented it.* This young prince, as we know, never accepted the throne, but forced upon it his brother Nintoku, who, like himself, was fond of literature, and did much to advance it. I have already mentioned † the measures ordered by the emperor Richiu for recording and reporting important facts. I may add, in the present connection, that he also (400 A.D.) caused the accounts of receipts and expenditures in the department which had charge of the precious metals, jewels, and other valuable things belonging to him to be kept in writing, and appointed Wani and another to perform the duty. This emperor, therefore, was prompt to turn to account the novel and imported art of writing.

In recalling facts like these it should be remembered that we are speaking of very primitive times, when the emperor lived in a mud house roofed with shingles, wore coarse hempen clothes, bore his own bows and arrows to the chase, and "carried his sword in a scabbard wound round with the tendrils of some creeping plant."

The affairs of Korea and China, and the struggles connected with the introduction of Buddhism into Japan, occupy the principal places in the public history of the country, from the fourth to the end of the seventh century. These

---

* Wani passed his life at the court of Japan, and from him descended two families, with whom literature became an hereditary profession.

† Page 56.

are dealt with in another chapter. It is well to observe, however, that throughout this period Japan continued to receive from Korea and China persons of skill in various trades and professions, including architects, doctors of medicine, musicians, dancers, chronologists, artisans, and fortune-tellers. Agriculture, including the laying-out of pasture-lands, was greatly encouraged; artificial irrigation was much extended; numerous canals were constructed, and additional public roads were made. A system of weights and measures was introduced (about 630 A.D.).

The emperor Tenji administered the affairs of the country throughout two, if not three, reigns. His uncle, the emperor Kotoku, after vainly pressing the crown upon him when Prince Naka-no-oe, and accepting it himself, practically left the government to him; and although the empress Samei, his mother, was by no means without a will of her own, she was fond of her son, and he of her; so fond was he of her that he mourned for six years after her death before ascending her throne; and it is probable that even during her reign he practically conducted the public business. He certainly did throughout the reign of Kotoku, during the nominal interregnum of six years, and throughout his own reign. He was a hard-working prince, and a great reformer, but I fear his reforms were sometimes fanciful. It was he, for instance, who introduced the system of giving arbitrary names to years and periods, which has proved so very troublesome to the historian. He also placed on his palace wall a bell and a box; the box for the reception of the complaints of dissatisfied suitors for justice, and the bell, that any one who considered himself unjustly condemned might ring it and demand justice.*
He did many useful things. He founded the first school in Japan, and established an education department; he ordered a census of the population; he suppressed a foolish practice,

---

* This emperor (Tenji), while yet a prince, invented and made a clepsydra, and when he came to the throne he placed it in a tower built for the purpose, and caused the hours to be struck by means of a bell or drum, as indicated by the clepsydra.

under which peasants took the names of emperors who left no successors, in order to perpetuate their memories; he regulated the sale of lands, established a system of fuse-signals round the coast, to give warning of invasion, and constructed fortifications in the provinces. He did two other things: he created the office of Dai-jo-Dai-jin, or prime minister,* which continues to this day, and is now held by Mr. Sanjo; and he created likewise the office of Nai-Dai-jin. To the latter post he nominated a personage named Nakatomi-no-Kamatari, who became the founder of the illustrious house of Fujiwara, which subsequently exercised so great an influence upon the fortunes of Japan. One historian (a Japanese) says: "Tenji-Tenno was a highly instructed man; he did much for the popularisation of learning. He endowed Japan with numerous and very useful political institutions, and corrected many abuses of administration. He was very prudent and economical; his palace, built at Asakura-Yama with timber in the rough, was very simple, and named by the people Kuroki-Nogosho or Kino-Marodono (Black-wood Palace, or Palace of Wood-in-Bark). Tenji-Tenno composed on this subject a piece of poetry, which in later times was chanted as a canticle at religious festivals." A silver mine was discovered in the isle of Tsushima towards the end of the seventh century, and the first observatory was then founded.

This was in the reign of the emperor Temmu, who also was a great reformer, causing the laws to be collected and revised, lives of the emperors to be written, reports on the state of the country to be prepared, the limits of provinces to be defined, and so forth. Up to his time the Japanese had worn their hair as it grew naturally; he ordered them by a decree to dress their hair. He likewise forbade them to prostrate themselves at the public ceremonies. The last reign of the seventh century (neglecting the first three years of Mommu-Tenno's) was that of the empress Jito, second daughter of Tenji, and widow of Temmu. The new

---

* More literally, "First Officer of the Superior House."

code of twenty volumes was issued in her reign. Like her father, she must have had a pretty strong will, for she commanded that one fourth of the population should be trained to the use of arms. She was also an advocate of woman's rights, for she took the, till then, unprecedented step of bestowing honorific titles upon women. She encouraged the culture of textile plants and of fruit-trees, and in her reign tiles were first applied to roofs, thatch only having been previously employed.

Before passing on beyond the seventh century, I will advert to a few facts connected with the progress of the country in education and art. In the year 514 a professor of the Chinese classics was invited and came from Kudara by order of the emperor Ketai. Three years later another came to succeed him. Here we have the beginning of the system of calling professors from foreign countries — a system in full force at the present day. The same emperor a few years later published a decree ordaining that the selection of men for the public service should be based upon their integrity and learning, to encourage the cause of morality and education. This was the origin of the system of appointing students to the imperial service from the university and provincial schools, which was for a long time prevalent in Japan. A Korean priest, named Kauroku, went to Japan in the reign of the empress Suiko (593), and presented books on almanac-making, one in astronomy, and one in divination, and we are informed that their pupils succeeded in their studies. The almanac was first made use of in the twelfth year of this reign. After Buddhism came in the pursuit of literature fell largely into the hands of the priests, and professorships were no longer filled by foreign scholars.

The development of art was not wholly neglected even in these early days. The first mention made of foreign artists was in the seventh year of the reign of the emperor Yuriaku (463), when, by his command, various artists were sent over from Kudara, and among them a celebrated painter named Inshiraga. Other artists followed, but none of their authenticated productions remain. Among the cultivated persons sent over to the empress Suiko by the state of Koma (in Korea), together with the subscription for the monumental statue of Buddha,* was a priest named Doncho, who was a painter of merit. At the end of the seventh, or the very commencement of the eighth, century, a painting department was created by the government, to which were attached four *gashi*, "artists," and sixty *gabu*, or sketchers. It was soon after abolished as a distinct department, and was incorporated with a department of architecture, in which a studio was formed. The chief object was, however, decoration; but in after times the charge of the office was entrusted from age to age to skilful painters. There were also private artists of note.

I have thought it well to make mention above of the introduction of various learned and practical arts, for ere long we shall be plunged into periods when the thoughts and aims of the emperors were diverted from the peaceful progress of the country, and when the military classes strode from end to end of it, "breathing and sounding battle," that (*pace* Tennyson) was often anything but "beauteous."

Hitherto the Mikados have been the central figures in Japanese history. Their lives were simple, as we have seen, or shall see by the glimpses of their palace interiors to be obtained in the course of this work; and as regards the palaces themselves, they were plain timber buildings, with thatched roofs, and displaying only the beginnings of artistic decorations. Indeed, the opportunities for building themselves fine houses must have been very few, inasmuch as nearly every fresh occupant of the throne changed the imperial residence from one place to another, and I have observed that one of the emperors changed his place of abode no fewer than three times during his reign. We are now approaching a time when these imperial wanderers began to think of creating an abiding city. In the early part of the eighth century, the empress Gemmei took up

---

* See chapter on Buddhism in Japan.

her residence at Nara, and this beautiful spot remained, with some interruptions, the imperial city during several reigns, so that people have got accustomed to speak, somewhat loosely it is true, of the "Nara dynasty." Great and splendid temples and pagodas were built there, and the first two Nara empresses, Gemmei and her daughter Gensho, did much to promote permanence in the institutions of the country, including that of an imperial capital. Their immediate successor, however, removed first to Kuni, and afterwards to Naniwa (Osaka), which his advisers considered would be a more convenient situation. Off and on, however, Nara remained the capital city for the greater part of the eighth century, and no period of its history was more glorious for Japan, if the promotion of literature, art, and religion constitutes the glory of a country. Several of its rulers in these palmy days were empresses, and impressed that fact upon the history of the period, among other things training women to be doctors of medicine. The history of Japan under the empresses of Nara will ever remain an honour to the sex. But before the end of the century, in the reign of the emperor Kuwammu, the capital was again transferred, this time to a site where it was destined to remain for more than a thousand years, and where, as a western capital, it still remains. The place was then called Kadzuno, afterwards and still Kioto, and often Miako. Here Kuwammu, who was by no means an economist, and once brought the public treasure down to a good deal less than nothing, constructed a splendid palace with a dozen gates, and built a city worthy of it. It contained twelve hundred streets, and while the plan of it was excellent, the buildings were of the first order. The palace was named Heian-jo, or Château of Peace. We shall hereafter learn that it proved to be a Château of Contention and of War, and was the very centre of those feuds and struggles which only terminated in the overthrow of the Shoguns in 1868.

With the founding of Kioto, and the establishment there of the throne, the ancient period of Japan may be said to have passed away, and the struggles of the middle ages to have commenced. In order to form a general acquaintance with the subsequent history of the country, we must take note of the rise of some of those great families which soon began to sway the state. One of these was the house of Fujiwara, the title of which we have seen created by the emperor Tenji, in the elevation of Kamatari to the office of Nai-Dai-jin, by the title or name of Fujiwara. Henceforth, for centuries to come, we shall see the Fujiwara suggesting, directing, controlling public affairs, close to the throne, and even sitting upon it in the persons of emperors sprung from its daughters. Under Mommu, a Fujiwara-no-Fuhito revised the ancient code; it was Fujiwara-no-Momokawa who got Kuwammu placed on the throne; it was the prime minister Fujiwara-no-Yoshihisa who acted as regent during the minority of the emperor Seiwa, after which the regency became almost hereditary in the family; and it was another Fujiwara prime minister (Mototsuné) who was created "Kampaku,"* a functionary who was empowered to take cognisance of all reports, etc., before their communication to the emperor, and therefore, doubtless, the most influential subject in the realm. We shall frequently see the Fujiwara playing prominent parts hereafter; not always in concert among themselves, not always loyal to their mikado; but for many a long year to come the mikados themselves were practically in their power.

Another family which was scarcely less ancient or eminent than the Fujiwara was that of Sugawara, which, although most distinguished by its literary fame, took for a time an active part in the politics of the country. The emperor Kuwammu (who was himself superintendent of the university while a prince) on ascending the throne appointed Sugawara Furuhito his tutor, requested him always to attend him, and always behaved to him with the respect due to a teacher. After the death of Sugawara, the emperor, in consideration of his services, granted his four sons allow-

---

* Literally, "the bolt inside the gate," but meaning "to represent the Mikado."—*Griffis.*

ances for providing the necessaries of life to enable them to pursue their studies, and to make their father's profession hereditary. These allowances were continued to their descendants.* In an application for a similar allowance for the Oye family, it is stated that "in consideration of the services of the Sugawara and Oye families in founding a college of literature,† to which students for many years resorted for instruction in literature, the children of the two families enjoyed the privilege of being taken into the imperial service, without regard to their abilities and ages." It was thus, by the pursuit of learning and of literature, that the Sugawara house obtained its position near the throne, which occasionally proved of great public importance. In the early part of the tenth century, this family made itself extremely popular in the person of its greatest representative, Sugawara-Michisané, who applied himself with sad results, so far as he was concerned, to lessening the alarming power of the Fujiwaras. Fujiwara-Tokihira and Sugawara-Michisané were both ministers, but the former chose to deem the latter a pretender, while the latter chose to deem the former an upstart, and one of a family of upstarts. The emperor Daigo compelled them, nevertheless, to work together for a time, for the good of the country, and it is not a little curious to find that by his order Tokihira composed an historical work in seventeen volumes, the

---

* An instance of the Sugawara family having to make application for such an allowance in the year 956 is recorded. Sugawara Fumitoki applied on behalf of his son Tadahiro thus: "This grant originated in my family, it being made to my forefather, Kiyogimi, and his three brothers at the same time. ... To assist one to succeed to his forefather's profession is the boundless benevolence of the great patron of literature, and to study and transmit the literary profession of one's ancestors is the duty of the children of the family. For this consideration, it is most humbly requested that, by the great favour of the emperor, the monthly allowance be granted to my son to assist him in pursuing his hereditary profession." He afterwards applied for an allowance for his second son.

† In confirmation of this we read elsewhere that "the two families of Sugawara and Oye established in the university a *bunsho-in* (composition-school), which was divided into East Hall and West Hall, the chief of the former being Sugawara, while the latter was directed by Oye."

Engi-Kaku, and that Michisané also composed an historical work in two hundred volumes, the *Ruijin-Kokushi*. The Fujiwara could not, however, long brook the hindrances and antagonisms of his colleague, and consequently, it is said, calumniated the latter to the emperor, and induced him to send Sugawara to a distance. A history written by an official Japanese states that he was nominated governor of Tsukushi (Kiushiu), and remained there till his death, after which the emperor repented of the injustice done to him, and honoured his memory by nominating him to a high rank. The people, grateful for the benefits rendered by him, built to him a temple at Kitano; and later, the emperor decreed to him still higher titles, even nominating him, in retrospect, prime minister. Mr. Griffis states that he died at Kiushiu, in the horrors of poverty and exile, and even that he starved to death—statements hard to reconcile with his alleged governorship. I know not which story is the correct one, but Mr. Griffis is certainly correct when he adds: " Michisané is now known by his posthumous name of Tenjin. Many temples have been erected in his honour, and students worship his spirit as the patron god of letters and literature. Children at school pray to him that they may become good writers and win success in study; some of his descendants are still living."

From the preceding paragraph it will be seen that, although the Sugawara family occasionally stationed a member close to the throne, and helped to counteract, even in its partial overthrow (in the exile of Michisané), the Fujiwara influence, it cannot be considered as a rival house. The Fujiwara, as we have seen, looked down upon it, and its rank was manifestly far below theirs. It has next to be observed that neither of these families had entered, so far as we have yet seen, upon a military career. The Sugawara were essentially a literary family; the Fujiwara absorbed the civil power of the crown; the opportunities, or rather the occasions, for military distinctions had not yet presented themselves. We have now to notice the rise of two great rival military families, the Taira and the Minamoto, whose pride and prowess were destined to flourish in many an awful field. and to cause even the waters of Japan to run red with blood. The Taira family were of imperial descent, deriving their origin from the emperor Kuwammu by a concubine. The Minamoto were likewise offshoots of the imperial family, descending from the emperor Seiwa.

The names of some of the four great families just adverted to were prominent on both sides of the revolt of Shohei and Tenkei to which I have made brief reference in tracing the Descent of the Crown. I do not propose to dwell upon this struggle here, because, although it involved a great deal of bloodshed, and lasted for the greater part of two years, it did not materially affect the future, nor greatly further the establishment of military power; as the governors of provinces were at the time civilians, and only assumed military functions for the purpose of suppressing the revolt. In the reign of Reizei-Tenno (968 A.D.), a number of influential persons, among whom was Fujiwara-Chiharu, conspired to revolt, but the government discovered the plot, and transported the conspirators. The Sa-Dai-jin Takahira was broken, and sent as a vice-governor of Kiushiu. "At this epoch," say the historians, "the Fujiwara family was exceedingly influential, and it was believed that Fujiwara Morotada, jealous of the power of his superior, Takahira, calumniated him, and caused his disgrace."

Here we will close this outline of the early history of the country, and in another chapter will attempt to trace the later history in which the Fujiwara, the Taira, and the Minamoto figured so largely. Let us conclude this present record with a quotation which will serve to show that the arts of peace were still pursued, and that even the names which, when our next chapter has been read, will be suggestive of battle and bloodshed have better and worthier associations. It was the emperor Ichijo whose reign was current at the close of the tenth century of our era, and the Japanese say: "Ichijo-Tenno was an educated man; he often examined personally the students of the university. His reign was marked by the works of several savants, among others Minamoto-Tsuneohu, Fujiwara-Kinto, Minamoto-Toskikata, and Fujiwara-Yukinari. All the four bore the title of Chiu-nagon; they were ordinarily designated by the *sobriquet* Shi-Nagon, or the Four Nagon. At this epoch also flourished several learned women."

ANCIENT STYLE OF JAPANESE ARCHITECTURE (A SHINTO SHRINE AT YOSHIDA, KIOTO).

CHAPTER VII.

THE TAIRA AND THE MINAMOTO—THE WARS OF THE RED AND WHITE FLAGS, 1000-1200 A.D.

The Taira red flag, and the Minamoto white flag—Indications of the struggles to come—Oppressive power of the Fujiwara house—Military tendencies of the Buddhists—Revolts of the Ainos—Yoshi-ye, afterwards Hachiman-Toro — Rising military power of the Taira and Minamoto—Their first contest at Kioto—The famous archer Tametomo — The great power of Taira-Kiyomori —A "cloistered emperor": immoral and conspiring—The Minamoto depress the Taira—The Taira revenge themselves: their ascendency—A conspiracy—The peasant girl Tokiwa becomes the mother of the renowned Yositsuné, the Bayard of Japan—His brother Yoritomo the founder of Kamakûra—Yoritomo marries Masago, of the house of Hojo—Hatred of the Taira and affection for the Minamoto—The city of Kamakura—Yoshinaka, the "Morning Sun General"—Overthrow and pursuit of the Taira: a prose epic thereon—Ascendency of the Minamoto—A review of the character and acts of Yoritomo—He becomes Sei-i-Shogun, "Barbarian Subjugating Great General"—His system of government—His royal court at Kamakura—His sceptre was his sword—Decay of his dynasty—His grave visited—What native historians say of him.

In one of the standard native histories of Japan it is stated that the descendants of Taira-no-Takamochi were for generations military vassals of the emperor, and "used a red flag"; and that the descendants of Minamoto-no-Tsunémoto were, similarly, military vassals from generation to generation, and "used a white flag." The two warriors to whom allusion is here made lived in the early part of the tenth century, and were the founders of the two rival families of *Hei* and *Gen*, or *Taira* and *Minamoto*; "and these colours were constantly displayed, in after years, in civil conflicts that caused as much bloodshed as the English wars of the

Red and White Roses" (McClatchie). I now invite the reader's attention to an account of these conflicts.

Very early in the eleventh century indications were given of the struggles which were to come. In Go-Ichijo's reign Taira-no-Tadatsune revolted, but was soon killed. Under Go-Reizei a formidable outbreak, fomented by Abe-Yoritoki, occurred in the province of Mutsu. Minamoto-Yoryoshi was nominated governor of the province, and sent against the rebels. Yoritoki perished, pierced by an arrow; his eldest son also was killed. The next emperor, Go-Sanjo, found the weight of the Fujiwara family so oppressive that he resolved to shake it off. He was an intelligent and energetic man, and for a time it seemed that by him the imperial power would be recovered for the mikados; but his premature death defeated this expectation. He reigned but three years. His successor, Shirakawa-Tenno, was also an energetic personage, and is said to have reduced the Fujiwaras to comparative silence and subordination, and to have himself governed the country. After reigning fourteen years he abdicated in 1086, but practically controlled the government for forty years after his abdication, during the reigns of Horikawa and Toba. But while he sought to control the Fujiwara, he gave way unwisely to the Buddhist priesthood, and it was in his reign that those gentlemen took to training troops, fighting among themselves, disturbing the peace of the capital, and even attempting to overawe the very emperor to whom they owed their excessive liberty.

In the reign of Horikawa there was another revolt in Mutsu. Mutsu is one of the eastern provinces of Japan, and then had a population largely consisting of Ainos, and of men of mixed blood springing from the conjunction of the Ainos with the wilder portion of the Japanese people. This time it was the son of Yoryoshi, Minamoto-Yoshi-ye, who was made governor of the province and sent against the rebels. It took years of war to bring these half-savage tribes into subjection, but the work was so well done that it brought great celebrity to Yoshi-ye, who came to be called Hachiman-Toro, signifying the eldest son of Hachiman, Hachiman being the Buddhist name of the Japanese war-god Ojin. In these victories of Yoshi-ye, following upon those of his father, we see the military fame of the Minamoto growing apace; they were also begetting in that family hope of great reward, and ambition to match. The government furnished occasion of complaint. For some reason or other it chose to treat the great services to the state which the Minamoto, father and son, had rendered as mere personal contests between them and the leading rebels, and refused to recompense them. The father was always exceedingly popular with the troops whom he commanded, treating them with paternal care; the son, for the same reason, became as popular, and gradually the troops came to regard themselves as vassals of the Minamoto. This growing influence of the house of Minamoto alarmed the court, and in the reign of Toba an edict was issued forbidding the military class (*samurai*) of the various provinces from constituting themselves vassals either of the Minamoto or of the Taira.

In the following reign some Japanese pirates took to ravaging the southern coasts of the country, and Taira-Tadamori was sent to pursue and disarm them. About the same time the haughty and powerful priests of the Enriaku-ji temples near Kioto again entered the city in arms to make reclamations, and Minamoto-no-Tameyoshi was charged by the emperor to repel them. Thus we see both the Taira and the Minamoto families serving the government loyally and heartily, and with perfect friendliness, down to this period, the middle of the twelfth century. Tadamori, the head of the Taira, received the island of Tsushima in reward for his services, but took up his residence in Kioto during peace. He had a son, Kiyomori, of whose name the reader will do well to take note.*

---

* "Tadamori came to Kioto to live, and while at court had a *liaison* with one of the palace lady attendants, whom he afterwards married.' The fruit of this union was a son, who grew to be a man of stout physique. In boyhood he gave equal indications of his future greatness and

We have now reached a time when the Taira and Minamoto are about to enter upon deadly strife, which thirty years afterwards terminated in the utter overthrow of the former. Their first contest, of which Kioto was the scene, which is known as the fight of the year Hogen, came about in the following manner. In the year 1156, when Go-Shirakawa was about to ascend the throne, there were two ex-emperors living, Toba and Shutoku, both of whom had, so far as we know, voluntarily abdicated. The ex-emperor Shutoku was, nevertheless, averse to the ascension of Go-Shirakawa, desiring himself to resume the imperial power. After conferring with the minister Yorinaga, he took up his position in the imperial palace, raised an army, made Yorinaga his war minister, obtained the support of Tameyoshi, the head of the Minamoto family, and prepared to attack the emperor. Go-Shirakawa meantime took up his quarters in the palace of Higasi-Sanjo, whither he was followed by his chief minister, Tadamichi, and others, and sent for Yositomo (Minamoto), eldest son of Tameyoshi, and for Kiyomori (Taira), and others, and ordered them to attack the rebellious ex-emperor. We here see the Minamoto family miserably divided in this unfortunate affair; Tameyoshi and his youngest son, Tametomo, in arms with the ex-emperor, and Yositomo, his eldest son, in arms against them on behalf of the new emperor. But we also see the heads

---

his future arrogance. He wore unusually high clogs — the Japanese equivalent for 'riding a high horse.' His fellows gave the strutting roisterer the name of *Kokêda* ('high-clogs'). Being the son of a soldier, he had abundant opportunities to display his valour. At this time the seas swarmed with pirates, who ravaged the coasts, and were the scourge of Korea as well as Japan. Kiyomori, a boy full of fire and energy, thirsting for fame, asked to be sent against the pirates. At the age of eighteen he cruised in the sea of Iyo, or the Suwo Nada, which is part of the Inland Sea, a sheet of water extremely beautiful in itself, and worthy, in a high degree, to be called the Mediterranean of Japan. While on shipboard he made himself a name by attacking and capturing a ship full of the most desperate villains, and by destroying their lurking-place. His early manhood was spent alternately in the capital and in service in the south. In 1153, at the age of thirty-six, he succeeded his father as minister of justice."— *Griffis.*

of the Taira and of the Minamoto on opposite sides in the contest.

The young Minamoto Tametomo twice gave advice which was rejected. He said first, "For the attack of a large number of men by a small number a night attack is best," and advised accordingly; that advice being rejected, he said, "This palace has but a single wall and a very shallow ditch, and is quite indefensible; we had better therefore go to Nanto to defend ourselves"; this counsel was also declined. Soon afterwards the attack of Kiyomori and Yositomo upon the Shirakawa palace was made, and met with so stout a resistance that the result remained long in suspense. Tametomo in particular fought with great bravery, and maintained his post with remarkable success. At length, however, Yositomo set fire to a part of the palace buildings to windward, thus throwing the rebel forces into confusion, in the midst of which Yositomo triumphantly drove them out. The palace was taken, and the ex-emperor Shutoku escaped to Nioizan in Yamasiro. Yorimaga was killed by a random arrow. Tameyoshi endeavoured to escape to the east, but was prevented by illness, and had to surrender to the emperor, who (somewhat barbarously, it would appear to us) ordered his son Yositomo to put him to death. Tametomo was made prisoner, but his punishment was commuted from that of death to exile in Osima, in Idzu.* The ex-emperor was banished to Sanuki.

---

* "The most famous archer Minamoto Tametomo took part in many of the struggles of the two rival families. His great strength, equal to that of many men (fifty, according to the legends), and the fact that his right arm was shorter than his left, enabled him to draw a bow which four ordinary warriors could not bend, and send a shaft five feet long with enormous bolt-head. The court, influenced by the Taira, banished him, in a cage, to Idzu (after cutting the muscles of his arm), under a guard. He escaped, and fled to the islands of Oshima and Hachijo, and the chain south of the Bay of Yedo. His arm having healed, he ruled over the people, ordering them not to send tribute to Idzu or Kioto. A fleet of boats was sent against him. Tametomo, on the strand of Oshima, sped a shaft at one of the approaching vessels that pierced the thin gunwale and sunk it. He then, after a shout of defiance, shut himself up, set the house on fire, and killed himself.... A picture of this doughty warrior

The new emperor only retained the imperial power for about three years, after which he abdicated—in order, according to some authorities, that he might wield the power the more absolutely in concert with the Taira Kiyomori, whose influence after the defeat of Tameyoshi was enormous. Mr. Griffis says of the emperor in question, Go-Shirakawa : "This Mikado was a very immoral man, and the evident reason of his resigning was that he might abandon himself to debauchery, and wield even more actual power than when on the throne. In 1169 he abdicated, shaved off his hair, and took the title of Ho-o, or 'cloistered emperor,' and became a Buddhist monk, professing to retire from the world. In industrious seclusion, he granted the ranks and titles created by his predecessor in lavish profusion. He thus exercised, as a monk, even more influence than when in actual office. The head of the Taira hesitated not to use all these rewards for his own and his family's private ends." Some readers may, like myself, experience difficulty in understanding how a person can at the same time " abandon himself to debauchery " and withdraw into " industrious seclusion," the industry being devoted to state affairs. I quote the passage, however, for its general interest.

The successor of Go-Shirakawa was Nijo, aged sixteen, who reigned seven years. In the first year of his reign occurred another great contest, known as the battle of Heiji (the year name), in which the Fujiwara, Taira, and Minamoto all took conspicuous parts. Fujiwara-no-Nobu-

---

has been chosen to adorn the greenback currency of the banks of modern Japan." — *Griffis*. It is proper to add that in the histories of Japan put forward by the present government, it is stated, apparently with full confidence, that Tametomo (instead of killing himself as just described) went to the Liu Kiu Islands; that he there married, and that his son became king of the country. Mr. Satow makes reference to this alternative account in a paper entitled

'Notes on Loo-choo,' read before the Asiatic Society of Japan. Mr. Satow says: "Very little appears to be known of the history of the Loo-choo anterior to the twelfth century, and its real annals commence with Sunten, who ascended the throne in 1187. Sunten is said to have been the son of the famous warrior Tametomo, who after the defeat of his party in the civil war, 1156, was exiled to Vries Island, and fled some years later to Loo-choo."

yori, having been a favourite of the ex-emperor (Go-Shirakawa), solicited for himself the appointment of commander-in-chief of the imperial guards, and was refused. Hearing that the refusal was given by the advice of another Fujiwara, named Michinori, whom the ex-emperor consulted in the matter, Nobuyori was greatly mortified, and absented himself from court on the alleged ground of illness. At this time Yositomo (Minamoto), seeing that he was always inferior in power to the Taira family, consulted with the malcontent Nobuyori, and agreed to seize with him the first opportunity of revolting. They raised troops, and during the absence of Kiyomori (Taira) from the capital, suddenly besieged and partly burnt the imperial palace. Michinori fled, but was captured and put to death. The young emperor and the ex-emperor were confined to a room in the palace—one of the great objects in this and all such outbreaks, down even to the revolution of 1868, being to obtain control of the sacred person of the mikado, who has always been the recognised source of all power in Japan. Nobuyori now made himself, not a mere commander of the guard, but chief minister and commander-in-chief to boot, and settled state affairs to his own taste. But there were troubles before him.

Kiyomori, having heard the disastrous news, hastened back to the capital, to see what could be done, but only to find that Nobuyori doubled the guard at every gate of the palace on hearing of his return. He and his party then resorted to a bold artifice, which proved successful. They set on fire a neighbouring palace, in the hope that the guards of the imperial palace gates would rush from their posts to put it out. They did so, and straightway the emperor and ex-emperor fled in disguise. Kiyomori and his son Shiyemori then attacked the usurpers, and drove them from the palace with great slaughter. Nobuyori fled to the ex-emperor and implored pardon, which would have been granted him but for the young emperor, who would not consent to it, and soon afterwards Nobuyori was executed—a not uncommon consequence of overweening ambition. Yositomo fled to the east, taking refuge on his way in the house of one Osada Tadamune (at Ushimi, in Owari), who, on the persuasion of his son, had him put to death, and sent his head to Kioto. In consequence of the great services which he rendered to the emperor in this latest contest, Kiyomori rose rapidly, and was ere long named Dai-jo-Dai-jin, or prime minister. For a long time previously the Taira and the Minamoto had rivalled each other in the pursuit and attainment of power, every warlike service being committed by the court to one or other of them. This rapid elevation of Kiyomori now secured for a time to the Taira an ascendency which placed them above the rivalry of the Minamoto: but only for a time, as we shall hereafter see. Kiyomori himself had dangers and troubles yet to encounter, in spite, and partly because, of his elevation.

A striking instance of the great power of the two or three noble families at this period of the history of Japan, and more especially, just then, of the Taira, is observable in the manner in which the imperial throne was disposed of, to which I have already adverted in some detail in the chapter on the Descent of the Crown. After Nijo came the babe-Mikado Rokujio, who abdicated at the age of five; and after him Takakura, who reigned from the age of eight to that of twenty. The histories say: "Takakura was a clement and well-informed prince, but as all power was in the hands of the Taira family, he was himself reduced to inaction." During his reign this power of the Taira, concentrated in Kiyomori, interfered greatly with the plans of the "cloistered" ex-emperor Go-Shirakawa, and caused him great annoyance. That becoming known, there was, of course, a Fujiwara ready to avail himself of it, as the influence of the Taira was more annoying to the Fujiwara than to any one else. Accordingly Fujiwara-Narichika and some others conceived the design—not very difficult of conception, one would think, to a certain class of persons—of getting Kiyomori assassinated. Among the conspirators were some of the Minamoto family, one of whom, Yukitsuna, disclosed the plot. One of the Fujiwara (Moromitz) who was implicated was put to death by Kiyomori; Narichika was first exiled to Bizen, and afterwards put to death by an emissary of Kiyomori; and numerous others were banished. Kiyomori, suspecting the ex-emperor of taking a part in the plot, was about to confine him, but the son of Kiyomori, named Shigemori (who is spoken of as a distinguished man and faithful subject, and as counterbalancing, while he lived, the excessive influence of his father), succeeded in dissuading him from the project. After the son's death, however, Kiyomori carried it out, and shut Go-Shirakawa up in the palace of Toba.

Here we must pause to note the Taira family in the hour of its greatest eminence, and the Minamoto in the time of its greatest depression. The conspiracy recorded in the last paragraph gave to Kiyomori the last incentive which the tyrant needs to give to his tyranny the fullest scope, namely, fear for his own life. He was in practical possession of the throne, upon which he placed, and from which he displaced, babes, youths, or whomsoever best suited his purposes or his passions. The emperor of the moment was his own grandson. All the imperial sources of honours and endowments were open to his family, his friends, and his retainers, and no nice scruples deterred him from giving them their full benefit. The usurpation which his foes had successfully attempted had been brought to a speedy end, and the usurpers were now either headless or exiled. The plot against his life had been stayed, and the chief of the plotters had been slain. The cup of his triumph was full. It is said that his tyranny and insolence were almost boundless. Meanwhile the Minamoto, once his rivals, were either dead, or flying in terror from the reach of his power, and from the wrongs and cruelties which his retainers were everywhere inflicting upon the survivors. Not satisfied with this, Kiyomori set his heart upon their extermination.

As one thinks of all this, one is ready to exclaim—

"Turn, Fortune, turn thy wheel and lower the proud;"

and we shall soon see that Fortune did so—turned her "wild

wheel, through sunshine, storm, and cloud." But there was a family whose fortunes we must hasten to pursue.

After the revolt and battle of Heiji, so fatal to Yositomo, and apparently to his house, his young wife, Tokiwa, whose beauty when a peasant-girl had won for her his love and protection as his concubine, fled with his three little sons. One of these was as yet but a babe, but a babe to be remembered, for it was he whose fame as a hero of chivalry is on every Japanese tongue. I have myself seen an immense native audience in Tokio strain and reach forward to catch the first glimpse even of a stage personation of this great character. "That babe at her breast was Yositsuné—a name that awakens in the breast of a Japanese youth emotions that kindle his enthusiasm to emulate a character that was the mirror of chivalrous and knightly conduct, and that saddens him at the thought of one who suffered cruel death at the hands of a jealous brother. Yositsuné, the youngest son of Yositomo, lives, and will live, immortal in the minds of Japanese youth as the Bayard of Japan" (Griffis).

Kiyomori arrested the mother of Tokiwa, and the daughter, hearing of this, after much suffering and exposure, went to the capital, and presented herself and her children to Kiyomori, imploring pardon. He, struck by her beauty, in spite of her many scruples, made her his own concubine, recompensing her by sparing the lives of her little ones. His retainers wished to slay them, but the pleadings of the mother effectually protected them. The children were afterwards sent to a monastery, their hair was shaved off, and they were put in training for the priesthood. Later, Yositsuné himself persuaded a merchant to take him to the province of Mutsu. There he was taken into the house of the prince of the province, a noble of the Fujiwara family, and trained in the military art.

But of more importance to this historic sketch is another son of Yositomo, who was twelve years old when his father fled, and whose life was spared on the intercession of a lady-relative of Kiyomori. This was Yoritomo, the founder of Kamakura, the greatest, in some respects, of the Minamoto—he whose strong, well-tempered swords with silver scabbards, whose bows and arrows, dresses, inkstands, and many other relics, are still shown at the temple of Hachiman in that ancient city, as we shall see hereafter. Although his life was not taken, he was banished to Idzu, under the charge of Taira officers. The guard kept over him was strict at first, but it was not such afterwards as to prevent Yoritomo from acting when the time came. It will be well for the reader to know and to observe that Yoritomo married Masago, a daughter of one Hojo Tokimasa, a man of good family, even of imperial blood, who gave him protection during his exile. His wife had much to do with the future development of affairs, as we shall see, and with the subsequent rise to great power and pre-eminence of her own, the Hojo, family. She long survived Yoritomo.

It was the year 1180 A.D. when the throne was vacated by Takakura-Tenno, and Antoku, a child three years old, was put into the vacant seat. This was a year before the death of Kiyomori, and when his power and tyranny were, as we have seen, at their height. The Minamoto, though without power themselves, found others with power whom the supremacy of the Taira perpetually galled. Advised by Yorimasa (Minamoto), an imperial prince, Mochi-Hito, determined to raise an army, and to attempt the reduction, and even the extermination, of the dominant family. With this object, and relying upon the general disaffection against the Taira, he issued a proclamation calling upon the whole population to range themselves under his flag. Yoritomo received the appeal, and was ready enough to respond to it. The influence of his family in the eastern parts of Japan, and more especially in that part known as the Kuanto,* was still great if only it could be exerted, and here was the opportunity. Yoritomo wrote to Yositsuné, who joined the enterprise

---

* Kuanto is a term variously employed, as regards the provinces included by it. It originally meant the whole of the eastern provinces; it is here used in the more restricted sense in which it is now usually employed, as comprising about eight of the provinces eastward of, and nearest to, the Hakoné mountain range. It therefore includes Tokio and Kamakura.

with alacrity, and soon an army was raised. The troops of Yoritomo, at first successful, met with a great reverse at the pass of the Hakoné mountains, and Yoritomo was obliged to flee.

The hatred of the Taira house and the affection for the Minamoto, however, enabled him to commence again the raising of troops and the pursuit of his object. But this time he applied himself to the work of organising forces in a more systematic manner. There being a family residence near to the village of Kamakura, where also had been built a temple to the god Hachiman, he fixed upon this place as his headquarters, and there drew his people about him, and in fact founded a city, the renown of which has now become a thing of the past. As we approached the place from the eastward, on the occasion of our visit, we found the country so hilly that when we knew we were close to its site we could not conjecture how a large city could ever have flourished there. The difficulty did not much diminish when one was pointed to the tomb of Yoritomo and the shrine of Hachiman on the slopes of the hills to our right, so restricted was the area of level ground in front. Upon this space—now cultivated fields—nevertheless, once stood the residence of Yoritomo, and beyond the Hojo palace. The level ground widens away to the south, and extends as far as the sea-shore, two or three miles distant. It must have been here that stood most of the ancient city, but few remnants of which now remain.

Yoritomo made personal progresses through the Kuanto, continually winning new troops to his standards, and fitting himself and his officers, no less than his men, for the great task of conquering the country. In the north, a cousin of his, Yoshinaka, inspired by his example, raised another army, and in the course of time marched southwards towards Kioto. In the meantime Kiyomori had died, and been succeeded by his son Munemori. As may be supposed, neither Kiyomori previously, nor he now, had been slow in taking their measures of defence. Kiyomori had, in fact, made the most solemn appeals to his family and retainers to crush the Minamoto; he died entreating them to show their regard for him in one way only—by hanging the head of Yoritomo upon his tomb. On one occasion the hostile armies faced each other on the opposite banks of the great and swift river Fuji Kawa, at the foot of the sacred mount of Fuji Yama, but neither party attempted to cross and bring on the fight. At length Yoshinaka from the north approached the capital, and Munemori sent out forces to resist him, under the ablest generals at his disposal. Yoshinaka overcame their resistance, completely defeated them, and marched triumphantly into the capital. The ex-emperor Go-Shirakawa remained in Kioto, but Munemori retreated westward, bearing with him the child-emperor, Antoku, and all the members of the Taira family, including Kiyomori's widow, the grandmother of Antoku. The cloistered ex-emperor was, need I say, delighted to see at last this great result brought about—the Taira tyrants in full flight, and the throne itself again vacant. "This prince," we are told, "soon organised a provisional government, and distributed rewards to Yoshinaka, Yoritomo, and others."

As Antoku was but five years old when he was carried off to the west by the Taira, and Go-Toba was his younger brother, he also must have been a very young child when the priest ex-emperor hoisted him with joy upon the throne. Go-Shirakawa, however, soon got troubled again, for Yoshinaka, pluming himself upon his great services, wished to be omnipotent. He was entitled Asahi Shogun, or Morning-Sun General, on account of the brightness of his sudden rising. He was given exalted social rank, and valuable appointments. But he was not satisfied with all this, and made the ex-emperor hate him by wishing to have everything his own way. He even threw Go-Shirakawa into prison. He also attacked the great monasteries of Enriaku-ji, executed their abbots, and stripped officers of state of their titles. To give effectual expression to his hatred, and to get rid of him, Go-Shirakawa endeavoured to get him assassinated—so at least says history—and although he was an emperor and a priest too, I fear we must accept the statement. But Yoshinaka had roused the antagonism of some one else, by showing himself jealous of his cousin Yoritomo, and acting in opposition to him. Wherefore Yoritomo sent in arms against him his brothers Yositsuné and Noriyori, and these generals settled the matter by defeating Yoshinaka's army and killing him. They then proceeded westward to operate similarly upon the Taira party.

There are many ways of telling the story of the final pursuit and overthrow of the Taira. One way is that adopted in a native historical summary, which curtly says, "After several battles, they obtained a decisive victory at Dan-no-ura." Another is that adopted by Mr. Griffis, who converts the story into an eloquent prose epic, in which Yositsuné, after burning the enemy out of the Fukawara palace, and again out of the castle of Yoshima, pursued them "as with the winged feet of an avenger," and drove them "like scattered sheep" to the Straits of Shimonoséki, then named Dan-no-ura. There the Taira clan were "hunted to the seashore," and turned "like a wounded stag" upon their pursuers. Ships were collected on both sides, and a terrible contest upon the waters ensued: "The combat deepened; the Minamoto loved fighting, the Taira scorned to surrender," continues our American prose poet. "Revenge lent its maddening intoxication. Life, robbed of all its charms, gladly welcomed glorious death. The whizzing of arrows, the clash of two-handed swords, the clanging of armour, the sweep of churning oars, the crash of colliding junks, the wild song of the rowers, the shouts of the warriors, made the storm-chorus of the battle. One after another the Taira ships, crushed by the prows of their opponents, or scuttled by the iron bolt-heads of the Minamoto archers, sank beneath the bubbling waters, leaving red whirlpools of blood. Those that were boarded were swept with sword and spear of their human freight. The dead bodies clogged the decks, on which the mimic tides of blood ebbed and flowed and splashed with the motion of the waves, while the scuppers ran red . . ." But enough! No, not enough; one sentence more: "The Taira, driven off the face of the earth, were buried with war's red burial beneath the sea, that soon forgot its stain, and laughed again in purity of golden gleam and deep blue wave." There, that is equally poetic, and far more pleasant than the other! The dethroned child-emperor, Antoku, was drowned in the arms of Kiyomori's widow. His mother was drowned in trying to save her child. Munemori was taken first to Kamakura, and sent thence by Yoritomo to Kioto, but was slain on the way there by his guards.

I have now to record of Yoritomo acts which humanity can never forgive, and history ought never to extenuate. He sought the assassination of his gallant brother Yositsuné, to whom he owed so much; he led troops against him, in the hope of accomplishing his destruction; and he eventually was the cause of his assassination in the house of a friend. The sending of Yositsuné to fight against their common cousin Yoshinaka, after his brilliant defeat of the Taira troops, and his capture of the capital—events of supreme advantage to Yoritomo—had at least a semblance of justification. But for him now to turn upon Yositsuné himself, after all the risks he had run, the battles he had fought, and the services he had rendered, was not merely to tarnish, but to stain, and to stain deeply and for ever, whatever honour he may have possessed. It is all very well for his apologists to speak of calumnies whispered in his ear, and of the dangers which sprang from the greatness and brightness of Yositsuné's renown on his return to the capital from his western campaign, after the overthrow of the Taira. But that Yoritomo caused Yositsuné to be slain no generous nature will ever remember save with sympathy for the one and hatred for the other. On returning from the west and from the capital, after his successive victories, Yositsuné was stopped at a village outside of Kamakura, opposite to Enoshima, and ordered to wait there his brother's pleasure. Tired of waiting, he returned to the capital, and there men in his brother's employ attempted his life. He escaped, and wandered a fugitive in many provinces, his wanderings terminating in the house of the prince of Mutsu, where his youth had been spent. The prince during his own lifetime protected him, but his retreat was discovered, and the prince's son had him put to death, and sent his head to

Yoritomo at Kamakura. If he dared to look upon it, I hope its aspect haunted him for the remainder of his life. Of Yositsuné it may be said that

> "His virtues
> Did plead like angels, trumpet-tongued, against
> The deep damnation of his taking off."

I cannot myself forget either that Yoritomo himself gained neither of the great victories over the Taira, or that he slew both the men who did gain them. Some victories he gained certainly, and among them this: He proceeded to Mutsu and attacked the young Fujiwara (Hidehira's son) who slew Yositsuné, or at least caused his death,* his offence being that he did not either slay or betray Yositsuné sooner! He vanquished the young fellow, of course, and seized the province. On his return he went to Kioto, and there he was received by the emperor and ex-emperor with such display as befitted the greatest subject of the realm, and a man already wielding all but supreme power.

On his return to Kamakura, Yoritomo proceeded to consolidate his power, to aggrandise his city, and organise measures for making his influence directly felt throughout the empire. His ambitious objects were greatly furthered by the arrival of a dignitary of the court from Kioto, authorised to confer upon him the exalted title of Sei-i-Shogun, which is said literally to mean "Barbarian-Subjugating Great General," but which practically signifies Greatest General, or General-in-Chief. This title was first employed four hundred years before, when it was bestowed

---

* It is said by some that Yositsuné preferred to commit, and did commit, *hara-kira*. There is likewise a tradition that he escaped from Japan, and became the renowned conqueror Genghis Khan. The account given in the official histories now published is, however, that which I have adopted in the text, viz. that the son of Prince Hidehira caused him to be assassinated, and sent his head to Kamakura. "The immortality of Yositsuné is secured. Worshipped as a god by the Ainos, honoured and beloved by every Japanese youth as an ideal hero of chivalry, his features pictured on boys' kites, his mien and form represented in household effigies, displayed annually at the boys' great festival of flags, glorified in art, song, and story, Yositsuné, the hero, warrior, and martyr, will live in unfading memory so long as the ideals of the warlike Japanese stand unshattered, or their traditions are preserved."— *Griffis*.

by the emperor Kuwammu on two generals in succession. Another Sei-i-Shogun was appointed two reigns later, but with this exception the title remained obsolete until Yoshinaka received, or rather assumed, it, just before he was killed. The conferring of this title upon Yoritomo was the greatest distinction that he could have received, and its bestowal was most favourable to the development of his plans. For this title, which was originally designed to give additional rank and power to a general, so changed its character after a time that the Shogun (to which form Sei-i-Shogun usually gets abbreviated) found himself the real master of the country. Yoritomo now founded a system of government which prevailed with little change down to the abolition of the Shogunate in 1868. The Ashikagas, the Toyotomis, and the Tokugawas all adopted it. That system, shortly stated, was to bring all the public business of the country into the hands of the Shogun, who appointed chiefs in all the provinces to conduct the local government in accordance with his instructions, but to do all this in the name of the emperor, whose nominal authority was allowed to remain intact. The system was introduced gradually and warily by Yoritomo. He first induced the court to appoint as governors of provinces a few men of his own name; he then got a military governor placed alongside of the civil governor in each province; and in lesser districts a somewhat similar arrangement was carried out, members of his own family, the Minamoto, being as far as possible placed in these offices, and instructed and controlled from Kamakura. The pretext for these appointments was at first the search for his brother. The provincial functionary was called a Shugo, and the fief-functionary an Iito, or Jito.

In this way, and in a thousand similar ways, he so increased his own power that the city which he created became an eastern capital; his seat became substantially a throne, and the sceptre which men saw extended above them was no other than his keen-edged, two-handed sword. The representative of the ancient race of the Mikados nominally ruled in Kioto, but Yositomo's son, who as a boy had been

sentenced to death, and only spared to be flung outcast into
exile and solitude, had become the virtual ruler, and held
his royal court at Kamakura like any monarch. Yoritomo,
nevertheless, founded no lasting dynasty, and the city which
he created was not an abiding one. The city of Kamakura
has vanished; not its glory only, but itself has departed;
the palace grounds are now ploughed fields; the huge brazen
god, the eastern Daibutsu, once the wonder and adornment
of a capital, we had to approach by a country lane, through
sand and slush; and save the temple of Hachiman, which
existed before Yoritomo was born, and the relics of himself
and others which that contains, but little remains to mark
the scene of his labours, his ambitions, and his successes.
Yes, one thing more remains; his grave still exists, and I
have stood beside it. A simple grave, high upon the hillside, bordered and railed with stone, and still bright with
flowers, cut and placed there by some living hands—whose I
know not. Then one heard again the low-voiced "Earth-
song":—

"How am I theirs, if they cannot hold me,
But I hold them?"*

That Yoritomo was a great and able man cannot be doubted.
"He is looked upon as one of the ablest rulers and greatest
generals that ever lived in Japan." But native historians,
while crediting him with abundant ability, both as a civil
and as a military chief, deplore his selfishness and cruelty.
One of them says that he obtained his results by encouraging
each of his officers to believe that he was a special confidant
of his master's plans, thus preventing them from combining
with each other; and then, when they ceased to be service-
able to him, casting them one after the other aside, and even
treating them with cruelty. Another historian says: "Yoritomo was a man of great *sang froid;* he was also exceedingly
energetic, and very just, for, while he punished the guilty
without pity, he recompensed every one who deserved it;
and consequently he was esteemed as well as feared by his
subordinates. He was very mistrustful, and destroyed

* 'Poems,' by Ralph Waldo Emerson.

several members of his family whose influence he feared. Notwithstanding this, he committed the error of having too much confidence in the Hojo (his wife's) family, to the members of which he gave so many important posts that the descendants of this family eclipsed those of his own." This was no doubt largely due to the fact that throughout his previous wars and labours Yoritomo was powerfully assisted by his wife and her father, Hojo-Yokimasa, who are said to have secretly intrigued with the object of transferring the influence of Yoritomo to themselves and their descendants. This scheme was so successful that, after the death of Yoritomo, although his son Yoriye succeeded him in the Shogunate, he bore the title only, the power passing, as we shall see, into other hands. As to the historian's assertion that Yoritomo was a "very just" man, I can only say that I am unable to reconcile this statement with his acknowledged practice of putting to death the "members of his family whose influence he feared." These historical "portrait painters" appear to me to lack scientific restraint, and to neglect while writing one sentence what they have just set down in a previous one. My own opinion of Yoritomo has already been stated; my admiration of him is certainly very limited.

GRAVE OF YORITOMO AT KAMAKURA.

CHAPTER VIII.

THE HOJO DOMINATION.

Family struggles of the Minamoto and the Hojo—Masago imprisons her father—Efforts of the emperor Go-Toba to assert the imperial rights—Contest between the emperor and his minister—Two brothers become Mikado and Shogun—Good and patriotic services of the Hojo house—Invasion of Japan by the Mongol Tartars—Fall of the Hojo—Masashigé, or "Nanko," whose temple is at Hiogo—Undertakes to restore the emperor—Escape of the emperor from Oki—Nitta Yosisada—His desertion from the Hojo to the imperial cause—His military success—The eastern provinces support him—His attack upon Kamakura—His appeal to the god of the sea—His victory, and overthrow of the Hojo—Taka-Uji, the first of the Ashikagas—Restoration of the emperor Go-Daigo.

YORITOMO died in the year 1199 A.D., and the struggles between his own family and that of his wife commenced at once. His son Yoriye succeeded him, as I have said, but Yoriye had been so trained by his mother, Masago, as to have become, as she alleged, too fond of his pleasures, and she accordingly forbade him to attempt the administration of the country's affairs, and formed a commission composed of her father and her father's friends to perform that duty. Yoriye falling ill, at the age of twenty-two, gave his mother an opportunity of further pursuing her policy, and she desired him to commit the administration of thirty provinces of the west to his younger brother Sanetomo, aged twelve, and that of twenty-eight eastern provinces to a very much younger child named Ichiman. The father-in-law of Yoriye, named Hiki-Yoshikazu, apprehending evil results from this divison of power, advised Yoriye to resist it, and even to get rid of the Hojo family, and transmit his power eventually to Ichiman. It is difficult to believe that Masago either instigated or concurred in the murderous events which followed, although history discredits her by the imputation ; and it will at least be well to put the primary blame upon her father, Tokimasa, who, it can scarcely be doubted, was the real cause of it all. Yoshikazu was assassinated, as was likewise the infant child of Masago, Ichiman. Yoriye was deposed, sent with his head shaved to a temple in Idzu, and there secretly assassinated ; and Sanetomo, a more supple son, and one who took as readily as his friends desired to the gentle pursuit of poetry and of what is often called religion, and to the companionship of the softer sex, was made Shogun in his stead.

But after a while a difference of interests, or at least a difference of desires, arose between Masago and her father Tokimasa, and with serious consequences. Tokimasa had a daughter born of a second marriage, who herself was married to one Hiraga-Toma-Masa. Taking this son-in-law into his special favour, Tokimasa wished to substitute him in the Shogunate for the effeminate Sanetomo. To this Masago strongly objected, so strongly that she imprisoned her father in the name of Sanetomo rather than submit to it. Then a son of Tokimasa, named Yoshitoki, who was a minister, persuaded Kugio, a son of Yoriye (who had become a priest), to assassinate Sanetomo, which he did quite effectually, shearing off his head, and getting his own sheared off in return by a soldier who pursued him. The direct line of the Minamoto being thus cut off, and Yoshitoki fearing to take a stranger and attempt to make him Shogun, sent to a relation of Yoritomo, and a Fujiwara, named Fujiwara-michi-ie, and instructed him to send his son Yoritsuné, aged two years, to be invested with the office, naming Masago, the widow of Yoritomo, as regent.

These events were not matters of indifference to the imperial court at Kioto. There existed at this time two ex-emperors, Go-Toba and Tsuchi-Mikado, and now a third was added, in the person of Juntoku, who abdicated and gave place to his son, Chukio-Tenno. This occurred in the fourth month of the year 1221 A.D. The real power at Kioto was, however, in the hands of the ex-emperor Go-Toba, who was always mortified, we are told, "by the annoyance and assumption of military men," and who witnessed with "fury" the conduct of the Hojo at Kamakura. The death of Sanetomo appeared to him to offer an opportunity for bringing back power to the imperial court. Go-Toba, it is true, owed his throne originally to the Minamoto house, who drove away the Taira, as we saw in the last chapter; and in gratitude for this he treated Yoritomo with the greatest distinction when he visited the western capital, Kioto. But now, with Yoritomo dead, and the leading scions of the Minamoto assassinated, and all the power and glory of the Kamakura dynasty (so to call it) passing into the hands of the Hojo, Go-Toba felt at liberty to assert, if he could, the rights of the imperial house.

After the assassination of Sanetomo matters proved worse instead of better, his minister Yoshitoki frequently paying no attention to the express commands of the emperor. Go-Toba therefore collected an army in the neighbourhood of Kioto, and despatched a secret ambassador to the eastern country to persuade the great families there to join his cause, and to help him destroy the family who had usurped alike the imperial power and the heritage of their friends, the Minamoto. Yoshitoki, having heard of this, seized the ambassador, burnt the imperial letter, and sent his sons Yasutoki and Tomotoki, and his brother Tohifusa, with an army of a hundred and ninety thousand men to Kioto, to attack the ex-emperor. Go-Toba called the ministers and courtiers together in council, and in concert with them resolved to resist with their troops the Kamakura army. The imperial army was, however, defeated, the court thrown into confusion, and Kioto carried by Yasutoki. The ex-emperor was then, to employ the language of one of my Japanese friends in Tokio, "caught with fear, and said, 'This matter did not come from my mind, but was the doings of my advisers;' whereupon Yasutoki made the chief advisers prisoners, and sent them to Kamakura, they being put to death on the way." In the seventh month the youthful Chukio (aged seventeen), after a reign of two months, was dethroned by Yoshitoki, adding a fourth to the ex-emperors then alive. The other three were all exiled, Go-Toba to Oki, Tsuchi-mikado to Tosa, and Juntoku to Sado. This affair became known in history as the " disaster of Shokiu."

The emperor placed on the throne by Yoshitoki after the deposition of Chukio was Go-Horikawa (grandson of the emperor Takakura), during whose reign the Hojo family were, of course, all-powerful throughout Japan. Yoshitoki, as *Shukken*, or minister, of the child-Shogun was the real master of Japan. He removed literally by thousands the enemies of the imperial court from their offices throughout the country, filling the vacant places by those who had been useful to him, reserving, let it be known, none of the spoils for himself. He therefore became as popular as he was powerful. At his death his son Yasutoki succeeded him in his office of Shukken, and his term of office was characterised by great goodness, economy, and laborious exertions on his part. He therefore became as popular as his father had been. He improved and extended the system of government established by Yoritomo, and among other useful things published a new Code of Laws. In the reign of the emperor Shijo, the Shogun Yoritsuné, accompanied by the Shukken Yasutoki, did homage to him; and when Shijo died, Yasutoki put Go-Saga, a son of Tsuchi-Mikado, on the throne, out of gratitude for the peaceful and conciliatory counsels which, subsequent to the disaster of Shokiu, the father had always given. In the reign of Go-Saga, Yasutoki died, and was succeeded as Shukken by his grandson Tsunetoki, and the Shogun Yoritsuné resigned his office in favour of his son Yoritsugu, aged six. In the next reign Tsunetoki gave way in his office as minister to his younger brother Tokiyori, whom the ex-Shogun Yoritsuné endeavoured to get assassinated. Tokiyori discovering this, sent the ex-Shogun to Kioto. After a while Yoritsuné aimed at the same object again, this time raising an army for the purpose. He was unsuccessful; all his accomplices were arrested; his son, Shogun Yoritsugu, was deposed and sent to Kioto; and Prince Munetaka, the second son of the ex-emperor Go-Saga, was taken to Kamakura by

Tokiyori, and made Shogun in his place. Soon afterwards, in 1260, the sixth son of Go-Saga was made emperor, so that the Mikado and the Shogun were now brothers.

It is unnecessary to follow all the changes that took place during the dominance of the Hojo family, either as regards the crown, the Shogunate, or the office of Shukken. We may hasten on to the fall of this great family. But it is fair to them to state that the period of their supremacy was marked by many good and patriotic services rendered to the country. Several of them exhibited as ministers admirable zeal and ability, one of them, Tokiyori, having made numerous journeys through the country in strict *incognito* for the purpose of personally observing the condition and the wants of the people. Some of the members of the Hojo family likewise did much to promote the study of literature and the progress of education. Hojo Akitoki founded, in 1240 A.D., a library in the village of Kanazawa, near the Bay of Yedo, at a few miles from Kamakura. This institution was used as a school through the nine generations of the Hojo family, and was much frequented by scholars and students. Some of the books are to be found scattered about the country at present, bearing the library marks. I have previously noted the publication of Yasutoki's Code. It has frequently happened in the history of Japan that power usurped by subjects has been used for the peace and to the advantage of the country. We shall hereafter see that this was the case with the Tokugawa dynasty of Yedo, which lasted for the greater part of three centuries. It was so at first, and for many years, with the Hojo rule; but as time wore on, their industry decayed and gave way to luxury, and from luxury followed excessive taxation, wrong, and tyranny, and "the whirligig of time" had to bring about "revenges."

During the domination of the rival families of Taira, Minamoto, and Hojo in succession, the country had been at peace externally, and all its warlike energies and resources, largely as they were exerted, were expended internally, Japanese only warring with Japanese. But in the reign of the emperor Go-Uda, who took the crown in 1275 A.D., the government and people suddenly found themselves threatened by an invasion from China, and one of the most formidable character. The Mongol Tartars, having overthrown the reigning dynasty of China, and obtained the submission of all the surrounding states, sent to Japan haughty demands for her submission likewise. Receiving in the first place no reply, and afterwards having ambassador after ambassador put to death, the king of the Geng prepared a mighty armada, and despatched it to subjugate his independent neighbour. The Mongol armada met with the fate which befell that which Spain launched against our devoted little country. The story of its defeat and destruction I briefly relate elsewhere, referring to it here only to give due note of it in the historic sequence of events.

The overthrow of the house of Hojo has unavoidably been briefly referred to in my account of the Descent of the Crown. I must now record the circumstances at greater length, avoiding repetition as far as possible. The period was the first half of the fourteenth century (A.D.), and the emperor Go-Daigo was on the throne of Japan. We previously saw that the question of the succession which Go-Daigo raised was but a pretext for a rupture with the house of Hojo, to the galling domination of which he earnestly desired to put an end. Aware of this, the Shukken, Hojo Takatoki, sent a general, Sodatoki, with three thousand men to Kioto. One of the imperial princes, learning from a spy that Takatoki intended to dethrone the emperor, gave the latter timely notice, and Go-Daigo escaped from his palace in a woman's carriage, and went to Kasagi-yama. By his orders Fujiwara-no-Morokata put on the imperial dress, personated the emperor, and went to the monastery of Hiyei-san. The priests gladly came about him at first, but dispersed on learning that he was not the emperor.

While at Kasagi the emperor was greatly troubled at his powerlessness and abandonment, and one day dreamed, it is said, of two boys making a throne under a large *kusunoki*, or camphor-tree, at the south side of the imperial palace, and calling him to sit upon it. He interpreted the dream as signifying that some one named Kusunoki would take up the imperial cause, and give him great help in his undertaking. He therefore called together the priests and inquired if they had heard of any one named Kusunoki, and one of the priests answered, "There is one called Kusunoki-Masashigé, who, on account of having quelled the robbers, was made Hioyenojo." The emperor then said, "That is the man," and at once sent for him to come to him at Kasagi. "I commit to your care," said the emperor, "the overthrowing of the revolters," and asked him what had best be done. Kusunoki was not wanting to the occasion. "The time will come," said he, "when there shall be no rebel who has not been overthrown. The eastern soldiers are very brave, but they are wanting in intelligence; as to bravery we cannot equal them, though we raise the armies of the sixty provinces; but as to intellectual resources, I have stratagems to practise upon them. But victory and defeat are the common incidents of war, and therefore, though one may suffer defeat in the beginning, we must not change our minds, or slacken in our undertaking. As long as your majesty knows that I am still living, your majesty need not trouble yourself about the matter." Something like a counsellor this for an imperilled and dejected emperor! This Kusunoki-Mashashigé is known to fame as Nanko, who is now worshipped in temples, and more especially in the large Shinto temple at Hiogo, which will be mentioned on the occasion of our visit hereafter. Masashigé then went to Akasaka to build a castle as a basis of operations. The emperor soon after vainly endeavoured to escape from the troops of Takatoki, who made him a prisoner. He was sent in exile to the island of Oki, and Kuwoogen-Tenno was raised to the vacant throne. Kusunoki-Masashigé, although with a comparatively small force, kept the troops of Takatoki in check for several months.

Then, while Go-Daigo was at Oki, Fujina Yasituna, one of the guards, took up the imperial cause, and recommended the emperor to escape from Oki and go to the province of Hoki. This the emperor succeeded in doing by night, with the aid of a fisherman, who carried him to the port of Chiba, where he obtained a passage in a small merchant vessel, and at last arrived at Hoki. There Nawa Nagutosi took up his cause, and defeated the imperial troops sent against him. After this, and in view of Masashigé's stout resistance, many generals declared in favour of Go-Daigo, who acquired sufficient strength and confidence to issue an edict for the overthrow of the Hojo family.

At this point a fresh warrior, who became one of the most renowned in the history of Japan, appeared upon the scene —Nitta Yosisada. He was a Minamoto, and an officer in the army of the Hojo family, and in the latter capacity had been sent to besiege Kusunoki. Doubting the justice of the Hojo cause, and being strongly averse to fighting against the rightful Mikado, he abandoned with his troops the army of the Hojo, and joined his forces to those of the emperor Go-Daigo. He charged himself with the great task of capturing Kamakura, and annihilating in its very centre and source the intolerable rule of the upstart family. He raised, or rather recruited, his force in one of the eastern provinces, Kodzuke, and marched towards the eastern capital. Once, when encamped,* he was startled to discover 2000 horsemen coming towards him, which every one about him took for a hostile force. They proved, however, to be kinsmen and followers of his from Yechiyo, who, hearing of his project, had come to aid him in his undertaking. The next day he collected his forces and marched into the province of Musashi, in which Kamakura is situated. An additional force of 20,000 men gathered to his standard as he advanced. But the Hojo minister, Takatoki, thought lightly of Nitta, and sent two of his kinsmen to repel him. Nitta pitched his camp at the north side of the river Iruma, and the Hojo generals halted their troops on the southern side, deferring their advance on account of the unexpected strength of which they found Nitta in command. Thereupon Nitta crossed the river and gave battle.

Both armies consisted of the hardy troops of the east ; both

---

* At a place called Kasagakeno.

were strong in cavalry, and accustomed to fighting mounted; and the battle-field was a plain. Commencing with bow and arrow work, they soon closed in hand attack, and, after charging each other more than thirty times, both forces retreated. On the following day they fought again at the village of Kumegawa, without attaining a decisive result; but the Hojo force in each contest lost double the number of the men whom Nitta lost. Takatoki now sent his brother Yasuiye with a reinforcement of many thousand men, who joined the Kamakura force by night. Next day Nitta, who was unaware of the reinforcement of his enemy, was defeated. His success greatly emboldened Yasuiye, who said, "I am sure some one from among the enemy will bring me Nitta's head." His troops, sharing the elation of their general, doffed their armour, and proceeded to enjoy a night of revelry. During the night Nitta fell upon them from three directions, and routed them with great slaughter. At the same time another body of Hojo troops were defeated, and driven towards Kamakura.

The great families of the eastern provinces now submitted to Nitta, who advanced to Sekido with 120,000 men. Here he divided his force into three parts, with the intention of attacking Kamakura from three sides simultaneously. To alarm the enemy he set fire to fifty different places around the city; but the Hojo had still an army of a hundred thousand men for its defence. One of Nitta's divisions was defeated and driven back, its general being killed. Then Nitta selected 20,000 of his best troops, intending to advance by night upon Kamakura by the sea-coast; but the enemy built a stockade across his route, and stationed vessels of war on the south side near the shore, so as to attack his troops in flank. Thus was the approach of Nitta effectually barred. The only road left him was past a jutting headland, near Enoshima, round which the tide washed more or less deeply.

And now occurred one of those incidents which strike the popular imagination, and stamp a lasting impress upon a nation's memory. What Nitta's private opinions were I know not, nor am I able to say how great or how little was his knowledge of the tides, and of the ebb and flow of the sea in Kamakura Bay; but his knowledge of men was no doubt great, and of his power of inspiring courage and hope in his troops he gave many proofs. At this crisis of his own and of his emperor's fortunes, he removed his helmet, bowed reverently towards the sea, and said: "Our sacred Mikado has been dethroned by his disloyal subjects, and exiled to a distant western isle; and I, Yosisada, being unable to bear such treachery, have raised this army for his rescue. O god of the sea, take pity upon my loyal heart, cause the tide to withdraw, and open a way for my army to pass!" Thus saying, he cast his sword into the sea, as a tribute of fidelity to the god whom he had invoked. At the break of day the tides withdrew, the war-vessels were drifted away, and Nitta marched upon the city, setting fire to the houses, and attacked the Hojo family in their own residence. The Hojo troops, after severe fighting, were utterly overthrown, Takatoki himself and his kinsmen either being killed or putting themselves to death. Nitta's invocation of the sea-god, and the casting of his sword into the sea, form an incident which Japanese historians delight to record, and Japanese poets to relate in the most stirring verse at their command. I confess to viewing the spot where it occurred with no small interest, as will be seen in the accounts of my visit to the city whose name recalls the fame alike of its founder and of its destroyer.

Kamakura captured, and the Hojo family destroyed by Nitta on behalf of the emperor Go-Daigo, it remained for the imperial forces to proceed to Kioto, there to re-establish the imperial name; and with it, it was fondly hoped, the imperial power, so long kept in abeyance by the Kamakura families. With this object, Ashikaga-Taka-Uji, one of the generals of the slain Hojo-Takatoki, now joined his forces to the imperial troops, and the combined army marched for the western capital. On its arrival the Hojo forces were driven out, the generals commanding them withdrawing eastward, and carrying with them the ex-emperors Go-Fushimi and Hanzano. Go-Daigo re-entered his capital, dethroned Kuwoogen-Tenno, and reascended the throne. He reorganised the ministries, appointed fresh governors of provinces, nominated as *Shugo* the generals Taka-Uji, Yosisada, Masashigé, and some others, and gave the high title of Sei-i-tai Shogun to his own son, Prince Morinaga, the heir to the crown.

SIX-SIDED TEMPLE OF KIOTO.

CHAPTER IX.

THE SIMULTANEOUS DYNASTIES.

Ambition of successful generals—Distribution of confiscated fiefs unsatisfactory—Discontent of Ashikaga-Taka-Uji—His abrupt departure from the court—His letter of accusations against Nitta—His capture of, expulsion from, and efforts to regain Kioto—The emperor consults Kusunoki (Nanko)—His wise advice rejected—His memorable address to his son—The great battle of Minatogawa—Kusunoki commits *hara-kiri*—His fame as a patriot—His son Masatsura defeats Taka-Uji's general—His interview with the emperor—His gallant death—Taka-Uji again enters the capital—Retreat of the emperor—Enthronement of Komio—Two emperors and two courts—Kioto and Yoshino—The northern and southern dynasties—Defeat and heroic death of Nitta—Ashikaga-Taka-Uji reigns at Kamakura—He makes the Shogunate hereditary in his family—Diversified views of his character—The murder of Prince Morinaga—The wars of the rival dynasties—The southern emperors—The legitimate sovereigns.

MONARCHS who owe their thrones to successful generals appear seldom to have pleasant and peaceful reigns. A triumphant army is a weapon so splendid and so powerful that he who grasps it firmly, so to speak, seems usually to cast about for opportunities of wielding it. The re-enthroned Go-Daigo soon found his crowned head lying uneasy on this account.

The overthrow of the Hojo family was succeeded by the confiscation of numerous fiefs, and in the distribution of these and many valuable offices the emperor gave cause for deep dissatisfaction. Those who had greatly aided him in the recovery of his throne received properties and offices of much value; but at the same time imperial princes, who had done nothing, and even some of the ladies of the court, likewise received many good things, and consequently great dissatisfaction arose in the military class. Unfortunately the Japanese, with all their politeness and natural delicacy, seem throughout their history to have lusted after place, property, and power in a way altogether worthy of the nations who have enjoyed a European training. Patriotism —I mean that form of patriotism which finds its chief reward in the privilege of serving one's country—appears to have been as rare among the great personages of Japan as among other nations. So far as love of country is concerned, it does not appear to matter much to what race or nation or religion or political faith men belong; the great bulk of them worship their poor, miserable, short-lived, worthless selves more devotedly than anything or anybody else. Happily a patriot occasionally towers above the swarming crowd, and shows us that nobleness is not altogether unknown among us; but it is impossible for me to write, or for others to read, these repeated records of the selfish uprising of military chiefs, without deploring the want of something nobler in their aims, and something stouter in their virtues.

Ashikaga-Taka-Uji (let the reader note the name, for we shall see much of the Ashikagas soon), although his services were not nearly so valuable as those of Nitta or Nanko (Kusunoki), and although he received the largest rewards, nevertheless took into his selfish head the belief that he was insufficiently recompensed, and even thought that he, or some one belonging to him, ought to have been set up at Kamakura in place of the Hojo chief. He was a wary and a wily personage, however, and waited a suitable chance for the exercise and display of his disaffection. As if to afford him such a chance, some of the former vassals of the Hojo after a time broke out in revolt, and Ashikaga-Taka-Uji requested permission to put them down. This granted, he further desired that he might be appointed Shogun, and charged with the government of the eastern provinces. This was refused, and he was appointed commander-in-chief of the eastern army. Annoyed with this, and his blood doubtless already running traitorously within him, he departed without taking leave of the emperor and the court, and being joined at Suruga by his brother Tadayoshi, defeated the Hojo rebels, and entered Kamakura. Warned by his abrupt and discourteous departure from Kioto, the emperor sent one of the Minamoto, named Tomomitsu, to Kamakura to recall him; but he refused to return, and soon afterwards appointed himself Shogun and governor of the eastern provinces. He handsomely rewarded his followers, invited the imperial troops to surrender and to join him, and seized upon the provinces of Nitta Yosisada and divided them among his own generals and other officers. By these means he gained great support, and then wrote to the emperor a letter making accusations against Nitta, and invited the western provinces to rise in revolt. Nitta presented a counter-statement to the emperor, clearing himself from Taka-Uji's charges, and preferring against him a list of crimes. Imperial troops were sent against Taka-Uji, but they were defeated, and he marched with his own forces into Kioto. He was, however, unable to hold it, and after several struggles was driven out, and escaped westward. There he reorganised his forces, and again began to fight his way towards Kioto, winning every battle he fought.

On learning this, Nitta reported the matter to the court, who were greatly alarmed, most of the imperial troops having left the capital. The emperor summoned Kusunoki to assist Nitta in repelling the rebels. Kusunoki, however —maintaining his old theory of the superiority of intellectual stratagems to mere fighting—warned the emperor that the troops of Taka-Uji were very numerous and brave, having been largely reinforced in Kiushiu and elsewhere, while their own troops were few and fatigued: "I humbly hope, therefore," said he, "that your majesty will recall Yosisada (Nitta), yourself retiring from the city for a time, and will allow Taka-Uji to freely enter Kioto. I will return to Kawachi, intercept their provisions and stores; their army will consequently dwindle away, while ours will increase daily; and afterwards, attacking the rebels on opposite sides at once, we may fairly hope to defeat them.

Yosisada, though he does not expressly say so, is, I know, desirous of this course being taken, for ultimate victory is the only thing to be sought after in war. I pray your majesty to reconsider the orders now issued." All the ministers and courtiers agreed with Kusunoki except one highly placed but stupid fellow (Sanjo Fujiwara-Kiyotada), who was both a bad reasoner and a fatalist, and who said: "Though the revolters may be strong, this will not be like other battles; and besides, whether we gain the battle or lose it, it will be so ordained of heaven, and we ought therefore to defend Kioto, and engage the enemy before he reaches it." The emperor followed this high-sounding advice, to his cost.

Kusunoki retired from the emperor's presence, and informed his brother and kinsmen of what had happened, and added, "The matter is now settled, and I can say no more." He soon after took leave of the emperor, and with his brother, his son, and other kinsmen and friends, went westwards to Sakurai. There he halted, and, instructing his son to go to Kawachi, made to him a speech which has become one of the most memorable of the many loyal speeches by which Japanese imperialists have distinguished themselves. He said: "Though you are young, you are eleven years old, and will therefore be able to bear in mind what I now say to you. We are about to engage in a battle on which the future destiny of the country depends. I think I shall not see you again, and it is almost certain that when you hear of my death the whole country will submit to Ashikaga. But nevertheless do not you think of your own fortune, and forget your duty to the emperor, whereby you might make your father's loyalty vain; but as long as you have even one follower defend the castle of Kongo-san, and give yourself up to your country. This is what I expect from you, and this is the greatest honour you can render to me." Thus saying, he gave to his son his sword—always a solemn and significant thing in Japan, but in this case much more so than usual, the sword having been given to Masashigé by the emperor himself. The gallant boy implored his father to allow him to fight and to die with him, but the father reprimanded him for this wilfulness, and caused him to take his leave. Masashigé then went to Hiogo (where his temple, as I have said, now stands), and there conferred with Nitta Yosisada, and banqueted the whole night long with him, as a parting celebration.

The great and decisive battle was soon after fought. In briefly recapitulating its incidents I will give the names of the places concerned for the benefit of those readers who may care to identify the scene of it. Taka-Uji leading the sea forces and Tadayoshi the land forces, the two proceeded to the attack of the imperial troops. Yosisada pitched his camp near Wadano-saki to resist Taki-Uji, and Masashigé fixed his at Minatogawa to encounter Tadayoshi. Yosisada appears to have been out-manœuvred, for, according to my information, "the van of the sea forces passed the camp of Yosisada, and when he pursued the enemy the whole force had landed at Wadanosaki." Then Masashigé—the rejection of whose counsel seems not to have in any degree lowered his ardour—joined with his brother, and made no less than seven successive and desperate attacks upon Tadayoshi, at one time coming extremely near success. Tadayoshi was unhorsed, and one of Masashigé's soldiers was on the point of capturing or slaying him, when a general officer of the rebel army by a violent effort interposed and saved him. Meanwhile Taka-Uji, learning of the dangerously persistent efforts of Masashigé against his brother, sent part of his force to aid the land force, and then attacked Masashigé's men from the rear. Masashigé turned upon them, and is said to have maintained an unequal contest with the greatest and most sustained valour, charging the enemy over and over and over again, to the number of sixteen times, and until no more than seventy horsemen remained to him. The battle was, of course, lost, and although Masashigé escaped from the field, he resolved, like many another valiant Japanese, not to survive the disgrace of defeat. He went to a peasant's house near Minatogawa, and there, taking off his armour, found that he had sustained eleven wounds. To his brother Masasuye he said, "What do you desire after death?" Masasuye answered, "I wish to be born again seven times over, that I may have lives enough to exterminate the revolters." Masashigé joyfully said, "That is right, indeed," and then the two brothers applied to themselves the fatal knife.

Thus, at the age of forty-three, perished one of the purest patriots of Japan; and with him perished several relatives and retainers in like manner. It is hard to reconcile the taking of his own life either with the charge delivered to his son at Sakurai, or with his own last words to his brother. It is strange that, while anxious for his son to devote his life to the emperor's cause, and desirous of re-living himself seven times for the good of that cause, he should throw away his own life, and the lives of his relatives and friends, at a comparatively early age, and in the plenitude of his prowess and personal power. The spurious sense of honour which caused many great and good men to resort to *hara-kiri* must have been deep-rooted indeed, and it is impossible to avoid either deploring it or censuring it. Still it would be idle to judge of Masashigé and others by our present sentiments respecting that form of heroism, and we must not forget the greatness of the man or the glory of the patriot in lamentations for his fate. Mr. Griffis shall pronounce for us his eulogium. Deploring, as we do, the mode of his death, but remembering that he acted according to the lights of his time, he says: "Of all the characters in Japanese history, that of Kusunoki Masashigé stands pre-eminent for pureness of patriotism, unselfishness of devotion to duty, and calmness of courage. The people speak of him in tones of reverential tenderness, and, with an admiration that lacks fitting words, behold in him the mirror of stainless loyalty. I have more than once asked my Japanese students and friends whom they considered the noblest character in their history. Their unanimous answer was, 'Kusunoki Masashigé.' Every relic of this brave man is treasured up with religious care; and fans inscribed with poems written by him, in fac-simile of his handwriting, are

KUSUNOKI MASASHIGÉ.

From HOKUSAI. Reproduced for this Work by a Japanese Engraver.

sold in the shops and used by those who burn to imitate his exalted patriotism. His son Masatsura lived to become a gallant soldier."*

Of this son of Masashigé, whom we saw sent away from his father at Sakurai before his last battle, I must narrate a touching incident, terminating in his death. In the year 1348 A.D., while defending the castle of Kongo-san, as his father had charged him to do, he conceived the idea of attempting to seize Kioto on behalf of his emperor, Go-Daigo; but before he could make the attempt, one of Taka-Uji's generals attacked him. He successfully resisted the attack, defeated the rebel general, and advanced towards the city. Hearing of this, Taka-Uji despatched against him an army of eighty thousand men, under experienced commanders. On learning of their departure, Masatsura went with the members of his family to the temporary residence of his emperor, and said: "Your majesty's late subject Masashigé (my father) overthrew the revolters with his little army, and put the mind of your majesty at rest; and when the revolters rose a second time, he fought them again, and died at the battle of Minatogawa. I was then only eleven years old, and he told me to go back to Kawachi, and there, collecting the remaining army, revenge myself upon the enemy of the empire. I have now come to years of maturity, having much feared hitherto that I should get ill and die, and thus be unable to fulfil the commands of my late father. Now that the rebels come with their whole army to attack us, and I feel that it is time for me to die, I humbly beg that I may be allowed to take leave of your majesty in your majesty's presence." Thereupon the emperor raised the blinds which screened him, and consoled him thus: "The victories of the last few days have tended to seriously baffle the plans of the revolters. I greatly admire

---

* Mr. Griffis, in the few lines which he devotes to the final doings of Kusunoki Masashigé, speaks of the address to the son and the bestowal of the sword as occurring *after* his last battle. But Sakurai is a long distance from the battle-field, as I can state from personal knowledge, and the facts are as I have recorded them in the text.

the loyalty of yourself and your father. Now the rebels are coming with their great army, and our fortune depends on the battle we are about to engage in; but I hope you will act according to circumstances, and will take care of yourself, as I consider you my only support." Masatsura went out from the presence "with tears in his eyes," and afterwards fought with the rebels at Sijo-Nawata. The battle raged from morning till evening, and Masatsura, after receiving many wounds, perished, first bowing twice towards the north, where the emperor was residing. His brother perished with him.

Ashikaga-Taka-Uji now again obtained possession of Kioto, the emperor Go-Daigo having previously fled to Yoshino. The victorious general treated the throne as vacant, and raised to it Prince Yuta-Hito (a brother of the temporary emperor Kuwoogen), under the name of Komio-Tenno. The country was not, however, so completely in the power of Taka-Uji or of Komio-Tenno as to destroy all the power and pretensions of Go-Daigo, and the consequence was that from this time (1336 A.D.) forward, for more than half a century, there existed a state of things which is indicated in the title given to this chapter. There were two emperors of Japan, and two imperial courts, at Kioto and Yoshino respectively. Both emperors were members of the same imperial family, but it was as the northern dynasty and the southern dynasty that the two branches became distinguished. That sitting at Kioto was known as the northern; that sitting at Yoshino, as the southern. The emperor Komio nominated Taka-Uji Shogun, Tadayoshi as Vice-Shogun, and his second son Moto-Uji as Governor of Kamakura.

Taka-Uji lived till the year 1357; but the second of his great antagonists, Nitta Yosisada (the first, Kusunoki Masashigé, having died as we have seen), was killed nearly twenty years earlier. Nitta was in the province of Echizen,*

---

* Echizen is the second of the seven provinces of the *Hokurokudo*, or "the route of the continent of the north."

when Taka-Uji sent one of his family against him with the army of the Hokurokudo.* The Ashikaga pitched his camp in Yechizen-Fu, but was driven thence by Yosisada, and fled to Asuka. Yosisada and Yoshisuké combined their forces and again attacked him, but were unable to dislodge him from the fortresses in which he had taken up his position, and which he had repaired and strengthened. The fighting still proceeded, and one day Yosisada put himself at the head of a small body of cavalry—fifty men only— and went to make an attack, but on the way encountered a body of three hundred horsemen, who surrounded him and his party, pouring arrows in upon them from every side. Yosisada's men, being without shields, had no alternative but to put spurs to their horses, and rush against the surrounding cavalry. Yosisada was pierced in the head by an arrow, and thereupon, after the fashion of the time and of the country, put himself to death. The rebels witnessed his self-destruction in ignorance of his identity, only discovering that it was the redoubted Yosisada after his death, when they found in his pocket an imperial letter containing the words, "In overthrowing the revolters I have to trouble you." On seeing this they knew that before them lay the dead form of the greatest of the antagonists of their rebellious chief, Taka-Uji. Nitta Yosisada was but thirty-eighty ears of age, and the circumstances of his death (in 1338) were worthy of the heroism and devotion of his life.

His great antagonist, Taka-Uji, who had "spoiled the purpose of his life," survived him, as I have said, for many years, enjoying, like Yoritomo and the Hojo, all but imperial sway at Kamakura. His descendants succeeded him in the Shogunate, which he made hereditary, and which remained in his family till the uprising and the wide-reaching of Nobunaga, in the latter half of the sixteenth century. I cannot say that I am an admirer of Taka-Uji, the founder of this Ashikaga line of Shoguns. Without a fuller knowledge of himself and his time I cannot, it is

* See note on previous page.

true, fully appreciate his character and his acts; but his adherence to the Hojo family until its overthrow by Nitta; his sudden transfer of his force to the imperial side when it thus became successful; his bidding for the command of the eastern expedition and for the Shogunate; and his traitorous use of the former in order to secure the latter—all these things combine to cast over his undoubted ability and generalship the shadow of studied disloyalty and of organised crime. Even those who speak of him—and some historians do so—as of a great, generous, and confiding man, admit that he was unable to repress the arrogance and the venality of his vassals, and state that during his administration the finances and the general business of the country lapsed into a deplorable condition. There are others who allege that an element of meanness, which took an almost unspeakable form, prevailed in his public life.* Certain it is that he plotted, and unjustly secured, the overthrow of the emperor's son, Prince Morinaga, and not his overthrow alone, but his long imprisonment in a wretched subterranean dungeon, into which we recently looked with disgust, at Kamakura, enticing him from it by a creature of his under a pretence of secret friendship, only to sever his head from his body as he stepped forth. Men capable and guilty of crimes like this must not be paraded in the pages of history as worthy examples of the race whose nobler impulses alone save them from being overwhelmed by fraud and wrong.

The existence of contemporary dynasties in Japan, with their capitals at no great distance from each other, led, as it was certain to lead, to almost incessant civil war. Go-Daigo died in the year 1338. In dying he left a testament enjoining upon his vassals the duty of remaining faithful to his son and successor, Go-Murakami, and to do all in

---

* Mr. Griffis says that Ashikaga Taka-Uji bribed the Mikado's concubine, and speaks of "his ally in the imperial bed." He also says that, partly by her means, he poisoned the mind of Go-Daigo against his own son, and got him seized, deposed, sent to Kamakura, and murdered in a subterranean dungeon.

their power to preserve his rights; and as he had generous partisans scattered throughout the provinces, the peace was not hard to keep. In the course of time, however, as the more distinguished and devoted members of his party died, his power began to decline. In the chapter on the Descent of the Crown I have made mention of the manner in which in the year 1391 the Ashikaga Shogun Yoshimutsu availed himself of this decline of power to bring about an agreement by which the two dynasties were merged into one. The convention then entered into was broken, and the crown was retained, as I have there shown, by the northern branch of the imperial house; but the southern emperors are nevertheless regarded by most Japanese historians as the legitimate sovereigns, the northern being spoken of as mere usurpers, forced upon a throne, and held there by the military power of the Ashikaga generals. But as both lines of sovereigns were taken from the legitimate imperial house which had descended from the sun-goddess, the sacredness of the sovereignty was not impaired.

KOREAN DOGS *

* These Korean dogs are placed at the foot of the imperial throne of Japan, probably in commemoration of the conquests of Japan in Korea.

CHAPTER X.

THE ASHIKAGA SHOGUNS.

Supreme power of the Ashikagas—Rivalries and contests—Capture and recapture of Kamakura—Assassination of Mochi-Uji—Assassination of Shogun Yoshinori—The imperial insignia carried off—Their recovery—Terrible contests in Kioto in the fifteenth century—Rebellion of Katsumoto—Partisan contests—Two large armies meet in the capital—Flight of the court—The city fired—The Mikado taken to the palace of the Shogun—The war of brothers—The Shogun Yoshimasa—Progress of the arts—The Shogun Yoshitané imprisoned, restored, and again deposed—Further battles in Kioto—The introduction of muskets and cannon—Decline of the Ashikagas, and rise of Nobunaga—Disturbed state of the country in the sixteenth century—Nobunaga's victory in 1560 A.D.—He is commissioned by the emperor to pacificate the country—He overthrows the false Shogun—Appearance of Tokugawa Iyéyasu—The battle of Anagawa—Conspiracy and overthrow of the last Ashikaga Shogun—Review of the Ashikaga period.

In previous chapters we have seen the Ashikaga house, in the person of Taka-Uji, strike the Minamoto from the heights of power to the abysses of humiliation, and drive the legitimate sovereigns from their throne and capital, establishing in their places a new imperial branch. During the existence of the two contemporary dynasties, the power of the Ashikagas was supreme within the limits of the northern dynasty, and continually encroaching upon that of the southern. When the two dynasties became one, their power became absolute over the whole country, and remained so until the appearance of Nobunaga in the sixteenth century. It is true that, after the reconsolidation of the imperial power in the hands, nominally, of Go-Komatsu, some troubles were experienced; but all difficulties were surmounted, and the Ashikagas became, as I have said, dominant throughout the land.

The period of their supremacy was not, however, free from rivalries and contests. The native historians tell us, for example, that trouble arose at Kamakura as follows. Taka-Uji, in his day, had nominated his second son, Moto-Uji, to the governorship of Kamakura and of the eastern provinces. One of Moto-Uji's descendants, named Mochi-Uji, who was very powerful, exceeded his authority by giving the title of "Kuwan-le" to his first minister, and by setting himself up as a rival to the Shogun. Learning this, a former minister of Mochi-Uji * turned against the upstart, made an uncle of the latter his chief general, and entered Kamakura by force of arms, driving out Mochi-Uji. The Shogun, however, treated this as a rebellion, and sent large succours and reinforcements to Mochi-Uji, calling also upon his great vassals of the eastern provinces to assist him. The consequence was that Mochi-Uji put the rebels down, and again took possession of Kamakura. Later, in the reign of the emperor Go-Hanazono, this same Ashikaga Mochi-Uji got into bad relations with the Shogun Yoshinori, and was assassinated by one of the ministers of the latter.†

Other troubles arose. Yoshinori conceived, we are told, the design of dispossessing one of the great vassals named Akamatsu-Mitsusuké, in order to give his domains to a member of his family named Akamatsu-Sudamura. On learning this, Mitsusuké, while deeply indignant, concealed his feelings, and invited the Shogun to attend a great festival which was to be celebrated at his house. Yoshinori went, and was assassinated. His son Yoshikatsu became Shogun in his place, and at once put to death the murderer of his father. As a further instance of the unsettled state of public affairs during this period, I may mention the case of Fujiwara-Arimitsu, a man of great eminence, who, having

---

* Named "Onesugni-uji-nori."

† This minister was named Onesugni-Norisané, and is said to have been a very popular man, and a great patron of letters. He founded a celebrated college, which was named the Ashikaga-gakko.

committed a crime, as a means of escaping punishment allied himself with others, and invaded the imperial palace with 300 men, and carried off the imperial insignia. The imperial troops pursued him, vanquished him, and put him and his two chief associates to death. A remnant of the rebel force escaped to Yoshino with the imperial symbols, and there attempted *une résistance suprême*, taking for their chief a prince of the blood, Tadeyoshi. One of the vassals of the deceased Akamatsu-Mitsusuké, hoping to reinstate, so to speak, the memory of his master by rendering a signal service to the government, went to Yoshino, slew Prince Tadeyoshi, recovered the imperial symbols, and carried them back to Kioto. As a reward to the family, the emperor commanded the Shogun to bestow the lands of Mitsusuké upon his nephew Musunori, and thus continue the forfeited domains in the Akamatsu family.

The emperor Go-Hanazono was succeeded, 1465 A.D., by Go-Tsuchi-Mikado, who reigned till the year 1500. His reign was made memorable by a series of terrible contests between subjects, which lasted for several years, and of which the capital itself, Kioto, was the scene. This extraordinary war appears to have arisen out of a miserable petty jealousy, the origin and development of which it is difficult for me to trace. The first incident which I can connect with it is the non-acceptance by the Shogun in the year 1467 of an entertainment offered him by his first minister, Hatekeyawa-Masanaga. It was usual for the Shogun to accept such an entertainment annually, in the first month of the year, and his refusal of Masanaga's, coupled with his acceptance of the invitation from one Yamana-Michi-Toyo, gave great offence. Among those who were most offended was another minister of the Shogun, named Hasokawa-Katsumoto. While the ill-feeling existed, Michi-Toyo visited the Shogun's palace, and obtained from him an instruction to Katsumoto to rescind an order of his, by allowing one Yoshinari to return to his home. Instead of obeying the Shogun's command, Katsumoto said, "I will go to the palace and answer the Shogun myself"; but instead of doing so, he gathered together troops to defend his house, and was there joined by the first minister, Masanaga. Meantime Michi-Toyo in like manner got troops together to defend the Shogun's palace from attack. The original quarrel having lain apparently between the first minister, Masanaga, and Yoshinari, the Shogun gave the singular order that these two alone, with their respective soldiers, should fight the matter out unaided by others. Yoshinari, at least, was content with this, and soon fell with his troops upon those of Masanaga, being secretly aided by Michi-Toyo. He was victorious in the fight, and took possession in Kioto of the principal residence of his enemy. Thereupon the people derided Katsumoto for not having assisted Masanaga, and attributed his abstention to fear. In consequence of these reproaches he shut himself up in his house, which was on the western side of the Shogun's palace; that of Michi-Toyo being on its eastern side. The Shogun, finding himself between these two fiery foes, did his best to reconcile them, but in vain. Katsumoto raised troops in the provinces of Setsu, Tango, Idsumi, Awaji, Awa, Sanuki, Tosa, Bichu, and Mikawa, which were then under his sway; and to these were added forces raised by Masanaga and other friends, the aggregate army of Katsumoto amounting to 160,000 men. Michi-Toyo raised troops in the provinces of Tajima, Inaba, Harima, Hoki, Iwami, Bizen, and Mimasaka, to which were joined the forces of Yoshinari and of other friendly personages, bringing the whole number up to 110,000 men.

These two large armies entered Kioto, frightening the poor citizens out of their wits, and forcing them to flee in all directions to escape the inevitable calamities of a war carried on within a peculiarly perishable city. The Shogun, Yoshimasa, issued a proclamation declaring that he would regard as his enemy him who should begin the fight. This did not, however, deter Katsumoto from attacking an enemy's house in front of the Shogun's palace, and carrying it. Katsumoto also obtained flags of the Shogun from the palace, and hoisted them over his own gates, and invited to his house Yoshimi, the younger brother and heir of the Shogun. This induced Michi-Toyo to attack Katsumoto, but without success. The grand dignitaries of the court, fearing like commoner people for their lives, fled from the city in different directions; and from this time forward Kioto became the scene of continual struggles, in which for a long time the troops of Katsumoto were usually victorious. On one occasion the army of Michi-Toyo set fire to the house of one Ishiki-Masa-Uji, and, as the wind was strong, 30,000 houses were burnt down. At about the same time the army of Michi-Toyo was reinforced by the troops of Nagato and Suwo, and thenceforward was continually successful.

It may readily be supposed that neither the Mikado nor the Shogun, nor their households, wholly escaped the influences of a war like this, carried on in the city in which both resided, and under the very walls of the palaces to which they were confined. Suspecting that his enemies were in communication with the Shogun's officers, Katsumoto compelled the Shogun to dismiss some of them; these, getting angry, declared that the Shogun himself was in favour of Michi-Toyo, smiling when his troops gained successes, and frowning if the fortune of war turned the other way. The only result of their attempted treachery was that Katsumoto put them all to death. Soon afterwards, Michi-Toyo made an unsuccessful endeavour to obtain possession of the person of the Mikado, in consequence of which both the Mikado and the ex-Mikado were brought by Katsumoto to the palace of the Shogun. Bad as matters were, they were made worse by circumstances (with the details of which I will not trouble the reader) which had the effect of bringing the Shogun Yoshimasa and his brother Yoshimi into the opposite camps, the latter being with Michi-Toyo and the former with Katsumoto. From this time the war was carried on as between the two brothers, and it continued for seven years, not having ceased when Katsumoto and Michi-Toyo both died, within a month or two of each other.

Yoshimasa, although embroiled, as we have seen, in frightful disturbances, is said to have been a "*grand amateur de plaisirs.*" It was he who introduced the art of ceremonial tea-making and tea-drinking, to which I shall have frequent occasion to refer hereafter. He also established the beautiful villa and gardens of Higashi-yama, which exist until to-day, and where he formed a fine collection of pictures and antiquities. Unfortunately he spent a good deal too much money, and caused the people to suffer in consequence. He was succeeded in the Shogunate by the son of his brother Yoshimi, named Yoshitané. In this reign (that of Go-Tsuchi-Mikado), notwithstanding its wars and tumults, the art of painting made great progress, as we shall note elsewhere. Suffice it here to remark that the celebrated families of Tosa and Kano, which have produced generations of celebrated artists, date from this period of the Ashikaga Shoguns.

In the year 1526 A.D., the emperor Go-Kashiwabara succeeded to the throne, but sat upon it only for a single year. The Shogun Yoshitané had previously been confined by Hosokawa-Masamoto, who had placed the nephew of Yoshitané in the uncle's high office. Yoshitané now escaped, and Masamoto was assassinated, Yoshitané again assuming the Shogunate. He was soon afterwards again deposed. The troubles of this reign were continued into the next—that of Go-Nara-Tenno, which lasted thirty years. Kioto was again the scene of grave disturbances, and the garrison and battle-field of hostile armies, raised by dissatisfied Shoguns and ministers, and by their friends and vassals. To add to the troubles and horrors of the time, the Portuguese arrived in the isle of Také in Satsuma, and taught these warring Japanese the use of firearms. In the following reign they added the use of imported cannon.

The reign of the emperor Oki-Machi, who came to the throne in the year 1558, and continued upon it for nearly thirty years, was as disturbed as that of his predecessor. During this reign an end was put to the power of the Ashikagas, both the emperor and the Ashikaga Shogun himself having summoned to their aid in quelling the disturbances of the capital and of the country a General Nobunaga, who afterwards became one of the most renowned men of Japanese history, and who changed the whole course of that history onward from his day to ours. The great fame of Nobunaga may be said to date from the second year of Oki-Machi's reign, viz. 1560 A.D. It will be obvious to the reader, from what has already been recorded in this chapter, that the great military domination over the whole country which the first of the Ashikaga Shoguns, Taka-Uji, had established, had gradually dwindled away, and that the Shoguns were fast becoming almost as powerless to govern the country in tranquillity as were the Mikados. The influence of the Shogun was, in fact, insignificant, and the lords of several provinces refused to recognise his authority, at least within their own domains.* The great families each maintained its own army, and rivalled their neighbours in military power, some having almost annual wars, and their generals occasionally achieving great military distinction. This being the state of things, one Imagawa Yoshimoto had taken the three provinces of Suruga, Totomi, and Mikawa, and now desired to take that of Owari. For this purpose he led an army of forty-five thousand men into that fruitful province, to attack the troops of the Ota family,† at the head of which was Nobunaga. He, on learning the news of Yoshimoto's advance from the keepers of the castles of Wasitsu and Maruné, resolved to attempt their rescue, and before starting gave a banquet to his retainers, where he is said to have exhibited great cheeriness, and to have danced, saying, "Men live for fifty years, which pass like a dream: we are born once, and it is our fate once to die." At the break of day he put spur to his horse, and went forth alone, or with only about ten men

---

* The following examples of this are cited in one of the Japanese histories: The family of Ota, in the province of Owari; that of Imagawa, in Totomi; that of Hojo, in Sagami; of Takeda, in Kai; of Uesagui, in Echigo; of Amako, in Idzumo; of Mori, in Aki; those of Ashina, Mogami, and Date, in Mutsu and Dewa; of Chosokabe, in the island of Shikoku; and of Shimadzu, of Otomo and of Riuzoji, in the island of Kiushiu.

† See last footnote.

following him; but when he reached Atsuta (where the sacred sword is enshrined, and which we shall visit hereafter), he was joined by about a thousand men. Proceeding onward, he gathered troops from the castles on his route till his numbers amounted to four thousand. Yoshimoto, who had pitched his camp at Okehasawa, and had routed the Owari forces from these castles, and set them on fire, in the flush of his success neglected to guard his camp, whereupon Nobunaga—who had given conspicuous proofs of personal prowess on his way thither—concealed his flags and drums, and fell upon Yoshimoto's army during a storm of thunder and rain, putting them to the rout, Yoshimoto himself being beheaded by one Mori Hidetaka. This great victory, which was gained in the year 1560 A.D., made the name of Nobunaga famous throughout Japan.

During these early years of this reign of Oki-Machi the Shogun Yoshiteru was assassinated, and his younger brother Yoshiaki, who should have succeeded him, was forced to flee to the province of Omi, another of the Ashikagas, Yoshihidé, being proclaimed Shogun. When the fame of Nobunaga became great, the emperor committed to him the task of pacificating the country. At the same time the exiled Yoshiaki besought Nobunaga to restore to him the Shogunate. Nobunaga accepted this double service, and, taking Yoshiaki with him, marched with a powerful army upon Kioto. Putting to flight all those who sought to resist him, he entered the capital, driving the false Shogun Yoshihidé out of it, and setting up Yoshiaki in his place. This occurred in the year 1568.

Two years later we find Ota Nobunaga in Echizen, attacking Asakura Yoshikagé, and capturing the castles of Tetsutsu and Kanasaki, then returning to Omi to put down one Nagamasa, who had risen there in support of Yoshikagé. When Nobunaga besieged the castle of Yokoyama in Omi, Yoshikagé sent help to Nagamasa, who encamped with twenty thousand men on the Mount of Oyori in Omi. In the battle which then ensued Nobunaga had under him a general, Tokugawa Iyéyasu, who subsequently became the founder of that so-called Tokugawa dynasty of Shoguns and Tycoons, which lasted, and was omnipotent in Japan, from the year 1600 down to our own time, that is to say, to the overthrow of the last Tokugawa Tycoon in 1868. We shall have occasion to take further notice of this great general hereafter. At this battle of Anagawa, fought in 1570, the generalship of Nobunaga appears to have been the most remarkable. Observing an unusual movement of torchlights one night in the camp on Mount Oyori, Nobunaga inferred that the enemy was arranging a daybreak attack, and gave orders for an immediate assault upon him before his dispositions were completed. The battle went untowardly at first for Nobunaga's army, the columns of both Iyéyasu and another general (Nobuteru) being defeated; but spirited and well-devised flank attacks being ordered both by Nobunaga and Iyéyasu, the day became theirs.

Unfortunately for himself and for his house, the new Shogun Yoshiaki, whom Nobunaga had placed in the seat of eminence, after a few years (about six, I think) became jealous of the great power of Nobunaga, forgot the services which the general had rendered him, and promoted an attempt to remove him by assassination. Nobunaga discovered the plot, and deposed the ingrate, in the year 1573. Thus ended the domination of the Ashikagas; and when one recalls the means by which it was established by Taka-Uji, and remembers the frequent and terrible intestine wars which prevailed throughout it, it is with a sense of satisfaction that one witnesses its overthrow. For more than two hundred years the high office of the Shogunate—the most exalted of all in the state save that of the Mikadoate—had been in possession of this Ashikaga family; from them it now for ever passed away. Established by the treachery of its founder, the Ashikaga rule was abolished because of the treachery of its last representative. The period covered by it was one of almost incessant civil wars, and of deplorable loss and suffering to the whole country. The two capitals,

Kioto and Kamakura, were perpetually assailed with storms of battle, and although the end had not yet come, the downfall of this pernicious family was the blest beginning of the end.*

* "So utterly demoralised is the national, political, and social life of this period believed to have been, that the Japanese people make it the limbo of all vanities. Dramatists and romancers use it as the convenient ground wherein to locate every novel or play the plot of which violates all present probability. The chosen time of the bulk of Japanese dramas and novels written during the last century or two is that of the late Ashikagas. The satirist or writer aiming at contemporary folly, or at blunders and oppressions of the government, yet wishing to avoid punishment and elude the censor, clothes his character in the garb and manners of this period. It is the potter's field where all the outcasts and Judases of moralists are buried. By common consent, it has become the limbo of play-wright and romancer, and the scape-goat of chronology."—*Griffis.*

TENTO: HEAVENLY LANTERN.

CHAPTER XI.

NOBUNAGA AND HIDEYOSHI.

Ota Nobunaga the son of a warrior—He adopts his father's profession—Fuller display of his character—Return of the pursuits and pleasures of peace—Public acts of Nobunaga—He is made "Great Minister of the Right"—Hideyoshi, afterwards the Taiko—Originally a *betto*, or groom—Was patronised by Nobunaga—He becomes a great general—Takes rank with Iyéyasu—The three greatest generals of Japan—Buddhists and Christians—Nobunaga protects Christianity and attacks Buddhism—Padre Organtin's interview with Nobunaga—The Jesuit church, or "Temple of the Southern Savages"—Persecution of the Buddhists—Luxurious priests—Splendid rituals and unseemly lives—The gorgeous temples of Mount Hiyei destroyed—Butchery and conflagration—Fortified temple of the Shin Buddhists in Osaka—Its siege and ultimate surrender—Its priests scattered—Nobunaga, attacked by rebels, slays himself—The "Later Hojo" of Odawara—Hideyoshi appoints a child-successor to Nobunaga—Himself takes the real power—Defeat of Shibata—The "Seven Spearmen of Sedsagataké"—Romantic deaths—Shibata slays his wife by her desire—Fighting in the Kuanto—The Later Hojo overthrown—Other rebels subdued—Hideyoshi declares war against Korea—Invades Korea and threatens China—Christians burnt at Nagasaki—The Jesuit priesthood—Ambition of Hideyoshi—He becomes the Taiko—His character reviewed—Anecdotes concerning him.

In the preceding chapter, in tracing the Ashikaga domination to its downfall, I have had to notice the rise of their destroyer, Ota Nobunaga. The son of a warrior who in the troubled times of the Ashikaga Shoguns had acquired provinces by means of his sword, Nobunaga took up the father's pursuit, and conquered for himself several important provinces in the south. We have already seen indicated both the spirit in which he lived, and the ability with which he raised and commanded troops. Both emperor and Shogun sought his masterly aid, and when the Shogun turned treacherous he felt no scruple in deposing him, or in leaving the Shogunate itself vacant as long as he lived, himself governing in the name of the emperor. Thus far, however, we have acquired but an imperfect representation of the man; his character will more fully appear in what follows.

From the time of his triumphal entrance into Kioto, Nobunaga distinguished himself by numerous useful acts, among which a native historian cites the reconstruction of the imperial palace (a matter of moment in a country where the Mikado bore a sacred character), the recall of those whom the civil wars had forced into exile, the repair of the roads and thoroughfares, the subjection of the troublesome Buddhist clergy (who had attained enormous wealth and influence, and often employed both for other than church purposes), and the pacification of the country. After years of commotion and bloodshed, the capital now enjoyed again the pursuits and pleasures of peace. In return for his great services the emperor made Nobunaga *Udaijin*, or "Great Minister of the Right."

Thus far it has not been necessary to make particular mention of one who must now take a place of much eminence in this historic summary; I refer to the great general Hideyoshi, better known in Japanese records as the Taiko, or Taiko-Sama. This renowned man owed nothing to birth or ancestry, being the son of a poor peasant. "While a mere boy he became a *betto*, or groom, to Nobunaga, who noticed the boy's monkey face and restless eyes, and encouraged him to become a soldier, which he did" (Griffis). In the wars in which Nobunaga was engaged prior to the overthrow of the Ashikagas, Hideyoshi had played a prominent part as a general, and divided with Iyéyasu the fame of ranking next to Nobunaga in military skill and promise of power. At the time of Nobunaga's assassination (of which I must presently speak) in 1582, Hideyoshi had been despatched to the west country to subjugate Mori, the prince of Choshiu, who had refused to recognise the new order of things as established by Nobunaga. At this point, then, we have before us three great and successful generals, Nobunaga, Hideyoshi, and Iyéyasu, all of whom were serving the emperor directly, without the intervention of a Shogun, and all of whom in turn became in succession, and in the order in which I have just arranged them, the virtual rulers of the country.

But although these three men—apparently three of the greatest in many respects that Japan ever produced—appear on the scene with swords in their hands, and as warriors of the first order, it was upon the religious history of the country that they stamped their will and temper most effectually. It is in other chapters that I trace in outline the rise and progress of Buddhism and of Christianity in Japan, but here, in outlining the history of the latter half of the sixteenth century, I must state a few facts connected with the momentous influences brought to bear upon both these religions by the successors of the Ashikagas. Buddhism had at this time been for many centuries the most favoured religion of the court and nobles, and had so prospered that it had risen far above that state of humility and unworldliness which all advocates of all religions are willing to accept in the beginning. It had indeed so prospered that its most influential priests had come first to covet, then to handle, and at length to wield those worldly weapons of the state which many religious dignitaries have been willing to employ when they have had a safe opportunity. We have in an earlier part of this book seen the boldness with which more than once the priests of Hiyei-san marched with troops from their mountain-monastery into Kioto to menace the emperor and coerce his ministers. Great and wealthy and proud, indeed, were the Buddhist *bozus* of Japan when the last of the Ashikagas was deposed by Nobunaga. And meantime, in the middle of this sixteenth century, not only had Christianity made its appearance in the southern and western parts of the country, but the great Jesuit missionary Xavier had landed at Kagoshima, found his way to Kioto, and preached, though with no visible success, the religion of the Virgin in the streets of the capital.

Nobunaga, in the day of his power, took the Christian

religion, in the form of Roman Catholicism, under his protection. In a Japanese work * is given the following account of the origin of this influential patronage. One of the Roman Catholic missionaries, Padre Organtin, had an interview with Nobunaga. Organtin was asked why he had come to Japan, and replied that he had come to spread his religion. He was told that he could not be allowed at once to preach it there, but would be further informed later on. Nobunaga then took counsel with his retainers as to whether he should allow Christianity to be preached or not. One of these strongly advised him not to do so, on the ground that there were already enough religions in the country. But Nobunaga replied that Buddhism had been introduced from abroad, and had done good in the country, and he therefore did not see why Christianity should not be granted a trial. Organtin was consequently allowed to erect a church, and to send for others of his order, who when they came were found to be like him in appearance. "Their plan of action was to tend the sick and relieve the poor, and so prepare the way for the reception of Christianity, and then to convert every one, *and make the sixty-six provinces of Japan subject to Portugal.*" †

This account shows that it was from no regard for Christianity, as Christianity, that Nobunaga permitted the Jesuit missionaries to pursue their calling in Japan; indeed he caused the Christian church that was built to be designated the Temple of the Southern Savages. There is even on record evidence which shows that after the new religion had made considerable progress under his protection, the suspicion that it was to be made an instrument for depriving the country of its independence induced him to

---

* The *Saikoku Kirishitan Bateren Jitsu Roku*, or "True Record of Christian Pastors in Kiushiu." I avail myself of the translation of J. H. Gubbins, Esq., of H.B.M. Consular Service in Japan.

† I have quoted and italicised these words because they furnish the clue to the tremendous persecution which befell the Christian converts subsequently. It must be remembered that the Buddhists had already made it clear that the promoters of an alien religion were not averse to the employment of it for quite other than religious objects.

meditate its overthrow. "Nobunaga," says the *Ibuki Mogusa*, "now began to regret his previous policy in permitting the introduction of Christianity. He accordingly assembled his retainers, and said to them : 'The conduct of these missionaries in persuading people to join them by giving money does not please me. It must be, I think, that they harbour the design of seizing the country. How would it be, think you, if we were to demolish Nambanji (the Temple of the Southern Savages)?' To this Meyéda Tokuzenin replied: 'It is now too late to demolish the temple of Nambanji. To endeavour to arrest the power of this religion now is like trying to arrest the current of the ocean. Nobles both great and small have become adherents of it. If you would exterminate the religion now there is fear lest disturbances be created even amongst your own retainers. I am therefore of opinion that you should abandon your intention of destroying Nambanji.' Nobunaga in consequence regretted exceedingly his previous action with regard to the Christian religion, and set about thinking how he could root it out." *

This change in the feelings of Nobunaga must have come late, and have had but little effect upon his public policy ; for it is certain that he greatly fostered the growth of the Christian religion in Japan, and enabled it to spread throughout the southern and western provinces. The province of Bungo became its headquarters, the prince of Bungo being himself a convert, but it also made its way throughout Kiushiu, crossed the Straits of Shimonoséki northwards, and found a centre at Yamaguchi in Nagato, and spread eastwards to Kioto and Sakai, and to other places near the centre of the empire. Nobunaga even established a Christian church in a castled town which he himself built in Omi. In a short time the Roman Catholic religion, under his patronage, numbered a hundred and fifty thousand proselytes.

Nobunaga, while thus extending in the first place toleration, and afterwards encouragement, to the Roman Catholic religion, was assuming a very different attitude towards the

---

* Translation of J. H. Gubbins, Esq.

Buddhist faith and its ministers. Moved, doubtless, by the wealth, the armed strength, the bold interferences of the Buddhist priesthood with secular affairs, and the alarming habit which they had acquired of "settling questions of dogma with their co-religionists by the arbitrament of the sword," Nobunaga resolved to reduce their pride and power to the utmost of his ability. He appears to have had no scruples of conscience to overcome in pursuing this object, for he is said to have "laughed at the worship of the gods, convinced that the bonzes (*bozus*) were impostors, abusing the simplicity of the people, and screening their own debauches under the name of religion."* Nor were these views without some basis in the luxurious and unseemly lives of the priests in his day, if we may believe the accounts that have come down to us. Mr. Griffis, who has studied the records of the period, after referring to the vast warlike monastery in Mount Hiyei, near Lake Biwa, the grounds of which, "adorned and beautified with the rarest art of the native landscape gardener, inclosed thirteen valleys and over five hundred temples, shrines, and priestly dwellings," tells us that the thousands of monks who were there congregated "chanted before gorgeous altars, celebrated their splendid ritual, revelled in luxury and licentiousness, drank their *saké*, ate the forbidden viands, and dallied with their concubines, or hatched plots to light or fan the flames of feudal war, so as to make the quarrels of the clans and chiefs redound to their aggrandisement. They trusted profoundly to their professedly sacred character to shield them from all danger." Moreover, "The bonzes (*bozus*) continually foiled his schemes, and he saw that, even if war between the clans ceased, the existence of these monasteries would jeopard the national peace. He resolved to destroy them." This resolution he carried out, in spite of the reluctance, and even of the remonstrances, of his generals and friends. Spending, and often hazarding, his own life in the cause of his sovereign, and for the purpose of tranquillising the realm, he stoutly

---

* Dr. Walter Dixon, in 'History of the Church.'

refused to spare those who had systematically opposed him, and aided his enemies. He reminded his supporters of the political crimes, the warlike antagonisms, and the sensual indulgences of the Buddhist priests; declared that their continued existence was full of peril to the state, and commanded that Hieyei-san should be burnt to the ground, and its priests put without exception to the sword. "The generals, incited by the speech of their commander, agreed. On the next day an awful scene of butchery and conflagration ensued. The soldiers set fire to the great shrines and temples, and while the stately edifices were in flames plied sword, lance, and arrow. None were permitted to escape. Without discrimination of age or sex, the toothless dotard, abbot, and bonze, maid-servant and concubine, and children, were speared and cut down without mercy."

In the chapter on Buddhism I have given an account of the doctrines of the Shin Buddhists, and in a later chapter shall describe the splendid entertainment which we received in Kioto from the heads of this religious body. One of the severest of the blows which Nobunaga struck fell upon this sect, which at that time possessed "an immense fortified temple and monastery," called Honganji, in Osaka. According to Mr. Griffis, whose account I will again quote, this establishment formed the retreat and hiding-place of Nobunaga's enemies. "The bonzes themselves were his most bitter haters, because he had so encouraged the Jesuits. They had taken the side of his enemies for over twelve years. At last, when some of his best captains had been killed by 'grass-rebels,' or ambuscaders, who fled into the monastery, he laid siege to it in earnest, with the intention of serving the inmates as he did those of Hiyei-san. Within the enceinte, crowded in five connecting fortresses, were thousands of women and children, besides the warriors and priests. Another frightful massacre seemed imminent. The place was so surrounded that every attempt of the garrison to escape was cut off. On an intensely dark night, under cover of a storm then raging, several thousands of the people, of all sexes and ages, attempted to escape from one of the forts. They were overtaken and slaughtered. The main garrison shortly afterwards learned the fate of their late comrades by seeing a junk, despatched by the victors, laden with human ears and noses, approach the castle with its hideous cargo. Another outpost of the castle was surrendered. In the second month of the siege, a sortie in force was repelled by showers of arrows and matchlock balls; but in the fighting Nobunaga's best officers were slain. The besieging army finally occupied three of the five in the network of fortresses. Thousands (twenty thousand) of the garrison had been killed by arrow and ball, or had perished in the flames, and the horrible stench of burning flesh filled the air for miles. The fate of the main body within the walls was soon to be decided. The Mikado, grieving over the destruction of so much life, sent three court nobles and a priest of another sect to persuade the garrison to yield. A conference of the abbot and elders was called, and a surrender decided upon. The castle was turned over to Nobunaga, and from that day until the present has remained in the hands of the government. Pardon was granted to the survivors, and the bonzes scattered to the other monasteries of their sect. To this day," concludes our author, "the great sects in Japan have never fully recovered from the blows dealt by Nobunaga. Subsequently rulers were obliged to lay violent hands upon the strongholds of ecclesiastical power that threatened so frequently to disturb the peace of the country; but they were able to do it with comparative ease, because Nobunaga had begun the work with such unscrupulous vigour and thoroughness."

The death of Nobunaga was brought about in a manner that illustrates the dangers of military ascendency. On this occasion, as on many former ones, the attainment of power in Japan by the force of arms was followed by the conspiracy of others to effect its transfer. One of Nobunaga's generals, named Akechi-Mitsuhide, moved by ambition, and by what he chose to deem an affront of his chief, set on foot a conspiracy against him, obtained the support of other officers, and surrounded with troops the temple in which he was residing. Nobunaga, on being attacked and struck by an arrow, deemed escape impossible, and therefore set fire to the temple, and slew himself. His son Nobutada shared the father's fate.

At the time of his death Nobunaga was preparing to go to the west to support Hideyoshi, who was engaged with Mori, the prince of Choshiu, as previously stated. On learning of the assassination of his chief, Hideyoshi came to an understanding with Choshiu, and hastened back to Kioto to attack the rebel and assassin Akechi, whom he defeated and slew. The country was not even then in full possession of that tranquillity which Nobunaga had sought for it, after his own stormful fashion; there was fighting in Kiushiu, and Iyéyasu was engaged in the Kuanto with the "Later Hojo" at Odawara. For during the early part of this sixteenth century a family known by this designation had begun to exhibit pretensions in the Kuanto, and in 1524 Hojo Ujitsuna attacked and carried the castle of Yedo, which remained in the possession of these Later Hojo for many years afterwards. The chief seat of the family was, however, at Odawara, near the shore of the Sea of Sagami.

Moreover, the eldest son of Nobunaga being dead, and having left a son, Hideyoshi occasioned new contentions and fresh hostilities by appointing this child-grandson nominal successor to the place and power of Nobunaga, himself retaining the real authority. The third son of Nobunaga, named Nobutaka, resisted this arrangement, being supported (and perhaps started) in his resistance by Shibata-Katuiye, one of Nobunaga's generals, who had married Nobunaga's sister. Hideyoshi was already in the province of Isé, with an army of seventy thousand men, engaged with one Kadsumasa, at Nagasima, when he heard of Shibata's approach. Leaving his principal generals at Nagasima, he took part of his forces and pushed forward to meet Shibata. Before any engagement took place, Nobutaka raised a separate force, and proceeded to the aid of Kadsumasa and Shibata, thus forcing Hideyoshi to change his plans. He did change them, so far as to fall upon Nobutaka, and drive him backward to Ogaki in Mino. Meanwhile, at a place called Sedsagataké, some of Hideyoshi's forces were suddenly fallen upon and wholly defeated. The victors were unwise enough to remain upon the field, learning which, Hideyoshi took fifteen thousand men, and fell upon them with such impetuosity and fierceness, and so much generalship withal, that they were utterly routed. In this battle, known as that of Sedsagataké, seven warriors armed with spears distinguished themselves so greatly that they became renowned thenceforward in Japanese history as "the Seven Spearmen of Sedsagataké." * When Shibata heard of the defeat of his friends, he fled to Hokusho in Yechizen, whither Hideyoshi pursued him, and where he besieged him. Seeing no way of escape, says the native historian, he dined with his friends, and then killed his wife, children, and retainers, and set fire to his castle. His friends followed his example, committing suicide. Another account says that after the parting banquet Shibata gave his wife permission to leave, and to marry again; but she (Nobunaga's sister, be it remembered) thanked him with tears, but declared she would die with her lord, and after composing a verse of poetry besought him to kill her, and received from him, as his best blessing, her deathblow.† Another sad incident of these struggles, by which the death of Nobunaga was followed, is recorded in the words, "Gifu was attacked and taken by Nobuwo, who compelled Nobutaka to kill himself," observing that Nobuwo was the second, and Nobutaka the third, son of Nobunaga, and the two, therefore, brothers!

Hideyoshi had other armed enemies to subdue. I have already mentioned that Iyéyasu was engaged, at the time of

---

* Their names are Kato Kiyomasa, Fukusima Masanore, Kato Kosiyakiro, Hirano Nagayasu, Wakisaka Yasuharu, Kasuya Takenori, and Katakiri Katsumoto, of some of whom we shall hear again.

† "Like true Stoics, Shibata and his companions put all the women and children to the death they welcomed, and for which they gave thanks; and then, with due decorum and ceremony, opening their own bodies by *hara-kiri*, they died as brave Japanese ever love to die, by their own hands, and not by those of an enemy."—*Griffis*.

Nobunaga's death, in fighting the Later Hojo of Odawara in the Kuanto. Several years later, in 1590, these Hojo were still unsubdued, and Hideyoshi had to raise his army to the enormous number of two hundred and fifty thousand men in order to make a fresh and more determined effort to put them down. After capturing by his generals castles held by the enemy in the provinces of Masashi, Kodzuke, Kadzusa, Shimosa, and Awa, he was compelled to subject the castle of Odawara itself to a seven months' siege, and then the capitulation resulted rather from dissensions among the besieged than from external stress. By this capitulation the latest effort of the Later Hojo family to gain the government of the Kuanto was completely frustrated. The great islands of Shikoku and Kiushiu, which have always been important integral parts of the country, also had to be subdued by Hideyoshi. At length, after ten years of warfare, the whole country became subject to his authority, and he rewarded his generals by parcelling out much of the land into fiefs under titles granted in his own name without reference to the sovereign.

There remaining nothing and no one to be conquered in Japan, and having a vast army and many warlike generals at his disposal, Hideyoshi turned his thoughts towards foreign countries in search of objects of conquest. In a later chapter will be found the story of his sitting in front of a hillside temple in Kioto, mourning the death of his child, and there conceiving the intention of subduing Korea, the conquest of which had been the dream of his life; and in a separate chapter will be found the story of its attempted conquest, and of the menace to which China also was subjected by him. It is sufficient to say here that as a pretext for disturbing the relations with Korea he sent an ambassador to the king, requesting him to furnish guides to conduct an expedition against China. The king refusing to do this, Hideyoshi declared war, and followed this up by hostile expeditions so effectually that, notwithstanding the assistance of China, the capital of Korea was captured, and two of the royal princes were made prisoners. Hideyoshi next prepared to invade China, but the emperor wished to make peace, and induced Hideyoshi to withdraw his troops. Subsequently, deeming a letter from that monarch insufficiently humble, he reorganised a new expedition against him. His troops were on the point of entering China when Hideyoshi died.

The policy pursued by Hideyoshi with regard to Christianity and Buddhism differed greatly from that of Nobunaga. At first, indeed, he seemed to favour the Roman Catholics, and continued the destruction of Buddhist monasteries. But there is strong reason for believing that he never was really favourable to Christianity, that during the lifetime of Nobunaga he remonstrated against it, and that when, after his assumption of the chief power, he appeared to favour it, he was only waiting to secure himself before exhibiting his hostility. In 1588, when Go-Yosei had succeeded Oki-Machi on the throne, Nobunaga issued a decree ordering the missionaries to assemble at Hirado, and prepare to leave Japan. They obeyed; but the decree not being followed by strong measures, they dispersed again, and placed themselves under the protection of the nobles who had become converts. The territories of these princes offered safe asylums, and in scattered districts the proselytising work was carried on in disregard of the edict. "Christianity was at its most flourishing stage during the first years of Hideyoshi's administration. We can discern the existence at this date of a strong Christian party in the country, though the turning-point had been reached, and the tide of progress was on the ebb. It is to this influence probably, coupled with the fact that his many warlike expeditions left him little leisure to devote to religious questions, that we must attribute the slight relaxation observable in his policy towards Christianity at this time" (Gubbins). Five years after the edict against the Roman Catholics, in 1593, nine missionaries, Franciscans and Jesuits, were arrested in Kioto and Osaka, sent to Nagasaki, and there burnt. Long before this time, however, the Jesuit missionaries and their converts, instead of commending their religion by the preaching of the gospel, by furnishing examples of godliness and charity in their own lives, and by the pure love of truth and virtue, had sought to spread their faith by the evil arts of corruption, abuse, and persecution. With the doubloons of Spain and Portugal, furnished as "alms," influence and support were purchased, the priests of the existing religions were insulted and attacked, their idols destroyed, their shrines and temples burnt. The people were in many places commanded to become Roman Catholics by their converted lords, the alternative being banishment and loss of all they possessed. "The bonzes were exiled or killed; and fire and sword, as well as preaching, were employed as instruments of conversion" (Griffis). With the measure they themselves thus meted, it was measured to them again, when the flames of Nagasaki were kindled; and if Hideyoshi began to beat them with whips, there came after him others who chastised them with scorpions, as we shall mournfully see hereafter.

Hideyoshi is remembered not only by his generalship, his invasion of the Korea, and his edict against the Roman Catholics, but also by his improvements of the cities of Kioto and Osaka, and by other works of civic and national usefulness. He will reappear in later portions of this work in connection with many such deserving labours. It was against difficulties that he had to struggle both in the attainment and in the exercise of power; for he was of birth so obscure that he could not himself trace his parentage, although when he had obtained eminence he asserted that he was of the Taira house, and sought to have himself designated Sei-i-tai Shogun. This title had, however, been hereditary in the Minamoto family, and could not be accorded to him. He then attempted to obtain the title of Kampaku; but this belonged to the house of Fujiwara. Fearing, however, to irritate him too much, the emperor bestowed it upon him, and also gave him the family name of Toyotomi. Years before his death he nominally surrendered his functions to his adopted son, Hidetsugu; but he in reality continued in the exercise of power until his death, under the name of

Taiko. "In his youth he had wedded a peasant girl; but as he rose step by step to eminence, he kept on marrying until he had a number equal to that of the polygamous English king Henry VIII.; but, unlike that monarch, he enjoyed them all at once, and caused none of them to lose her head" (Griffis).

The incidents of the invasion of Korea furnish us with many very instructive glimpses of the character of Hideyoshi. On one occasion the king of Korea sent him a letter of congratulation, accompanied by "some of the poor productions of our country, which we beg you will refrain from laughing at immediately," these presents consisting of horses, falcons, saddles, harness, cloths, skins, etc. Hideyoshi suggested that the ambassador should return to Korea without waiting for an answer; but, not unnaturally, they preferred to wait for one. When they got it, it was found to be one which they could not possibly receive. After many emendations it was brought to the following form, which can hardly be considered remarkable for either modesty or courtesy :*
"This empire was of late years brought to ruin by internal dissensions which allowed no opportunity for laying aside armour. This state of things roused me to indignation, and in a few years I restored peace to the country. I am the only remaining scion of a humble stock, but my mother once had a dream in which she saw the sun enter her bosom; after which she gave birth to me. There was then a soothsayer, who said, 'Wherever the sun shines, there will be no place which shall not be subject to him. It may not be doubted that one day his power will overspread the empire.' It has, therefore, been my boast to lose no favourable opportunity, and taking wings like a dragon I have subdued the east, chastised the west, punished the south, and smitten the north. Speedy and great success has attended my career, which has been like the rising sun illuminating the whole earth. When I reflect that the life of man is less than one hundred years, why should I spend my days in sorrow for

---

* The following translations are by Mr. W. G. Aston.

one thing only? I will assemble a mighty host, and, invading the country of the Great Ming, I will fill with the hoar-frost from my sword the whole sky over the four hundred provinces. Should I carry out this purpose, I hope that Korea will be my vanguard. Let her not fail to do so, for my friendship for your honourable country depends solely on your conduct when I lead my army against China."

The following is an account by Korean ambassadors of their reception by Hideyoshi: "The ambassadors were allowed to enter the palace gate borne in their palanquins. They were preceded the whole way by a band of music. They ascended into the hall, where they performed their obeisances. Hideyoshi is a mean and ignoble-looking man, his complexion is dark, and his features are wanting in distinction. But his eyeballs send out fire in flashes—enough to pierce one through. He sat upon a three-fold cushion, with his face to the south. He wore a gauze hat and a dark-coloured robe of state. His officers were ranged round him, each in his proper place. When the ambassadors were introduced and had taken their seats, the refreshments offered them were of the most frugal description. A tray was set before each on which was one dish containing steamed *mochi*, and *saké* of an inferior quality was handed round a few times in earthenware cups, and in a very unceremonious way. The civility of drinking to one another was not observed. After a short interval, Hideyoshi retired behind a curtain, but all his officers remained in their places. Soon after a man came out, dressed in ordinary clothes, with a baby in his arms, and strolled about the hall. This was no other than Hideyoshi himself, and every one present bowed down his head to the ground. Looking out between the pillars of the hall, Hideyoshi espied the Korean musicians. He commanded them to strike up all together as loud as they could, and was listening to their music when he was suddenly reminded that babies could despise ceremony as much as princes, and laughingly called for one of his attendants to take the child and to bring him a change of clothing. He seemed to do exactly as he pleased, and was as unconcerned as if nobody else were present. The ambassadors having made their obeisance, retired, and this audience was the only occasion on which they were admitted to Hideyoshi's presence."

BUDDHIST PRIEST.

CHAPTER XII.

IYÉYASU, THE FIRST TOKUGAWA SHOGUN.

The founder of the Tokugawa dynasty—His birth and native district—His castle in Suruga—He establishes himself in the Kuanto and founds Yedo—He becomes sole regent—Governs well, and is conspired against—A western army brought against him—The famous battle of Sekigahara—Iyéyasu's victory—Is created Shogun in 1603—Revolt of Hideyori, a son of the Taiko—Osaka attacked and its castle besieged—Peace concluded—Second revolt of Hideyori—Osaka again attacked and carried—The fate of Hideyori—The Tokugawa family firmly seated in the Shogunate—Multiplication of Jesuit missionaries—The edict of expulsion against them—Apprehensions in Japan of foreign conquest—Consequent persecution of the Christians—The extirpation of Roman Catholicism from Japan attempted—The Spanish Inquisition imitated—Crucifixion, strangling, drowning, and worse—Revival of learning—Iyéyasu takes education and literature under his care—He takes control of the mines—Peaceful relations with Korea renewed—Foreign commerce encouraged—Public roads and highways improved—Death of Iyéyasu—His " Legacy "—His feudal system of administration—Daimios, Samurai, Hatamoto, and Gokenin—Yedo and its castle—Origin of the famous Tokugawa temples of Shiba, Tokio—Story of Son-o the priest.

WE have already had occasion, more than once, to notice the important part played in the wars of Nobunaga and Hideyoshi by Tokugawa Iyéyasu. We have now to observe this great general more closely, and with good reason, for he it was who founded the Tokugawa dynasty, so to call it, of Shoguns and Tycoons. This dynasty gave two centuries and a half of peace to Japan, and fell but a few years since, in our own time, when a storm of internal and external forces raged in Japan, leaving behind a restored, a liberated, and a progressive empire, presided over by the legitimate sovereign.

Tokugawa Iyéyasu was born in 1542 at Okazaki, a town in the province of Mikawa, where his ancestors, belonging to the famous Minamoto family, had established themselves. Okazaki is on the main Tokaido road, about twenty miles eastward of the great city of Nagoya. It will be seen hereafter that Okazaki was one of our resting-places after resuming our inland journey at the last-named city. The province of Mikawa is separated from that of Suruga only by that of Totomi, and it was in Mikawa and Suruga that Iyéyasu first obtained possessions. In Suruga, at the town then known as Sumpu, but now as Shidzuoka, he built himself a castle, and this town has ever since remained intimately associated with the Tokugawas. We shall see presently that it was here that Iyéyasu spent the closing years of his life in the encouragement of art and literature; and later on, when we ourselves visit Shidzuoka, we shall find that it was hither that the last of the Tokugawa Tycoons retired, and it is here that he now resides. Sumpu is, however, on the western side of the Hakoné mountain range, and although this place became the most closely associated with the Tokugawas in their personal relations, it is the city of Tokio (formerly Yedo), the present eastern and principal capital of the empire, that expresses the dynastic greatness, so to speak, of this line of governing Shoguns. The temples of Shiba and of Wooyeno in Tokio, and the rich shrines of Nikko, eighty miles farther north, were the most splendid manifestations of the wealth and power of the Tokugawas, while the capital itself, Tokio, a city of a million of souls, is one vast monument of their greatness. Some of the finest temples of Shiba and Wooyeno were destroyed at the time of the revolution, but the city which Iyéyasu founded has become the centre of the modern empire, and will doubtless grow in wealth and beauty as the country advances along the path of constitutional freedom and good government. The manner in which Iyéyasu came to establish himself in the Kuanto as well as at Sumpu in Suruga was this: After the death of his father, he had gradually increased the family domains in Mikawa, and became very influential there. In Hideyoshi's time, however, he received from that general an order to surrender to the government his Mikawa properties, and some other, and accepted in exchange for them five of the eastern provinces, including that in which Yedo, now Tokio, stands. It appears that Hideyoshi suggested to Iyéyasu the merits of the great plain of Yedo as a site for the capital city of the Kuanto, and Iyéyasu had already commenced the building of it when Hideyoshi died. It may be well to remark here what has not before been stated, viz. that Hideyoshi and Iyéyasu at one time ranged their armies against each other, but Hideyoshi subsequently prevailed upon Iyéyasu to restore peace between them, and induced him to visit Kioto and make his submission to the emperor.

Before his own death, Hideyoshi caused his adopted son, Hidetsuga, whom he had nominated his successor, to be put to death, on the ground that he was *un libertin et un homme cruel*, and had subsequently nominated his own son, Hideyori, his successor. Hideyori being very young and inexperienced, however (but six years old, in fact), Hideyoshi in his will appointed a council of regency, composed of Tokugawa Iyéyasu and others. The others having died, Iyéyasu soon found himself the only regent, and so governed the country as to win increasing popularity from day to day. The result was, as usual, jealousy of his power, and a conspiracy to overthrow it. One of the former favourites of Hideyoshi set himself to work to bring about the old crime of assassination, persuading some of the most influential Daimios that it was the wish of Hideyori to have Iyéyasu put to death. This led to a strong combination against him—a combination that was doubtless strengthened by the apprehension that Iyéyasu contemplated setting Hideyori aside and taking to himself the governing power of the realm. Others again objected alike to Iyéyasu and to the son of Hideyoshi, viewing both as mere upstarts, without any real claim or just pretension to govern the country. Nor were the family of Nobunaga idle, some of them seeking to assert their claims to the executive government. To make the position of the country still more complex and dangerous, there was the army that had returned from Korea without employment, under leaders who had gained victories, and longed to achieve others. The result of all these complications was, after many hesitations, war—war between an eastern army led by Iyéyasu's generals, and a western army led by his enemies in league, including the partisans of Hideyori, and of the pretenders of Nobunaga's family.

The battle fought between these two armies, at a place called Sekigahara, in the year 1600, was one of the greatest and most decisive ever fought in Japan. Unfortunately the manuscript accounts which I have obtained of it so abound with names of persons and places, and run into so many details, that greater time and labour than I can devote to the matter are essential to a full and clear description of it. It may be well to state, however, that the site of it was an undulating plain, at the foot of a mountain range, through which plain runs the great high road, the Nakasendo, connecting the capitals of Kioto and Tokio by a northern route, just as the Tokaido connects them by a southern route. The intrusion of the Owari Bay into the southern coast of Japan forces the Tokaido so far northward at Nogoya, or rather at Miya, as to bring these two great thoroughfares within fifteen miles of each other, and Sekigahara is on the Nakasendo, near to this point of approach, and at a distance of about nine miles to the east of Lake Biwa. The castle of Ogaki was the stronghold of the western army, the castle of Gifu that of the eastern. Both Ogaki and Gifu are in the province of Mino; and, speaking generally, the provinces east of Mino had submitted to Iyéyasu and the eastern army, while those to the west for the most part had submitted to the western army. The castle of Otsu, on Lake Biwa, a few miles to the south-west of Ogaki, was held for the eastern army—a circumstance which materially influenced the action of the western commanders.

A council of war was held, and the relative merits of remaining within the castle and of leaving it were warmly discussed. It was decided to leave it, on the ground that their force (one hundred and twenty-eight thousand men) was so much greater than that of Iyéyasu (seventy-five thousand) that it would disappoint and discourage the troops if they failed to go out and crush the enemy. Accordingly the western army marched forth at night from the castle of Ogaki, and took up its position at Osekimura. When Iyéyasu heard that the western army had come out into the open he was glad, and issued orders to advance upon it, himself leading the centre of his force. About the break of day they reached Momokubarino, but it was so foggy that objects a few yards in front could not be seen. The two armies, still advancing, met at Sekigahara, the western force avoiding battle at first, in the hope of enticing the easterns into a less favourable position. Iyéyasu, however, resolved to bring on the fight, and ordered an attack. Fire was opened with arrows and bullets, to the sound of drums and bugles, and an awful battle ensued. The fighting was bravely carried on upon both sides for several hours, the eastern troops, who were so greatly outnumbered, suffering most severely. At one time the eastern army was about to retreat, but the coming up of its reserves, under Hachisuka Yorishiye and others, restored the balance of fighting force, and prolonged both the struggle and the uncertainty of its issue. The two armies were now so equally matched that they advanced together and retreated together, and together swayed to and fro, neither army being able to bring the battle to a decisive point. Meanwhile two generals, Hidemoto and Hideaki, with their troops, held aloof from the fight, upon the mountain side, in apparent uncertainty as to which side they should join. The eastern army therefore fired a shot towards their camp to test their intentions. Upon this they descended the mountain slope and fell upon the western troops, throwing them into disorder. At this critical moment—critical for Iyéyasu, for his house, and for the empire of Japan—that great captain ordered a general advance of his troops, which was carried out with such force and enthusiasm that the whole western army was utterly routed, and pursued with great slaughter by the victorious eastern troops. Most of the western leaders were killed, and others driven into hiding for their lives. The heads were cut off all those who were overtaken, to the number, according to native histories, of a third of the whole western army. Iyéyasu pursued his advantage with such zeal and determination that Kioto, Osaka, and even the distant provinces of Choshiu and Satsuma—indeed the whole of Japan—very soon submitted to him. He was in 1603 created Sei-i-tai-Shogun by the emperor, and that place and title remained hereditary in his family until the overthrow of the Tokugawa Shogunate in 1868. Some of his successors took to themselves the title of *Tai-Kun* (sometimes written " Tycoon " by strangers), signifying " High Prince." This title was never given by the Mikado, and was a mere assumption of the Shoguns, who were always, and in the days of their greatest power, officers of the Mikado. As soon as Japan came into contact with the outer world, and began to make treaties, the pretended royal power of the Tai-Kun broke down, and the authority of the Mikado, or emperor, was asserted.

Neither the battle of Sekigahara nor the other military successes which followed it finally disposed of Hideyori, the son of Hideyoshi, who gave trouble to Iyéyasu long after he attained the Shogunate. That office, in fact, Iyéyasu held for a couple of years only, making it over in 1605 to his son Hidétada; himself exercising, however, in his retirement, as much power as he pleased. In the year 1614, Hideyori, on the recommendation of one Ono Harunaga, raised an army at Osaka for the purpose of recovering, if possible, the power of his (the Toyotomi) family. Iyéyasu thereupon brought together troops to attack Osaka. Many of those who suffered defeat at Sekigahara, and had since lived in concealment, found their way to that city, and joined Hideyori. None of the lords of provinces joined him, but he raised altogether about fifty thousand men. There was much disappointment at the comparative smallness of this force, but the rebels had gone too far to retreat. Near the end of the year 1614, Iyéyasu and his son Hidétada reached Fushimi, seven miles south of Kioto, and advanced on Osaka, completely surrounding it, " so that there was not an inch of space left around the castle of Osaka." The investing army numbered, say the native histories, half a million of men. The stockades erected outside by the Osaka forces were carried with a rush, and the castle itself was closely besieged. Iyéyasu offered Hideyori peace on one of the three following terms: 1. That the outer works of the castle should be destroyed, and the moat filled in; 2, that Hideyori should remove to Yamato; 3, that he should deliver up his mother as a hostage. After a time, Hideyori accepted the first of these stipulations, and peace was concluded.

It did not last long, however. Scarcely had Iyéyasu withdrawn and dispersed his forces, before Hideyori again raised the standard of revolt, and this time collected a force of a hundred and twenty thousand men. At first declining to believe, or pretending not to believe, this news, Iyéyasu refused to act; but the proofs of rebellion soon became so manifest that he was compelled once more to bring large forces together and march westward. In the fourth month, the van of the eastern army reached Kioto, and soon afterwards in the following month Iyéyasu and Hidétada arrived, and proceeded with the combined army towards Osaka. Hideyori divided his army into three divisions, retaining the general command himself, and made various attacks upon the eastern troops as they approached the city. At length the castle was reached, attacked, and set on fire, and after terrible fighting and bloodshed the rebels were completely beaten.

In the course of the battle, when the eastern troops had succeeded in breaking into the castle, Hideyori and his mother Yodokimi were removed into a storehouse, and Hideyori's wife (who was a daughter of the Shogun Hidetada) was sent to her father in the eastern army. Iyéyasu sent officers to guard the storehouse and protect its inmates, and despatched a messenger to the latter saying that he did not forget his past intimacy with the Taiko, and that if they would come out of the castle to him he would spare their lives, sending Hideyori to Koya, and giving his mother a pension of twenty thousand *kokus* of rice. The western general in command sent back to say that Hideyori and his mother were under great obligations to Iyéyasu for his liberality, and would come and thank him in person if he would provide them with *kagos* (the sedan-chairs then in use) in which they could pass safely through the many thousands of troops that surrounded them. While these messages were passing, however, some of Iyéyasu's troops attacked the storehouse with guns, and Hideyori then said, "I am a son of the Taiko, and it is my fate that I should come to this," and then he put himself to death. Yodokimi, his mother, commanded her attendant to kill her; and then their principal generals committed *hara-kiri*, and "accompanied them in their death." Thus the Toyotomi family became extinct, and with them became extinct too the many troubles which they occasioned. This was the last great battle fought upon the soil of Japan prior to the revolutions of our own time, and therefore the last fought there for two hundred and fifty years. Its effect was to place the Tokugawa family upon the seat of the Shogunate for the same period.

Thus much of the military doings of Iyéyasu. Let us now consider his action with reference to the religions of the country. He, like his predecessor, was in the early days of his supremacy busily occupied in subduing those who refused to acknowledge him, and consequently allowed the Jesuits to pursue their own course without determined interruption. A hundred of these foreign priests consequently established themselves in Kioto, Osaka, and Nagasaki. But in 1600, after the victory of Sekigahara, which so fully confirmed his power, he issued an edict of expulsion against the missionaries. The Jesuits state that he withdrew this edict, on account of the threatening attitude of some of the converted nobles who had previously supported him; but the Japanese accounts do not confirm this. The Roman Catholics had, however, made so much progress in the country that Iyéyasu was doubtless obliged to exercise prudence and patience in putting his hostility into practice. The converts numbered nearly two millions, and there were Christian churches in every province of Kiushiu, except two, and also at Kioto, Osaka, Sendai, and Kanagawa. In eight provinces only of Japan had the new religion gained no footing. Remembering this, but remembering also that from the beginning the spread of Roman Catholicism had been associated with apprehensions of foreign conquest; that the Christian converts of rank and power had been induced by the missionaries to employ their influence in persecuting the unconverted, and in offending and injuring the existing priesthoods of the country; that the Buddhists in particular (to whom Iyéyasu was favourable) had suffered the most terrible slaughters and spoliations from Nobunaga, the protector of the Christians; and that the revolts of Hideyori, culminating in the bloody battles of Osaka, had been in large part promoted by the Jesuits, whom he entertained, and whose patron he was—it is not surprising that when the time came Iyéyasu resolved to expel the foreigners, nor is it surprising, though it is most deplorable, that "the decree of expulsion directed against the missionaries was followed by a fierce outbreak of persecution in all the provinces in which Christians were to be found, which was conducted with relentless severity "* (Gubbins).

* Mr. Griffis states that in 1611 Iyéyasu obtained documentary evidence of what he had long suspected, viz. the existence of a plot on the part of the native converts and the foreign emissaries to reduce Japan to the position of a subject state. The chief conspirator, Okubo, then governor of Sado, to which place thousands of Christians had been sent to work the mines, was to be made hereditary ruler by the foreigners. The names of the chief native and foreign conspirators were written down, with the usual seal of blood from the end of the middle finger of the ringleader. With this paper was found, concealed in an iron box in an old well, a vast hoard of gold and silver. In the chapter which follows upon the foreign relations of Japan, I adduce further evidence on this subject, and quote one author, Montanus, who attributes the Shogun's repressive measures, the consequent revolt of Shimabara, and all its train of evils, to the alleged forging by the Dutch of a letter which threatened a Portuguese conquest of the country.

It was under Iyéyasu that the extirpation of Roman Catholicism from Japan commenced in earnest. There had been persecutions before his time—the burning of the nine missionaries at Nagasaki, for example—but they were all of a more or less local character. It was Iyéyasu's edict of 1614 which opened the vials of wrath upon the devoted heads of missionaries and native converts alike. The processes of detection and of punishment bore a startling resemblance to those which the Spanish Inquisition had just before employed, and with which some of the Jesuit missionaries to Japan were probably but too familiar. Mr. Gubbins, of our consular service in Japan, in the able paper to which I have frequently referred, tells us that a special service, called the Christian inquiry, was organised to devise methods for detecting, arresting, imprisoning, and punishing the Christians, who were subjected not to death only, but to tortures and horrors far more terrible than any death that is at once swift and certain. Even crucifixion, strangling, and drowning—all of which were resorted to—were merciful punishments compared with others that were sometimes inflicted upon the unfortunate converts of the Jesuit priests. "We read of Christians being executed in a barbarous manner in sight of each other, of their being hurled from the tops of precipices, of their being buried alive, of their being torn asunder by oxen, of their being tied up in rice-bags which were heaped up together, and of the pile thus formed being set on fire. Others were tortured before death by insertion of sharp spikes under the nails of their hands and feet, while some poor wretches, by a refinement of horrid cruelty, were shut up in cages, and there left to starve with food before their eyes." It is sad to remember; but it must in justice to the Japanese be said that religious persecutions and tortures such as these were unknown in Japan before the Jesuit missionaries of Spain and Portugal found their way there. Until their appearance every Japanese was free to worship at any shrine or temple which pleased him, and it was, sad to say, from the missionaries that Japan learnt to introduce loss and shame and suffering and torture and death into matters of religion.

I have previously spoken of Tokugawa Iyéyasu as one who encouraged the peaceful arts. It might be fairly said that the revival of learning dates from his accession to power. For six hundred years before his time the empire of Japan had been torn by the struggles and competitions of military commanders, and although the brief intervals of peace had often been turned to good account, as I have previously shown, it was not possible for either art or literature to become speedily and progressively developed under the Taira, the Minamoto, the Ashikagas, Nobunaga, and Hideyoshi. Iyéyasu gave the country peace, and even before that peace became settled and lasting (by the destruction of Hideyori) he took education and literature under his care. Soon after the great battle of Sekigahara, he founded (in 1601) at Fushimi, near Kioto, a school for the encouragement of literature; and in 1614 he established another at Kioto, placing at the head of it a learned man named Seikuwa. Seikuwa had in early life been a priest, but had abandoned the priesthood for scholarship, and in face of many difficulties "undertook the restoration of moral education." Under the patronage of Iyéyasu he did much towards the accomplishment of his object. We are told on good authority that after "general peace and order were established under the Tokugawa family, each Daimio became possessed of his own land, and provided for the education of his vassals, and the people living in his dominion." In the account to be given hereafter of our visit to Shidzuoka, the residence of Iyéyasu, I shall have occasion to make further mention of the services rendered by him personally to literature; but it is proper to mention here that he ordered several Chinese works to be printed by means of movable types formed of wood and of copper, and that he caused valuable books to become objects of special search and inquiry, with a view to their collection and preservation.

Before the time of the Tokugawa Shogunate the Daimios, or provincial princes, had possessed for their own advantage the gold, silver, and other mines included in their domains, converting the produce into money as they saw fit. Iyéyasu, however, took the mines of the country into his own hands, and placed them under the direction of one Okubo-Nogayasu, upon whose advice he had acted in centralising the control. Okubo took vigorous measures for working and letting the mines of Idzu, Sado, and Iwami, which chiefly consisted of gold and silver, and returned considerable revenues. Later on numerous other mines were discovered in different parts of the country, and became an important source of income. Iyéyasu also took an active interest in the foreign relations of the country. He sent back to Korea the prisoners made at the time of Hideyoshi's invasion, and renewed peaceful relations with that country, which sent an ambassador to Japan, and continued to do so at each change of Shogun, the princes of Tsushima being always charged to receive the Korean ministers. During Iyéyasu's time some Dutch ships arrived at Sakai (near Osaka) and sought permission to trade with Japan. Iyéyasu sent for one of the captains, and made many inquiries respecting foreign countries. Having learnt that there existed foreign countries in Europe, Asia, Africa, and America, he conceived the design of opening commercial relations with them. Several English vessels likewise arriving from the Philippines, Cambodia, Annam, Macao, etc., he gave audience to their captains, authorised them to trade, and gave them letters to their respective sovereigns. He likewise sent a Japanese ship to visit the Spanish possessions of the New World. A Japanese subject was also sent to Italy to study the religion and manners of that country. He further sought to renew friendly relations with China, sending the emperor a letter through the king of Loo-choo. In that letter he explained that different countries produced different products, and that it would be wise to exchange produce with each other, each supplying the other with its own superfluity, and taking in exchange what the other had in abundance. The letter was not answered, but many Chinese merchants went to Japan to carry out its objects. Iyéyasu also applied himself vigorously to internal improvements, including the repair and the making of public roads, and more particularly the perfecting of the great highway between the emperor's capital and his own, *i.e.* between Kioto and Yedo, known as the Tokaido. The regulations laid down by him were both comprehensive and detailed, and tended immensely to facilitate internal communication.

Iyéyasu died in March 1616, at the city of Shidzuoka, where the last years of his life were peacefully spent, and in the following year his remains were removed to Nikko, where his son had erected for them a splendid shrine. He was deified as Gongen Sama, and is there worshipped under that title. He left behind him a legal treatise or code, now celebrated as the " Legacy of Iyéyasu." A learned barrister who has resided in Japan* has made a careful study of this work, and arrived at the following results respecting it. It is a compilation of old laws and not a series of new ones, but is original in so far as it contains the maxims of government by which the successors of Iyéyasu were to be guided. The leading principles of it, so far as these are concerned, are as follows : The relation of the Shogun to the Mikado was to be one of reverential homage, the theoretical supremacy of the latter being strengthened in every way—whereas former Shoguns had often treated the Mikado with rudeness or contempt. The respect formerly paid to the relatives of the Mikado, and to the old court aristocracy, was to be continued. To inferiors the Shoguns were to behave with courtesy and consideration, not pressing upon them harshly or tyrannically. The places of government of the lesser Daimios were to be frequently changed, ostensibly to prevent misgovernment, but really to avoid endangering the power of the Shoguns. Finally, peace was to be preserved in the empire as long as possible. " To assist the people," says Iyéyasu, " is to give peace to the empire ;" and certainly he and his

---

* Mr. W. E. Grigsby, B.A., of Balliol College, Oxford, and of the Inner Temple. Mr. Grigsby says, " Doubts have been cast upon the authenticity of the 'Legacy,' but even if it be not his own composition it undoubtedly embodies the policy of Iyéyasu, and is of historical value."

successors gave Japan the benefit of this assistance for two and a half centuries.

The arrangements of Nobunaga for the government of the country after his death failed, as we have seen, and Hideyoshi seized the government. His arrangements equally failed, and Iyéyasu succeeded to his power, and revived the high office of Shogun. The plans which he laid down worked so successfully for two centuries and a half after his death that it is worth while to take brief note of them. In the first place, Iyéyasu made a careful redistribution of the lands, so devised as to place his nearest relatives and most trusted friends in the most important positions, and thus to put as much check as possible upon doubtful feudatories. The chief vassals of the crown who possessed or came into possession of a revenue exceeding ten thousand *kokus* of rice were designated Daimios. These, although of equal nominal rank with the Shogun, were really his subordinates (and in large part his nominees), and had to perform acts of homage to him. The number of the Daimios is officially stated to have been two hundred and forty-five, of whom eighteen of the oldest and most powerful were called *kokushiu*, " ruler of province "; about a hundred and thirty were called *fudai*, all of whom were created Daimios by Iyéyasu in reward for their services as generals or retainers of his—about a third of the number being members of his own family! and the remainder, of somewhat inferior grade, were likewise promoted from among those who had supported Iyéyasu along the road to power. Some of the *kokushiu*, or most powerful order of Daimios, had descended from the feudal barons of Yoritomo, while they had subsequently won their provinces by the sword. They had been either defeated or conciliated by Iyéyasu, and in making his dispositions he took care to interpose his own nominees as far as possible between and around those who might otherwise combine against him. He similarly protected the Mikado's capital, Kioto, in order that his person might be secure from seizure.

The Daimios exercised independent authority within their

own domains, residing with their retainers in walled towns, and ruling separately over provinces or districts which provided within themselves everything which they required—thus realising, as has been said, the idea of independence which the Greek states strove in vain to accomplish. The power of Iyéyasu as Shogun had to be asserted and exercised with some prudential restraint over the *kokushiu* Daimios, but the *fudai* were wholly subject to him, and he could change their places or vary their revenues at will. The executive government of the Shogun was composed of Daimios whom he could thoroughly trust, the subordinate posts being held by retainers of his own family or its connections. The Daimios possessed the power of granting out their lands, but they could not add to them, even by conquest, without the Shogun's permission, and the fundamental condition of their Daimioates was, of course, that of military service.

Below the Daimios came their two-sworded retainers, the *samurai*, upon whom, usually in return for military service, grants of land had been bestowed. These formed at once the military and the educated class—" the backbone of the nation " (Mounsey). In fact the Daimios farmed out their lands to the *samurai* in return for their military services. These *samurai* possessed the right of sub-feudating their land grants on the same condition. " Military service was incumbent on every one who held lands ; and so far was this theory carried that a vassal who was not able to perform the service by reason of age or sickness, abdicated in favour of his son " (Grigsby). As the lands were escheated to the Daimio in the event of death without an heir, the practice of adoption became common. If the vassal proved faithless to his superior, his property was forfeited.

The Shogun—himself the chief of the Daimios—had a special class of vassals, called *hatamoto*, upon whom he chiefly depended for service about his person in war time, and from among whom the officials of the Shogun's government were chosen. They are said to have numbered eighty thousand throughout the country, the larger part residing in the Shogun's capital, Yedo. There was another class, of whom (having reference to a subsequent period) Mr. Griffis says: The *gokenin*, many of the descendants of Iyéyasu's private soldiers, were inferior in wealth and rank to the *hatamoto*, but with them formed the hereditary personal following of the Shogun, and constituted the Tokugawa clan proper, whose united resources amounted to nearly nine million *koku*. "The Shogun, or chief Daimio of the empire, had thus unapproachable military resources, following, and revenue, and could overawe court and emperor above, princes and vassals beneath." All the above classes, of less rank than the Daimios, were *samurai*, of whom very diverse accounts indeed are given. Even the same authors sometimes describe them as the life and soul of the country, the impersonations of chivalry and valour, "the class which for centuries monopolised arms, polite learning, patriotism, and intellect," and at other times denounce them as a class of whom "the majority spent their life in eating, smoking, and lounging in brothels and tea-houses, or led a wild life of crime in the great cities." The truth no doubt is that they enjoyed the best opportunities for acquiring education and culture, as the military class often do in times of peace; but enjoying at the same time a free command of time, the majority wasted their opportunities, as they too frequently do, while the minority made a better use of them, and balanced the dishonour of the many by their virtues and distinctions.

While working out the arrangements sketched above, by which he secured the power of his dynasty by the strongest and most widespread ties of personal fealty, Iyéyasu did not neglect to provide also for his successors the strength and the *prestige* which a great and castled city would afford to his successors. He was the founder and the builder of Yedo, now Tokio, the modern capital of Japan. In the common order of things, and with a man of less ability and originality than he, the restoration of the Shogunate would have resulted in the rebuilding of Kamakura in greater beauty and splendour than ever. But Kamakura was not the best site for an eastern capital, and this Iyéyasu and his advisers discovered.

The castle of Yedo was founded in the middle of the fifteenth century. A few huts of fishermen at that time existed along the beach of the bay of that name, and thence stretched away inland the wide plain of Musashi, covered with reeds and sedge,* but dotted here and there with small villages on elevated spots. Its builder was a general named Ota Dokuan, whom the Kamakura authorities had stationed on the rising ground of what is the present suburb of Shinagawa (of Tokio), in order to guard against attacks from the east during the troublous times then prevailing in that part of Japan. The rivers which flow into the Bay of Yedo appeared to him of great importance both for transport and for defence, and it is recorded as a fact that in later times, whenever war broke out in that part of the country, the first care of the commandant of Yedo Castle was to throw forward a detachment of troops to the bank of the branch of the Tonégawa which flows into Yedo Bay, in order to prevent the enemy from crossing that river. If successful in the field, these troops inflicted a severe check upon the advancing foe; if themselves worsted, they could always fall back upon the castle. In 1456 Ota Dokuan, convinced of the advantages of the site, commenced building this castle of Yedo on part of the ground which it at present occupies. Dokuan appears to have been a poet as well as a general—indeed most Japanese of education are poets after a fashion—and in the year 1474 he collected sixteen literary guests within his new residence and held a poetical meeting,† himself composing a poem in which was the picturesque verse—

"To my hut adjoins a fir-tree plain, and hard by rolls the sea;
The lofty peak of Fuji is seen from below the eaves." ‡

In 1590, after the Later Hojo had been overthrown by

---

* Here and occasionally in the remainder of this chapter I derive my description, sometimes literally, from Mr. McClatchie's paper on "The Castle of Yedo."

† Many of the verses composed on this occasion are still preserved.

‡ There is at present a platform in the grounds of the castle from which I have seen the peak of Fuji.

the success of the siege of Odawara, as previously recounted, Hideyoshi had bestowed upon Iyéyasu the eight provinces to the east of the Hakoné barrier, known collectively as the Kuanto, instructing him at the same time to fix his residence at Yedo, which he immediately did. The castle of Yedo, however well situated, and however charming the views of sea and mountain which it enjoyed, appears to have been at this time a poor sort of a construction, for an old account tells us that its inclosure was limited in extent and unsightly in appearance, the flights of steps being built of old ships' boards. On Iyéyasu taking possession of it one of his attendants remarked, "In such a place as this my lord cannot receive guests; I pray that it may be put in repair." It is characteristic of the great general that he laughed and replied, "What a womanish idea! There is time enough for talking of repairs!" He immediately set to work, nevertheless, to provide for the military strength of his stronghold, surrounding it with a vast cordon of fortresses, bestowing each with grants of land upon officers high in his confidence. There were thirty-two of these outlying defences, including Koga and Sekiyado in the province of Shimoda, Iwatsuki and Kawagoye in Musashi, and Odawara in Sagami, all of which continued to be the fortified residences of influential Daimios down to the restoration of 1868. The castle of Yedo itself was likewise taken in hand by its new master, who greatly enlarged its inclosure, excavated its broad moats, threw up their great earthern embankments, and built its many gates and bridges. It is said that three hundred thousand labourers were employed on these works. A native account says, "Until that time it was merely a small fortification, but during the period Keicho (1596–1615) the site of the castle grounds was widened, and it was made a grand structure as it at present stands, being an immense castle immutable for myriads of years." Within the vast area of the castle grounds were located many palaces for the ministers and chief officers of the Shogun's court and government, including some of the greatest and most favoured of his

Daimios. Around this great castle there naturally gathered many other residences, the number of which became very great in consequence of the Shogun requiring the Daimios to reside at short intervals in Yedo, and to leave their wives in residence there during their own absences in the provinces. When the necessity of accommodating the lesser Daimios, the *hatamoto*, the *gokenin*, and also the manufacturing, trading, and labouring classes in numbers proportioned to the requirements of a great military and government capital is taken into account, it is not surprising that Yedo soon grew to be, what it now under another name remains, the largest city in Japan.

In concluding this chapter I must borrow from Mr. McClatchie's story of the castle of Yedo the following account of the manner in which the since famous Shiba temples of Tokio became first connected with the Tokugawas, observing that during our stay in Tokio, with Admiral Kawamura, we resided in the immediate vicinity of this beautiful Shiba district, and passed almost daily through the temple grounds. The temple of Zojoji (by which name it was known) was at the time situated on the shore, and as Iyéyasu was riding into Yedo, and was approaching the main entrance of the castle, the incumbent of the temple, named Genyo Son-o, stood before his gate to see the procession go by. From the archives of the temple comes the following account of what passed, as recorded there by the good priest himself:—

"My lord, riding on horseback, was just passing in front of the temple gate, when, strange to say, his horse stood still of himself, and would not advance. My lord looked to left and right, and perceived a priest before the gate. He gave orders to his attendants, saying, 'Inquire what priest that is.' They therefore questioned me, when I replied, 'The temple is of the Jodo sect, and my own name is Son-o.' But before the attendants had repeated him my answer, my lord caught the words as he sat on horseback, and said, 'Then you are Son-o, the pupil of Kanyo?' (Kanyo was the priest of the temple of Taijiuji, in Iyéyasu's own province of Mikawa.) I could only utter in response an exclamation of surprise. 'Then I'll halt awhile at your temple,' said he, and he entered Zojoji. My lord next observed, 'I wish to take a meal by myself in this temple to-morrow morning, but it is quite unnecessary for you to make any extensive preparations,' and with these words he went on his way. True to his promise, he arrived early next day. I was in the greatest delight, and offered him a humble repast. Then said my lord, 'My sole reason for stating my desire to take a meal here this morning was as follows. For a general to be without an ancestral temple of his own is as though he were forgetful of the fact that he must die. Taijiuji, in the province of Mikawa, has of course been the temple of my forefathers for generations back, but what I have now come to ask of you is to let me make this my own ancestral temple here, and enter with me into a compact as between priest and parishioner.' With tears of joy, I assented. He with all reverence pronounced his acquiescence in the Ten Buddhist Precepts, and then went back to the castle. After this he was pleased to remove Zojoji to Sakurada, but on the grounds that it rendered the frontage of his castle too confined, it was shortly afterwards (in 1598) removed once more to its present site to the west of the sea-beach at Shiba."

From these incidents, and from the patronage of the Tokugawa family which of course followed them, the temples of Shiba derived their subsequent splendour, and their priests advantages of incalculable value, not the least of which was the high privilege accorded to the head priest of riding in his palanquin up to the very entrance-hall of the castle, instead of dismounting at a gateway lower down, like meaner mortals.

MIKADO'S PALACE, KIOTO.

CHAPTER XIII.

THE TOKUGAWA PERIOD (1603-1868).

Iyéyasu's successor, Hidétada—He sends a subject to Europe to study its religions—Decides against Roman Catholicism—Founding of the Wooyeno temples—Another empress reigns—Iyemitsu, the ablest of the Tokugawas—Foreign intercourse forbidden—The construction of sea-going vessels prohibited—The Christian revolt of Shimabara—Their castle seized and afterwards besieged and captured—Massacre of the Christians—An army of "martyrs"—The fatal rock of Pappenberg—"Christ" becomes a name of terror throughout Japan—Evil effects of foreign intercourse—Home enterprises of Shogun Iyemitsu—A prince-priest at Nikko—The emperor Go-Komio—Yedo ravaged by fire—Shogun Iyetsuna—His encouragement of literature—Maritime commerce of the country—A literary Shogun (Tsunayoshi)—His lectures at his court—The Dutch traveller Kaempfer—Tsunayoshi's defective finance—Changes in the coinage—Suppression of smuggling—A scientific Shogun (Yoshimune)—The observatory of Kanda—The calendar reformed—Prosperity of the country in the eighteenth century—The "Rice Shogun"—A census taken in 1744—Art and industry developed—Spread of public instruction—Russian demands upon Japan—Attack upon a garrison in Yezo—Spread of the Dutch language—Decline of the Tokugawa power—The long peace engenders luxury and decay—Violent opposition to foreign intercourse—Review of the Tokugawa period—List of the Tokugawa Shoguns.

THE period covered by the heading of this chapter extends from the elevation of Iyéyasu to the Shogunate in 1603 down to the excitements and changes that brought about the revolution of 1868. We have already seen that Iyéyasu's son Hidétada had succeeded, at least nominally, to the Shogunate twelve years before the father's death; but on that event happening, in 1616, he promptly proceeded to Kioto to do homage to the emperor, and prove his fidelity to him. This was during the reign of Go-Mino-o-Tenno, but the ex-emperor Go-Yozei took advantage of the occasion to address Hidétada as follows: "Your father has gone from us, and it will now be for you, who have the happiness to become Shogun in a time of peace, to pursue the studies necessary for learning all that a good administrator ought to know. Your father, less happy than you, attained to power while civil war was ravaging the country, and he consequently was unable to do all that he desired in this respect. Be you zealous, laborious, and faithful to your sovereign, and above all chase from your mind the fallacious dreams of ambition." Hidétada, profoundly moved by these simple but wise words, conformed himself all his life, we are told, to these counsels, and examples of this have been recorded. Desiring more definite information about Christianity, he sent one of his subjects, Ibi-Masayoshi, to Europe to study attentively the principles of that religion. At the end of several years Masayoshi returned to Japan, and was immediately called to the palace to make his report. Hidétada listened attentively all day and night without interruption till his report was finished; and when, during the audience, his courtiers suggested that he would injure his health by so much fatigue, the Shogun replied: "You speak of my fatigue, gentlemen, but what is that in comparison with the fatigues, I would even say with the troubles, the privations, and the dangers which Ibi-Masayoshi has not shrunk from undergoing in order to faithfully fulfil his mission?" The result of Hidétada's reflection upon the report thus made to him was the conclusion, that the Roman Catholic religion would be injurious to Japan, and he renewed the interdiction which already forbade its practice in the country.

It was from the Shogun Hidétada that the eminent ecclesiastic (Dai-Sojo) named Tenkai obtained an authorisation to construct a temple at Shinobu-Gaoka in Yedo, since so well known as Uyeno, or Wooyeno. The government undertook to bear the costs of its construction, obtaining the requisite funds from several of the Daimios. The temple was named Kuwan-ei-ji, and Tenkai was appointed to the charge of it. A short time before the government had ordered the construction at Shiba, in the inclosure of the temple of Zojoji, both a mortuary chapel and a tomb dedicated to the ex-Shogun Iyéyasu. From these beginnings sprang the famous Tokugawa temples and burial-places of Shiba and Toyeizan, or Wooyeno, the beauty and renown of which have cast somewhat into the shade temples and burial-places more deserving of celebration by reason of their greater antiquity and solemnity.

In the year 1630, an incident occurred in the sovereignty of Japan which deserves note for more than one reason: a lady once more ascended the imperial throne, and was destined to occupy it for fourteen years. The emperor Go-Mino-o had made the daughter of the Shogun Hidétada his empress, and by her had a daughter, who received the too troublesome name of Too-Fuku-no-in. From the time of the empress Shotoku, who, it will be remembered, reigned twice over, eight centuries and a half before, no lady had occupied the throne; but now the highest station in the realm was occupied by one who was—and probably because she was—the daughter both of the nominal and of the actual sovereign. She reigned under the title of Miosho-Tenno until 1643, her brother Iyémitsu, who had succeeded his father Hidétada as Shogun in 1623, visiting Kioto to do homage to her at the time of her ascension.

Iyémitsu distinguished his term of rule or office in many ways, and, after Iyéyasu, has been pronounced the ablest of the Tokugawas. He certainly carried out the feudal policy of his grandfather Iyéyasu even beyond the lengths to which he bore it. Iyémitsu it was who prescribed to the Daimios the rule of residing in their own provinces and in Yedo alternately, he himself meeting them outside of his castle, reswearing them to their allegiance, and taking their signatures to the compact in their own blood—a not unusual mode of sealing solemn covenants in Japan. These formalities were gradually made more and more stringent by him, the Daimios being pushed more and more from the position of equality to that of vassalage. But that it was not merely as a Tokugawa that Iyémitsu acted is shown by many incidents, of which it will suffice to cite one. In writing to the governor of Nagasaki he said: "If my dynasty (that of the Tokugawa) should be made by intestine wars to disappear, the shame would recoil upon me only; but if an inch of our soil were to pass into the hands of foreigners, the disgrace would be a national one."

This sentence is referred to by native writers in connection with the revolt and massacre of Roman Catholics at Shimabara, which occurred during his government, as a proof that the object of Iyémitsu in interdicting the foreign religion and exterminating its advocates was to avoid political complications which, in his opinion, must have led either to wars with foreigners, or to insurrections in the country. But however this may be, Iyémitsu, seeing that the edicts which had been directed against the Christians remained without effect, took steps for their enforcement, and in order to check that foreign intercourse which seemed to him so injurious, as furthering the spread of Roman Catholicism, he went to the length of forbidding, under pain of death, the construction of vessels large enough to proceed to sea. He so completely reversed the policy of Iyéyasu as regards foreign trade that he forbade the admission to Japanese ports of any foreigners, excepting only the Chinese and the Dutch, and allowed these to trade only to the single port of Nagasaki.

In 1637 came the famous revolt of Christians at Shimabara to which I have just adverted. In the autumn of that year the peasantry of a district in Hizen (the westernmost province of the great island of Kiushiu, and that in which Nagasaki is situated)—a district in which large numbers of converts had been made—broke out into open rebellion against the government. They seized the castle of Shimabara, repaired and armed it, and prepared to meet any forces which the Shogun might send against them. When the number of the rebels, amounting, it is said, to thirty thousand, is considered, and when it is also remembered that Hizen is the most distant from Yedo of all the provinces of Japan (exclusive of off-lying islands), that mountains and seas separated the rebels from the Shogun's capital and military centre, and that the communications by sea were of the most unsatisfactory kind, it will not be surprising that three months were spent in reducing Shimabara, and that it was at last accomplished by the aid of Dutch cannon from Nagasaki. The resistance of the Christians was bravely and desperately maintained against the investing forces, but it ultimately of course gave way before the unlimited means of the government, and the "army of martyrs," as many will consider them, was massacred by the victorious soldiery. The Roman communities scattered over the country were hunted out, and either banished, tortured, or put to death.

Then it was that from the rock of Pappenberg (a pretty, peaceful island near the entrance to Nagasaki harbour, which at first sight seemed to me to have no side sheer enough for the murderous purpose) the poor converted Japanese were hurled headlong to the sea, and onward into that other world—so far off in the midst of life, and so near in the hour of death. The name of Christ became an object of shame and terror throughout Japan. "For centuries the mention of that name would bate the breath, blanch the cheek, and smite with fear as with an earthquake shock. It was the synonym of sorcery, sedition, and all that was hostile to the purity of home and the peace of society. All over the empire, in every city, town, village and hamlet; by the roadside, ferry, or mountain-pass; at every entrance to the capital stood the public notice boards, on which, with prohibitions against the crimes that disturb the relations of society and government, was one tablet, written with a deeper brand of guilt, with a more hideous memory of blood, with a more awful terror of torture, than when the like superscription was affixed at the top of a cross that stood between two thieves on a little hill outside of Jerusalem. Its daily and familiar sight startled ever and anon the peasant to clasp hands and utter a fresh prayer, the bonze to add new venom to his maledictions, the magistrate to shake his head, and the mother to find a ready word to hush the crying of her fretful babe " (Griffis). So thoroughly was the *Jashiu Mon*, "corrupt seat," supposed to be eradicated, that there was thought to remain nothing of it save " an awful scar on the national memory." Besides the terrible " name " of which Mr. Griffis has written in the above passage so strongly, that author considers that the only apparent results to Japan of nearly a hundred years of Christianity and foreign intercourse were " the adoption of gunpowder and of firearms as weapons, the use of tobacco and the habit of smoking, the making of spongecake, the naturalisation into the language of a few foreign words, and the introduction of new and strange forms of disease," among which the Japanese count a scourge that must here be nameless.

Before the time of Iyémitsu Japan had possessed three kinds of copper money, coined in the country; but so much of this had been employed by the Buddhists for casting monster bells and images of Buddha that the deficiency had to be supplied by the purchase of Chinese money, which was paid for with gold from the Japanese mines, valued far below its real worth. Iyémitsu put an end to this costly arrangement, and himself struck a new coinage in copper. This Shogun also did much to improve the Tokugawa capital, erecting watch-ladders for the prompt detection of fires, cutting canals and building aqueducts for improving the water supply, and in other ways perfecting and aggrandising the city of his family's pride.

During the period of Iyémitsu's reign, so to call it, the empress Mioshio was succeeded on the throne by the emperor Go-Komio, who ascended it in 1644. Nothing serious happened during his reign of ten years, but there were internal troubles which it may be well to note. There was a revolt against the Shogun by one Yui-Shosetsu, which proved so great a failure that the worst effect of it was the suicide by *hara-kiri* of the rebel. A more significant indication of the dangers that then existed may be found in the fact that the priest Tenkai (whom we just now saw appointed to the charge of the Wooyeno temples, but was subsequently sent in charge of those at Nikko, and who appears to have been a wary and influential friend of the Tokugawas) urged the successive Shoguns to induce the court at Tokio to send a prince of the imperial blood to become a *bozu* at Nikko, his object being to secure for possible emergencies one who could be set by the Tokugawas upon the throne in the event of a vacancy occurring by means of successful rebellion or otherwise. In pursuance of this purpose Prince Shucho-Shinno was sent to Nikko, and there entered holy orders. It is also an important fact that we read in native histories the statement that Go-Komio-Tenno was an instructed and energetic man, and was proposing to possess himself of the governing power when death surprised him. He died in 1654, and was succeeded by a younger brother, in whose reign Yedo was ravaged by a terrible fire, many of the inhabitants being lost in the flames. The Shogun's ministers ordered several of the Daimios to return provisionally to their provinces, forbade the too rapid reconstruction of the city in order to avoid extravagant expenditure, and issued ordinances against luxury and waste. These wise measures, it is said, prevented the prices of wood and of other articles from rising excessively, and thus saved the sufferers from the fire from much of the further evil of pecuniary distress. Iyémitsu had died, be it noted, in 1649, and therefore in the previous reign, and had been succeeded in the Shogunate by Iyétsuna, who retained it for thirty years. The emperor Reigen commenced his reign in 1663, and from that time to 1680 he and the Shogun Iyétsuna held their respective high offices contemporarily. Their joint rule was not without points of interest.

Iyétsuna appears to have given great encouragement to literature. He caused to be composed and published an historic work of three hundred and ten volumes by Hayashi-Harunatsu. Under his patronage a Tokugawa, the prince of Mito, opened an establishment where he commissioned several great scholars to compose a detailed history of Japan. This work became very celebrated under the title *Dai*

Nihon Shi, which was given to it by command of the emperor. The Shogun's government also created about this time a department charged with the conduct of astronomical observations; and the period was further noted in respect of science by the works of Seki, a celebrated mathematician, who founded an important school known as that of Sekiriu.

A curious anecdote concerning countrymen of ours, belonging to this period, is told in illustration of the strong aversion which the Japanese then felt towards the Portuguese and Spanish, whose missionaries had introduced the religion which had become so hateful to them, and whom they believed responsible for all the misery and bloodshed which had fallen upon the country in the various persecutions by which that religion had been sometimes favoured and sometimes resisted. The story is that an English vessel arrived at Nagasaki, and sought permission to trade with the natives; but the Dutch residents having informed the local authorities that the king of England had married a Portuguese lady, the captain of the vessel was ordered instantly to leave the port.

Meanwhile, the Shogun's government encouraged maritime commerce within its own limits, one instance of which may be cited in connection with the growth of the eastern capital. The sudden foundation and development of the city of Yedo, and the rapid increase in the number of its inhabitants, made it largely dependent upon other and more or less distant provinces for its supplies of provisions. The supplies from the southern and western provinces were easily obtainable; but those from the fruitful provinces of the north, such as Dewa and Mutsu, for example, which grew large crops of cereals, reached Yedo with great difficulty and irregularity. A rich merchant of the city, named Kawamura-Yasuhara, who was thoroughly acquainted with the circumstances, obtained the concurrence of the government, and established a regular service of junks for bringing down provisions from the northern provinces. He constructed a number of well-built vessels, manned them with picked sailors, and prescribed for them specific cargoes, times of sailing, and so forth. Those running from Mutsu had, of course, merely to coast round to Yedo, a distance of less than four hundred miles; those from Dewa had to make their way down the western coast to Shimonoséki, and thence by the inland sea and the south-eastern coast to Yedo, a distance of very nearly two thousand miles. The establishment and successful working of these two lines of vessels greatly simplified the provisioning of the city, and conferred many benefits upon the government and people. A sum of money was awarded to the enterprising merchant for his services, and he was soon afterwards empowered to improve the rivers of Osaka, and to cut the canal of Ajiwaka.

The rule of Reigen-Tenno and Shogun Iyétsuna was succeeded by that of the emperor Higashiyama and the Shogun Tsunayoshi, which lasted into the eighteenth century, terminating in 1708-9. The native histories say that Tsunayoshi was well-versed in literature and science, and gave great encouragement to both. He even made himself an instructor of others, assembling the princes and high functionaries about him, and expounding to them passages from the classics of the country. He also built in Yedo, and liberally endowed, a temple dedicated to Confucius. It was in his time that the celebrated Dutch doctor Kaempfer, whose great work on Japan is known to many, visited the country. The Shogun gave him frequent audience, and facilitated his acquisition of the knowledge which he desired. In the educational history of the country Tsunayoshi occupies a very prominent position. He was the patron of the celebrated Tokushin, who was the second son of Shimsai, himself a distinguished literary man and priest, and son of the famous Confucian sage and priest Doshun. Doshun was the *protégé* of Iyéyasu, and had great influence at the court of Yedo. When he died in 1657, at the age of seventy-five, he left behind him works on a hundred and thirty different subjects, and a hundred and fifty volumes of essays. He was succeeded by Shimsai, who again was succeeded, as we just saw, by Tokushin. To him

Tsunayoshi gave a residence within the castle ramparts at Yedo, and directed him to remove the temple of the sage his grandfather Doshun to Ushima, "where it was built with great magnificence, and called Tai-sei-den." In the following year the Shogun personally visited the temple, and performed the ceremony which had been instituted in honour of Doshun, endowing the temple with a permanent fund for the education of numerous students.

Seldom before had learning been so prosperous, " for now everybody, from the nobility down to the masses of the people, began to appreciate literary studies." Availing himself of the friendship of Tsunayoshi, Tokushin obtained from him permission to abandon the shaving of his head, which, as a teacher of Confucianism, he had hitherto been obliged to submit to. Tsunayoshi likewise gave him a secular title of high rank, and made him president of the college. All the scholars throughout the empire now abandoned the custom of shaving the head, and a general impulse to study was everywhere felt. The Daimios, seeing Tsunayoshi so favourable to learning, imitated his example, and except in ancient times the literary class had never before been so much respected or encouraged.* I am afraid that Tsunayoshi's judgment was somewhat defective in one important branch of science—that of finance, for having been extremely liberal, and given away more money than could be spared, he made a very unscientific attempt to restore the treasury balance by merely changing the designations and nominal value of the coins in circulation.

The reign of the next emperor, Naka-Mikado, extended from 1710 to 1735, a period during which three Shoguns successively carried on the government of Yedo, viz. Iyénobu, Iyétsugu, and Yoshimuné. The first of them,

---

* The learned Sorai, or Ogin Soyemon, was a retainer of Yanagisawa Yoshiyasu, who was a favourite of the Shogun Tsunayoshi, and we read that "on every occasion that the Shogun visited Yoshiyasu, Soyemon had the honour of delivering in his presence lectures on the Chinese classics" ('Outline History of Education in Japan,' from which other brief quotations in the text are taken).

Iyénobu, promptly set about correcting the error made by his predecessor in dealing with the coinage, by amending the altered money and restoring it to its former condition. Finding that this suppressed one half of the current coinage, he issued a new coinage, of smaller size, but of an alloy of suitable value. These changes were not completed within the brief period (three years) of his tenure of power, and had to be concluded by his son and successor, Iyétsugu. But although Iyénobu's rule was of such brief duration, he made an effectual mark upon the history of his country. He took great pains to allay and subdue the warlike spirit which the people had been accustomed to cherish for many a century, and successfully directed their thoughts to polite and peaceful pursuits.

While Iyétsugu was Shogun, strong measures had to be taken to subdue the smuggling propensities of the natives and of the Chinese at Nagasaki. The Daimios of the west coast received orders to take energetic measures for the suppression of contraband proceedings. About the same time there arrived in one of the islands of Satsuma some Catholic missionaries, speaking the Japanese language, and wearing the Japanese costume. The prince of Satsuma arrested them, and sent them to Yedo, at the disposition of the Shogun. They were there interrogated concerning their object in coming to Japan, and replied that their only object was to spread their religion. After they had been further questioned respecting scientific and other matters, they were thrown into prison, and died there soon afterwards.

Yoshimuné, the third of the Shoguns of Naka-Mikado's reign, took great interest in astronomy and other branches of science, and his first act, it is said, was one for the encouragement of literature. He established a professorship the holder of which was to deliver lectures on Chinese classics to the Shogun himself, and his court. Another step in the same direction was the circulation through the writing schools of the city of texts from Chinese moral philosophy, to be used as copies for the pupils. Before

A Country Scene.

becoming Shogun, Yoshimuné had exhibited a great taste for astronomical and calendrical studies, and as soon as he attained to power he set about giving effect to his wishes on these subjects, getting made a large celestial globe for his own use, and himself inventing an apparatus for determining the meridian altitude of the sun. In the last year of his reign he built the observatory of Kanda, in Yedo, and placed therein the large celestial globe before referred to. He much consorted with scientific men, sending for one Nishigawa Joken, from Nagasaki, and employing another to advise him respecting the revision of the calendar. He obtained a European calendar, and recognised the precision of it; but fearing to disturb the populace, he refrained from adopting it. He interested himself in the criminal laws, ordering minimum punishments for offences, permitting the friends of persons who were thought to be unjustly condemned to demand a revision of the judgment, and forbidding the use of torture save where flagrant proofs of culpability existed, and the accused, notwithstanding, obstinately refused to confess the truth. He revised and completed the criminal code in a form in which it continued down to our own time. He caused to be published a collection of all the laws promulgated from Iyéyasu's time onward. He likewise greatly interested himself in agricultural and industrial questions, being the first to introduce the culture of sugar-cane into Japan, and making himself master of the art of extracting and refining the sugar obtained from it. History says that many other industries were equally promoted by him. He likewise caused Dutch, Korean, and Chinese horses to be imported into Japan for improving the native breed. Agriculture so flourished in his reign, and the price of rice was consequently brought so extraordinarily low, that he obtained the name of *Kome-Shogun*, or "Rice-Shogun." He improved the system of taxation, making provision for remissions of taxes in time of dearth. Further, he took a lively interest in medical works and studies; caused a manual of practical hygiene to be widely circulated among the country populations; and founded in Yedo a free hospital for the poor. A census made after his death showed, in 1744, the population of Japan to be 26,080,000 souls. The reigns of the next succeeding emperors, two in number, were signalised by profound peace, with abundant rice crops, and consequently by an extraordinary development of art and industry. "All the clans of Japan entered eagerly upon the path of progress." Another empress, Go-Sakura-Machi, ascended the throne in 1763. She was sister to the last preceding emperor (Momozono), and daughter of his predecessor (Sakura-Machi), and she assumed the imperial power on account of her nephew, the heir to it, being too young to reign. She reigned eight years, and then made way for him by abdicating. He reigned for nine years (ending 1779), under the same title as his father, Momozono, with the prefix "Go," signifying "Momozono the Second." His reign was not altogether a satisfactory one, owing to the circumstance of the Shogun, Iyéharu, having a minister who was equally corrupt and powerful, and who caused many serious disorders in the administration of the country.

The next emperor, Kokaku, enjoyed a long reign—from 1780 to 1816. One of its early incidents was the removal from office of the corrupt minister, Tanuma, and the appointment in his place of Matsudaira-Sadanobu.* The new minister effected great economies, corrected many abuses, and appointed to the offices of the state the most capable men he could find. His general direction of the administration, under the Shogun Iyénori, was excellent. The courts of Yedo and Kioto appear to have been on good terms, for upon the imperial palace in Kioto being burnt down, Sadanobu, by Iyénori's orders, rebuilt it on a far larger

---

* Matsudaira is the name of a village in Iyéyasu's native province of Mikawa, and it was adopted as a family name by nearly all those vassals of the Tokugawas who held their lands by virtue of direct grants from Iyéyasu. When the Tokugawa dynasty was overthrown in 1867, there were more than fifty Daimios bearing this surname.

scale and with greater splendour than before. This Shogun likewise greatly increased the university of Shohei, and threw it open for courses of public instruction, to which every one was admissible. The spread of public instruction had, in fact, by this time become, under the fostering care of the Tokugawa Shoguns, a subject of rivalry among the provinces and local governors of Japan.*

In the first year of Kokaku's reign a famine ravaged Japan, and it is recorded that the district of Yonesawa escaped from its effects by virtue of the administrative excellence of the governing prince, who distinguished himself above all others by the wise economies which he practised, and, at the same time, by the substantial encouragements which he bestowed upon the culture of tea, of the silkworm, etc., and also upon letters and the fine arts. But the most important events of this reign, as observed from the standpoint now occupied by us, were the repeated unsuccessful demands of Russian vessels to trade with Japan, the attack by Russians of a Japanese garrison in the island of Yezo, and the consequent attention which was given to the coast defences of the country by the minister Sadanobu. Important for like reasons was the great spread of the Dutch language in Japan which became observable in this reign, many scientific works being translated from Dutch into Japanese, and the number of students of the foreign tongue increasing from day to day.

The Shogun Iyénori, to whom I have made reference already, held the reins of power in Yedo for half a century, viz. from 1787 to 1837, and was consequently contemporary not only with the emperor Kokaku, of whose long reign I have just spoken, but likewise with his successor, the emperor Ninko, whose reign began in 1817 and continued down to 1846. Both Iyénori and Ninko have therefore been contemporaries

---

* The most celebrated establishments were the Ii-Shu-Kuwan, of the province of Higo; that of Meirin-Kuwan, of the province of Nagato; the Zoshi-Kuwan, of Kagoshima; the Kojo-Kuwan, of Yonesawa; the Seitoku-Sho-in, of Sakura; and the Yokendo, of Sendai.

of men no older than myself. The history of their time shows plainly enough that the beginning of the end of the long and prosperous domination of the Tokugawas was already appearing. This is clearly inferable from two of the more significant of the signs of their times: one was the general luxury

KEIKI, THE LAST OF THE TOKUGAWA SHOGUNS.

and extravagance of the country; the other was the increasing interference of foreigners. Regarding the first of these, it must be confessed that it is a deplorable tendency of human nature to turn even the blessings of peace into evils. In the very heart of the sweetest and maturest fruit the destroying worm is engendered; in the midst of stirless air, above an ocean without a ripple, the cyclone begins to spin and advance. Among men it is the same. What says our own laureate?

"Why do we prate of the blessings of Peace? We have made them a curse."

And what says the native historian of Japan under the Tokugawas? "The profound peace which Japan had enjoyed for so long a period had engendered the taste for luxury and show, so that the treasury had become impoverished, and the Shogun was obliged, in order to repair the breaches made in it, to strike a new coinage of inferior quality, and to alter the old coins." Poor Shogun! Poor people! But more serious than the financial difficulty, and more significant, were the perpetually renewed efforts of foreigners to force Japan to trade with them. Iyénori was so resolved to maintain the policy of isolation, and of that national independence which was considered to be jeopardised by foreign intercourse, and was at the same time so vexed to find foreign vessels continually appearing in Japanese ports with troublesome demands, that he gave orders to the Daimios to fire upon every foreign vessel that approached the shores of Japan. Later on he so far modified this as to provide for shipwrecked persons being protected and cared for, and to limit the attack upon foreign vessels to cases in which they were thought to be approaching with hostile intentions.

The last emperor of Japan, Komei-Tenno, reigned from 1847 till February 1867, and then dying, was succeeded upon the throne by his heir-apparent, the present emperor. The Shogun Iyénori was succeeded in 1837, after his fifty years of rule, by Iyéyoshi; he was followed in 1852 by Iyésada, and he in 1858 by Iyémochi. All that need be said of these Shoguns, and of the emperor Komei, will appear in other chapters, in which one will require to take note of the circumstances of that revolution which swept the Tokugawa dynasty away, and sent the last of its Shoguns, Hitotsu-bashi-Yoshinobu, into that learned leisure at Shidzuoka to which the first of them, Iyéyasu, voluntarily retired more than two and a half centuries before.

Those readers who have read this sketch of Japanese history thus far will, I think, draw two inferences from it with much confidence: 1, that whenever the excitements and troubles of war have for a time ceased, an innate love of art, literature, and education has given many evidences of its existence; and, 2, that whatever may have been the faults or shortcomings of Iyéyasu and his successors in the Shogunate, their dominion proved for much more than two centuries a great blessing to their country, endowing it with peace, with plenty, and with a springtime for all those intellectual pursuits the harvest of which the country has scarcely yet commenced to reap. Japan has since abandoned its exclusiveness, and committed its future fortunes to what are called freedom and civilisation, which, however great their advantages, will unhappily bear with them forms of loss and suffering and wrong which were altogether unknown to the Japan of the Tokugawas. Let us earnestly hope that the concurrent blessings may greatly outweigh all these.

This chapter may be usefully concluded by the following list of

THE TOKUGAWA SHOGUNS.

Iyéyasu	1603–1605
Hidétada	1605–1623
Iyémitsu	1623–1650
Iyétsuna	1650–1681
Isunayoshi	1681–1709
Iyénobu	1709–1713
Iyétsugu	1713–1717
Yoshimuné	1717–1745
Iyéshige	1745–1763
Iyéharu	1763–1787
Iyénori	1787–1838
Iyéyoshi	1838–1853
Iyésada	1853–1859
Iyémochi	1859–1866
Yoshinobu	1867–1868

CHAPTER XIV.

THE REVIVAL OF THE IMPERIAL POWER.

Long-standing grievances of the princes of Choshiu and Satsuma—Their projects for restoring power to the emperor—Literary influences of like nature—American demands for commercial intercourse—Defensive preparations—Commodore Perry presses the American demands—Russian demands—Renewed visit of Commodore Perry—The Shogun yields—The imperial court resists—Arrival of the English—An English treaty—The tremendous earthquakes of 1855—Wreck of the *Diana*—Further defensive preparations—The Shogun resolves to abolish the law against foreign intercourse—Continued resistance of the court—The Daimio Ii created chief minister of the Shogun—He concludes treaties with foreign governments—Death of the Shogun—The "Swaggering Prime Minister" is murdered—Agitation for the expulsion of foreigners—Despatch of Japanese envoys to Europe—The Mikado orders the Shogun to court—The emperor again free to assert his power.

THE author of the 'Kinsé Shiriaku,' a history of Japan from 1853 to 1869,* has taken great pains to compile from official sources a chronological record of the events which transpired in Japan from the arrival there of Commodore Perry's American squadron in 1853 down to the capture of Hakodaté in 1869, this last event being the conclusion of the

---

* In a short introduction to his translation of this native Japanese work, Mr. Ernest Satow says: "The author, for what other reason than a dislike for notoriety does not appear, has chosen to conceal his identity in the Preface under the fictitious name of 'The Rustic Annalist of the Pepper Mountain'; but as he has half revealed it on the title-page, which announces that the work is printed for Yamaguchi Uji, there can be no indiscretion in stating that he is an ancient official of the Foreign Department as it was constituted under the administration of the Shoguns, and now an official of the *Mombusho* or Education Department. These two facts are presumptive evidence of impartiality." For any use that I may make—and I shall make much in this chapter—of the 'Kinsé Shiriaku' I shall be indebted to the translation and notes of Mr. Satow.

revolutionary troubles which attended the overthrow of the Yedo Shoguns, and the restoration to supreme power of the Mikado, or emperor. It will not be possible, however, for any one to thoroughly understand the strange and dramatic events of this period, without carrying his mind back to that which occurred long before Commodore Perry sailed into the Sea of Sagami, and into the history of Japan. It will be in the recollection of the reader that when the death of Nobunaga occurred, Hideyoshi was engaged in the west with the prince of Choshiu, who refused to recognise the authority of Nobunaga; and although Hideyoshi concluded a peace with the prince before returning to the east to secure the chief power, and if possible the Shogunate, for himself, there could not be, and there was not, any establishment of cordial relations between the upstarts of the east (whether Hideyoshi or the Tokugawas) and the great quasi-independent princes of the west. In those days the prince of Choshiu saw his provinces reduced from ten to two, and the prince of Satsuma had five out of his eight taken from him; and neither they nor their descendants ever forgot or forgave the usurpations, as they considered them, of the Tokugawas; but through two centuries of peace those descendants waited and watched for the opportunity of overthrowing the usurpers and recovering their broad and valuable domains. The obvious way to this object was the rescue, as they might well consider it, of the legitimate sovereign of them all from the thraldom imposed on him by a single family of generals—a way which, if successfully pursued by themselves, would possess the double advantage of destroying the domineering Shogunate and of winning to themselves the chief favour and confidence of the liberated emperor. The cardinal principle of their policy consequently was the restoration of the imperial authority of the Mikado, and this principle the Satsuma and Choshiu clans were carefully trained to keep continually in view.

It may be thought by some that this principle was identical with that which the first of the Tokugawas, Iyéyasu, had himself laid down in his "Legacy" for the guidance of his successors, when he affirmed that "the relation of the Shogun to the Mikado was to be one of reverential homage," and that the supremacy of the monarch was to be in every way strengthened. But in view of the acts of Iyéyasu, and of the form in which he organised the government of Yedo, it cannot for a moment be doubted that the homage to be paid, and the supremacy strengthened, were both to be of a kind that was compatible with the retention of the actual government in the hands of his own successors. Any homage which involved weakness in the authority of the Shogunate, and any supremacy which would bring that into subjection, were doubtless as far from the intentions as from the acts of the Tokugawas. Nor is it at all difficult to understand how the exaltation of the Mikado might well be an object, both of those who would set him free and of those who had wrested his authority from him and wished to keep it. The Tokugawas dared not assail the nominal sovereignty of the Mikado. To have done so would have been to affront the entire nation, for the entire nation viewed the sovereign and the sovereignty alike as sacred, ordained of the gods, hallowed by time, and revered through all the strifes of twenty centuries. The isolation of the Mikado, which was so indispensable to the Shoguns, could not, therefore, be obtained by his removal, or even by his visible depression; but it could be secured by his greater exaltation, by increase of the homage paid him, by the further adoration of his sacredness, and the fuller recognition of his theoretical supremacy. Hence the policy of Iyéyasu and his successors. The princes of Choshiu and Satsuma, on the other hand, recognised in the Mikado's sovereignty and authority the only available instrument for the smiting down of the Shoguns. Round themselves it was impossible, and would for ever remain impossible, to rally the support of other princes and Daimios, and to gather the military forces even of the west country, unless a higher purpose than any centred in themselves could be presented. But such a purpose, higher than any other, and one at all times dear to the people, was the assertion of the greatness and power and glory and authority of the Mikado; and with this set before them, with this presented to the nation when the favourable time arrived, they might well hope to contrive another turn in Fortune's wheel, and such a turn as would "lower the proud" Shoguns, and bring back to themselves at least as much as the usurpers had torn from them.

While the princes of Choshiu and Satsuma were thus watching and preparing through the seventeenth, eighteenth, and part of the nineteenth centuries for the overthrow of the Yedo Shoguns, other influences were springing up which greatly tended to promote their object. One of the most important of these was the revival of learning and literature to which the Shoguns, and the Tokugawas generally, themselves so much contributed. Mr. Satow has pointed out that the great history of Japan, the *Dai Nihon Shi*, which the prince of Mito wrote in the seventeenth century (with the aid of many Japanese and Chinese scholars), did so much to recall the country to a sense of the Mikado's position that the prince may be regarded as "the real author of the movement which culminated in the revolution of 1868"; and this prince of Mito was a grandson of Iyéyasu. From his time forward there frequently appeared scholars and authors who revived the interest of the Japanese in the ancient religion and history of the country, each work of theirs bringing more and more home to the mind of the people the rights and privileges of the sovereign—rights and privileges many of which were known to be kept in abeyance by the system of government enforced from Yedo. In 1827 another history of Japan was published,* in which the author records the history of the great military families (Taira, Minamoto, Hojo, Ashikaga) that had usurped the powers of the Mikado. "This work had to pass the ordeal of the censorate at Yedo, and some of the volumes were repeatedly purged by the censors before they were allowed to be published. The unmistakable animus of this great book is to show that the Mikado is the only true ruler, in whom is the

---

* The *Nihon Guai Shi*, or 'External History of Japan,' by Rai Sanyo.

fountain of power, and to whom the allegiance of every Japanese is due, and that even the Tokugawas were not free from the guilt of usurpation" (Griffis). Thus, by force of that literary activity which successive Tokugawas had encouraged, their own domination was coming into disrepute, and the day for which the western princes had so long been waiting was beginning to dawn.

But while the Shogunate was thus becoming slowly undermined from internal forces, external forces were beginning to seriously press upon it from without, and the two causes combined brought about its overthrow. We have already seen, in the last chapter, the pressure which the repeated demands of foreigners put upon the Shogun Iyénori, and the warlike edict which he issued in consequence. We have likewise observed that the violence of his resolve to have every foreign vessel that approached the coast fired upon, had speedily to be subdued, and his warlike ardour restrained in presence of peaceful vessels. The attack made by the Russians upon a Japanese garrison in Yezo, although repelled, was a note of alarm which continued to resound at the Bakufu* of Yedo. While the Shogun was opposing the admission of foreign vessels to their ports of Japan, a Dutch man-of-war arrived at Nagasaki with a letter from the king of Holland counselling him to open the country, and renew relations with other powers. The Shogun replied that he could not change the traditional laws of Japan.

When Komei-Tenno commenced his reign, Iyéyoshi was Shogun. In his time two American vessels arrived at Uraga, near the entrance to the Bay of Yedo, their captains formally requesting that commerce between Japan and their country might be permitted. The Shogun gave the same answer as his predecessors, and ordered the Daimios of the coast provinces to press forward the defences of the coast. The Dutch government again advised the Shogun that various powers were arranging to send ambassadors to

---

* "Bakufu" is the term applied by its opponents to the Shogunate, from *Baku*, a curtain (the curtain of a general's tent), and *Fu*, a government office.

Japan, to press for treaties of commerce, the only result being more urgent orders to proceed with the defences. The Shogun removed the existing restrictions upon the sizes of vessels, and the prince of Satsuma, by permission, built and presented to the government two ships of European type, the prince of Mito following his example by building and presenting to the state another. Persons skilled in the use of firearms were ordered to instruct troops in the art, and the example being followed by others, European arms, and the European military system, came largely into operation. The governor of Nagasaki was ordered to form an arsenal, and a few years later a dock. The Satsuma clan also established a naval arsenal and a European rope factory, and the Hizen clan built a gun foundry.

In 1852 the Shogun was informed by the king of Holland that the United States was about to send a squadron into Japanese waters to again urge the making of a commercial treaty, and on the 7th of July 1853 Commodore Perry arrived at Uraga with a squadron of four ships, and sent up his demand for a treaty of amity and commerce. "In those days," naïvely says the native historian, "all classes of the nation were so accustomed to a peaceful and enjoyable existence that the suddenness of the event caused great excitement." The ancient custom of refusing foreign vessels admission to any other port but that of Nagasaki was explained to the commodore, "who, however, would not listen." The Bakufu ordered the Daimios to guard the neighbouring coast, and reported the affair to the imperial court, who commanded the Shinto priests at the shrines of Isé to offer up prayers for the sweeping away of the "barbarians."* On the Bakufu explaining to the American that the general opinion of the nation must be taken on the subject, he sailed away, promising to return before a year had elapsed. On the clans being consulted, some pronounced in favour of a treaty, and some in favour of repelling all advances of the foreigner. The latter appear

---

* This term, as employed by the Japanese, meant little more than "outsiders."

to have predominated. At about this time the Shogun
Iyéyoshi died, and was succeeded by Iyésada. Sir Ruther-
ford Alcock, in his 'Capital of the Tycoon,' gives what "is
said to be the palace chronicle" of the mode of Iyéyoshi's
death, according to which he was stabbed by one of his
officers. His prime minister, who was suspected of insti-
gating his destruction, committed *hara-kiri*.

In the following month a Russian ship entered Nagasaki,
with the object of establishing friendly relations, in order
that the northern boundary question concerning the island
of Saghalin might be discussed. This visit stimulated
still further the predominant desire to put the country in
a state of defence. The ex-prince of Mito, who had been
confined to his secondary palace at Yedo for having melted
down all the Buddhist bells in his district into cannon, and
for similar acts, was released, and appointed a commissioner
for superintending maritime defences. He was instructed
to make extensive military preparations:—this prince, we
are told, always had at heart an increase of respect for the
Mikado and the expulsion of the foreigners, and he was
celebrated for his energy and courage. Soon afterwards
(in October) permission to build war-vessels was given to
all the Daimios, the red ball on a white ground being
chosen as their distinguishing flags. The construction of
the forts of Shinagawa, which are now such conspicuous
objects off the city of Tokio, was commenced during this
month, and many large cannon were cast. The expenses
were levied upon Yedo and the surrounding villages, and
upon the rich merchants of Osaka.

In February 1854, long before the year had elapsed,
Commodore Perry again appeared with his war squadron,
anchoring about twenty miles from Yedo.* He there

---

* The Japanese account, in the 'Kinsé Shiriaku,' says the "American envoy again arrived with his ships, anchoring this time at Shimoda in Idzu, and demanded the same things as had been urged in the letter presented in the previous year. He waited until the fourth month, when the Bakufu promised," etc. On his second arrival in Japan, however, on the 13th of February 1854, Commodore Perry really passed beyond his former anchorage off Uraga to within about twenty miles of Yedo, as I

renewed his demand of the previous year. After a delay of three months the Bakufu agreed to sign a treaty under which kind treatment should be shown to shipwrecked sailors, and permission should be given to obtain wood, water, provisions, coals, and other stores needed by ships, and for ships to anchor in the ports of Shimoda and Hakodaté (in the south of the Island of Yezo). These privileges were soon afterwards accorded to the Russians and the Dutch. Thus was in part broken down, without hostilities, and by the concession of the Shogunate or Bakufu, that refusal to admit foreigners which had become an established custom of the country, and which many of its most influential men considered indispensable to its security and happiness. And let the reader note that by this concession the Shogun made himself responsible for a policy which was hateful to the great western princes of Choshiu and Satsuma, to the great eastern prince of Mito, and to many other influential personages, who were at the same time eager to see the Mikado restored to the exercise of his sovereign powers.* The Americans throughout the preceding negotiations considered themselves to be in communication with the emperor of Japan, and only subsequently discovered that the Shogun was no emperor, and had no power to conclude treaties with foreigners.

have stated in the text. He was pressed and entreated to return to Uraga, where the representatives of the Japanese government awaited him, in a building prepared for the purpose, but stoutly refused, and declared that his intention was to go to Yedo itself for his answer. Eleven days afterwards, as the Japanese authorities still urged his return, he moved his squadron several miles up the bay, and anchored off Kanagawa, above Yokohama, within sight of the capital. On the 10th of April, after concluding a treaty, he again put his squadron under weigh, and in spite of the most urgent dissuasions went up so close to the capital as to satisfy himself that "the city of Yedo can be destroyed by a few steamers of very light draught of water and with guns of the heaviest calibre." After making this discovery, so gratifying to the commodore, but less so to the million of harmless inhabitants, his vessels steamed away to their original anchorage of Uraga, and a few days afterwards on to Shimoda.

* It will be well for the reader to bear in mind, in reading this chapter, that the rich provinces of Mito, Owari, and Kii were bestowed by Iyéyasu upon three of his sons, and that the Kii branch of his family supplied in the direct line the first seven of the Tokugawa Shoguns.

And here I would point out that the view which many persons at home have vaguely taken of the events of the imperial restoration of 1867 is altogether erroneous. From observing the present state of things, in which the emperor and his court are among the best friends of foreign intercourse and modern progress, and from remembering that the Tokugawa Shoguns were so long strenuously averse to it, they draw the inference that the Mikado and his court were all along contending against the Shoguns for the objects now realised, and that the sweeping away of the Shogunate and the opening up of the country to foreigners were the results of an imperial policy long pursued with these objects, and reaching its climax in 1867-68. Nothing could well be further from the truth. The court of Kioto was in 1854, and for several years following, vigorously averse to the admission of foreigners, and the granting to the American envoy of the terms before stated by the Shogun was made, by his powerful enemies, the occasion of bringing themselves and the court into closer accord, with the view of resisting the Shogun's action in the matter. How it happened that, although the policy of concession ultimately triumphed, those who at first most opposed it triumphed with it, while the Tokugawas who commenced it came to grief and overthrow, will appear hereafter. Meanwhile it may be well to note that in making the concession to Commodore Perry without the authority of the Mikado, the Shogun assumed an imperial authority with which no reasonable theory of his government could endow him, and for which nothing but the direst exigency could have furnished a satisfactory excuse. One can easily conceive how readily his adroit enemies at the court of Kioto would construe this act against him, and what a cry it would give them in appealing to the country on behalf of the Mikado when the time arrived for doing so.

While troubles, external and internal, were thus preparing, the English made their appearance upon the scene, and those who know what sort of men we are abroad, and how we generally bear ourselves in the East (and one may say in the west, north, and south too) to people weaker in ships and arms than ourselves, may well imagine that our appearance did not greatly contribute to the tranquillity of the government of Japan! We had come to blows with Russia in those days (about the Holy Places), and our admiral in the Pacific, Rear-Admiral Sir James Stirling, went to Nagasaki, made known that fact, notified the Japanese that we might have to do some fighting in the vicinity of their shores, and requested them to supply us, belligerents as we were, with wood, water, and provisions if required. Although the Shogun could not have been able at that time to fully appreciate either our greatness or our wilfulness, he knew enough of both to grant the permission required, restricting the visits of our war-ships to Nagasaki and Hakodaté. Hence an English treaty, which was not, however, ratified.

To increase the anxieties of these unhappy Japanese, who must already have become quite sure that foreign intercourse was not in point of fact destined to add to the tranquillity which they had enjoyed under the dynasty of Yedo, Nature intervened about this time to further disturb their peace by an unusual succession of earthquakes. Through several of the provinces of the south,* on one occasion, a tremendous earth-wave passed, heaving the land like water into waves, opening the ground in many places, throwing up mud and water, rolling the sea in upon the shore and sweeping off the people, driving the ocean up the rivers and flooding the country, bringing landslips down from the mountains, casting down the cities and setting them on fire, and otherwise converting four hundred miles of country into a scene of desolation and ruin. In one night seventy separate shocks occurred, and in fourteen months more than eight hundred had to be endured. During the course of these tremendous shakings and heavings of the earth the city of Yedo was visited by one of the worst, which threw down more than

---

* Suruga, Mikawa, Totomi, Isé, Iga, Setsu, Harima, and the great island of Shikoku.

fourteen thousand dwelling-houses, and nearly two thousand of the fireproof storehouses in which the citizens place their property for safety. One hundred and four thousand citizens lost their lives. Nor did the foreigners escape from these terrors: our Russian friends in particular discovered that we "barbarians" were not to have everything our own way in the ports of Japan, for the Russian frigate *Diana*, which was lying in the port of Shimoda, was caught up by the sea, whirled round and round forty-three times in thirty minutes (although not constructed upon the circular type of Admiral Popoff), and flung upon the shore with such violence that she suffered irreparable injuries—showing that if Japan could only enter into an offensive and defensive alliance with her earthquakes she might dispense with war-ships and fortifications, and accomplish a great economy.

Notwithstanding the concessions which it had already made to foreigners, the government felt that defensive preparations were still urgently necessary, and accordingly the princely houses of Sendai and Satake were ordered to garrison the coasts of Yezo; men were sent to Nagasaki to learn how the Dutch worked steam vessels, and batteries were erected at the mouths of the Osaka River. The court went so far as to give orders to melt down all the bells of the Buddhist monasteries throughout the country, to be "cast into cannon and muskets"; but on the princes of Chionin and Rinnoji opposing the measure, it was abandoned. As may well be supposed, not only was the treasury of the Bakufu pretty low by this time, but the princes and Daimios had been called upon to make large contributions to the state defences. An illustration of this is recorded: both the Mikado's palace in Kioto and the Shogun's castle in Yedo had been burnt down, as the shrines of the Shoguns at Shiba and Wooyeno had previously been. All these the Shogun commenced to rebuild, but he refrained from calling upon the clans to contribute towards the expense, as had theretofore been done, although "the Bakufu treasury was reduced to a very low ebb."

In October 1855 Rear-Admiral Stirling returned to Japan,

and next year Mr Townshend Harris arrived from America at Shimoda, with full powers from his government, and with instructions to reside in Japan, and requested permission to present his credentials to the Shogun. "The Bakufu was driven to its wits' end by the repeated visits of the foreigners,"* and, evil portents increasing, the burden of affairs was found too great for the Shogun's minister, and a new one was appointed, with rank above his colleagues. Hitherto the Shogun, notwithstanding his concessions, had preserved as far as possible, or endeavoured to preserve, the law of the Tokugawa Shoguns, dating from 1639, providing for the exclusion of foreigners. But he now was made to feel, by the repeated arrival of armed squadrons and vessels from abroad with fresh demands, that the persistence in that policy would result in war. A letter from the head of the Dutch Factory at Nagasaki confirmed this view, saying, "I advise you to be careful, for in intercourse with foreign countries disputes often arise out of the smallest matters, let alone questions of right and wrong." A man of experience this! "To be ignorant of your own weakness is certainly not the way to preserve your country from danger. It was for this reason that China some ten years ago lost part of her territory after the opium war, and that the province of Canton is now a desert." The ministers took this to heart, and decided that the law of 1639, and with it their bearing to foreigners, must be changed in order to preserve peace. Whereupon the ex-prince of Mito took offence, and declared his unwillingness to have any further share in public affairs. This feeling rose, or sank, to disgust with the prince and his council when they heard that, yielding to the persistent pressure of the "American Harris," the Shogun had resolved to give that envoy an interview in Yedo, in spite of the custom which prohibited the entrance of foreigners into the city. Their annoyance was shared by the princes of Kiushiu, Owari, and most of the other members of the Extraordinary Council. A written protest against the proceeding was handed in.

---

* 'Kinsé Shiriaku.'

Mr. Harris was, nevertheless, received officially in Yedo by the Shogun, and afterwards saw the ministers, explaining his demands: Unrestricted trade between both countries in all but gold and cereals, without any official interference;* the closing of Shimoda (the earthquake having shaken its reputation), and the opening of Kanagawa (near Yedo, and adjoining Yokohama) and Osaka; the residence of a minister plenipotentiary in Yedo, and conclusion and ratification of a detailed treaty. The Shogun now appealed to the Mikado and court at Kioto for its consent, sending ministers to explain the critical state of affairs, and to ask for sanction; but some of the court nobles (*kugé*) strongly opposed the measure. Mr. Harris now began to perceive that he had all along been dealing, not with a secular king, as he and other foreigners had supposed the Shogun or Tycoon to be, but with an officer who had a monarch over him, and, getting impatient of the long delay of his mission, he threatened to go to Kioto himself, and there arrange the matter. The Shogun therefore endeavoured to persuade the court to give way, but in vain. At one time the principal court minister (Kuambaku) was talked over, and empowered the Shogun to deal with the foreign question as he found best, but eighty-eight court nobles reproached him for the decision, and the proceeding was then stopped.

About this time Ii Kamon no-Kami† (of whom I shall hereafter speak as Ii) was created Tairo, or chief minister, by the Bakufu, and, the Shogun Iyésada being childless, the prince of Kiushiu, Iyémochi, was chosen as his successor by Ii.

The earthquake which shook Yedo so terribly in 1855 was succeeded in 1856 by a storm which destroyed more than a hundred thousand lives there, and now, to complete the

---

* The fairness of this demand, coming from America, must be admired. It suited the United States to force this upon Japan; but would they submit to have it forced upon themselves by us? "Do unto others," etc.

† Ii was the Daimio of Hikoné, a fief and town on the eastern shore of Lake Biwa. He was the head of the *Fudai* class of Daimios, and therefore closely allied to the Tokugawas. *Kamon-no-kami* was his title at the imperial court. His personal name was Naosuké.

usual trio of calamity, an epidemic of chorera in 1858 swept through the land, and "about thirty thousand people died in Yedo alone."

But neither earthquake, storm, nor cholera could stay the determined on-coming of the Christian powers, and in July of this year (1858) American and Russian men-of-war went to Yokohama and informed the over-worried government that they would be followed in a few days by the English and French squadrons, all of them being determined to conclude treaties of peace and amity with Japan—of course by force of sword and musket and cannon, if not otherwise. In view of those terrors, and fearing lest some unlucky "accident" should set the Christian cannon blazing at the poor people, Ii waited no longer for the consent of the court, but concluded a treaty with Mr. Harris at Kanagawa, affixed his seal to it, and reported the transaction to Kioto. Immediately afterwards the Russians, English, and French entered Japan, and obtained treaties from him on the model of the American treaty—and therefore *not* such a treaty, be it observed, as they would have ventured to try and force upon each other! * The result was that a widespread agitation for the "expulsion of the barbarians" arose throughout the country, and Japan's two centuries and a half of peace were past.

On the 15th of August the Shogun Iyésada, who had for some time been ill, died, and left to Iyémochi such an inheritance of trouble as no Tokugawa had ever before succeeded to, and as no Japanese had ever before believed possible. It had been the pride of Japan that its shores had never been successfully invaded, and that no foreign foot had ever trodden its soil for long without permission. But now the foreigner trod the streets of Yedo itself as he listed, and

---

* For fuller details respecting the proceedings of the various foreign ministers in Japan at this and later periods the reader may with great advantage refer to Mr. Mossman's 'New Japan,' published by Murray (London, 1873)—a book full of valuable information, but necessarily written without the knowledge we now possess of the difficulties and dangers which beset both the Mikado and the Shogun twenty years ago. Hence the accusations of bad faith, etc., which the author sometimes levels at the Japanese.

the grim mouths of the foreign squadrons grinned protection to the intruder, and what appeared to be derision to the proud islanders in their deep-felt abasement. No wonder that a cry of resistance and resentment arose all over the land. It was a wail of anguish from a humiliated and overborne people, on its passage from two thousand years of independence into a state of unknown subjection for a period unknown, possibly for ever. The excitement of the military class manifested itself in repeated acts of violence, and the members of the foreign legations in Japan could only move about the streets of Yedo and its suburbs at the risk of their lives. They were frequently mobbed and assaulted, and on one occasion three Russians, an officer, a steward, and a sailor, were savagely murdered at Kanagawa, which had been made a treaty port, but which had been practically set aside in favour of Yokohama. Soon afterwards an interpreter of the British Legation was likewise murdered; but as he was a Japanese, and, according to Mr. Mossman, ill-tempered, proud, quarrelsome, and violent, it was, no doubt, a straining of the facts to connect him with the antagonism to foreigners. Both the Russian and British ministers found themselves unable to obtain due redress for these wrongs, owing to the inability of the Shogun's government to contend with the powerful influences that beset it on every side.

The accession of Iyémochi to power caused many anxieties to the opponents of the Bakufu's policy. Iyémochi was but twelve years old, and Ii, who was called by some "the Swaggering Prime Minister" (a personage wholly unknown among ourselves), would naturally wield his full authority. He very soon asserted his will in the choice of a person to be nominated head of the Tokugawas and successor to Iyémochi. The powerful princes of Owari and Echizen, with several others, advised that Hitotsubashi Giobukio, otherwise known as Keiki,* who was of man's estate, much esteemed by his

---

* Keiki is the son of the prince of Mito, and had been adopted into the house of Hitotsubashi, being sometimes designated as in the text, and at other times as Hitotsubashi-Yoshinobu. I shall for convenience call him Keiki. He is the ex-Shogun now residing at Shidzuoka.

father, and had a certain reputation, should be selected. But the prime minister, Ii, rejected their advice, and nominated the prince of Kii, another boy of twelve. In consequence of this appointment, and of the foreign treaties, the princes of Owari and Echizen, and the ex-prince of Mito, went to the castle to confer with the Shogun, but Ii denied them the interview, himself personally overruled their remonstrances, and disgraced the three princes by forbidding them to reappear at the castle. When the court heard of this, and of Ii's personal luxury and indulgence in theatrical and other amusements, he was summoned to Kioto, but excused himself from going on the ground of his public duties. The court then secretly advised Mito as follows: "The Bakufu has shown great disregard of public opinion in concluding treaties without waiting for the opinion of the court, and in disgracing princes so closely allied by blood to the Shogun. The Mikado's rest is disturbed by the spectacle of such misgovernment, when the fierce barbarian is at our very door. Do you therefore assist the Bakufu with your advice; expel the barbarians, content the mind of the people, and restore tranquillity to his majesty's bosom." The Mikado and his court evidently knew less of the power and character of the "barbarians" than was desirable. Meanwhile the prime minister had his spy, one Nagano Shiazen, at Kioto, and learnt from him all that was going on, which was very much more than I can undertake to narrate. He therefore despatched a minister (Manabé Shinosa) to Kioto, and he, with the aid of the Shogun's resident, threw three court nobles into confinement—including the present prime minister of Japan, Sanjo, whose acquaintance I lately had the honour of making in Tokio—put some of the conspiring *samurai* to death, and arrested and carried off to Yedo thirty other disaffected persons—disaffected, that is, towards himself. Thus ended the year 1858.

But the imperious acts of Ii did not come to an end with the year. After receiving repeated representations from Prince Mito concerning the respect due to the Mikado and the expulsion of the foreigners, the prime minister and his colleagues turned upon the prince, recounted his acts of disloyalty to them (as they were pleased to consider them), told him he had failed in his duty to the Bakufu, and ordered him off into perpetual confinement in his castle of Mito. Keiki they likewise forced into retirement for having coveted the Shogun's office. Shortly afterwards they made the princes of Owari, Echizen, Tosa, and Uwajima resign to their sons their posts as Daimios and betake themselves to private life in their private *yashikis* or residences. Twenty other persons of some importance were condemned for conspiracy, some to imprisonment and some to exile, while several were sent into eternal exile by being put to death. In the summer of this year, 1859, the ports of Kanagawa, Nagasaki, and Hakodaté were opened to foreigners, and permission was given to Japanese to trade with them. In the early part of 1860 Japanese envoys were despatched to America for the first time; but before the end of March Ii's administration came to an abrupt end, he himself being despatched to a more distant land, and one from which there is no returning. I must let the author of the 'Kinsé Shiriaku' tell the story of his taking off:—

"When Ii Kamon-no-kami punished the princes of Owari, Mito, and Echizen, all classes held their breath, and looked on with silent affright. From that moment his power increased daily, but a few *ronins** conspired to assassinate him, and, watching for an opportunity, approached his palanquin one day as he was proceeding to the castle, under the pretence of presenting a petition. Snow happened to be falling heavily, and rendered every object indistinct, so that the escort, taking the men to be ordinary petitioners, scarcely noticed them. Suddenly the head of the train was attacked, and the commotion which ensued in that quarter drew away the attention of the guards at the side of the palanquin. The petitioner profited by his opportunity to cut down the bearers and to reach the palanquin, and a number of confederates sprang up instantly, who succeeded in slaying the chief minister and in escaping with his head. The escort engaged the men who had attacked the front of the train, and fought vigorously. Four, including Nagoshi Gengi and Kusakabé Naiki, were killed on the spot, while Kusakari and nineteen others were wounded.

* *Samurai* who had left their masters' service, and did what they could for a living.

The affair occurred so suddenly that they were unable to assist their master, and on looking round were horrified to see what had happened. They pursued the *ronins*, but could not overtake them. This affair, known as the Sakurada outrage, occurred on the third day of the month (March 23)."

The assassins were all Mito men. Some were killed at the time, and the remainder gave themselves up, and were put to death, first recounting the sins of the man whom they had slain, which included the disgrace of the princes, the imprisonment of the court nobles, the slaying of *samurai* at Kioto, and the being frightened by the empty threats of the foreign barbarians into concluding treaties with them without the sanction of the Mikado, and under the pretext of political necessity. "These crimes being such as neither gods nor men could pardon, they as the representatives of the divine anger had chastised him." They prayed that death might be inflicted on them, and the Bakufu readily granted their prayer.*

From this time the advocates of the expulsion of foreigners continually increased, batches of them stirring up strife in Yedo, in Hitachi, and in Shimosa, and as foreign merchants and other strangers were continually arriving in the country, the Bakufu, who earnestly desired to protect them, had much difficulty in doing so. Their efforts were not always successful in this respect, for on the night of January 14, 1861, Mr. Hewsken, the American Secretary of

---

* Mr. Mossman says, in 'New Japan': "At first it was supposed that they had all been killed or captured, but this could not have been the case, as the head of the Regent was said to have reached the Daimio Mito, who was in a stronghold on his own territory. When this old man of sixty saw the grey head of his enemy he spat upon its face, muttering maledictions. It was then secretly conveyed to Kioto, the capital at that time of the Mikado, and there exposed at a place of execution in the city especially set apart for nobles or princes condemned to decapitation. Over the ghastly trophy a placard was placed, stating: 'This is the head of a traitor who has violated the most sacred laws of Japan—those which forbid the admission of foreigners into the country.' After two hours' exposure, the same intrepid retainers who had brought the head took it away, and afterwards made their way into Yedo, where, during the night, they threw it over the wall of Ii Kamo's palace, from whence he had sallied out in pride and power on the morning of his death."

Legation, was murdered. The number of the disaffected *ronins* increased, in fact, to such an extent that they proceeded into the provinces of Kodzuké and Shimotsuké, both situated to the north of Yedo, and there levied charges upon the peasants and tradespeople. The Bakufu ordered the house of Mito to arrest and curb them.

On the 5th of July English blood was first shed. Some *ronins* attacked the house occupied by the English in Takanawa, the southern suburb of Yedo; the assailants were repelled by aid of the Japanese guards,* and several *ronins* were killed. Some of the guards were also killed and wounded, and two of the English were wounded. The native historian adds: "The English minister was angry, and said such ruffians only existed because the Japanese government could not rule its own country"—which was partly true, but was scarcely consistent, perhaps, with politeness on the part of an uninvited guest, who by his presence was stirring up these troubles. "Remarking that in future it would be useless to appeal to reason with such a people, he retired with the French and Dutch representatives to Yokohama, *in order to prepare for an attack with troops*.† The Bakufu made ten thousand apologies, and the affair, after some difficulties, was peaceably settled." And it is well for the credit of England that it was so settled, and that the British arms were not then, at least, turned upon people who were doing their best to protect our intrusive countrymen, and had shed the blood of their guards and risked their own lives in defence of them. The British force attacking the very troops that had fought for and saved their countrymen would have been a spectacle for gods and men! However, from this time onwards English troops were always stationed at Yokohama, to guard against surprises, and they were commonly called the "Scarlet Regiment," from the colour of their clothing. The Bakufu

---

* The English accounts complain of the conduct of the Japanese guard, but they admit that the bodies of the two assailants who were killed bore abundant proofs of the vigour with which they had been repelled by Japanese swords.

† This statement is by a Japanese. The italics are mine.

ordered the house of Mito to arrest the assailants of the English residence, but they effected their retreat. In escape of further troubles, the ex-prince of Mito died in September 1861. The remaining incident of this year was the marriage of the younger sister of the Mikado to the Shogun Iyémochi, to show to the world that the imperial family and the house of Tokugawa were politically one.

On the 21st of January 1862 Japanese envoys were despatched to England, France, Russia, Holland. Prussia, and Portugal, for the first time, and a few weeks afterwards another minister of the Bakufu was attacked by *ronins* on his way into the castle, for having, as documents found on them alleged, followed up the policy of the deceased prime minister Ii, " and commanded learned scholars to collect precedents for the deposition of the emperor, his intention being to depose the Son of Heaven." The minister escaped with a wound in the shoulder, but the Bakufu dismissed him, and increased the salaries of several of the court nobles.

The ferment throughout the country still increased, the *samurai* of several clans deserting and joining the *ronins*. At Fushimi, near Kioto, there was fighting between the disaffected and the retainers of Shimadzu Idzumi, the father of the prince of Satsuma. Another unhappy incident occurred at the English residence at Yedo, one of the guard murdering two Englishmen in the garden, and then committing suicide. The English and their allies demanded satisfaction, and received the dead body of the murderer, and an apology. The commander of the guard was removed. In English accounts of these transactions, the greatest horror of the massacres is, of course, expressed, and the gallantry with which our representatives remained at their dangerous post is very properly extolled. But it is fair to observe that writers who show themselves very capable of painting in the darkest colours the wrongs done to ourselves, somehow fail even to notice the wrongs to which the Japanese had to submit. The insults which they had to endure—and down to this moment have had to endure—from the foreign press in Yokohama, were of the most galling nature; and as an example of the acts which English authors can recount with placidity, when directed against the natives, I may quote the following from Mr. Mossman's 'New Japan': "Among the imports at Yokohama was a tiger from Singapore, brought over by a Dutch trader. The Japanese customs refused at first to let it be landed, while the shipmaster would not take it back. In this dilemma *it was resolved that it should be let loose on shore*, which horrified the officials, and they gladly admitted the animal, while the importer sold it for ten times its cost." Mr. Mossman, who has a Christian horror of Japanese offences, has no word of complaint to direct against those who treated the Japanese thus insolently.

Moved by oft-repeated horrors, and the inflammatory condition of the whole country, the Mikado sent to Yedo requiring the Shogun to go to Kioto with *all* the Daimios, ascertain the opinion of the country, expel the barbarians, and "so calm the indignation of his Divine Ancestry." He further required that a sort of cabinet be formed of five great princes, to be consulted on public affairs; that Keiki should be appointed guardian of the Shogun, and that the ex-prince of Echizen should be made prime minister. For two hundred and thirty years—since the time of Shogun Iyémitsu—the personal homage of the Shogun to the emperor had been neglected, and most people came now to hear of it for the first time. The sensation created by the imperial command must be imagined. The Shogun resolved to comply with all the emperor's instructions. The former acts of the Shogun in imprisoning and banishing court nobles and Daimios had previously been cancelled, and Keiki and the ex-prince of Echizen received the appointments above-named. The Bakufu established at Kioto a protectorate, and appointed Matsudaira Higo, prince of Aidzu, to fill the office. The time which the Daimios had to pass compulsorily in Yedo was lessened, and they were now authorised to keep their wives and eldest sons at home on their domains—a serious blow to the city of Yedo, of course. The Bakufu confiscated a large part of the lands of the late prime minister Ii, on account of his alleged crimes. Meanwhile in Kioto the imperial court commanded the princes of Satsuma, Choshiu, and Tosa to act in concert for the repression of disorders, and the word "Sat-cho-to," compounded of the three first syllables of their names, became a popular expression of the influence and popularity of the princes.

We have now seen how it happened that a combination of internal and external causes brought the long prosperous Shogunate of the Tokugawas into such a coil of difficulties that the power of the Mikado was again at liberty to assert itself, and Kioto once more able to issue its commands to Yedo. With this revival of the imperial authority I may fitly conclude this chapter.

RICE-CUTTING.

CHAPTER XV.

THE FALL OF THE SHOGUN.

The Mikado commands the Shogun to expel the "barbarians"—The Ashikaga images beheaded and pilloried—A day fixed for the expulsion—Assassination of Mr. Richardson—The English revenges—Bombardment of Kagoshima—Indemnities paid—The closing of the ports urged—Choshiu fires upon foreign ships—Bombardment of Shimonoséki—Internal difficulties of the country—Dismissal of the Choshiu clan from Kioto—Rebellion of the *ronins*—Choshiu attacks a Satsuma ship—Troubles in the north—Fighting in Kioto—Return and disgrace of the envoys to Europe—Hostile parties—Choshiu repels the attacks of the Shogun's forces—Death of the Shogun—The foreign squadrons go to Hiogo—The Mikado yields and approves the treaties—Reconciliation of Choshiu and Satsuma—The last Shogun, Keiki—Death of the Mikado—Abdication of Keiki.

THE year 1863 was a trying period for the government of Japan. It opened with a new assertion of the imperial power in the form of a message from the Mikado to the Shogun at Yedo declaring that the Bakufu must clear away old abuses and entirely reform the constitution, and so give peace to the imperial mind; also that he must go to Kioto in the spring, issue his orders to the clans, and proceed without further delay to the expulsion of the barbarians. One of the bearers of this message was the minister Sanjo, now prime minister at Tokio. In pursuance of a previous imperial order, an amnesty for all political offenders since 1858 was decreed, and pensions were granted to the widows and orphans of all who suffered death for their opinions. But the troubles of the country were far from ceasing. The house building for the British Embassy was set fire to, and on Keiki arriving at Kioto the *samurai* and the *ronins* pressed him concerning the expulsion of the foreigners.

He could but temporise with them, and temporising so disgusted them that they cut off an unfortunate fellow's head, and sent it as a blood-offering to Keiki to further the expulsion. They also—which was even more objectionable to some persons—cut off the heads of the images of three of the Ashikagas,* which were enshrined in the Toji temples, and pilloried them in the dry bed of the river. The Tokugawas understood the hint, no doubt. The prince of Aidzu arrested the offenders, and Choshiu pleaded for their lives; but in vain, for Aidzu and Echizen were obdurate. In April the Shogun went to Kioto, presented himself at court on the day of his arrival, and took up his residence in the castle of Nijo. The prince of Satsuma left Kioto without waiting for leave, and proceeded to Kagoshima (in his own province), on the pretext of silencing slander and preparing to expel the foreigner. During this period the court daily deliberated upon the latter subject, and at length sent the prince of Mito to Yedo to superintend the closing of the ports. All the maritime princes were sent home to prepare for war. Pressed continually by the clans (through their *samurai*, and by the *ronins*) to fix a date for the expulsion, the ex-prince of Echizen resigned his post, and slipped quietly away to his province.

It becoming at length impossible, apparently, to further postpone the matter, the Shogun and his high officials went to court, and the 25th of June was then fixed upon as the day for expelling the foreigners. The Bakufu was instructed to communicate the news to all the clans, and, affecting to obey, privately resolved to do nothing. The Mikado next proposed to visit a famous war-god shrine,† and there deliver to the Shogun the sword emblematic of his authority to expel the barbarians. The Shogun fell conveniently ill, and could not go; and Keiki, who went

---

* Taka-Uji, his son Yoshinori, and Yoshimitsu.

† Otokoyama in Yamashiro, also called Iwashimidzu, on the left bank of the Yodogawa, 15 miles from Kioti. It is a shrine to the memory of Ojin-Tenno, the deified emperor there worshipped under the title of Hachiman Daibosatsu.

as his proxy, fell no less conveniently ill at the shrine
itself, and descended from it. The *ronins* were furious, and
insisted upon the Mikado himself taking the field, asking
that they might be allowed to march in his van. The
court contrived, however, temporarily to appease them. But
the *ronins* in Yedo gave a great deal of trouble. The Bakufu
tried to collect and train them into an organised force; but
they comprised many lawless ruffians, who plundered the
citizens, and were preparing to attack Yokohama. The
Bakufu had, at last, to appeal to the clans to arrest these
rascals, and thus restored tranquillity.

At this time occurred a further cause of trouble with the
English. Shimadzu Saburo, a near relation of the prince
of Satsuma, was travelling from Yedo to Kioto, and when
passing through a place called Namanugi, not far from
Yedo, some English people rode up to the head of his
train—a sad insult to the Japanese, whether done in
ignorance, heedlessness, or otherwise. "A native who
would attempt to cross, walk, or ride into a Daimio's procession would, according to invariable custom, meet with
instant death" (Griffis). The Yedo authorities, it is said,
had previously requested foreigners not to go on the road
in question on that day. The three men of the party were
promptly attacked by the escort, and one of them, Mr.
Richardson, was unfortunately killed, as he probably would
have been in any such case in Japan in those days, and as he
was more certain than ever to be at a moment when, as we
have seen, the whole land was aflame with excitement, and
with hostility to foreigners. I shall not dwell long upon the
subject. Saburo said: "The English insulted me, and my
escort punished them." The English said to the Shogun,
You must arrest and execute in the presence of our officers
the person who was the cause of the act—signifying Saburo.
If you cannot do this, we shall demand an indemnity of
500,000 dollars from the Bakufu, and we will go to Satsuma
and take 125,000 dollars there also. Delay occurring, the
British men-of-war—those omnipresent ministers of pure
and stainless justice—were called upon to speak with their

persuasive voices in favour of the payment, and the Bakufu understood the nature of their eloquence so well beforehand that they paid the fee (only £100,000!), and thus got them to go away again, without putting themselves to the trouble of doing anything. Before the matter was thus happily settled (so far as Yedo was concerned), and the bright unselfish honour of Great Britain vindicated, the poor people of Yedo (who had nothing whatever to do with the matter), warned by a proclamation, had to pack up their property and take refuge in the country around, lest the guns of H.M.S. *Havoc** should shed their blood and involve them in ruin.

But the matter was far from being over with Satsuma. On the 12th of August a squadron of seven British men-of-war appeared off Kagoshima, and demanded the further indemnity of 125,000 dollars. The English account of the transaction proves, of course, that all this was quite right and necessary, and that although the squadron purposely went to make "reprisals," the fighting was really brought about by the Japanese! But the Japanese view the matter differently, and say that when the Satsuma clan were about to reply to the demand for money " the English seized the man-of-war belonging to the clan without the slightest provocation." At any rate a battle occurred. We bombarded both the forts and the city for a couple of days, with a net result which Mr. Griffis sums up thus : " The explosion of magazines, partial destruction of the batteries, a conflagration which reduced factories, foundries, mills, the beginnings of a new civilisation, to ashes, the sinking of five Loo-choo junks, the firing of the palace of the prince, besides the slaughter of human beings, whose number Japanese pride has never divulged." The £25,000 pounds was shortly after paid !

The most prejudiced prince, the densest Daimio, the rudest *ronin*, could scarcely be so foolish after all this as to speak of the Christian English any more as "barbarians." They had only to look at the *Havoc* steaming away from Yedo

---

* The corvette *Pearl*, and " perhaps another vessel," as Mr. Satow says, were ordered up to Yedo to maintain our honour upon this occasion.

with £100,000; to see her steaming off a second time with the £25,000 sent from Satsuma; and above all to look at Kagoshima after the bombardment and the conflagration, to become convinced that the British at least were a highly civilised and Christian nation, whatever might be the condition of other foreigners. It is just conceivable, nevertheless, that a less highly "civilised" power might have made more allowances for the difficulties and the distress of the country we were forcing ourselves upon, and for the extreme prejudices and excited feelings of the people whose observances our cavalcade rode roughly into; and so allowing, might have been content with less money, less blood, less destruction—in a word, less vengeance—for the impulsive acts of a few swashbucklers under sudden provocation. What insufficient allowance we made for the circumstances of the Shogun's government, under its trying conditions, may be inferred from the fact that our insistence upon the prompt payment of the indemnity for Mr. Richardson's offence and punishment, and its consequent payment by the Bakufu, led to the deprivation and confinement by the court of the minister who paid it without the imperial sanction, which could not have been obtained.

At length the urgency of the court (acted on by external influences) to get the ports closed was so great that all reluctance had to be overcome, and the foreign residents then at Yokohama were notified that, after doing all that ingenuity could suggest to avoid it, the Bakufu was compelled to ask their assent to the closing of the ports. The foreign representatives referred the agents of the Bakufu to the treaties, argued against the proposed step, warned them of the consequences that would follow, and advised a reference to their respective governments. The Bakufu consequently prepared to send ambassadors to foreign nations. But meantime, foreseeing that the foreigners would fight for the observances of the treaties that they had succeeded in extorting, the works of defence had been proceeding, and the prince of Mori had, in particular, been constructing batteries at Shimonoséki, in Choshiu, commanding the western entrance to the Inland Sea. On some Dutch, French, and American vessels passing into the Shimonoséki Straits against the prohibition of the Japanese—an American vessel anchoring in a forbidden place—warning and firing ensued. The American war-ship *Wyoming* afterwards thereupon proceeded to the place, destroyed two Choshiu war-ships, and shelled the batteries, the Choshiu clan inflicting upon her no small loss and injury. French and Dutch ships likewise shelled the batteries. The English squadron also took a turn at them somewhat later; but I will defer fuller mention of the circumstances until I have to record my visit to the straits. Suffice it here to say that our squadron proved as worthy of itself and of us at Shimonoséki as it had done at Kagoshima.

One cannot help pitying the people at this time. When the Choshiu clan was engaged with the foreign squadrons, the men of the Kokura clan stood idly by, believing the action of Choshiu was contrary to the Bakufu's wishes; and so it was, for soon afterwards envoys of the Bakufu arrived at Choshiu to reprimand them for firing on foreign vessels without orders. But at the same time the court at Kioto issued a proclamation to the clans remonstrating with some of them for "putting their hands in their pockets and looking on quietly when the barbarian ships had been attacked," and telling them that the emperor was profoundly distressed by such conduct, and that "it was the duty of all the clans to try and achieve the work with all possible speed." Moreover, the internal difficulties of the country were increasing, alarming complications exhibiting themselves in Kioto.

We saw before that the clans of Satsuma and Choshiu had been called upon to preserve order in Kioto, their first consequent duty being to guard the imperial palace. The court dismissed the Satsuma clan from this duty, or privilege, which therefore devolved upon the Choshiu men. A breach between this clan and the Bakufu now happened, on account of the reprimand above referred to for firing on foreign vessels; and the nobles of the court likewise became divided on the subject, some supporting Choshiu, and others detesting that house. Another party occupied a neutral division; "but the court," says the 'Kinsé Shiriaku,' "cherished a secret dislike to the clan." On their advice, however, the emperor consented to undertake a progress to Yamato to exhibit his intention to take the field against the foreigners, and this becoming known, the fear arose of his falling into their hands, the possession of the Mikado's person being always a matter of the first importance in revolutionary times. Sharing this fear, both court and Bakufu endeavoured to shake off the house of Choshiu, and on the 30th of September 1863 the princes of Nakagawa and Aidzu, with other nobles and military men, met and resolved to dismiss Sanjo and other court nobles and the Choshiu clan. Satsuma and the other clans were called on to guard the palace gates, the emperor's progress to Yamato was countermanded, and Sanjo and the other six offending nobles were doomed to punishment for high treason. The Choshiu *samurai* started for their own province, the seven nobles with them, these latter being deprived of their titles and rank, and eighteen other court nobles being punished with them, for having acted in concert with the Choshiu men. The Mori family were prohibited from entering the capital, and troops were levied for its defence in the adjacent provinces. Proclamation was made to the puzzled people assuring them that previous proclamations had been misleading, but that any which might now appear were to be taken as the expression of the will of the Mikado.

Meanwhile the disaffected *ronins*, disgusted with the long delay in expelling the barbarians, broke out into open rebellion at Gojo in Yamato, and were only defeated and dispersed after much severe and repeated fighting. Nor was the capital, Kioto, itself much longer preserved from bloodshed. One Hirano Jiro, seeing that Princes Nakagawa and Aidzu had their way at court, got possession of one of the seven deprived nobles, Sawa, and with a hundred men prepared to enter Kioto to present a petition to the emperor. The peasants attacked them, and the Bakufu ordered the clans to do the same; but it required three days of bloodshed to subdue them, some of them escaping westward with Sawa. The court now so far gave way to the representations of the Bakufu as to despatch a mission to the foreign courts respecting the closing of the ports, whereupon the advocates for swift expulsion fled enraged to Choshiu.

The year 1864 opened with an incident which heightened the ill-feeling between Choshiu and Satsuma. The former clan were so bent upon firing into foreign vessels, that one day they opened fire on a strange craft without waiting to make quite certain of her nationality. Seeing that she was of European build was sufficient for them, and swiftly the batteries blazed forth upon her. Thirty of the crew were killed, and both ship and crew proved to belong to Satsuma, which, as we saw previously, had adopted the European model. Then was Satsuma angrier than ever with Choshiu.

At this time both the emperor and the court showed themselves somewhat inconsistent, for after having steadily pursued the expulsion policy so long, they now turned round upon the noble Sanjo and others who had supported it, and called upon the Shogun to punish them, and to assist in otherwise carrying out the imperial wishes. This approximation of Mikado to Shogun, or of Court to Bakufu, was a compliment which the latter returned by contributing to the shrines of Isé, and by providing that Shoguns and Daimios, on succeeding to their offices, should present themselves to the emperor; that the western Daimios should pay court at Kioto on their way to Yedo; that all the clans should make presents of produce to the emperor, and that the playing of music should be stopped for a time after the death of a prince of the blood. "In the fifth month the imperial court formally placed the direction of affairs in the hands of the Bakufu, which was ordered to punish Choshiu and the seven runaway nobles."

Trouble now again arose in the provinces to the north of Yedo, some of the retainers of the prince of Mito taking to arms in Hitachi and Shimotsuké, and repeatedly repulsing the forces sent against them by the Bakufu. While the discouraging accounts of this dangerous outbreak were arriving from Yedo at Kioto, that city itself became the scene of still worse trials and dangers. The Choshiu people having vainly endeavoured to vindicate themselves to the emperor in letters which received no answers, an armed party of them now arrived at Fushimi, near Kioto (by way of the sea and of Osaka), and asked in a letter why Sanjo and his companions had been punished for obeying his majesty's own wishes by endeavouring to expel the foreigner? The Bakufu ordered part of this force away, but others arrived in the vicinity of the city, and it was thought that the Choshiu clan had really come to coerce the court. The city was full of other troops, some of whom pressed for permission to attack the Choshiu clansmen. A conflict being imminent, the inhabitants of Kioto packed up their goods and hastened away, as the people of Yedo had in the previous year hastened from the English "Havoc." The Choshiu men, finding they were to be attacked, precipitated events by making a sudden advance upon the city on the 20th of August 1864. After severe fighting, in which the Satsuma and Aidzu clans greatly distinguished themselves, the Choshiu forces were defeated with much slaughter. The principal part of the city was destroyed by fire, and the roads were strewn with killed and wounded in numbers exceedingly great in proportion to the forces engaged. The loyal Daimios and *samurai* were praised and promoted for the victory, and carried their heads higher than ever; the rebels had theirs taken off, and displayed in public places.

The Japanese embassy to Europe now returned (August 1864), wiser than when they left. Reaching France first, their proposals were rejected and an answer refused. Seeing what Europe was like, and how great was its wealth and power, they thought it useless to proceed farther, and returned home—to be reprimanded by the Bakufu, and sent with reduced incomes into private life. But to send the "barbarians" into private life was a more difficult matter, and unhappily they once more thought it desirable to take some Japanese money—and a good deal of it too! After the bombardment of Shimonoséki, they returned to Yokohoma and asked for it. "We expect," said they, according to the native account, " to get an indemnity of three million dollars for this business. We will be guided by your decision, whether we shall go back to Choshiu and take it, or whether the Japanese government will undertake to receive it and give it to us." The Bakufu replied, "Our government will take it from Choshiu and give it to the nationalities interested." "This settlement having been arrived at, the foreigners pressed every day for payment of the indemnity, and the Bakufu was at its wits' end." In the old days it used to be, "Your money *or* your life." But those old days were dark, uncivilised, unchristian days; in these days it is, "Your money *and* your life"—" life " at Shimonoséki, and "money" at Yedo. No wonder the Bakufu was at its wits' end. With a costly rebellion raging in the east, and with an expensive war on hand in the west to punish Choshiu for its demonstrations against the foreigners, here were the foreigners themselves demanding dollars by millions on account of the very same business !

It is not worth while to attempt to narrate here either the political or the military conflicts which in those days took place between the "Righteous Party" (Seigito) and the "Wicked Party " (Kanto) or the " Vulgar View Party " (Zokuren-to) and their antagonists, nor need one enter into the details of the Bakufu war upon Choshiu. Some of the fighting in the west country must have been pretty severe, however, for the native historian whom I have so frequently quoted in this chapter tells us that in a battle on the 10th of September at Kuwa and Obata " the noise of artillery resounded on all sides, causing the hills to roll down into the valleys." The Choshiu troops usually got the best of the fighting, being better armed, more lightly clad, and drilled more perfectly. While they fought with muskets, the eastern troops fought with swords and spears, and were burdened with surcoats and armour. The success of these Choshiu insurgents, added to his many other anxieties, proved too much for the Shogun Iyémochi, and on

COOLIES QUARRELLING.

From HOKUSAI. Reproduced for this Work by a Japanese Engraver.

the 19th of September 1866, at Osaka, he retired from this world's troubles.* He was the last of the Tokugawas who died in possession of the quasi-royal throne of the Shogunate. Keiki, who was at this time under orders to make a personal effort with fresh troops against Choshiu, now declined to proceed there, and obtained leave to consult the friendly princes, the result of their deliberations being that the court ordered the operations against Choshiu to be abandoned. Terms were offered and accepted, and the western men returned in great triumph to their native province. The life of the Shogun and the treasury of the Bakufu had been exhausted upon them in vain.

A year before the death of the Shogun, however, the European powers and the United States had extorted the consent of the Mikado to the treaties, viz. in November 1865. The English, French, and Dutch squadrons went into the Inland Sea, and anchored off Hiogo (which Kobé now adjoins), which was the nearest convenient anchorage to the Mikado's capital. Dissuasions were in vain: there they went, and thence they sent the letter demanding his majesty's approval of the treaties. Persuaded by Keiki and others, and knowing his inability to fight the combined squadrons, the emperor yielded to the pressure of the allies, and gave his general consent to the treaties. Thus the treaties between Japan on the one side, and European and United States on the other, were, rightly or wrongly—let it be well remembered —extorted by armed force, and yielded by Japan at the cannon's mouth; and were so extorted from, and yielded by, a government wholly ignorant of the art of treaty-making, and altogether incapable at the time of protecting its own interests. Now that Japan has abandoned its old exclusive-

---

* At the end of 1865 the Shogun, upon whom both the internal and the foreign affairs of the country pressed with crushing weight, had memorialised the emperor to permit him, on account of his health, to retire in favour of Keiki. The request was refused. Later on he had again fallen ill, at Osaka, and Keiki had to undertake to go westward in his stead. "The Shogun was agitated by constant anxiety," and no wonder. Had his heart been examined after death, "Foreigners" and "Choshiu" are the words that would have been found most deeply graven there.

ness, cultivated international relations, and educated itself to fulfil imperial duties, it is entitled by every principle of justice and morality to an unfettered revision of its treaty obligations.

Long before the court and the Bakufu made war upon Choshiu, that clan had come to an understanding with Satsuma, by the wish and at the suggestion of the latter. The Satsuma men began, after a while, to regret the feud between two such powerful and neighbouring clans, especially at a time when the empire itself was in the greatest peril from foreigners. Foremost among those who saw and urged this was Saigo, who afterwards became minister of war under the reformed government, and still later achieved a sad and evil distinction as the leader of the Satsuma rebellion of 1877. He it was who first put the two warring clans into friendly negotiations by the despatch of a secret messenger to Choshiu, and thus initiated a movement which ended in a peaceful understanding between them—an understanding which was of immense value to Choshiu during the remainder of its contest with the government, as it converted into a secret friend the clan which of all others was the best armed and most expert in war, and which would otherwise have been in the field against it.

Keiki, who now, as we shall see by-and-by, leads at Shidzuoke the peaceful life of a private gentleman with artistic tastes, had the office of Shogun forced upon him in the opening of the year 1867; and very soon after (Feb. 3) the emperor Komei died, and was succeeded by the heir-apparent, the present emperor. About midsummer the representatives were once more at Hiogo, congratulating the new tenants of the highest offices of the state, and making "certain requests"—among others the opening of Hiogo, to which the imperial court now assented. It is a common enough thing to find English and American writers speaking of the new Shogun, Keiki, as a weak and vacillating man, but to me he appears to have acted with signal wisdom on several critical occasions, one of which comes here to notice.

The power and pride of the Tokugawas were now rapidly

diminishing—had, in fact, already become so small that, instead of controlling all the action of the state, as the Shogun was aforetime wont to do, he now referred all matters of importance to the emperor for decision. We saw the imperial power reviving in the last chapter, and now, after the triumph of the rebellious Choshiu, and the success of foreign interference, men began to feel that the division of the supreme authority was one of the causes of their troubles, and that the power of the lawful hereditary sovereign should be restored in all its fulness to him. The prince of Tosa expressed this view strongly in a letter to the Shogun, and said, " You should restore the governing power into the hands of the sovereign, and so lay a foundation on which Japan may take its stand as the equal of all other countries. This is the most imperative duty of the present moment." The Shogun concurred in the view, and patriotically, on the 19th of November 1867, sent in his resignation to the Mikado. There was much hesitation, it is said, on the part of the court, and many suspicions of unfairness were entertained, but the resignation of the Shogun was proclaimed, and on the 3rd of January 1868 a decree announced that the government of the country was henceforth in the hands of the imperial court.

INSCRIPTION WRITTEN BY THE PRESENT EMPEROR AT NARA.

CHAPTER XVI.

THE IMPERIAL RESTORATION COMPLETED.

Shogun Keiki attempts to regain his power—He marches to Osaka—Goes with armed forces towards Kioto—The battles of Fushimi—Victory of the imperial troops—Honours granted to Choshiu and Satsuma—The foreign representatives received by the " Heaven-King "—The emperor's oath to promote representative government—The ex-Shogun submits—His friends remain in rebellion—The warfare with the rebels—Preservation of the Nikko shrines—Fighting at Wooyeno, in Kioto—Destruction of the Tokugawa temples—The *Shogitai* and the " Shreds of Brocade "—Further military contests—The victories of Generals Yamagata and Kuroda—The " Wicked Party " and the " Righteous Party "—The Okubo memorandum—Reforms of the New Empire—Suppression of the naval revolt—Admiral Enomoto—Rewards to the victors.

IT was now that the ex-Shogun Keiki exhibited a change of purpose which probably furnishes the chief ground for that accusation of vacillation which is so freely alleged against him; but in judging of his acts, those who wish to be fair will bear in mind the excitements and dangers of the period, of which this sketch of mine can convey but very imperfect ideas. On the day on which the Shogun's office was abolished (January 3, 1868), the forces friendly to the Shogun and to the Tokugawas generally were sent away by the court, and the guardianship of the palace approaches was committed to the clans of Satsuma, Tosa, and Geishiu. Irritated by this affront, and by the court acting without even consulting him, Keiki changed his views of the position, and, summoning the Aidzu clan and other adherents, expressed to them his belief that the favoured clans were conspiring to mislead the young emperor. He also availed himself of a former order of the court, made at the time of his resignation being sent in, and directing him to continue the conduct of affairs, and now declared that he would act upon that, and assemble a council of princes as was then provided. On the night of the 6th he marched with his retainers and friends to Osaka. I must not omit to mention that prior to all this, in 1867, the seven banished princes had been recalled, and the honours and titles of the house of Mori restored. The present prime minister, Sanjo, was consequently again back at Kioto, where he once more took a leading part in court affairs.

In the city of Yedo the peace became seriously disturbed, and by order of Keiki the Satsuma Yashiki was burnt, and the *ronins* who held it were made prisoners. Keiki likewise requested the court to dismiss all Satsuma men who had any share in the government, which the court declined to do. Henceforth there was fierce antagonism between the Satsuma clan and the Tokugawa. The court sent conciliatory messengers to Osaka, to dissuade Keiki from resentful measures, and to request him to go to an interview with his majesty at Kioto with a small escort only. He promised compliance, but subsequently yielded to the persuasions of the princes of Aidzu and Kuwana, and resolved to proceed to Kioto with those clans in force, "to remove from the emperor his bad counsellors." On learning this, the court stationed the Choshiu and Satsuma clans to bar the way to the capital, and block up the Fushimi and Toba roads. The orders were to let Keiki enter the capital with an escort, but not accompanied by a large force. The clans of Aidzu and Kuwana were to be refused admission absolutely.

There consequently ensued some of the severest fighting ever known in Japan, many of the heroes of which are still alive. It was not on a very large scale, the defenders of the capital numbering only about 6500, the attacking force being reported as 30,000 strong. On the 27th of January, the Tokugawa messengers having announced the intention of Keiki's troops to force the barriers, and the main body afterwards approaching, the Kioto forces opened fire upon them with artillery. Their fire was returned with musketry, and severe fighting ensued. Both parties retired early in the evening. At midnight the loyal troops fell upon the troops bivouacking on the Toba road, and drove them in consternation before them. Reserves coming up, the battle was renewed, but after two hours of hard fighting, with fluctuating fortune, the eastern troops were defeated. Next morning at eight the combatants fought again, upon both the Fushimi and the Toba roads, and fought with desperate courage and persistency. "At last the enemy (the rebels) was put to flight on the Fushimi road, while from Toba he advanced with greater determination than ever; and his ferocity was terrible," says the native historian, naïvely adding: "Some of the rebels' bullets actually struck the gold brocade standard of the Mikado, which the commander-in-chief, Prince Ninnaji, had ordered to be carried before him as he advanced!" At length victory declared itself for the loyal troops, and the rebels were driven in all directions, "the fugitives trampling on the dead and dying in their hurry to escape." But owing to the greatly superior numbers of the rebel troops the contest was not yet over. On the following (the third) day, at dawn, the imperial troops attacked the rebels in Yodo. After many displays of personal valour, they carried the castle about noon, driving the rebels in a body to Hashimoto. On the opposite bank of the river, at Yamazaki, the Tsu clan, from Isé, surrendered the barrier to the loyal troops without fighting, on the representations of an envoy sent to win them over from their rebellious position. On the 30th, the rebel force in Hashimoto was attacked, both directly from Yodo and flankwise from Yamazaki, and after suffering heavy losses, broke up and fled to Osaka, whence Keiki, the princes of Aidzu and Kuwana, and other officials had escaped eastwards in a man-of-war. The castle of Osaka was burnt.

The successive victories which the Satsuma and Choshiu clans had so valiantly won against the army of Keiki, exalted by the final success of Osaka, brought great honours to them. The clans of the neighbouring provinces, some of whom had been disloyal, all now submitted to the imperial arms. Tokugawa Keiki, the ex-Shogun, and his followers were deprived of all their honours and dignities; an army was sent to subdue him, called the army of chastisement, and was placed under the command of the imperial prince Arisugawa, "a brocaded banner and a sword of justice being granted to him." The foreign representatives at Kobé declared themselves neutral in the coming contest, forbidding the sale of arms to either party. They were informed that Kioto would thenceforth be the seat of government, and the emperor made everywhere a proclamation of protection to foreigners.

It was out of the power of the emperor and his court, however, to repress altogether the hostility to foreigners which was so strongly felt by the *samurai* and others, and consequently a Frenchman got wounded in Kobé, and a body of French sailors were fired upon at Sakai (near Osaka), some of them being killed. This brought, of course, more demands for money and life upon the unhappy government, which they thought it best to submit to. Twelve Japanese were executed, and a hundred and fifty thousand dollars had to be scraped together and paid: other demands were likewise yielded to. A further trouble arose with the English. The emperor having arranged to receive the foreign representatives at Kioto, some *ronins*, alike violent and foolish, made an attack upon the English representative, wounding some of his escort. "The Japanese officials and the English guards repelled the attack, and killed the *ronins*, so that nothing serious resulted. The representative, however, returned home without going through the ceremony." On the 26th, the English representative had an interview with the Tenno ("heaven-king"), the Dutch, American, and French representatives having been already presented to him on the 23rd. "They congratulated his majesty," we are told, "on the magnificence of the imperial rule, and gave renewed promise of friendly relations."* Thus peace and quiet seemed to be once more restored to the sacred capital, Kioto, and the people "gave themselves up to rejoicing."

The first notable use to which this renewal of tranquillity was put by his majesty (the present emperor) was that of assembling the court nobles and territorial princes, and making oath before them that a deliberative assembly should be formed, and all measures be decided on by public opinion; that impartiality and justice should form the basis of his action, and that intellect and learning should be sought for throughout the world, in order to establish the foundations of the empire. Although there were many ready to support him in further civil war, and some who urgently pressed him to continue it, Keiki, who was now in Yedo, resolved to make his submission to the emperor, and forbade his retainers to resist the imperial troops, himself retiring into the monastery at Wooyeno, in Yedo. His retainers were disgusted with him, and determined to fight the matter out without him. Meanwhile the imperial forces were advancing towards the city. At Katsunuma, on the Kofukaido,† the Tokugawa vassals stockaded the road, and attacked them from the hills. The army forced the stockade, whereupon the rebels broke down the bridges in front of them, and repeated their tactics, also setting fire to houses as a further check. They were at last overcome, and most of them either killed or captured. In other places resistance to the government troops was offered and overcome. On the army reaching the environs of Yedo, the most earnest appeals were made to the general commanding (General Saigo) to induce him and the imperial prince commanding in chief to accept the peaceable submission of the ex-Shogun Keiki, which was eventually agreed to, and the city thus saved from assault. The castle, the men-of-war, and all firearms were to be given up, and various severe punishments inflicted, Keiki being banished to Mito. Keiki assented, but many of his retainers withdrew northwards in large bodies.

* 'Kinsé Shiriuku.'   † The eastern part of the great Nakasendo road.

It is needless to pursue the details of the warfare which ensued between the rebels and the imperial forces in various parts of the country. That warfare was, however, of a very serious nature, as some of the rebels had been highly drilled in European style, and were commanded by able leaders. The principal fighting was between Yedo and Nikko, in Shimotsuké, at Yuki, Nagareyama, Oyama, Utsunomiya, and Imaichi. The splendid mausoleums and temples of Nikko were only saved from assault and destruction by an appeal made by one of the imperial leaders (I believe by Admiral Kawamura) to the Tokugawa rebels, cautioning them that resistance there could only result in the ruin of those magnificent memorials of the grandeur of the Tokugawa dynasty. This fate unhappily befell the finest of the similar shrines and temples of Toyeizan, at Wooyeno, Yedo. These were seized upon by an extremely disaffected and reckless set of rebels, who assumed the name of *Shogitai* ("the band which makes duty clear"), and whose conduct so excites the native compiler of the history of the period whom I have frequently quoted that his eloquence for once rises above the calm level of historic narration, and breaks into quite a storm of anger and denunciation. "There is no law or order amongst a heterogeneous body of this sort (literally an assemblage of rooks). When they walked forth for amusement they carried long swords in their girdles, wore high clogs, put on the airs of swashbucklers, and swaggered as much as possible." The loyal troops wore a piece of brocade sewn on to the clothes as a mutual sign, and the inhabitants used to secretly ridicule them, calling them *Kingiré*, or "shreds of brocade." "If the *Shogitai* met with a 'shred of brocade' in the streets, they immediately heaped all manner of insults upon him, and attacked or killed him with their swords. A large number of loyal soldiers were murdered in this way. The townspeople all feared the powers of the *Shogitai*, who became highly elated, and the indignation of the troops of the various clans was so strong that they petitioned for leave to inflict chastisement." It became necessary to drive these rascals out of Wooyeno, and it was found to require some very hard fighting to effect the object. Some of the finest of the temples, and much of the town in the vicinity, were burnt down before the imperial troops completed and secured their victory. After this, the "shreds of brocade" became respected in the city, the finest of the Tokugawa shrines in Yedo having been sacrificed to the rebellious spirit of Tokugawa partisans, persisted in after the head of the clan had shown them a wiser and better way. In consequence of this wanton resistance of the partisans of Keiki's cause, first near Nikko, and now at Wooyeno, the pensions granted to the Tokugawa clan were greatly curtailed. The eastern troubles were now, however, over, or nearly so, the only other being the seizure of the Hakoné mountain pass by one Hayashi Shonoské, aided by the Odawara people. These latter were promptly visited by an imperial force, and suffered a loss of some of their territory, Shonoské escaping to the north. The Kuanto was now wholly at peace again. An offer of the court to show further clemency to the Tokugawas, and to take some of their retainers into its own service, tended to its still further pacification.

An expedition sent to subject the Aidzu clan, and others joined with them, failed, however, to overthrow the combination at Shirakawa in Oshiu, the castle of which was then occupied by the rebels. Reinforcements were sent, and early in August the rebels were driven away, and the castle —one of great strategical importance—was retaken by the imperial troops. The latter then advanced upon the castle of Tanagura, which was also held by the rebels, and carried it. It took a longer time to drive the rebels from the castle of Iwakidaira. The defence of this was stoutly maintained, and the artillery thundered so tremendously on all sides that it was enough, according to Mr. Uji, "to crumble heaven and earth into ruins." Eventually, however, the resources of the defenders were exhausted, whereupon they set the castle on fire, and escaped along the sea-shore, thus abandoning the whole district to the imperial army. At Nagaoka, in the province of Echigo, the Tokugawa runaways and their allies gave the loyal forces a great deal of trouble, falling upon them by night, severely defeating them, and driving many of them into the river to drown. Owing mainly, however, to the high spirit and skilful generalship of General Yamagata, the present commander-in-chief of the army of Japan, and of General Kuroda, now colonial minister, the imperial troops were rallied, and made a stand. A few days afterwards they fell upon the rebels in a dense fog at daybreak, coming upon them while they slept, and not only defeating them, but driving them out of the city of Nagaoka, which again passed into loyal hands. Many of the inhabitants were executed for conspiring with the rebels, and aiding and abetting them in their evil work.

But the troubles extended still farther north, the town of Akita, in the province of Ugo, serving as their centre. At times the imperial forces were in isolated and dangerous positions, and at times sustained terrible defeats, filling the court with alarm; but reinforcements were sent, and the war continued—war by day and by night, nocturnal sorties being much in fashion during this northern campaign. The fluctuations and uncertainties of the contest were due not only to changes in the number and quality of the forces engaged, but largely also to the difference in the arms with which they fought, the greatest of these differences being due to the fact that the loyal troops had by this time become armed with American breechloaders. The fate of the campaign was determined by the siege of Wakamatsu, which, in November 1868, fell into the hands of the loyal troops, the rebel clans then submitting and giving up their arms. The rebellion once more exhibited itself in this part by a revolt of the Nambu clan, but that was effectually subdued in a single engagement. Down in the east, at Mito, some members of the Wicked Party, with some hundreds of associates, entered the town, but the Righteous Party resisted them, and the court subsequently sent the neighbouring clans to chastise the offenders, the ringleaders undergoing decapitation for their crime. There were still additional anxieties and resistances for the new government in store; but before mentioning them it will be well to note a few facts of other than military importance.

In the midsummer of this year (1868), the name of the city of Yedo was changed to that of Tokio, signifying "Eastern Capital," with the intention, it is believed, of preparing the public mind for that transfer of the imperial court from Kioto to Tokio which soon after took place, in accordance with the spirit of a memorial submitted some time previously by the councillor of state Okubo, who took an active part in all the great political changes which we have been reviewing. No man did so much as he, probably, to promote the adoption in Japan of the better elements of European civilisation, and for his services he received, ten years afterwards, that not unfrequent reward of patriots, death by the hands of assassins, in a manner to be hereafter narrated. In his highly remarkable memorial, Okubo complained of the seclusion of the emperor, and of the inconveniences of Kioto as a capital, in view of the changes passing over the country. "Since the middle ages our emperor has lived behind a screen, and has never trodden the earth. Nothing of what went on outside his screen ever penetrated to his sacred ear; the imperial residence was profoundly secluded, and naturally unlike the outer world. No more than a few court nobles were allowed to approach the throne, a practice most opposed to the principles of heaven. Although it is the first duty of man to respect his superior, if he reveres that superior too highly he neglects his duty, while a breach is created between the sovereign and his subjects, who are unable to convey their wants to him. This vicious practice has been common in all ages. But now let pompous etiquette be done away with, and simplicity become our first object. Kioto is an out-of-the-way position, and is unfit to be the seat of government." He went on to recommend Osaka as a temporary capital. This memorial had a great effect, and probably led to the subsequent adoption of Tokio as the seat of government.

In this year the chronological period was changed to that of

Meiji (enlightened government), and a proclamation issued providing for one chronological year-period only for each reign (whereas the year-period had previously been frequently changed on occasions of less note); a government *Gazette* was published, for making known to the country the administrative decrees; paper money was manufactured as a temporary device for meeting the excess of expenditure over income— being first issued in the spring of the next year, 1869; and the building of lighthouses was commenced under English superintendence. On the 16th of November the emperor arrived in Tokio, and there received from Prince Arisugawa, the commander-in-chief, the brocade banner and the sword of justice, in token of the pacification of the north and east. The rebellious princes of Aidzu, Sendai, Yonezawa, and other heads of clans were condemned to punishment one degree less than death, and to seclusion, the territories of the chiefs being reduced by one third, and the succession given to a member of each family. "The troubles of the empire were now nearly at an end," says one who wrote several years before the Satsuma rebellion.

It remains to make brief reference to the naval incidents of the revolution which has been described, in which the chief part was taken by my distinguished friend Admiral Enomoto Kamurijo, lately the minister of Japan at the court of St. Petersburg. In the year 1863, this officer, together with Akamatsu Daisaburo, now an admiral and a member of the Japanese admiralty, and others, were sent to Holland to have a man-of-war built, and to study the art of naval warfare. In the autumn of 1867 they returned to Japan, on board the new Dutch-built ship, named the *Kaiyo-Maru*, having acquired a large amount of experience in Europe. When the differences arose between the Bakufu and the court, Admiral Enomoto considered it his duty to hold the ship under his charge at the disposition of the former, by whom the order to build it had been given, and later on, for reasons which may be conjectured, he adhered to the Tokugawa cause, even after the ex-Shogun Keiki himself had abandoned it. When the clans of the north and east finally surrendered, after the capture of Wakamatsu by the loyal forces, the rebel chief Otori Keiske, who had displayed the utmost skill and bravery in the command of his forces, sought shelter on board the *Kaiyo-Maru*, which was at that time lying off the Sendai shore, with several other war-vessels of the Bakufu. After consulting Admiral Enomoto, he decided to proceed to Hakodaté, in the great northern island of Yezo, and employ that town and port as a base of future operations. It required some fighting to accomplish their objects, but they soon succeeded in capturing not only Hakodaté, but the fortress of Matsumae likewise, after which they proceeded to other conquests. Unfortunately for them, the *Kaiyo-Maru* struck, during a gale of wind, upon an unknown rock off Esashi, and although Admiral Enomoto and his companions remained on board for four days, and succeeded then, when the weather moderated, in landing with their arms, the ship a few days after became a perfect wreck, and "the rebels felt," says the rustic annalist, "like one who has lost his lantern on a dark night." But they had other vessels to fight with, and more fighting ensued, resulting in the success of the insurgent force, after which the forces elected Admiral Enomoto as governor-general, and he at once proceeded to make all secure as far as possible, and to develop the rich resources of the island. The government, on learning all this, ordered the Tokugawa family to subdue the revolters, and the ex-Shogun volunteered for the service. His offer was, however, declined, and the prince of Mito charged with the duty, the government being in possession of an American ironclad to assist in the operations. This vessel, with several others, and a large military force, was sent north, and after a stout resistance, during which several naval engagements and land battles occurred, and hundreds of lives were lost, the insurgent vessels were all, one after the other, destroyed, and Enomoto and his companions compelled, on the 26th of June 1869, to surrender. His personal qualities, his skill and bravery as a seaman, and his European experience led ere long, not only to his pardon, but to his appointment to high office

CHAP. XVI.] *IMPERIAL RESTORATION COMPLETED.* 287

under His Majesty's government, in which I have myself known him to render signal service.

The government was now in a position to apply itself to the reward of those who had greatly served it during the struggles of 1867–68, which had happily terminated in the restoration of the governing power in all its fulness to the Imperial House, and in the suppression of all rival pretensions. Pensions and gratuities were granted to the princes Arisugawa and Ninnaji, to General Saigo, to the heads of nearly a hundred of the clans, and to more than a hundred other persons. A shrine was erected in Tokio for the celebration of rites in honour of those who had fallen in the three decisive contests, viz. at Fushimi, at Wooyeno, and at Wakamatsu.

FARM IMPLEMENTS.

CHAPTER XVII.

FOREIGN RELATIONS OF JAPAN.

The early foreign relations of Japan with Korea and China—Attempted invasion of Japan—The Armada of the Mongol Tartars—Naval battles —Bravery of the Japanese—A miraculous storm aids them—Total destruction of the invaders—An ex-Shogun accepts from China the title " King of Japan "—Indignation of his countrymen—Beginning of intercourse with Portugal, Spain, England, and Holland—Foreign jealousies and treacheries—The Jesuit missionaries—They attack the Buddhist priests—Consequent reaction against Christianity—Fears of foreign invasion and domination—Interdict against the " Kirishitan " religion — An extraordinary proclamation — Japanese views of our religion—Other edicts against Christianity—Persecutions—Hideyoshi's invasion of Korea—Capture of the capital—Korea overrun—A singular parley—China helps Korea—The army of Japan triumphant—Its navy sustains a defeat—Japan contends for six years against both Korea and China—Withdraws on the death of Hideyoshi—The Island-kingdom of Loo-choo—Japan's recent war against Formosa—Her recent relations with Korea and China—Disputes with Russia—Surrender to Russia of Saghalin—Acquisition of the Kuriles and of the Bonin Islands.

In the early days of its history, and through many a long century, almost the only external relations with which Japan concerned itself were, naturally enough, those entered into with its nearest neighbours, Korea and China. In the chapter on the early history of the country I have explained how, even before the birth of Christ, the first communications between Japan and Korea arose, with the result of making one of the small Korean kingdoms tributary to the Mikado of Japan; and I have likewise set forth the manner in which Japan first entered into relations with China, under the reign of the warrior-empress Jingu Kogo. In her reign it was, as we also saw, that books are said to have been introduced into Japan from Korea, the first written characters having been brought over from that country at a much earlier date, viz. in the year 157 B.C. It is unnecessary for the purposes of this work to trace the fluctuation of Japan's relations with her neighbours throughout the early centuries of our era. Suffice it to say that the Korean kings all became tributaries of the Mikados, and that Japanese armies were on several occasions transported to Korea to compose the quarrels of these kings, and to enforce payment of tribute to their own sovereign.

Diplomatic intercourse between Japan and China may be said to date from the end of the sixth century, in the reign of the Japanese empress Suiko; and after the Zui dynasty of China was superseded by that of To, this diplomatic intercourse between the two countries was continued. It is said that in the reign of the emperor Mommu (697-707); one Awada-no-Mabito was sent by Japan as an ambassador to China. He had received a good education, which had not been thrown away upon him, and was so fine a fellow both in feature and in deportment that on his disembarking in the province of So, the Chinese, struck by his splendid bearing, could not help observing, "We have often been told that there was in the east a very happy, very polished, and very educated people; this must be so, since their ambassador has so noble an appearance." Arrived at the capital, Awada was received most graciously by the empress Buko, as was only natural under the circumstances. This flattering little story is carefully, and with pardonable vanity, preserved in the historic memory of Awada's countrymen.

In the ninth century, in the early part of the reign of Koko-Tenno, the king of Shiraki, in Korea, sent an embassy of no less than forty-eight persons to Japan; but as they were the bearers of a letter which was considered unsatisfactory, the emperor refused to receive them at his court, an indication of the pride which Japan had come to display in dealing with her tributary states of the Asiatic continent. In the following reign Korean pirates began to show themselves upon the coasts of Kiushiu, but were promptly driven off. Ere long, however, they went with a fleet of forty-five vessels and attacked the Japanese island of Tsushima, which lies near the Korean coast. They were again defeated and driven away, with a loss of over three hundred killed, and of many vessels and large quantities of arms. Korea still payed its tribute, and China continued to send its ambassadors to the Mikado. Early in the tenth century a rebel subject of the king of Shiraki wrote to the governor of Kiushiu requesting permission to become a tributary of Japan, but was very properly reminded that a subject could not enter into relations with a foreign country. A few years afterwards the dynasty of Kin was replaced on the throne of Shiraki by that of Wo, and the new king gave to his realm the name of Korai (Korea), and sent ambassadors to Japan, but the emperor refused to receive them. A new embassy sent some time afterwards was similarly treated. Permission was, however, given for the carrying on of commerce between the two countries. Early in the tenth century the Korean king again sent ambassadors, who were again refused reception at court, their rejection this time being followed by preparation for war on the part of Japan—a timely measure, as shortly afterwards the Koreans attempted an invasion, and were repulsed.* By this time the diplomatic relations between Japan and China had become interrupted, and although, on the extinction of the Chinese dynasty of To, and the establishment of that of So, the new emperor gave an audience to the Japanese *bozu* Chonen, and expressed his admiration of the immemorial age of the Mikado's dynasty (as stated in the opening of the chapter on the Descent of the Crown), it was nevertheless found that diplomatic relations between the two countries could not be renewed, and only their priests and merchants were able to maintain relations. We thus see that after centuries of official intercourse, Japan ceased to have relations with either Korea or China.

I have already† noticed the origin of the invasion of

---

* In the reign of the emperor Sanjo a Korean army attempted another invasion, and landed on the coast of Kiushiu; but they were totally destroyed by the Japanese garrison.

† See chapter on the Hojo Domination.

Japan attempted in the year 1275 by the Mongol Tartars. The threatening letter of the founder of the Geng dynasty having been received at the imperial court, the council, before replying to it, sent it down to Kamakura for discussion. Hojo Tokimune considered the letter an insolent one, and dismissed the Chinese envoys without an answer. On the Geng king sending another envoy (one Chorioitsu), the local governor of Kiushiu, acting under orders from Kamakura, drove him away at a speed exceeding that at which he came. Envoy after envoy followed, but always with the same result, that of being sent back again to China without having been allowed even to land. Then the Geng king sent a force of ten thousand troops to invade the island provinces of Tsushima and Iki, both of whose governors were killed in their unsuccessful defence. The generals of the west were thereupon summoned with their forces to repel the invaders, who, after some fighting, during which they lost their leader, "fled away." But the king of the Mongolians nevertheless persisted in sending ambassadors to hold intercourse with the Japanese government, ten of whom stationed themselves at Nagato, and refused to leave without a reply to the royal letters. Thereupon Hojo Tokimune sent for them to Kamakura, and gave them an answer which was perfectly conclusive to themselves at least, for he caused the whole ten of them to be there and then beheaded. Knowing what would follow, Tokimune took immediate steps for resisting the coming invasion.

He appointed Hojo Sanemasa to the command of the defensive forces in the west, ordered the army of Kioto to accompany him on the service, sent eastern troops to replace the Kioto army, and in many other ways prepared to give the Mongolians a reception worthy of themselves and worthy of Japan. Sanemasa built himself a castle in Kiushiu, and when in 1279 yet another ambassador of the Geng made his appearance, he accorded to him the same reply as his predecessors had been vouchsafed at Kamakura. Thereupon, seeing that diplomacy was vain, and diplomatists only slain, the king of the Geng applied himself in earnest to the invasion of the Morning Land. He appears to have foreseen that the task he had set himself would prove an arduous one, for he built very many war-ships, of sizes and armaments unknown in Japan, and collected an army of a hundred thousand men for the purpose.

In the fourth month of the year 1281 the invading armada approached the castle of Daizafu, and was met by the officers of Sanemasa and by his warriors with such courage, skill, and impetuosity that although the numbers of the defenders, both in ships and men, were small by comparison, the invaders underwent great slaughter. The smaller and lighter boats of the Japanese were readily destroyed and sunk, but their deficiencies in material strength the proud defenders made good by their valour. When their vessels failed them they swam to the enemy, climbed upon his decks, put his crews to the sword, and fired the ships. One gallant fellow, Kusana Schichiro, attacked them with two small vessels, and wrought wonders of war upon them. Alarmed by the heroism with which they were met, the invaders formed their war-ships in line, and connected them with iron chains, in order to ward off the attacks which were made upon them with so much spirit. The Japanese were not, however, to be thus kept at bay, but still contrived to close upon them in spite of all the missiles hurled against them by guns * and catapults. "Kono Michiari advanced," says a native account, "and though his elbow was shot through with an arrow he still advanced, and at last, taking a mast down, and using it as a ladder, he entered the enemy's ship, and made Okansha (one of the leaders of the armada) prisoner." With men like this to deal with, the invaders found it impossible to effect a landing, and withdrew to Takashima. "The whole nation," says Griffis, "was now roused. Reinforcements poured in from all quarters to swell the host of defenders. From the monasteries and temples all over the country went up unceasing prayer to the gods to ruin their enemies and save the land

---

* " Bow-guns shooting heavy darts were mounted on their decks."—*Griffis*.

of Japan. The emperor and ex-emperor went in solemn state to the chief priest of Shinto, and, writing out their petitions to the gods, sent him as a messenger to the shrine of Isé. It is recorded, as a miraculous fact, that at the hour of noon, as the sacred envoy arrived at the shrine and offered the prayers—the day being perfectly clear—a streak of cloud appeared in the sky, which soon overspread the heavens, until the dense masses portended a storm of awful violence." As a matter of fact a tremendous storm—whether originated or not at the shrine of Isé—did arise, and smote with "awful violence" the Chinese fleet, and the Japanese fully availed themselves of it by adding their destructiveness to that of the typhoon. Of the whole invading army, a hundred thousand strong, only three men returned to China to tell the terrible story. The gods of Isé became more revered than ever, and Hojo Takimune's name appears upon every scroll of Japanese heroes and patriots. China has not again attempted to conquer Japan, and the sacred soil remains unsullied by the foot of a successful invader. Ten thousand Koreans had formed part of the invading army; of these three thousand with great difficulty regained their country.

In 1401, when the Ashikaga Shoguns were in power, an incident occurred which has contributed to their shame in Japan, far more than the treachery of their founder, Taka-Uji, or than any other act of theirs. A change of dynasty had just taken place both in Korea and in China, that of Li having succeeded to that of Shin in the former country, and that of Ming to that of Yen in China. The ex-Shogun Yoshimitsu then sent ambassadors to China, to renew with the new emperor the ancient diplomatic relations between the two countries, and made these envoys the bearers of presents and of a letter by which some sort of suzerainty on the part of China was acknowledged; in return for which submission, Yoshimitsu was offered and accepted the title of King of Japan. In any case the act would have been one of treason, both to the Mikado and to the country; and happening as it did within little more than a hundred years after the overwhelming defeat by Japan of the Chinese army of invasion, it added to its treasonableness the wanton humiliation of a brave and independent nation. For such an act no one could be forgiven by the Japanese; and Yoshimitsu never will be forgiven. It is strange that *he* should have committed it, for he it was who put an end to the competition of the two emperors, and brought back the imperial power into the hands of one man. He was, moreover, the first of the Ashikaga Shoguns who had the leisure to carry out reforms in the government and administration of the country, and it is said that he effected great improvements in both.

It was the middle of the sixteenth century, when the Ashikaga domination was approaching its end, that the Portuguese began to influence Japan by their presence. They went there originally for trading purposes, Satsuma and the island of Hirado being the ports which they most resorted to. The English and the Spaniards likewise appeared upon the scene at about the same time. The Dutch arrived at Hirado in 1610. All of these being civilised peoples, there was then, as there was before, and as there is still, a great deal of envy, jealousy, mistrust, and even hostility existing between the rival merchants, and still more between the rival priests and saints who soon followed them. "To the natural rivalry of teachers of a different school, we must add the effects," says Mr. Satow, "of the international enmity which existed between the Portuguese of Macao and the Spaniards of Manila; and when the Dutch and English came upon the scene, they in their turn endeavoured to excite the suspicions of the Japanese rulers against their hereditary foes the Spaniards. We have evidence of this from European annalists."* I have, in a former chapter, pointed out that the great persecutions, reaching to almost total extermination, which afterwards befell the Christian sects of Japan, under Iyéyasu, were largely due to apprehensions of foreign conquest; and it seems

---

* 'Transactions' of the Asiatic Society of Japan, vol. vi. pt. 1.

certain that these apprehensions were stimulated, possibly they were engendered, by the treachery of the rival foreigners. Mr. Satow, after quoting one instance in which the Dutch brought to the notice of the Japanese authorities forged letters threatening invasion, seized by them in a native vessel, goes on to say : " We know that both the English and the Dutch in those days did all in their power to prejudice the rulers of Japan against the Portuguese and Spaniards, whether missionaries or merchants, and even two centuries ago the Dutch were accused of forging a letter which purported to be written by the Portuguese bishop in Nagasaki to the Viceroy at Goa, and from which it appeared that the Spaniards and Portuguese had formed the design, not only of converting the Japanese to Christianity, but under the cloak of religion of bringing the whole country under their rule ; and this letter, having first concealed it on board a Portuguese vessel bound for Goa, they caused to be discovered by the Japanese authorities."* To the discovery of this forged letter are attributed by Montanus those repressive measures of the Shogun which provoked the insurrection of Shimabara and all the horrors which followed in its train.

It has been well said by Mr. Gubbins that Japan was never perhaps in a state of greater internal discord than when the foreign missionaries first landed on its shores. The reader will remember what has already been said of the troubles of the reigns of Go-Nara-Tenno and of his successor, Oki-machi. The feudal barons were warring with each other "by the aid of mercenary bands, which roamed at large, the terror of the country people, ready to enrol themselves under any banner which could pay for their services," and, as I have before said, the Portuguese brought not the composing doctrine of Christ's love—not peace and goodwill—but the use of firearms, and the doubtful blessing of imported cannon. With them came the Jesuit mission-

---

* This story may be read in Mercklein's Appendix to Caron's 'Japan,' and Arnold's annotations thereon, pp. 285, 286.

aries. Their sphere at first was a very restricted one, their only port of supply being in the island of Hirado, and even there supplies arrived but once a year from the traders of Macao. It is said that these missionaries were also much hindered in their work by want of funds, deriving their only support from the Pope and the king of Portugal, sources which proved to be sadly irregular. They had often consequently to resort to alms for their maintenance. The Spanish Franciscan friars were more fortunate, some of the northern ports being opened to Spanish trade, and therefore to Spanish religion. No men are wiser or more politic in the rules of action and standards of conduct which they set up for themselves than the Jesuits; few men, if any, have made more glaring mistakes than they have made in the practical pursuit of their objects. It appears beyond all doubt certain that, as the Roman Catholic missionaries made progress in Japan, they became less wise, less prudent, and less just in the course which they pursued, they or their converts making war upon the Buddhist priests, whom they called devils, overthrowing their gods and temples, and commanding the people either to become instant converts to Christianity or to take themselves off from their families, their homes, and all they possessed.

"The Daimio of Bungo at one time, during war, destroyed a most prodigious and magnificent temple, with a colossal statue; burning three thousand monasteries to ashes, and razing the temples to the ground. The comment of the Jesuit written on this is, 'This ardent zeal of the prince is an evident instance of faith and charity.' This does not, however, sound like an echo of the song once heard above the Bethlehem hills, few echoes of which the Japanese have yet heard" (Griffis). Any account of the reaction against Christianity in Japan, and of the expulsion of Christians from it by Iyéyasu, which omits from consideration the wrongs and persecutions inflicted by the Christians themselves upon the members of other religious sects, must of necessity be one-sided, and far from complete. These wrongs and persecutions fed, if they did not light, the flames of fear and hatred which drove Christianity from the land.

But it was not, let it be frankly acknowledged, the Roman Catholics alone who were to blame; the Protestant Dutch and English added abundant fuel to the fire. They stirred up the Japanese, as we have seen, not merely to religious resistance of the Romish missionaries and their work, but to political resistance likewise, and to political resistance excited by the worst of all alarms, that of the hostile invasion of their country. And, as Mr. Satow has pointed out, there was yet another source of alarm and agitation springing from " the hostility of renegade Christians towards the religion which they had abandoned," several examples of which have come down to us. One notable instance may be cited. In 1611, a priest who had been expelled from a Kirishitan (Christian) temple in Yatsushiro in Higo, arrived at Sumpu (now Shidzuoka), where Iyéyasu lived, and lodged a complaint against his superior, who was sent for, and after full inquiry pronounced in the wrong, and punished. Out of gratitude for the justice done him, the expelled priest gave the following account of Kirishitan principles* :—

"The king of Namban [Spain and Portugal, then under one crown] devoted the revenue of the five countries which composed his dominions to the following objects. Every year, under the name of merchant-vessels, ships were sent to Japan laden with gold, silver, precious gems, woven fabrics, and articles of *vertu*, for the purpose of recommending to everybody the evil religion. The Bateren and Iruman (brothers, or friars) annually prepared a record, in which was inserted the number of persons who had been induced to join the religion in that year, and the valuable goods were distributed among them in proportion. From ancient times the Namban men in this cunning way had been wont to send valuables and commodities to Luçon, Hisupaniya [probably New Spain], and other countries in the Southern Seas, where at first they obtained the loan of a very small piece of ground, on which they then built a temple, and began secretly to teach Kirishitan. The ignorant inhabitants of those countries believed in their doctrines, and, finally becoming allies and partisans

---

* Satow's translation.

of the Namban men, enabled the latter to take possession of the land without any trouble. The barbarians then proceeded to send governors to the countries they had seized, took possession of the land, its valuable produce, and of all the gold and silver as their own property, and every three years sent these treasures to their own country."

Other Christian priests were summoned to Sumpu, and were subjected to a searching examination, which elicited corroborative evidence. Then it was that Iyéyasu issued his decree of 1614, strictly interdicting "Kirishitan" throughout the empire. A general beheading of the Christians ensued. The proclamation was one of the most remarkable official documents ever put forth by a government. It begins by reciting the old (Chinese) notion of the positive principle being the father, the negative principle the mother, by whom man is begotten, and man the completion of the Three Powers; and avers that the unfathomableness of the positive and negative principles being called God, man, in his uprising and sitting down, in moving and in being still, is not independent of God for a single moment. "He is the form which divinity takes." Japan is called, the proclamation goes on to say, the land of Buddha, and rightly so, for it is the country where the Divine Brightness reappears, the native land of the Sun. The Lotus of the Law, in a golden saying, a miraculous passage, says: "The power by which Buddhas save the world resides in their perfect omniscience, whereby they make happy all living beings, wherefore they make manifest immeasurable Divine Power." God and Buddha are the same in meaning, "just as if two halves of a tally be placed together." By the divine aid the law of Buddha was searched for in China, found, brought to Japan, and has been handed down from teacher to teacher in unbroken succession. "But the Kirishitan band have come, not merely sending their merchant-vessels to exchange commodities, but also longing to disseminate an evil law, to overthrow right doctrine, so that they may change the government of the country, and obtain possession of the land This is the germ of great disaster, and must be crushed." Japan honours God and reveres Buddha. The principles of benevolence and right-doing are held to be of prime importance, and "the law of good and evil is so ascertained that if there be any offenders they are liable, according to the gravity of their crime, to the five punishments of branding, nose-slitting, cutting off the feet, castration, and death." By oath shall be determined the offence and its punishment, and the distinction between guilty and innocent shall not err by a hair's breadth. Criminals of every degree are detested by Buddha, God, the Trinity of precious ones, mankind, heaven, and all living things. Whether by crucifixion or burning in the furnace, punishment shall be meted out, for this is the way, encouraging the good and chastising the evil. It proceeds: "Though one may desire to keep down evil, it accumulates with ease; though one desire to advance in good, it is difficult to hold by, and therefore a watch must be kept. In the present life it is so, and in the next not even all Buddhas past, present, and to come can save from the reproaches of the King of Hell, nor can the successive generations of our ancestors succour us. Fear and tremble!" The faction of the Bateren (Christian priests) rebel against this dispensation, disbelieve "in the army of the gods," blaspheme the true law, violate right-doing, and injure the good. "If they see a condemned fellow they run to him with joy, bow to him, and do him reverence: this, they say, is the essence of their belief. If this is not an evil law, what is it? They truly are the enemies of the gods and of Buddha." "If this be not speedily prohibited, the safety of the state will assuredly be hereafter imperilled; and if those who are charged with ordering its affairs do not put a stop to the evil, they will expose themselves to Heaven's rebuke. These people must be instantly swept out, so that not an inch of soil remains to them in Japan on which to plant their feet, and if they refuse to obey this command they shall pay the penalty." Iyéyasu then breaks out into a proud vaunt, which was not unnatural, seeing the passage from civil wars and sufferings to a state of peace through which he had zealously conducted the country: "We have been blessed by the commission of Heaven to be lord in Japan, and we have wielded power over the realm for years past. Abroad we have manifested the five Cardinal Virtues, while at home we have returned to the doctrine of our Scriptures. For these reasons the country prospers, the people enjoy peace." Then, after a few quotations from the sacred books, he concludes: "Quickly cast out the Evil Law, and spread our True Law more and more; for the way of the gods and the Law of Buddha to prosper in spite of the degeneracy of these latter days is a mark of a good ruler. Let Heaven and the Four Seas hear this and obey!"

The rules issued with this edict to guide the priests who were to test the orthodoxy of their parishioners were not less remarkable than the edict itself. The first was perhaps the most remarkable; it ran: "Because the Kirishitan law teaches that those who despise death can pass through fire without being burnt, or be plunged into water without being drowned, and that those who die by shedding their own blood are saved, the law of the empire is most strict: therefore you must examine such as make light of death." Another of these rules said: "The god whom they adore is called Godzu-Kirishitan-Teidzu-Butsu, and Teidzu calls himself Daiusu (? Deus). By the help of this god, if they look in a mirror, they see the face of a god, but if they have changed their religion they appear as dogs. This is a mirror of the Evil Law." After giving thirteen other indications by which the suspected may be brought under examination, the rules conclude by saying: "If a single one of these fifteen articles be disobeyed, the culprit shall be subject to divine punishment from Bonten Taishaku (Brahma Sakra), the Four Great Heavenly Kings, the Dark Officers of the Five Hells, Tensho-Dai-jin-Gu of Isé in Japan, Hachiman Daibosatsu, Kasuga Daimio-jin, also of his patron-god, and of all the gods of the sixty and odd provinces of Japan."

Other edicts againt Christianity followed, and in 1654 a circular was issued to the Daimios directing that all foreign vessels which might put into Japanese harbours to negotiate should be referred to Nagasaki, whence they were to be sent home. If they fired, efforts were to be made to sink them, but they were not to be pursued if a favourable breeze enabled them to escape. Rewards were offered for the discovery of Christians, and punishments threatened against the mayors of villages and against the friends and relations of any Christians who might be concealed. One of the tests applied was that of requiring a suspected person to trample upon a portrait of Christ, to facilitate which a modelled portrait was cast in copper at Nagasaki, and lent to the neighbouring Daimios. These edicts and arrangements remained in force, and were, Mr. Satow states, notified upon village notice-boards, down to the year 1868. The whole crew of any junk in which a missionary reached Japanese shores were, says the same authority, to be put to death, but pardon and rewards were promised to any of the crew who should turn informer. The carrying of letters or messages to Christians was prohibited under pain of severe punishment. The persecutions went on, the discovery of Christians occasionally occurring for several years, but in 1686 " the few remaining had learnt how to conceal their belief and the practice of their religion so well, that the Council issued a circular to the chief Daimios of the south and west, stating that none of the Kirishitan sect had been discovered of late years, owing perhaps to laziness on the part of those whose duty it was to search for them, and enjoining vigilance" (Satow). Traces of the Christian religion and people lingered in the country down to our own time, when the renewal of relations with Christian foreigners was forced upon Japan, as we have seen. All state resistance to the exercise of the Christian religion is now abolished in Japan, but Christians themselves, so called at least, have spoken with so many unpleasing voices to the Japanese—voices of command, voices of menace, and even voices of war—that years must pass away, and time must be given for our milder virtues to exert their attractions, before the Japanese can be expected to become enamoured of our religion.

The consideration of the foreign relations of Japan as affected by the introduction of Christianity has carried us beyond a point to which we must now return, viz. the reign, so to call it, of the Taiko Hideyoshi, and more particularly that invasion of Korea which has made his name much more memorable than it would otherwise have been. Soon after his acquisition of power, Hideyoshi turned his attention to the external relations of the country over which he ruled, and despatched an envoy to complain of the long neglect of the Koreans to send ambassadors to Japan. His envoy, one Yuyaji Yashuiro, was a curious fellow, who chaffed and taunted the Koreans, and gave himself airs and "lost his head," speaking metaphorically; he consequently failed in his mission, returned home in discredit, and there lost his head in the other and more prosaic sense. A second envoy, Yoshitoshi, met with no great success at first, but discovered that the Korean government were deeply aggrieved by the acts of some Japanese pirates who had a few years previously made a descent upon their coast and carried off some of the inhabitants, whom they induced to act as guides in their subsequent piratical expeditions. Yoshitoshi, on learning this, despatched a colleague to Japan, and had eleven of these Korean marauders brought back and handed over to justice, to the great satisfaction of the Korean government, who then consented to send ambassadors to Japan. These ambassadors arrived in Kioto in the summer of 1590, and both the treatment which they received and the letter which the Taiko wrote have already been set forth at the end of the chapter on Nobunaga and Hideyoshi. That treatment and the letter taken together induced the Korean ambassadors to inform their government on their return that war with Japan was certain. The Korean government accepted the position, and rejected the proposals of Hideyoshi's messengers, sending to him in reply a despatch in which they compared his contemplated invasion of China to an attempt to measure the ocean in a cockle-shell, or to that of a bee proposing to sting a tortoise through its armour.*

Korea had been at peace for two hundred years when

---

* See a paper on this invasion of Korea by Mr. W. J. Aston, in pt. 2 of vol. vi. of the 'Transactions' of the Asiatic Society of Japan, from which I condense the brief account of the invasion which follows.

the Taiko launched the forces of Japan against her. Not only was she therefore unprepared for war, but the people responded reluctantly to the demands made upon them by the government. The actual defensive force raised in 1591 was comparatively small, and it was wholly destitute of firearms. The Japanese, on the other hand, were at the time well accustomed to war; there were large numbers of experienced commanders and veteran troops awaiting employment, and some thousands were armed with the terrible matchlock. Moreover, as war upon China as well as upon Korea was in contemplation, the war strength of the country was vigorously put forth. An immense force, variously estimated at from 300,000 to 480,000 men, exclusive of sailors and camp assistants, was assembled at Karatsu (then Nagoya), in the north of Kiushiu. Hideyoshi, who was to have commanded in person, was dissuaded from doing so, but nevertheless proceeded to Kiushiu, and took up his temporary residence near Karatsu. One hundred and thirty thousand men, reinforced afterwards by fifty thousand more, crossed over to Korea, under the command of the generals Konishi Yukinaga and Kato Kiyomasa. Konishi's division landed first, in the spring of 1592, and captured the town of Fusankai and two neighbouring castles. On the arrival of Kato's division, he and Konishi advanced towards the capital by separate roads, the other generals occupying the towns taken, and advancing by other routes. No serious obstacles were met with; castle after castle was deserted on the approach of the main divisions of the army, or surrendered after a feeble resistance, and fear and trembling fell upon the capital. The inhabitants fled, the troops deserted, and seventeen days after the landing of the first Japanese, the king retreated towards the frontiers of China, sending the royal princes to stir up the remaining provinces to more vigorous resistance. A Korean author has described the royal journey northwards:—

"With a retinue the scantiness of which told a melancholy tale of desertion in the hour of danger and misfortune, the king made his first day's march, followed as he passed along by the lamentations of the inhabitants, who complained that they were being abandoned to the mercy of the invaders. His household was mounted on farm horses, no food had been provided for the journey, and a drenching rain fell during the whole day. Wretched with fatigue and hunger, they reached their lodging at Kaishung late at night, lighted by the glare of a public building which had been set on fire by the king's orders to deprive the Japanese of materials for rafts with which to cross the river which flows to the south of that city. Food had been provided here for the king and his suite, but the kitchen was invaded by hungry guards and attendants, and barely enough was saved for the king's supper. His less fortunate household had no food until the following day, when they were allowed to share with some soldiers their rations of boiled rice. Riyen [the king] did not feel safe until he had reached the fortified town of Pingshang, on the northern bank of the Taitong-Kiang, in the province of Pingang-to. Here it was resolved to make some stay, and to await the progress of events."

Three days after the retreat of the king from the capital, Konishi and Kato reached it, and soon afterwards advanced northward with their combined forces. On a Korean army disputing the passage of a river, the advance of the Japanese army was checked for some days. A feigned retreat drew a Korean force across the river, and this force was so assailed and cut up that the whole Korean army took flight. Unhappily, the Japanese commanders now quarrelled, and cast lots to determine the course each should separately pursue, and to Kato was thus assigned the conquest of the north-eastern province, extending for three hundred miles along the Japan Sea, and to Konishi the subjugation of the province of Pingang-to. Kato is said to have traversed nearly the whole of the immense region allotted to him, where he captured two of the princes of the blood, and many Koreans of rank, afterwards settling for a time with his troops "in the fertile region which surrounds the inlet known to Europeans as Broughton Bay." Konishi's progress was equally successful all the way to Pingshang, where he was joined by some of the other Japanese troops under Kuroda and Yoshitoshi, who had arrived by another route. Another attempt was now made to negotiate, and the circumstances of the parley were so picturesque that I quote their description as given by Mr. Aston :—

"A Japanese, unarmed and alone, appeared on the bank of the river, and planted on the gravelly strand a branch of a tree with paper hanging from it as a signal that he wished to communicate. He was observed from the opposite shore by some Korean officers who had ascended a tower in order to reconnoitre the Japanese position, and a man was sent across in a boat to inquire what was his business. The Japanese produced a letter addressed to 'Ri Tokukei,'* with which the Korean messenger returned. This letter asked for an interview at which to discuss the conditions of peace, and a meeting was accordingly arranged between Ri Tokukei and Yoshitoshi. Gensho, a priest, who had been Yoshitoshi's colleague in his mission to Korea, was also present. The interview took place in the river, the skiffs which contained the two negotiators being moored side by side in the middle of the stream. After the usual greetings had been exchanged, Gensho opened the conference by saying that it was the refusal of the Koreans to allow a passage for the Japanese army into China which had brought on the present war, and that even now, if a single road were thrown open for this purpose, their kingdom might escape destruction. But the Korean negotiators knew that such a concession would be fatal to the hope they entertained of speedy aid from China, and replied that the unprovoked invasion of his country was inconsistent with the peaceful professions of the Japanese, and that if they really wished to conclude peace they must withdraw their forces before the negotiation could proceed further. A blustering speech from Yoshitoshi brought the interview to a close, and the two boats returned to their respective sides of the river."

Konishi now applied himself to the capture of Pingshang, which was well garrisoned and well supplied, and had the river between its defenders and the Japanese. The Koreans prepared for a strenuous defence, and the prospects of a successful resistance seemed so favourable that the inhabitants, who had fled on the enemy's approach, returned, and assisted the garrison in their work. The Japanese were without boats, and were unacquainted with the fords of the river, so that their first demonstrations against the town were without result.

---

* Ri Tokukei had previously filled the office of entertainer of the Japanese embassy; hence the mention here of his name.

After a while the Japanese, who were observed to have relaxed in their vigilance, themselves became the object of a night attack. The Koreans, however, managed the attack badly, and although they were at first successful, and inflicted severe losses upon the Japanese in men and horses, they were ultimately driven back to the river bank. "There they found that the boats which had brought them over were now moored in mid-stream, the men in charge of them not daring to approach the shore where their countrymen were so hard pressed by the enemy. Many were drowned, and although the bulk of the army recrossed by the fords, this had the disadvantage of betraying their position to the Japanese, who were not slow to make use of their information. They crossed the river on the same evening, and the city of Pingshang was at once abandoned by the garrison, disheartened by the failure of their enterprise of the previous night. Large quantities of arms had been flung by the Koreans into ponds within the city, but the stores of grain fell into the hands of the Japanese." Meantime the king had fled still farther northwards, and had even reached the frontier city of Ichin, the news of the fall of Pingshang causing fresh desertions from his court, and the pillage of the army rice-stores by the people.

So rapid had been the victorious progress of the Japanese armies through the country that the Chinese government, both provincial and imperial, suspected the Koreans of connivance with their objects, and hesitated to send any reinforcements whatever. After some delay they sent a small force to serve as a guard to the king, but even this small force withdrew to the frontier on hearing of the fall of Pingshang. Later on, in compliance with the most urgent appeals for military aid, accompanied by offers of subjection to China in return for it, a Chinese force of five thousand men was sent to attack the Japanese in Pingshang. The latter allowed the new-comers to enter the city and penetrate its narrow lanes, and then fell upon them and totally defeated them, slaying their general, and forcing them to retreat with so much impetus that they never stopped till they found themselves at home again in their own province of Laotung.

But now came a turn in the tide of war. While the army of Japan was thus triumphant, the navy of Japan underwent a great defeat. The invading fleet lay at a place called Konchi, a little to the west of Fusankai (where the first landing was effected), and gradually the Koreans, who at first sank their vessels out of fear of their enemy's, gathered courage, built a new fleet, and appeared off the inlet in which the enemy was anchored. Drawing the Japanese out to sea by a feigned retreat, they suddenly turned upon them. "In the engagement which followed, the superior artillery of the Koreans, together with a new kind of warjunk, in which the fighting men were protected from the enemy's fire by screens of planking, insured them a complete victory." The Japanese were compelled to retire to Fusankai, and to abandon a plan which had been devised for prosecuting the campaign in the north-west with the land and sea forces combined. This decisive check is thought not only to have restrained the further progress of the invading army, but also to have preserved China itself from a Japanese invasion. The Koreans everywhere gained heart, and began to give the Japanese forces a great deal of trouble. The Chinese likewise prepared to offer more serious resistance to the Japanese arms, and got in readiness at Peking an army of forty thousand men, gaining time for its preparation by securing an armistice of fifty days, with the aid of an envoy who promised peace, and who was subsequently disclaimed by the government. For some months, down to the end of 1592, no great change in the position occurred, but on the whole the advantage was with the Koreans. At the time named the Chinese army arrived, and a series of struggles which lasted for six years was commenced. During these years several hard battles were fought, Japan bravely contending year after year against the combined forces of Korea and China on the enemy's soil, among hostile populations, and separated by the sea from their reinforcements and supplies. "Reserves from Japan were despatched to Korea, and the Japanese were on the point of invading China, when, in 1598, the death of the Taiko was announced, and orders were received from their government to return home. A truce was concluded, and Korean envoys accompanied Konishi to Japan" (Griffis). The comment of the same author upon this invasion may be concurred with: "The conquest of Korea, thus ingloriously terminated, reflects no honour on Japan, and perhaps the responsibility of the outrage upon a peaceful nation rests wholly upon Hideyoshi." Sir Harry Parkes, our minister in Japan, has made the following comment upon the invasion, of like tenor with the former: "The insight into Hideyoshi's character which it affords is very interesting; he appears to have had all the faults of a man of low origin intoxicated by the great triumphs which he had won by his sword over the feudatory chiefs of his own country. In his communication with Korea he did not hesitate to assume imperial designations, and he seems to have plunged his country into this bloody and unnecessary foreign war without consulting his nominal sovereign." The same thing occurs in countries other than Japan, and down to the present moment. We shall presently have occasion to recur briefly to the relations between Japan and Korea, with reference to recent affairs. Suffice it here to say that from the wrongs inflicted upon Korea by the Japanese during Hideyoshi's invasion that country has never recovered. Mr. Satow says "there appears to be good ground for believing that Korea once enjoyed a much higher degree of civilisation than, as we learn from recent sources of information, is the case in the present day; and when we consider the extent of the ruin wrought in that peninsula by the Japanese armies in the end of the sixteenth century, and the general difficulty experienced in countries where the civilisation is Chinese of recovering from such disasters, we shall not be surprised to find the modern Koreans far behind their neighbours in the practice of the useful arts, though in former ages it was to them that the Japanese went for instruction."

Korea and China were not the only regions in which Hideyoshi asserted himself outside of Japan proper. The island kingdom of Loo-choo was also made to feel the pressure of his power. In the middle of the fifteenth century, when the three so-called sovereignties of these islands had become merged in one,* the king of Loo-choo sent an acceptable tribute of a thousand strings of cash to the Ashikaga Shogun Yoshimasa. After this the Loochooans traded with Japan, in the port of Hiogo, down to about the year 1580, when Hideyoshi sent the king a peremptory message through the Daimio of Satsuma, demanding arrears of tribute. For the sake of peace the young king sent him a shipload of presents, which appeased the Taiko's appetite for the time. Trouble again arose, however, under Hideyoshi's successor, Iyéyasu, from the king of Loo-choo (acting under the advice of a minister, one Jana, who courted favour with China) ceasing to communicate with Japan. The prince of Satsuma, on his own application, was empowered by Iyéyasu to chastise the disloyal acts of the king, and to take any measures that seemed necessary to him. A Satsuma fleet of war-junks sailed in March 1609, and in the course of a few months captured the capital, and carried the king off, the prince of Satsuma holding him in confinement for three years at Kagoshima. "From this date the kingdom of Loo-choo became subject to the princes of Satsuma, the Shoguns not caring, or perhaps not venturing, to interfere with the conquest made by Iyéhisa (the prince who had conquered the king). The only marks of homage which were required

---

* "Very little appears to be known of the history of Loo-choo anterior to the twelfth century, and its real annals commence with Sunten, who ascended the throne in 1187. Sunten is said to have been the son of the famous [Japanese] warrior Tamétomo, who after the defeat of his party in the civil war of 1156 was exiled to Vries Island, and fled some years later to Loo-choo. Sunten was succeeded by his son and grandson, after whom the throne was occupied by descendants of the ancient sovereigns during five generations. The son of the last being a child only five years old, the people set him aside, and elected the governor of Urasoyé, named Satto, to be their king. From him is descended in a direct line the present sovereign Shotu, who is the thirty-fourth since Sunten." — Satow's 'Notes on Loo-choo,' in 'Transactions' of Asiatic Society of Japan.

by the house of Tokugawa from the kings were a submission to reinvestiture upon the accession of a new Shogun, conveyed through the medium of the prince of Satsuma, and the despatch of embassies to Yedo to return thanks on the succession of each Loochooan sovereign" (Satow). Fifteen embassies went to the Shogun's capital between 1611 and 1850. Investiture, it should be observed, was also received from the court of Peking. When the change of government recently took place in Japan, the king of Loo-choo sent ambassadors to congratulate the emperor, and received the rank of "Kuwa-zoku," the same as was accorded to the former Daimios and dignitaries of the court.

Later on, in 1873, a Loo-choo junk was wrecked upon the eastern coast of Formosa, and the crew massacred, and some say eaten, by the natives. The internal state of Japan at the time was such that some foreign diversion for the troops was thought very desirable, but before attacking the Formosans, who were subject to China, the government of Japan thought it best to appeal to the Chinese government for redress. Mr. Soyeshima, a highly placed and distinguished Japanese, was therefore despatched as an ambassador to Peking, and obtained an audience with the Chinese emperor. "The Japanese ambassador stood upright," as Mr. Griffis excitedly and somewhat comically exclaims, " before the Dragon Face and the Dragon Throne, robed in the tight black dress-coat, pantaloons, and white necklinen of western civilisation, bearing the congratulations of the young Mikado of the Sunrise to the youthful emperor of the Middle Kingdom." The Chinese government disclaimed control over the people of Formosa, and thus left the Japanese government free to chastise them itself. While the embassy was in China, a Japanese junk was wrecked on Formosa, and its crew plundered and ill-treated, so that on the return of Mr. Soyeshima there was more reason than ever for a hostile expedition to that country, and one was accordingly undertaken. The expeditionary force, of about three thousand men, sailed from Nagasaki in May 1874, under the command of Saigo Tsukumichi, the present minister at war. The expedition was perfectly successful; the Formosans were defeated in several encounters, and eighteen of the chiefs with their tribes submitted themselves unreservedly to General Saigo. Then, when Japan had thus performed the service which China had declined, the government of the latter protested against the action of Japan, declared it illegal, and claimed to possess that control over Formosa which it had previously disclaimed. War between China and Japan appeared to be on the point of breaking out. The Japanese government, however, proved itself as capable in the field of diplomacy as in that of war, and despatched Mr. Okubo, one of its ablest men, to discuss the question with the court of Peking. So well was his mission accomplished, that China, after many conferences and exchanges of documents, recognised the legitimacy of what Japan had done, and paid to its government as indemnity for its expenses a sum of 500,000 *taels*, promising to make the lives and property of any who might be shipwrecked upon Formosa secure for the future.

We must now briefly revert to the relations with Korea. When in 1867 France was proposing to send an expedition against Korea, the Shogun desired to send an ambassador to attempt to avert the war; but the changes then coming over the government of Japan prevented the departure of the embassy. When the new government was established, orders were given to the prince of Tshushima, whose province is nearest to Korea, to announce to its government the new *régime*. Since the withdrawal of the Japanese army from Korea in 1598, the government of that country had continued to send formal congratulations to the Tokugawa Shoguns as they succeeded to power; but when notified of the emperor's resumption of the governing power in 1868, Korea declined to acknowledge the Mikado, deeming him in league with the western barbarians. "It treated with contumely the Mikado's envoys who were sent to re-establish direct intercourse between the two countries, and reduced the small Japanese community at Sorio to the position formerly held by the Dutch at Decima (in Nagasaki). The attitude of the Koreans towards this settlement became indeed so menacing in 1873 that the Japanese government withdrew all but very subordinate officers from that place" (Mounsey). Hence arose in Japan, and particularly among the discontented *samurai*, or military class, a cry for war with Korea. But the cabinet was divided on the subject: the war party included Saigo Takamori (who afterwards rebelled), Itagaki, and Soyeshima; the peace party was headed by Iwakura, who had just returned from Europe, and considered that further war at that time would bring financial ruin on the country. The peace party prevailed, and in October 1873 Saigo and Itagaki resigned their offices. But the war feeling continued, and led to so much trouble that two years later, at the close of 1875, the government so far yielded to it as to resolve to force Korea into better behaviour. The Koreans afforded abundant pretexts, if not justifications, for it, by refusing to receive the Mikado's envoys (partly on the ground that they appeared in European dress), and more specifically by firing from a fort upon the boats of a Japanese man-of-war which was surveying the coast, and had entered the river leading to the capital for the purpose of revictualling. In January 1876 the Mikado despatched General Kuroda, now colonial minister, as his ambassador to Korea, associating with him Mr. Enouyé, now minister of foreign affairs. They were supported by several men-of-war and transports, but succeeded in framing a treaty of amity without resort to arms,* to the great credit and advantage of the government in the minds of all reasonable people, but without giving satisfaction,

---

* "They were supported," says Mr. Mounsey, "by a mixed squadron of seven men-of-war and transports, and with this imposing force, the strength of which they greatly exaggerated in the eyes of the Koreans by painting port-holes on the transports, and by other similar stratagems, they so overawed the government of Séoul, that without having recourse to force they speedily succeeded in obtaining the signature and ratification of a treaty by which permanent diplomatic relations were at once established between the two countries, and three Korean ports were to be opened at a given date to Japanese commerce. The expedition returned in March."

as may be conjectured, to the turbulent military spirits of the country. Soon afterwards a new commercial convention was signed, and a Korean ambassador proceeded to Japan to present to the emperor the respects of the Korean king.

The negotiations between Japan and Russia respecting the island of Saghalin next require notice. For the greater part of a century (from 1790) this island had been the cause of more or less ill feeling between the governments of the two countries, the Russian settlers drifting downwards from the north, and the Japanese upwards from the south, always intensifying the frontier question, and often raising on the part of Russia the question of mutual trading. At the commencement of the present century, the Russians renewed their efforts to open trade with Japan itself, the Czar sending a letter to the Shogun, asking for a commercial treaty. The ambassador bearing the letter went to Nagasaki, to which place similar applications were always referred. After waiting for several months he received a communication maintaining the old policy of seclusion, and commanding him to quit the port immediately. About the same time a few Russians who had landed for trading purposes on the island of Itorup were seized and imprisoned. In 1806,* two small Russian men-of-war arrived at Kushunkotan, the principal Japanese settlement of Saghalin, first firing "poison-smoke-guns," then landing, pillaging, and setting fire to the place. They carried off with them seven or eight Ainos and a Japanese soldier. Before leaving, they nailed up on the *torii* of the temple of Benten a copper plate thus inscribed :—

"I. It is unjust of the Japanese to prohibit trade with Russians in Saghalin.

"II. If the Japanese should change their minds and wish for trade, they may send a message to Saghalin or Itorup.

---

* I derive these facts from an interesting paper on " Russian Descents in Saghalin and Itorup in the years 1806–7," by Mr. W. J. Aston, printed in the 'Transactions' of the Asiatic Society of Japan, vol. i.

"III. If the Japanese persist long in refusing justice, the Russians will ravage the northern parts of Japan."

The copper tablet was sent to Yedo, where it was taken as equivalent to a declaration of war, and steps were immediately taken to repel future attacks, both in Yezo and on the main islands of Japan. Mr. Aston quotes from the diary of an official who was travelling northwards about this time, giving a lively picture of the bustle and excitement along the great northern highway. The roads were thronged with couriers carrying despatches in oilskin covers, and with troops equipped in the old fashion, with bows and arrows, spears, and occasionally matchlocks. To escape the burdens of the transport service, many of the farmers abandoned their holdings and concealed themselves among the hills. When the train of a Daimio or governor passed, the road was cleared by a man proceeding ahead of it, shouting "Shitani! Shitani!" the signal for every one to squat by the roadside till the great man passed. Then came twelve foot soldiers in files of six each; then two blowers of the war-conch, two drummers, eight matchlock men, two ammunition-bearers, two arrow-bearers, eight archers, three *samurai*, three men carrying emblems of the governor's rank, eight men to bear his private matchlocks, bows, and lances, more foot soldiers and halberdiers, and then the governor himself on horseback, his horse being led by two grooms. After him came six *samurai*, two doctors, and a dozen men bearing his sandals, umbrellas, camp-stools, baggage, and tea and luncheon appliances; two men to preserve order, two leading spare horses, and two with straw shoes for the horses, subordinate officials and their attendants bringing up the rear. The whole body numbered one hundred and twenty-three persons, of whom thirty-six were fighting men.

In the spring of 1807 the Russian war-ships again appeared at Itorup. Landing at Naiho, they pillaged and fired the settlement, the inhabitants fleeing to Shana.

Proceeding to Shana, the Russians fired into a body of Japanese and Ainos who endeavoured to open negotiations with them, and after some hours of light fighting on shore re-embarked. The Japanese were so pleased with their easy repulse of the long-dreaded enemy that they neglected all precautions, and soon after dusk the Russians again landed, and, getting unobserved close to the castle, discharged a volley of musketry, that frightened the garrison, and sent them scampering off to the hills, with the cry of *waré ichi*, or *sauve qui peut!* Their leader committed *hara-kiri*, and the rest made their way under great privation across country to the western end of Itorup, and thence by boats to Kunashin, and ultimately reached Hakodaté. The Russians next day burnt everything. Their next appearance was off Hakodaté, where they took everybody by surprise. They, however, sailed harmlessly away, merely capturing, rifling, and burning a Japanese war-junk as they went. They visited other parts, after the fashion of their visits to Naiho and Shana, and even rifled and burnt several junks off the harbour of Soya, in the north of Yezo. On landing their prisoners at Rüshin they charged one of them to deliver the following message, which was taken down in Japanese. I quote it, as it sets forth the object of these depredations, and illustrates the relation between the two countries. It was addressed to the governor of Matsumaye :

"The distance between Russia and Japan being but small, our emperor sent his officers across the sea to request that trade between the two countries might be permitted. If due inquiry had been made, and a treaty of commerce concluded, all would have been well; but although our officers went repeatedly to Nagasaki, they were sent away without an answer. These things took an unpleasant turn, and our emperor commanded us to give you a specimen of his power in return for your refusing to listen to his first request. If you persist in refusing his offers we will take all your northern territory from you, and if possible get an answer out of you in that way. The red men [as the Russians were called by the Japanese] can always come to Saghalin and Itorup and chase you about.

"If you comply with our wishes, we shall always be good friends with you; if not, we will come again with our ships, and behave in the same way as we have done before this year."

In 1862 the Saghalin boundary question pressed for solution, and Japan sent envoys to Russia to discuss it with the government there. They proposed to fix the fiftieth parallel of latitude as the boundary, because it marked the division between the Aino and Smelenkur tribes. They proposed that Japan should send officers to govern the natives in their southern portion of the island, and produced a map in which the respective divisions were coloured red and green, with the fiftieth parallel dividing the two. The Russians appear, from Japanese accounts, to have replied as follows : " On what grounds do you call this your territory? If we were to consult an impartial person, he would decide that the island belonged to Mantchuria. Besides, no Ainos are to be found north of the fortieth parallel, and you have quite disregarded the positions of the tribes in your unjustifiable desire to take the fiftieth parallel as your boundary. How is it possible for us to accept this ? There is nothing in the island by which a boundary can be properly laid down, and under these circumstances, if you insist upon laying one down, it will give rise to complications between the two powers. We are naturally averse to having our frontier undefined, but we are equally averse to defining it on insufficient grounds, or on such as do not suit our convenience. Let us, therefore, leave the matter as it is for the present, permitting our respective subjects to occupy the island in common, as was provisionally determined by the treaty concluded with Japan at Shimoda. At some future day, when we have both examined the locality, we can confer again. But if you still find it absolutely necessary to settle something, we will take Aniwa Bay (at the extreme south of Saghalin) as our boundary "—that is to say, would take the whole island to themselves ! The Japanese chronicler naïvely adds, " Although Takenoüchi [their ambassador] and his colleagues perceived from the evasive nature of their arguments that their design was to seize the whole island, they were unable to refute the reasoning of the Russians because they were insufficiently acquainted with the locality."

The Shogun's government, on the return of the embassy, desired to send a second mission, composed of persons who knew the geography and condition of Saghalin, but had so many pressing, confusing, and alarming matters in hand between 1862 and 1867 that it was prevented from carrying out its intention. The Russians, according to Japanese statements, took advantage of this long interval to extend their settlements in Saghalin, and when the Bakufu became aware of this, "it was highly alarmed," and forthwith despatched in 1867 another embassy on the subject to St. Petersburg. I have not the Russian account of the matter before me, and cannot therefore give it; but the Japanese account is this: "On arriving at St. Petersburg, Koidé produced the agreement made by Takenoüchi and his colleagues in 1862, and proposed to discuss the question on the basis of the nature of the localities. The Russians feigned never to have heard of the arrangement,* and offered in exchange for Saghalin certain of the Kurile Islands, which belonged to them; but Koidé and his colleagues denied their jurisdiction over the Kuriles, and upbraided them for their disingenuousness. The argument became warm, until the Russians at last said: 'It is not a matter about which we ought to wrangle; let us both colonise and occupy it?' Koidé and his colleagues consulted together, saying, 'Though we have exhausted all possible arguments, the fact remains that their colonies extend south of the fiftieth parallel. It is our fault for putting the negotiation off so long.' Eventually they made a convention by which the island was to be occupied jointly by Russian and Japanese subjects, and returned home in the following spring to report the result of their mission." At a later period the government of Japan sent Admiral Enemoto as minister plenipotentiary to the court of St. Petersburg, and the difficulty was ended, much to the advantage of Russia, by Japan surrendering Saghalin

---

* There surely must be some error in this, as it would have been quite impossible to ignore an "agreement" that was "produced"!

altogether to Russia, and itself taking possession of the Kurile Islands.

The restored Japanese government have taken the Bonin Islands likewise under their care, having in 1871 despatched a government steamer with a commissioner and about a hundred colonists to settle in Peel Island. Rules and regulations were drawn up in English by the Japanese commissioner and his assistants, but they do not appear to have been much enforced. They are now, however, within the jurisdiction of Japan, whose mariners were the first to discover them, and gave them a name at least as early as 1593.

STONE IDOL OF RENRETZU.

CHAPTER XVIII.

THE REFORMS OF THE LAST TEN YEARS.

Surrender of the principalities—Abrogation of the clan system—Division of the country into Fu, Ken, and Han—A new army created—An imperial navy established — Japanese commercial steamships—The police force—Revision of the laws—The codes of 1871 and 1873— Repeal of barbarous laws—Abolition of torture—The central convict establishment—Gold and silver equally esteemed formerly—A new monetary system — A national paper currency — Diminished gold reserves—The yen, or dollar — The Japanese "trade dollar"—New postal system—Land telegraphs—Improved educational system—The university of Tokio—Despatch of students abroad — An education department created—Female schools—Interest taken by the emperor and empress in education—The Tokio female normal school—Other reforms and improvements.

THE establishment of the imperial government in Tokio was followed by many reforms in the administration of the country. There was obviously much to be reformed, the feudal system not having as yet been got rid of. In the second year of Meiji* (1869) a most important step towards its final disappearance was taken. The princes of Satsuma, Choshiu, Hizen, and Tosa addressed to the emperor a collective memorial requesting his authorisation to surrender their principalities and subjects into his hands. Several other princes having followed this example, the emperor consented, but in order to avoid the probable evils of too suddenly breaking the bonds that held the people to their respective lords, the names of the clans were preserved, and the princes received the title of Chi Hanji, or governors of clans. One tenth of his former revenues was assigned as a

---

* See *ante*, pp. 284-85.

rental to each of these chieftains. In this way the feudal power was hopelessly broken down, and the government of the country firmly centralised; but the arrangement adopted soon proved, as was conjectured, but a step towards further changes. It soon became necessary to abolish the feudal system altogether, and in 1871, after lengthened communications between the Daimios and the officers of the new government, the clan system was wholly abrogated. The country was then divided, for administrative purposes, into three Fu, thirty-five Ken, and one Han. Each Fu is administered by a *chiji*, or governor, each Ken by a *rei*, or prefect, while the Han is governed by a *wo*, or vassal-prince of the emperor. The Hokkaido, or the great island of Yezo, is under the government of a colonial minister, who is at the same time minister of agriculture. The three Fu are districts centred in the great cities of Tokio, Kioto, and Osaka respectively. Tokio having become the new capital, the residence of the emperor, and the seat of government, the offices of the various ministers and departments are established there, together with the supreme court, and the various foreign legations. There is also at Tokio a foreign quarter conceded for the residence of Europeans and Americans. The Ken extend of course over the whole country.

The form of government adopted for the general administration of the national affairs will be described in a succeeding chapter; in this I propose to notice the improvements made in other ways. The army necessarily had to undergo a complete change—had, indeed, to be created, the military (*samurai*) having been under the old system the vassals of the Daimios, who now ceased to exist as local lords. Under that system, it is true, each Daimio was bound to furnish a contingent of troops proportioned to his revenues; but it was obviously necessary now to organise an army under wholly new conditions. The new army was consequently formed under a conscription law by which all males between the ages of seventeen and forty are made liable to serve three years with the colours, two years in the first division of the reserve, two years in the second division, and the remainder of the period of his liability in a militia, or what has been called "a sort of landwehr." Nearly seven millions of men are thus made liable to military service, and from this immense number recruits are taken by lot to fill up the vacancies in the regular army as they occur. The normal strength of the army is 35,560 in peace, and 50,230 in time of war.* The troops have been highly trained, chiefly under French officers, but the period of military tutelage is now nearly or quite at an end. The imperial guard is a fine body of men, chiefly selected from the *samurai* class, and may be considered the flower of the army.

We have already seen the government in possession of vessels of war employed in the suppression of the rebel navy in Yezo. The imperial navy has subsequently been largely developed, chiefly upon the pattern of the English navy, which has contributed to its instruction and train-

---

* Mr. Griffis gives the following tabular figures, which I have had occasion to slightly correct:—

		Number in each Regiment or Company.		Total in each Branch.	
		Peace.	War.	Peace.	War.
Infantry	14 brigades, or 42 regiments	640	960	26,880	40,320
Cavalry	3 regiments	120	150	360	450
Artillery	18 companies	120	150	2,160	2,700
Engineers	10 "	120	150	1,200	1,500
Military Train (Commissariat)	6 "	60	80	360	480
Marine Artillery	9 "	80	100	720	800
Total				31,680	46,250

And the Imperial Guard:—

Infantry	2 brigades, or 4 regiments	3,200
Cavalry	1 regiment	150
Artillery	2 companies	300
Engineers	1 company	150
Military Train		80
		3,880

ing some of its ablest commissioned and non-commissioned officers. There has lately been added to the naval force of Japan three ships of the latest European type, all to a certain extent protected by armour, and all armed with Krupp guns of the best pattern. A fine "naval establishment, with dry docks and extensive workshops and storehouses, exists at Yokosuka, a few miles below Yokohama, and there are other important naval appliances, as we shall hereafter note, at Nagasaki. The navy of Japan will doubtless be further developed as the financial strength of the government increases; but however this may be, a well-organised navy was one of the advantages which ensued upon the change of government ten years since. The assistance of the government was likewise given, or is said to have been given, to the organisation of a Japanese commercial navy on a considerable scale; and when the Satsuma rebellion recently broke out, "the government," says Mr. Mounsey, "had the use of the fleet of thirty-eight merchant steamers belonging to the Mitsu Bishi Company, which receives a large subsidy from the treasury on condition of placing its vessels at the disposal of the state when required to do so. They had thus complete command of the sea."

The constitution of a police force speedily engaged the attention of the reformed government, and its embodiment and training were carried out with great success. Eighteen thousand picked men have been drilled into a body which is now everywhere remarkable throughout Japan—remarkable for the good appearance (in European costume) of the men, their orderly demeanour, and the jugdment with which they interpose where necessary. They possess in no small degree the confidence of the people, who regard them as at once their protectors from disturbance and their authorised officers in all cases of irregularity and disorder. It is quite astonishing to observe the influence which these police exert. Nor is this due only to the obedient spirit of the people. The revolution, followed as it was by the dismissal of the *samurai* from their former functions and privileges, put the country into a condition in which there was very much indeed for a trained police force to do, and the duty has been performed with wonderful success. So important a body, indeed, have the Japanese police become, that they rendered most valuable military services during the late rebellion in Satsuma, and have even excited the rivalry and jealousy of the imperial guard itself. A slight skirmish or two has taken place between men of the two forces, and careful observers have seen in this, and in the feelings thus exhibited, a possible source of danger, springing from the very efficiency of the civil force. It is to be hoped, however, that these difficulties have been of but a passing character, or have ceased with the necessity for employing the police for military purposes. During our stay in Japan a commission of high officers of the police force was despatched to Europe, to improve their acquaintance with our police systems.

The laws of Japan have undergone great changes since the revolution. Two codes have been promulgated, one in January 1871, entitled "Chief Points of the New Fundamental Laws," and the other in May 1873, "The Revised Fundamental and Supplementary Laws." Under the government of the Shoguns the criminal laws of the country were in a very complicated state, because, while there was a general system based upon the Chinese Codes of Ming and Tsing (or Ching), there were also many local modifications of these in operation in different parts of the country under the authority of the princes and Daimios. The reformed Code of 1871 was also based upon the Chinese code just named, but with modifications adapted to the altered conditions of the country. The further Code of 1873 enacted additional modifications, based mainly upon the laws prevailing in Europe. Before the revolution the punishments for crime had been both rigorous and cruel; death was the usual punishment, and death accompanied by tortures was the penalty for aggravated crimes. "The commissioners who drew up the new code (of 1871), recognising that the true principle of punishment existed not in extreme and vindictive severity altogether disproportioned to the gravity of the offence, but in the certain infliction of the punishment, entirely eliminated from the new code those barbarous modes of execution which had characterised the old, largely curtailed the list of crimes for which death was enjoined as the penalty, abolished merciless and excessive whippings, and for the majority of offences prescribed the punishment of imprisonment with corrective labour, or, in other words, penal servitude. . . . By the second code (of 1873) many of the laws contained in the first were abrogated or amended, new ones which experience had shown to be necessary were added, and further proof given of the humane feeling by which the government was actuated by the still further curtailment of the list of crimes punishable by death, and by the almost total abolition of corporal punishment."* In explanation of the resort to torture under the old system adverted to above, it may be well to explain that it arose from the fact that in those days no condemnation could be carried into execution without the confession of the accused, and that torture was resorted to in order to elicit the confession of crime. Under the new codes this necessity for confession is abolished, judgments being based upon proofs of guilt or innocence. During our stay in Tokio we visited the central convict establishment, and found the prisoners engaged not only in learning and exercising various ordinary trades, but also in producing porcelain and lacquer work, and even in drawing, painting, and practising other branches of the fine arts.

The money of the country has undergone a radical change. When Japan was first penetrated by foreigners, under the compulsion of the fleets of Europe and America acting, more or less, together, the Japanese ideas concerning money and standards of value were so peculiar, and so peculiarly local, that they esteemed gold no more highly than silver, and readily bartered the one for the other, weight for weight. Neither the civilisation nor the Christianity of the foreigner

---

* 'A Summary of the Japanese Penal Codes,' by Joseph H. Longford, Esq., of H.B.M. Legation, given in the 'Transactions' of the Asiatic Society of Japan.

was forcible enough to suggest any objection to a free use of this chance, and the gold of Japan was rapidly bought up— so, at least, I have been informed—for its weight in silver. It is possible that the Japanese do not love or admire us any the more for taking advantage of their ignorance, and of our presence in their country under threats of battle and death, by carrying off their property in this fashion; but they have already got far away from the conditions under which alone such doings were possible. They now know the relative values of gold and silver as well as we do ourselves; they have established a monetary system in which gold is adopted as the nominal standard, and have created a mint and issued a coinage in gold, silver, and bronze, which compares favourably with that of any other country.

Under the Shogunate the only paper money existing was that of the clans, who obtained permission to issue it for purely local purposes, its circulation being limited to the clan which employed it. Under the new government the trade and commerce of the country have been much facilitated by the issue of a national paper currency, available throughout all the Kens of the country. It is to be regretted that the great expenses incidental to the change of government; to the pensioning of the Shogun and his Daimios with their vast arrays of retainers; to the creation of an army, navy, and police force, and of many other costly but more or less necessary institutions, and of numerous public works; and, added to all this, the great and cruel charge of the Satsuma rebellion—that all these have had the effect of so far diminishing the gold reserves as to greatly depreciate the paper currency. But this is an evil which, with the economy the government is now practising, and with the improved income which the government may fairly look for from a revision of the existing tariffs, will, it is at least to be hoped, soon pass away, and relieve the new government from the chastening but painful condition of having a national currency at a considerable discount. This passing condition should not, however, blind us to the great improvements in the form of the currency which have been introduced during the last few years, and which have been an enormous relief to the manufactures and commerce of the people.

The unit of the new currencies of Japan is the *yen*, or dollar, its decimal submultiples being the *sen* (or cent) and the *rin*. In the last report [*] of Mr. Consul Flowers, the following passage occurs: "The unit of exchange between Japan and foreign countries at the Treaty Ports is the Mexican dollar, and against this coin all native currency, whether silver, gold, or paper money, is estimated in value at so much per cent. premium, or so much per cent. discount. As a general rule the actual circulating medium between Japanese and foreigners is the *yen satsu*, or paper money issued under the auspices of the government, but not redeemable against bullion. The value of the *yen satsu*, therefore, fluctuates according to the capacity of the people to take them, and although they were, in 1877, at a discount of about eight per cent. against gold *yen*, such is the confidence of the people in the good faith of their government, that they have previously been actually at a premium of one or two per cent. against the gold they are supposed to represent." Mr. Flowers further states, as I have already done, that owing to the additional issue of paper money necessitated by the civil wars in Satsuma (the cost of which, he says, is estimated to have been in round numbers some forty millions of *yen*), *yen satsu* have since been constantly below par. It should be stated that the government have coined and issued a Japanese trade dollar which is intended to take the place of the Mexican dollar in commercial transactions. The new coin is identical in weight with the American trade dollar, being four grains heavier than the silver *yen*. As a consequence of the recent visit to Japan of that able officer of the crown His Excellency Pope Hennessy, governor of Hong Kong, this Japanese trade dollar is now accepted in our colony as the legal equivalent of the Mexican dollar, and is coming into general use throughout the east.

[*] Dated Hiogo, April 15, 1878.

In 1871 the European system of postage was adopted and carried out by the new government of Japan, in a manner which has won the admiration of all foreigners. Prior to that date there did not exist any national system of postage whatever, owing to the peculiar circumstances of a country under the feudal system. Private enterprise had chiefly to be depended upon for the conveyance of correspondence. The government postal system was commenced in the year just named, with a service between the capital (Tokio) and the great commercial city of Osaka, and so rapidly was the system developed and extended that within five years from that time mail routes of more than thirty thousand miles in length were in active operation, "and six hundred and ninety-one post offices, besides one hundred and twenty-four receiving agencies, eight hundred and thirty-six stamp agencies, and seven hundred and three street letter boxes, had been established. The number of letters, packets, etc., forwarded in 1876 was about thirty millions, being an increase of twenty-nine per cent. over the number carried in 1875, and ninety-eight per cent. over that of 1874."* The development thus indicated has still gone on. The postage for an ordinary letter in the large towns is one cent ($\frac{1}{2}d.$), and two cents ($1d.$) for the rest of the empire. Postcards are carried for one half these charges. In 1875, a money-order system was adopted, and within two years there were three hundred and ten offices where orders could be obtained or cashed. The number has since increased. Post-office savings banks were likewise opened in 1875, and appear likely to prove successful.

Great progress has been made with the introduction of the system of land telegraphs, which chiefly (on account of the limited extent of the railroads) follow the common roads of the country. I have elsewhere mentioned the extraordinary conjunction of the ancient and the modern which

---

* Mr. Mounsey's Report on the Finances of Japan. I give these figures, as they are the latest which I have before me in a convenient form.

is presented to the eye by the appearance of telegraph wires and posts through the more primitive parts of the country. Most of the principal towns have already a telegraphic service, and it is intended to extend it to the chief towns of all the Kens. I propose to take note of the railways of Japan, and of their contemplated extension, in a later chapter.

One of the most remarkable developments of Japan under its new government is to be seen in the creation of its educational organisations. Up to the time of the Shogun's downfall, the great colleges and schools of the country had been almost exclusively established and carried on for the benefit of the nobles and of their military retainers, the two-sworded *samurai*. The merchants, agriculturists, tradesmen, artisans, and labourers were excluded from the schools of the sworded gentry, and had to educate their children in the best way they could by means of private schools. That the education of these classes was, nevertheless, not altogether neglected, may be inferred from the fact that on the downfall of the Shogunate a large proportion of them were found to be sufficiently instructed for the ordinary purposes of their business, being " able to read, write, and keep their accounts "—reading, writing, and keeping accounts by Japanese methods being no small matter, be it remembered. With the new government the exclusiveness of past times disappeared, and the blessing of education was recognised (as we at last, but quite recently, came to recognise it in England) as at once the natural inheritance and the national obligation of all the people. The attempt to improve and extend education was made at the very commencement of the new order of things, by the establishment of an education board.

The civil wars which followed the first resignation of the Shogun, and lasted as we have seen for a year or two afterwards, had the unpleasant effect of turning the school-buildings into quarters for the troops, and burdening the medical schools and hospitals with the care of the sick and wounded. However, in the very year in which the

Shogunate was abolished (1868), the Education Board reopened the Foreign Language School and the old Confucian College, both of Yedo. The medical school and hospital were likewise brought under the new board. In the following year the Confucian College was converted into a university ("Daigakko"), and placed at the head of the national system of education. In the same year provision was made for translating and compiling text-books for Japanese schools from foreign languages, under the supervision of a Bureau of Translation. In 1870 the emperor and his government gave repeated further proofs of their interest in the education of the people by proclaiming favourable general laws for the foundation and management of colleges, high-schools, and primary schools; by authorising the provincial governments to select promising pupils for education in the Foreign Language School at the government expense; and by sending students abroad for the study of western science, literature, and medicine.

In the year 1871 a still greater step was taken in the same direction, by the formation of a government department of education ("Mombusho"), in which all educational affairs were vested, the charge of the department being entrusted to Mr. Oki Takato, the present minister of justice, a gentleman of high education and great administrative powers. The method of appointing students to the Foreign Languages Medical Schools by the provincial governments was abolished, and these schools thrown open to all who passed satisfactory examinations. Mr. Tanaka Fujimaro, then chief secretary of the department, was sent to Europe with the Japanese embassy, as a commissioner to report upon educational matters in foreign countries. This gentleman is now the acting minister of education, and is universally respected for the success with which he performs the arduous and intricate duties of his high office. In the year 1872 a female school was opened in Tokio, for imparting education both in Japanese and in English to girls—the first step taken in Japan towards the elevation of woman, from her traditional inferiority in the east to the high level upon which western women live and move, and devise contrivances for attaining to higher levels still. Many other girls' schools have followed, and in Japan now as here woman is decidedly " looking up." Many other important measures were taken during this year (1872) for improving education; new educational laws were proclaimed, bringing the provincial schools under the regulations of the central department; two millions of *yen* were voted for the use of that department; a bureau of superintendence was organised; and the educational officers of the provinces were assembled at a convention in the capital, to discuss and settle the details of school-work, and to further the spread of elementary schools throughout the empire. It is unnecessary to pursue this summary of educational improvements, but it will be proper to say that they were throughout made under the close personal attention of the emperor and empress, who rival Nintoku and some other of the ancient sovereigns of Japan in their care of the people, and in their diligent devotion to their interests. It was under the special patronage of the empress that the female schools were commenced, and again, in 1874, her majesty intimated her desire " to contribute the sum of five thousand *yens* from her private purse, for the purpose of promoting the education of her sex in the empire."* This amount was therefore applied to the establishment of the Tokio Female Normal School, to which I may have occasion to make particular reference hereafter. The school was opened by the empress in person in 1875.

It would be easy to extend this chapter by reference to the many works of public utility which the government has entered upon, and in greater or less measure carried out, including the admirable lighthouse system which I elsewhere speak of, the improvement of public roads and bridges, the construction of iron works and silk and paper

---

* 'Outline History of Japanese Education,' from which most of the facts in the above educational summary are derived.

factories as an incentive to private enterprise, and so forth. But I think I have already said sufficient to indicate roughly both the nature and the extent of the reforms which have been carried out in Japan since the revolution of 1868, and to show also the spirit in which the government of the country is now carried on. Many additional illustrations of all these points will arise in the narration of our travels, and of my visits to the public establishments of Tokio, Kioto, Osaka, Nagasaki, Nagoya, and other cities. No sufficient idea of the difficulties with which the new government has had to grapple will be obtained, however, without reference to the financial circumstances of the country, or without regard to the strain thrown upon the departments of the state by the Satsuma rebellion, which subject will now be separately dealt with.

IMAGE OF KUYA-SHONIN.

CHAPTER XIX.

THE SATSUMA REBELLION.

Mr. Mounsey's book—Seething state of Japan politically in the early days of the new empire—Saigo of Satsuma—The Shimadzu family—Shimadzu Saburo again—Saigo's hatred of the Tokugawas—Romantic story of Saigo and the priest Gassho—Recall of Saigo to Satsuma—Dissatisfaction of Saburo—An embassy sent to Kagoshima—Supposed political manifesto of Saigo—He takes office in Tokio—Becomes commander-in-chief—Takes offence and withdraws to his province—Saburo remonstrates with the imperial government—Satsuma remains independent—Its *samurai* disaffected—The first outbreak crushed—The removal of stores and arms from Kagoshima resisted—Admiral Kawamura's mission of peace—The rebel army constituted—Prince Arisugawa appointed to the chief command of the imperial forces—Investment of the castle of Kumamoto—Repeated contests—Kiushiu placed under martial law—Admiral Kawamura's attempted mediation—The rebels driven into Hiuga—Their repeated efforts to capture Kagoshima—They are forced into the open—Surrounded—Escape of Saigo—He captures Kagoshima—Is forced to withdraw—The lions in their lair—Taken in the imperial toils—The death and burial of Saigo—A speech by the emperor.

THE story of this rebellion—the latest and it may be hoped the last against the authority of the Mikado's government—has been so well and so fully told in Mr. Mounsey's volume on the subject,* that I would gladly dispense here with all record of Saigo's revolt, were not some brief account of it essential to the plan of this work as laid down before the appearance of his book. But although I cannot wholly omit reference to this trying rebellion, I shall content myself with giving a brief sketch of it only, which will amount to

---

* 'The Satsuma Rebellion.' An episode in modern Japanese history. By Augustus H. Mounsey, F.R.G.S., etc., London. John Murray, Albemarle Street, 1879.

but little more than an abstract of Mr. Mounsey's narrative, leaving the reader to resort to that narrative itself for a fuller and more worthy record.

The chapters that have preceded this will have given the reader some knowledge of the seething state of the political world of Japan during the later days of the Shogunate and the early days of the reorganised empire. Both the Shogun's court at Yedo and the imperial court at Kioto were split into rival and contending factions, the lords of Satsuma and of Choshiu, who were the first in Japan to adopt the arms and arts of western warfare, proving themselves too powerful for direct subjugation by either court. And while thus possessing, and likewise exerting, a certain independence with regard to their own sovereigns, they were among the most determined of all the clans in their resistance to that invasion of foreigners which for centuries the entire Japanese nation had been accustomed to regard with dread and detestation. When at length the foreigners came, and would insist upon remaining, while regarding themselves as Christians and envoys of civilisation, they were regarded by the Japanese as little better than barbarians, coming with flashing steel, rattling musketry, and thundering cannon, to threaten, to bully, and to compel an unoffending nation to do their bidding. Among those who took a leading part in the events of those days was Saigo of Satsuma, who, as we saw earlier, effected the reconciliation of his own clan with that of Choshiu, and induced both to make common cause against the wrongful acts, as he deemed them, alike of the government of Japan and of the foreign governments who were worrying the land. In pursuing this policy Saigo was only following out what had been for centuries before the policy of the Shimadzu family, to which belonged the lords of Satsuma. Hideyoshi and Iyéyasu each had his troubles with this house, whose domains being situated at a long distance from the capital, on a separate island, and nearest to the southern and western nations, were favourable to the cultivation of an independent spirit. Perhaps of all Japanese the Satsuma clan most habituated themselves to habits of pride and self-sufficiency, and most regarded with jealousy both internal and external control. Since 1858 the active head and leader of the clan has not been the actual head, owing first to the infancy and subsequently to the political indifference of the latter. The real active head has been that Shimadzu Saburo whose train it was through which Mr. Richardson and his party broke on the Tokaido, at the time when he was cut down and slain. Saburo is uncle of the present, and brother of the late, Daimio of Satsuma, and it was his life that the British minister demanded to have sacrificed with ignominy, in the presence of the British officers, on account of the Richardson affair. It was on his account that Kagoshima was bombarded by us, and, in view of the state of affairs that then existed, and especially of the haughty and independent bearing of Saburo and his clan, it is not improbable that the Shogun's government saw with satisfaction the attack of the English upon the capital of Satsuma. Moreover, it was well understood that Saburo and his friends were the most urgent and pertinacious of all those who, at that time, were contriving the restoration of the imperial power to the Mikado, and the attendant overthrow of the Tokugawas. When the imperial power was finally restored, the Mikado acknowledged in a letter to Saburo that for many years he, Saburo, had been the chief upholder of the imperial cause, and that it was to his efforts that the restoration was mainly due.

Saigo, who was a Kagoshima man, was thoroughly imbued by the Satsuma spirit, and had risen by his own efforts to a position of great influence in the counsels of the clan. He became the chief leader in what may be called an imperialist school in Satsuma, the primary aim of which was the overthrow of the usurped authority of the Tokugawa Shoguns. "The Shogun's government used every means in its power to suppress their teaching, and in 1858 it succeeded in arresting most of the members of this school, amongst them being Gassho, a priest of Kioto, and an intimate friend of Saigo. After a brief interval of imprisonment, Gassho managed to escape, and made his way to Saigo's house in Satsuma. There taking counsel together, these two men came to the conclusion that their cause was desperate, and agreed to drown themselves rather than fall into the hands of the Shogun's emissaries, whom they knew to be on their track. Accordingly, as they were being conveyed across the bay from Kagoshima to the island of Sukurajima, they both jumped overboard. The boatmen picked them up, but the priest was dead, and Saigo, already insensible, was with difficulty recalled to life. Thereupon the Satsuma authorities, fearing lest the Shogun's government should accuse them of harbouring its enemies, and yet determined to save Saigo, banished him to Oshima, a small island off the southern coast of the principality. His leisure there no doubt afforded him leisure to ponder over the affairs of his country, and it is not improbable that he there became convinced of the impossibility of expelling foreigners and restoring Japan to its previous state of isolation—a conviction which was confirmed by the subsequent bombardment of Kagoshima" (Mounsey).

After the bombardment just mentioned, Shimadzu Saburo recalled Saigo to Satsuma, where he immediately took a leading part in the politics of the country, and exercised great influence upon the neighbouring clans. At the battle of Fushimi, and during the last days of the Shogunate, he rendered great services to the emperor, and he likewise contributed to the suppression of the revolts in Echigo which ensued. He received for his services a considerable pension, which he was compelled against his will to accept, and which he expended, it is said, upon a military school. Thus the great services which both Shimadzu Saburo and Saigo Takamori had rendered to the emperor were clearly recognised, and further recognition of the services of the clan was made in the appointment of many other Satsuma men to office under the government, including Okubo, Terashima, and Kawamura. In 1869, however, Saburo and Saigo appear to have become dissatisfied with their positions, having expected still more eminent acknowledgments and higher posts of influence than they had received, and in 1870 this dissatisfaction induced them to suggest or obtain, on other pretexts, the imperial consent to the withdrawal from Tokio of the Satsuma troops who were there to guard the emperor and his counsellors. These troops spread in their native province the complaints of their chiefs, and Satsuma thus early became a thorn in the side of the government which it had done so much to create. A special embassy was sent to Kagoshima "to appease the wounded pride of the clan." The court noble Iwakura, an able and distinguished statesman, was selected as the representative of the emperor, and accompanied by Okubo. In January 1871 a sword was taken by him and presented to the shrine of the late Daimio of Satsuma, and as the result of the mission the three great clans of Satsuma, Choshiu, and Tosa agreed to send troops to the capital to protect the government, and to form the nucleus of an imperial army. Iwakura, however, had witnessed with alarm the independent military activity of the province he had visited, for, as Mr. Mounsey tersely puts the case, "Satsuma was as feudal as ever." It has become known that before consenting to send forces to the capital, in concert with Choshiu and Tosa, Shimadzu and Saigo had vainly endeavoured to induce those clans to join them in upsetting the then-existing government. In May 1871 Saigo went up to the capital, and soon afterwards there appeared in the newspapers a sweeping political manifesto believed to express his views. It provided for the retention of the governing powers by the Mikado, the perfecting of a great military power, the abandonment of steam power and railroads, etc. A lasting system, "which need not be changed for a thousand years," was to be established. The Satsuma chiefs accepted less than this document asked, but they brought about a reconstruction of the public departments. Saigo took office as a Sangi (councillor of state), and soon brought about the abolition of the "clan" system. On August 29, 1871, the rank and authority of the Daimios was formally abolished. Saigo's chieftain, Saburo, disapproved of this and other changes, and blamed Saigo for the part he had taken in them. After a while (in August 1873) the government

A Bridge at Kintai, Province of Suwo.

induced Saburo to visit Tokio; thither he went with some hundreds of armed retainers, dressed in the old war costume, and each bearing the two swords of the *samurai* class. Saigo was appointed commander-in-chief of the emperor's army as a compliment to Satsuma, but Saburo nevertheless remained discontented.

About this time (1873) the Korean difficulty, adverted to in the chapter on Foreign Relations, sprang up, and the cabinet became, as I have there stated, divided upon it. Saigo led the war party, and with the *samurai* "'War with Korea' became a popular cry." This military class was full of discontent with the arrangements incidental to the changes of government in their own country, and the Korean outcry was but one vent to their disaffection. Both for them and for Saigo, however, a successful foreign war, which he would lead and they would make, would, they might well hope, open new and alluring prospects. The nobles Sanjo and Iwakura—then as now prime and vice-ministers respectively—saw well the dangers of the time, and induced the cabinet to decide against the war scheme, whereupon Saigo and his friends resigned office, and, in spite of an imperial order to the contrary, he and Yeto Shimpei, another of the ministers, withdrew to their provinces. Saigo retained, nevertheless, the office of commander-in-chief of the army. Yeto placed himself at the head of a revolt of the *samurai* of Hizen, which the government forces suppressed, Yeto and others being executed. Saigo refused to return to the capital. The government, however, contrived to appease the still-lasting discontent of Saburo by giving him high rank, and by despatching the expedition against the Formosan Islanders, many Satsuma *samurai* being among the forces sent, and the command in chief being given to Saigo's brother. Saigo himself was not pleased with this expedition, and in the event it seems to have stimulated rather than to have allayed the demands of Saburo. In April 1875 the latter memorialised the emperor, asking permission to resign his offices, and formally protesting against the use of foreign dress, the employment of foreigners, the change of the calendar, the multitude of officials, the increase of public buildings, the adoption of foreign drill, the toleration of Christianity, the permission to intermarry with foreigners, and so forth. His requests were refused, as the government now felt strong enough to refuse them, and he was persuaded to accept a high but nominal office in the emperor's household. Saburo and the *samurai* were further appeased for the time being by the government reviving the idea of an expedition to Korea, unless its demands were complied with. All this time Satsuma virtually remained independent, refusing to have to do with any but Satsuma officials, and employing its energies in providing warlike men and materials. Even when the expedition to Korea took place early in 1876, Satsuma was not satisfied with its peaceful results, but on the contrary made the renewal of amicable relations with that country the ground of further dissatisfaction. Another cause of discontent to the Satsuma clan occurred in March 1876, when the government resolved to enforce its existing prohibition against the wearing of swords by any but the regular troops of the government. "The older generation of *samurai* still clung to the practice of constantly wearing the two swords—the brightest emblems of honour in their eyes—as one of their most valuable privileges, and to them the interdict was most distasteful. To Shimadzu Saburo it appeared like the *coup de grâce*, the knell of all his hopes and dreams of a return to the old order of things in Japan. He left Tokio at once (April 5, 1876) for his home at Kagoshima, and the spectacle of the few followers who accompanied him, carrying their swords in cotton bags, is said to have convinced him at last that his part in politics was completely played out" (Mounsey).

The country began now to perceive that the Satsuma chiefs were becoming "irreconcilables," and the newspapers began to cry out: "What is going on in Kagoshima? and, What is Saigo doing? are the principal questions asked by the people. If the government wishes to preserve peace in the country, what policy should it adopt? As we said before, both parties cannot long exist." Satsuma was preparing, but the government also was preparing, bringing its army up to thirty thousand men, and its navy to nine men-of-war and eight steam transports. Nevertheless no disturbance yet arose, and the government took advantage of the calm to decree in August 1876 the compulsory commutation into capital sums of all the hereditary pensions and allowances that had previously been granted to the ex-Daimios and *samurai*.

In October 1876 came the first outbreak. Higo is the central province of the great island of Kiushiu, and adjoins Satsuma, Kumamoto being its principal town. Dressed in the old style of Japanese warriors, in hemlet and chain armour, and armed with swords and halbards, about one hundred and seventy of the *samurai* fell by night upon the government barracks of Kumamoto, and either slew or wounded three hundred of the imperial troops. One half of the insurgents, afterwards finding themselves unsupported, committed *hara-kiri*, twenty-nine surrendered, and the remainder were killed or dispersed. Minor disturbances, easily suppressed, occurred in the northern parts of Kiushiu, and across the Straits of Shimonoséki, in Choshiu, a serious outbreak soon afterwards happened. The leader, Mayébara, collected some five or six hundred fighting men, but the government acted with promptitude, and crushed the rebellion in a fortnight. Satsuma remained quiet, and peace prevailed throughout the remainder of 1876. Mr. Mounsey, in an able discussion of the spirit and attitude of Saigo at this period, points to the conclusion that he was aiming at the establishment of a military despotism of which he should himself be the head, under the Mikado, and according to him it was to be in substance, if not in form, the case of Yoritomo, Taka-Uji, Nobunaga, Hideyoshi, and Iyéyasu over again; according to destiny, it was to be far otherwise.

In January 1877 the government commenced to quietly remove the arms and munitions of war stored in the arsenals of Kagoshima. The Satsuma *samurai*, in opposition to this, broke fully armed and repeatedly into the stores, and carried off all the arms and powder which they could get away.

They also forcibly interfered with the loading of a government transport with powder which the government had purchased. The vessel got away, and reported these facts to the imperial government. Admiral Kawamura, then vice-minister of marine, and a Satsuma man, was forthwith despatched to Kagoshima in a swift vessel. The vice-governor of the town informed him that the military men had taken to arms in consequence of their belief that the government was about to attack Satsuma and had sent emissaries to assassinate Saigo. The emissaries had been captured, and had confessed the plot, and that Saigo and Saburo had thereupon, after vainly endeavouring to restrain their followers, retired to their country houses. Admiral Kawamura denied the allegations against the government, declared that as a Satsuma man, and a relation, friend, and comrade of Saigo, he would have joined him had they been true, and stated that the Mikado had sent him to ascertain the causes of discontent, and to reassure the Satsuma men. The vice-governor then undertook to arrange an interview with Saigo, and left the admiral's vessel for the purpose. But soon afterwards, five boats filled with armed men approaching the ship with hostile intentions, Admiral Kawamura steamed across the bay in order to avoid a collision, which must have made a peaceable solution of the difficulty hopeless. The vice-governor again went on board, stated that an interview with Saigo was impossible, and that, in point of fact, the time for negotiations was passed. The differences between the Satsuma clan and the government, which the Satsuma chiefs had so much helped to bring into being, had therefore to be settled by the diabolical arbitrament of war. His imperial highness Prince Arisugawa-no-Miya was appointed commander-in-chief of the imperial forces for the suppression of this most serious and deplorable revolt. Saigo assembled his forces in Kagoshima, there embodied them into companies, regiments, and divisions, and sent them forth in the middle of February (1877) to the number of fourteen thousand men. On the 17th he marched after them with a picked bodyguard of fifty men.

He could have added largely to the number of his forces, but he preferred, for the time at least, to employ only those who had been trained in his own " private schools," as he called them. "He assumed to act as commander-in-chief of the Mikado's land forces, a post which he still nominally retained, and in this capacity he sent orders to the general in command of the nearest imperial garrison at Kumamoto not to move until he himself should arrive to give further instructions" (Mounsey).

The march was to the Straits of Shimonoséki, whence he proposed to cross into Choshiu, and thence onward by the great western road to Kioto. He, however, met with resistance from the imperial troops at the castle of Kumamoto, which he was forced to invest. He flooded the castle on three sides, and guarded the fourth with an army division, marching forward with the main body to Minami-no-séki, where he was confronted by two divisions of imperial troops, which had been brought there by means of the utmost exertions on the part of the imperial government and its commanders. At the first encounter the rebel forces were defeated, and driven back upon the town of Takasé, and upon the following day were forced three miles further southwards. On the 3rd of March the imperialist forces failed to carry the town of Yamaga, on the river Takasé, and had to wait for reinforcements. Meanwhile Admiral Ito (now commander-in-chief at Yokohama, from whom my son and I received many kindnesses while in Japan) was despatched with three men-of-war, carrying 1100 infantry, 800 marines, and 700 armed police, to Kagoshima, arriving there on the 8th of March. On board were General Kuroda (minister of the colonies), in command of the military forces, and an imperial envoy, Yanigawara, a court noble, by whom the Mikado pressed upon Shimadzu Saburo the duty of remaining loyal. The military forces landed in Kagoshima without resistance—in fact there were no troops left behind by Saigo to offer resistance. After removing all the powder and spiking the guns the troops were re-embarked, and the squadron returned to Nagasaki. This abandonment of the enemy's capital proved afterwards to be a great mistake.

The castle of Kumamoto, violently attacked, still held out under Colonel Tani, and large reinforcements were sent to the imperial army. General "Yamagata Ariaki [now the general in command of the army] took the command of the advanced divisions of the imperial army, and Admiral Kawamura cruised off the coast of Bungo, in order to prevent the passage of malcontents from the mainland" (Mounsey). Repeated and bloody contests in detail took place between the imperial and rebel forces, in which thousands of lives were in the aggregate lost on either side, the advantage on the whole being decidedly in favour of the imperial troops, who forced the rebels south of Uyeki. Towards the end of March General Kuroda, having landed at Hinaku, marched northwards, captured Udo, and appeared before Kawajiri. In the north of Kiushiu other outbreaks against authority occurred, and the government consequently placed the whole island of Kiushiu under martial law. They also levied and despatched to the seat of war large additional forces, the conduct of these operations in the capital devolving upon General Saigo, the present minister of war, and brother of the rebel general. The garrison of Kumamoto nobly held out, until at length, after fifty-five days of siege, Saigo had to execute a retreat southwards, which he is said to have done in a "most masterly manner."

During the siege Admiral Kawamura attempted to stay the effusion of blood by appealing in writing to Saigo to remember the difficulties in which the country was placed, and to cease to weaken the power of his country by prolonging the rebellion. He promised, if Saigo would submit, to urge the government to show to him all possible leniency, and then (in view doubtless of his relationship to Saigo) he concluded by saying, "If it be your intention to die, is it not better for you to die in your country's cause than to die rebels, disgraced and dishonoured? Let me entreat you to put this question to yourself, and endeavour to come to a right decision." Saigo replied in a most angry and offensive letter, telling the admiral that his answers were one-sided, and concluding with the insulting words : " So greatly do we differ from the views expressed by your excellency, that we think your excellency must be out of your mind, or speaking under the influence of nightmare. When your excellency has exhausted all your talents, you had better come to Kumamoto and ask our pardon. We beg to inform your excellency that this is the last time we shall hold any communication with you."* Compromise was clearly impossible with Saigo in the state of mind to which he had by this time brought himself.

Forced from Kumamoto, the rebel forces resolved to make a stand in Hiuga and Bungo, and also to reoccupy Kagoshima, from which they had all along been drawing plentiful supplies of men, food, and munitions of war. The imperial commanders were, however, beforehand with them in this matter, and Admiral Kawamura, with Generals Takashima and Oyama, occupied the city—which was sacked and almost deserted on their approach—with 7000 infantry and police, an artillery force with eight field-pieces, and a body of engineers. On the 20th of April the rebel army was attacked in three positions which they had taken up in force, and were driven from all of them and split into three corps. Forcing their way southwards, the imperialist forces entered the Satsuma territory on the 4th of June, and, fighting several successful battles, occupied various strong positions within it. Higo was therefore restored to the Mikado's government, but the mass of the rebels had made their way into Hiuga, the eastern province of Kiushiu. The position of the rebellion at this time, four months after its outbreak, has thus been well summed up by Mr. Mounsey :—

" The successes of the imperialist arms were not gained without very considerable losses, and as the rebels still held all Hiuga and Osumi and the greater part of Satsuma, whilst numerous bands of

---

* Mr. Mounsey gives the correspondence complete in his book on this war.

them overran Bungo in several directions, there was no prospect of a speedy termination of the war. Reinforcements were still demanded by the imperial generals, and more troops and policemen were constantly sent down from Tokio to the scene of the struggle. Ten thousand men were drafted into the regular army, and the large proportion of youths and old men in their ranks showed the strain that was being put on the government resources. As the war lasted it became each day more destructive and more bloody; towns and villages were burnt by both sides, and quarter was neither asked nor given by either. Driven back to their homes, the rebels fought with increased determination, and an address which Prince Arisugawa issued to the army about this time affords evidence of the feelings which animated the troops on both sides. He reminded his men of their successes before Kumamoto, but pointed out that the rebels were now hard pressed and were driven to desperation, so that additional watchfulness and valour were called for in order that the soldiers of the imperial army should not be taken unawares and defeated. The honour of the army was concerned in carefully guarding against any negligence which might give the enemy an undue advantage. Meantime the war in Bungo was carried on with varied success. The rebels took the towns of Saeki and Usuki on the sea-coast, and held them for some time. But being inferior in numbers to their opponents in this quarter, and probably the least efficient in arms, etc., of their corps, they were gradually forced towards the southern frontier of the province, and about the 24th of June entirely driven out of it, and obliged to retire to the neighbourhood of Nobeoka."

The most desperate attempts to capture Kagoshima were made by the rebels under Kirino, "the most adventurous of Saigo's lieutenants." On the 6th of May they made a determined attack upon it, but were repelled by Admiral Kawamura, whose artillery and rifles inflicted great losses upon them. The attack was nevertheless repeated, and earthworks were thrown up to keep the admiral's troops from assailing the rebel positions. On the 23rd of June, General Kawaji (now at the head of the police of Japan)[*] entered the town from the south, bringing reinforcements, which enabled Kawamura to make a general attack upon

---

[*] Since this was written I have heard with much regret of the decease of this gallant officer, whom I had the pleasure to meet in Tokio, and who left for Europe during our stay in the capital. He subsequently returned home, but only to die there.

those positions, some of which were captured, together with some of the enemy's guns. Other imperial forces arriving, Kirino was obliged to retreat northwards, which he did in good order, all the province of Satsuma now coming again under imperial command. The rebels, however, still held the province of Hiuga, Miyako-no-jo being their headquarters in the south, Nobeoka in the north, Saigo holding the centre at Miyazaki. The imperial troops which were sent against these positions, intending to penetrate between them, and thus separate the rebel positions, were continually harassed by the Satsuma guerilla forces, who were lightly attired, and knew the country well. On the 24th of July, however, Miyako-no-jo fell, and its fall was recognised by all as the beginning of the end. The escaping rebels retreated northward in small bodies.

Miyazaki was, with other towns, carried on the 31st of July, and northwards the fast-falling star of Saigo's imagined empire still pointed the way. Early in August there remained to Saigo but the single stronghold of Nobeoka, whither wended the remnants of his forces. But the imperial troops got there before them, and took possession of the castle on the 14th of August. They had, therefore, to defend themselves in the open. Reduced to less than ten thousand men, and with but a few rounds of powder, and that of very inferior quality, left to them, "they manfully contested every inch of ground, but were finally driven to an eminence near the centre of their position, and there completely hemmed in." At a council of war the hopelessness of their position was recognised, and orders were given for the troops to lay down their arms, whilst Saigo and those who were beyond the pale of possible mercy fought to the death. But the troops refused to surrender, preferring to die fighting for Saigo. In this emergency Saigo, Kirino, and other of the rebel generals determined to fly, and leave the mass of their men without excuse for further fighting. Accompanied by two hundred faithful *samurai*, they fell by night, during a thick fog, upon some of the imperial troops, threw them into disorder, carried off from their camps such supplies of food and ammunition as they could transport, and, passing beyond the imperial lines with these spoils, " disappeared amongst the mist-covered hills." The rebel army then surrendered, the war was considered at an end, and the disbanding of the temporary forces was commenced.

To the alarm of the government a telegram arrived in the capital on the 3rd of September announcing a rebel victory near to Kagoshima. Fresh troops and police were immediately despatched by sea from Tokio, and Nagasaki was put into a state of defence. Avoiding main roads, and advancing by secret or unfrequented paths, Saigo and his comrades had made their way towards Kagoshima, falling at one time upon the rearguard of a body of imperial troops that had been sent by sea under the command of General Miyoshi to defend the town, and had landed at Kajiki. This force vainly attempted to prevent Saigo from entering the town, which he passed into on the 10th of September. The only imperial troops in the place were some recruits, about a thousand in number, who were readily driven to the harbour-side. The civil authorities fled to a man-of-war. Saigo called by proclamation for fresh forces, and they speedily began to come in. Admiral Kawamura came in with the fleet from cruising off the coast of Hiuga, and landed a few miles to the north of Kagoshima. Joining his men to those of General Miyoshi, he marched upon the town to take Saigo in the rear. Saigo thereupon withdrew to the summit of a hill called Shiroyama, dominating a large part of the town, carrying with him guns, ammunition, and provisions, and there intrenching himself with about five hundred devoted followers. These were all of them, as Mr. Mounsey well says, "*samurai* of the *samurai*; all probably personal friends of their chief; all determined to sell their lives dearly, and all equally determined to die rather than surrender—five hundred lions driven back, after a long and weary chase, to their lair—no longer able to spring, but still capable of grappling with jaw and claw all that came within their reach." The imperialist chiefs surrounded the hill with fifteen thousand men, so placed and so sheltered by trenches and earthworks that every man composing such sorties as were attempted was destroyed. The rebels were hopelessly taken in the imperial toils.

On the 10th of September a bombardment with shell and mortar-fire was commenced, and under shelter of this the imperialist covered approaches were carried towards the hill-top, and feigned attacks were made to harass the rebel remnant that had already been reduced by nearly one half its number. On the 23rd of September, two of the " lions " came down from the lair to Admiral Kawamura, and asked (probably without Saigo's authority or knowledge) if the life of their chief would be spared. The admiral could now offer no conditions, but demanded an unconditional surrender, leaving all the rest to the mercy of the Mikado. He promised to wait till five in the afternoon, and added that if no communication reached him by that time he would give orders for the final assault. He kept his word, issued his orders, and before the next dawn, under cover of " a tremendous shower of shells," the assaulting parties went up to the summit, and poured a deadly fire into the rebel camp. Saigo fell wounded, and one of his lieutenants (Hemmi Jinroda) performed the friendly office of shearing off his general's head " with one blow of his keen heavy sword," that he might not fall alive into the hands of the imperialists. His generals and a hundred of his men fell around him, the remaining two hundred being taken prisoners, many of them in a wounded condition. The imperial loss was but thirty men. Although I have had the facts recounted to me more than once by eye-witnesses of this scene, I shall let Mr. Mounsey perform for me the melancholy office of describing the conclusion of this ghastly tragedy:—

" On the day succeeding the combat, the dead were brought down from the battle-field into the town for identification and burial. In the cemetery of the small temple of Jokoji, a broad trench had been dug, and near it the corpses of the fallen had been laid out side by side. It was then that the bodies of Kirino, Beppu, Hemmi, Murata, and the other leaders were recognised. All bore traces of the deadliness of the fight, and many were literally covered with wounds. Close to the body of Kirino lay the headless trunk of a tall, well-formed, powerful man, with a bullet-wound in the thigh and a stab in the stomach. Whilst the officers of the imperial army were discussing as to whether the body was that of Saigo or not, a head was brought in by some soldiers. It fitted the trunk, and was recognised as Saigo's head. It was disfigured and ghastly, clotted with blood and earth. Admiral Kawamura, the senior officer present, reverently washed the head with his own hands, as a mark of respect for his former friend and companion in arms during the war of the restoration. The bodies of Saigo and the leaders mentioned above by name were placed in coffins. The other corpses were wrapped in blankets. Saigo lies in the centre of the large grave where all are interred, and the rest are placed in rows on either side of him. Over the grave stands a large wooden tablet on which are inscribed the names of the dead, and the date on which they fell. Thousands of the people of Satsuma have since visited this grave, and there offered up their prayers; and, in the popular belief, the spirit of their once great general has taken up its abode in the planet Mars, and his figure may there be seen when this star is in the ascendant."

It is unnecessary for my present purpose to do more than state that the putting down of this formidable rebellion in 1877 cost the country eight and a quarter millions sterling, and to add that the officers engaged in the work received imperial decorations of the Order of the Rising Sun, and the men money gratuities. It may be interesting to quote Mr. Mounsey's translation of the words in which the Mikado conferred upon his relative, Prince Arisugawa, the highest decoration it was possible to bestow. His majesty said :—

"I, who by the will of Heaven am Emperor of Japan, descending in one unbroken line for ten thousand years, confer on you, Prince Arisugawa, a man of the highest merit, Commander-in-Chief of the Army, and President of the Senate, this decoration of the highest class of the Order of the Chrysanthemum, and you are herewith invested with all the dignities and privileges appertaining to the said order."

The prince was also created a field marshal.

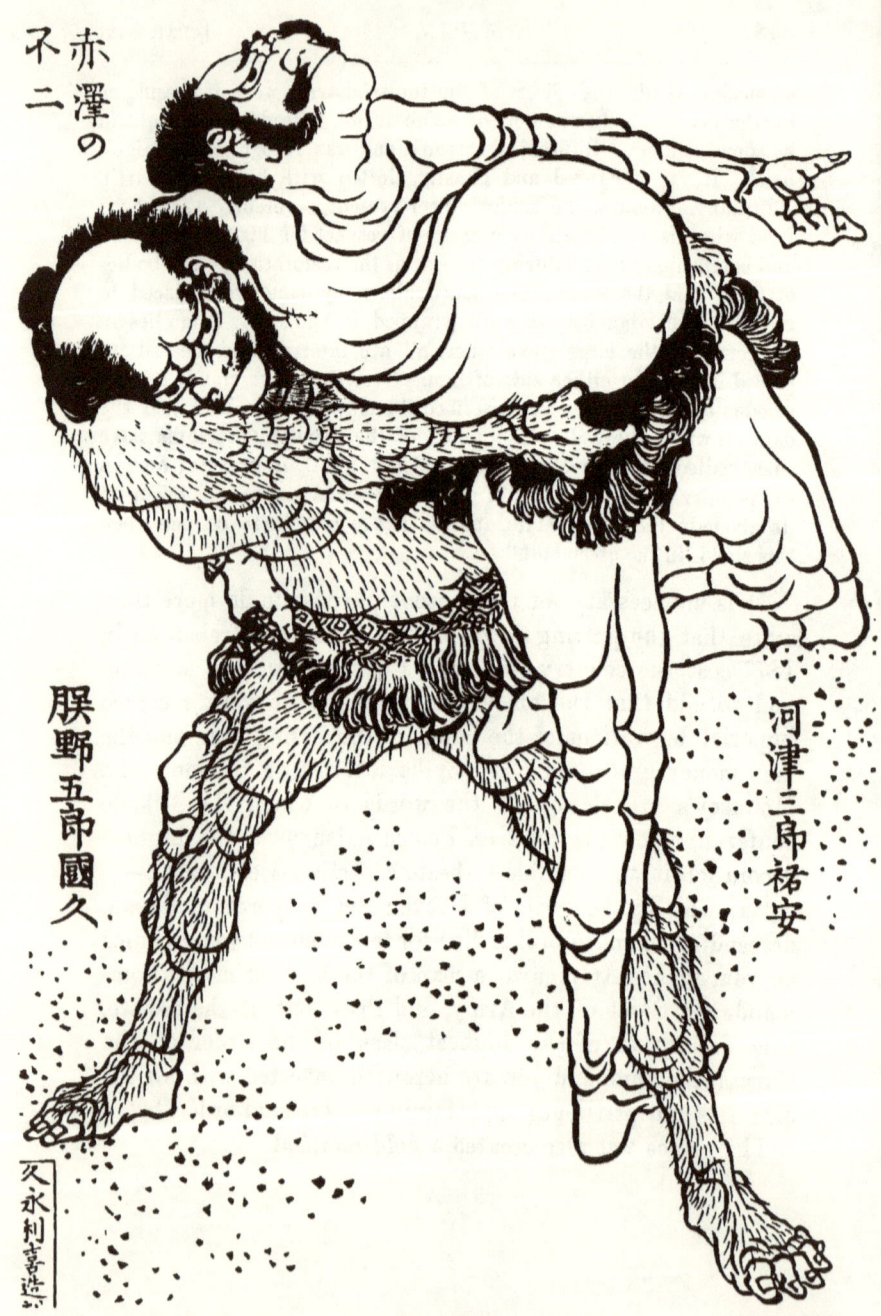

KAWADSU-NO-SABURO and MATANO-NO-GORO, two celebrated warriors, retainers of YORITOMO.
From HOKUSAI. Reproduced for this Work by a Japanese Engraver.

CHAPTER XX.

THE EMPEROR AND THE EXISTING GOVERNMENT.

The reigning emperor—The distracted empire to which he succeeded—His suppression of successive rebellions—Simplicity of his court—Reception by his majesty—The troubles of his reign—Its peaceful triumphs—The constitutional objects of the emperor—The new form of government—List of the cabinet—The prime minister Sanjo—The vice-minister Iwakura—Attack upon his life—Mr. Terashima, late foreign minister—Mr. Ito, the home minister—Mr. Okuma, the finance minister—His financial reforms —A Japanese Gladstone — General Saigo, minister at war—Admiral Kawamura, minister of marine—Enouyé Kawori, the new foreign minister—Attack upon him—His mission to Korea—Oki Takato, minister of justice—The conduct of business in Japan—General Kuroda Kiyotaku, the minister of agriculture and the colonies—His administration of Yezo—The senate—Progress of free institutions.

INTERESTING as Japan has been in the past on account of its romantic history, its singular religions, and its marvellous arts, it can hardly be questioned that the present emperor, his family, and his ministers have taken, and are taking, no less interesting parts in the great dramatic development of their country.

Those who have read the recent history of Japan, even hastily and ineffectively described as it may have been in this work, will remember in what a coil of domestic and foreign difficulties his country was enwrapped when, on the 3rd of February 1867, the young emperor, Mutsu-Hito, succeeded to the ancient throne. The forces of Choshiu had returned to their homes at the triumphant termination of their revolt against the Shogun. The Shogun's government, defeated by these rebels, and with a treasury exhausted in the vain attempt to subdue them, saw other great Daimios breaking away from it, and leaving it almost powerless against its enemies at home, and utterly incapable of resisting any more that invasion of the "barbarians" which had set in from abroad. The very foundations of the proud Tokugawa dynasty had been crumbling from beneath the feet of Iyémochi so rapidly and so irrevocably that, as the native historian says, "the Shogun was agitated by constant anxiety, and on the 19th of September (1866) he died at Osaka." A month before his own death the emperor Komei—whom, like his predecessors, the Tokugawas had so isolated and deprived of power that he had but them to cling to even when they themselves were actually falling—offered, as we saw, the appointment of Shogun to Keiki, he repeatedly declining it, and accepting it only when the emperor insisted upon its acceptance. Scarcely was the new occupant of what was then esteemed the throne of the Tokugawas seated upon it, when, like his deceased Shogun Iyémochi, "agitated by constant anxiety," the emperor Komei died. The Mikado's throne thus vacated, and rocking dangerously upon political earthquakes, so to speak, amid the din of foreign cannon and the clashing of rebellious arms, was that to which the present emperor then succeeded.

A mere youth of fifteen, the emperor came upon the scene, in the highest place, amidst that sudden outburst of European lights and systems which had just broken upon Japan through the long twilight of its insulated life. Within less than a year from his ascension he abolished the Shogunate. He then proceeded to put down the rebellion of the ex-Shogun, and many another rebellion in various parts of the country; shifted the seat of government to the maritime city of Yedo, and modified the immemorial and exclusive despotism of the Mikados' rule by commencing to govern with the advice and assistance of a cabinet. He also began, as we shall presently see, to lay the foundations of municipal and political government by and for the people; established a widespread system of elementary education; founded universities, colleges, hospitals, and schools of science and art; created an army, a navy, and a police force, which are the admiration of all who know them; and has furnished a model of domestic excellence, economy, and orderly life to all his ministers and people. I had the honour of presentation to his majesty very soon after our arrival in Tokio, and have no hesitation in acknowledging the interest with which I looked forward to it. A special reception by such a ruler of such a country, at such a period of its history as this, would have been a privilege conferred upon any one, and was the greater when conferred upon myself, whose only personal claim to it was the faithful execution of certain business engagements.

The palace in which the emperor now resides is in many respects a makeshift, although situated in beautiful gardens, and possibly sufficient for the requirements of a court so simple in its ceremonies and its functions of state as that which his majesty has been content to establish. It was, in the days of the Tycoons, the *Yashiki* of the lords of Kiushiu, and is situated just outside one of the gates of the grounds of the former castle of Yedo. It is a purely Japanese residence, with the exception that in some of its walls glass panes are substituted for paper, the ante-room is furnished in European style, and the audience-chamber is supplied with a chair or throne, also of European style. I was accompanied to the palace by his excellency Admiral Kawamura and by Flag-Lieutenant Hattori, of the imperial navy, who has served in several of our ships, speaks English like an Englishman, and on this occasion as on many others during my visit kindly officiated as interpreter. It is needless to detail the incidents of the visit beyond saying that his majesty wore a uniform of European fashion, and was attended by the two imperial princes Arisugawa-no-Miya and Higashi-Fushimi-no-Miya, the former of whom, as we know, was the commander-in-chief in Satsuma during the suppression of the rebellion. The prime minister, Sanjo Saneyoshi, and two or three other ministers, were likewise present. His majesty did me the honour of addressing to me the following observations, which, as being his, the reader will excuse me for publishing, although, if modesty alone had to be regarded, I would gladly withhold them.

The emperor said: "It gives me great pleasure to see you visit my country from such a distant land. The three men-of-war, which by my particular desire were constructed under your special care, have duly arrived, and are very successful. I do not doubt that the success of these ships is entirely due to your able and skilful management. I wish you future prosperity and good health."

I need hardly say that my reply was the briefest possible expression of grateful thanks for the honour done me, and of the pleasure I had enjoyed in working for his majesty. On leaving the presence, tea and confections were served in the ante-room, and, in accordance with a pleasing Japanese custom, the confections were afterwards sent to our residence, in trays bearing the imperial crest. The impression made upon my mind by this presentation to the emperor was that Japan is now ruled by a monarch who possesses in a remarkable degree the qualities which command the respect and loyalty of mankind. Young as he is (being but twenty-seven years old at the date referred to), the anxieties and labours of his arduous reign have told seriously upon him. Many are the troubles he has had to bear, affliction after affliction descending upon him. In addition to great griefs of state—revolts and rebellions coming in swift succession in the early years of his reign, followed in later days by the defection of one trusted minister, the murder of another, and the attempted assassination of a third,—in addition to these, he has had to bow to the sorest of all imperial and domestic woes, the loss of the children of his love, and the consequent failure (for the time at least) of the succession to his heirs. The countenance of the emperor is, as it must be, sad, grievously so for one so young; but with its sadness is mixed an earnestness and proof of purpose which show that trouble has not lessened in him the sense of his great responsibilities, as the head of a nation numbering nearly thirty-three millions of souls, and undergoing in a few years the changes and transformations of many centuries. I was repeatedly informed by those who knew the emperor well that he is second to none in the empire in solicitous regard for the well-being of the people, and that in point of ability and practical statesmanship there are but few of his countrymen who could venture to compete with him. For my part, remembering the antiquity of his dynasty, the singular conditions under which it has existed for many a long century, the strange and sacred-seeming seclusion from which it has emerged in his person, the vitality with which it has outlived the long lines of military usurpers, the persistence of its struggle against foreign intrusion, the wisdom with which it accepted that intrusion when it became inevitable—the courage with which its present representative has faced all dangers, conquered all enemies, given strength and peace and freedom to the people, and won for himself the respect of all the nations of the earth—I say, remembering all these things, for my part I know of no more interesting or worthy figure in contemporary life than this youthful emperor of the Land of the Rising Sun. No doubt his majesty has had the advantage of wise and good men for advisers, and is at present assisted by a cabinet of men at once well-acquainted with the condition of the country and desirous of leading it along the paths of progress. But the choice of capable ministers is one of the best evidences of wisdom in a sovereign, and the present emperor has given such abundant proofs of great personal qualities that his name and fame will for ever remain associated with both the military and the peaceful triumphs of his reign.

During our stay in Japan we had many opportunities of making personal acquaintance with the men who at present constitute the government of the country. And here it may be well to mention that the government is at present necessarily of a very centralised character, and must remain so while the country is being prepared for the adoption of a popular or representative system. Those who are conversant with the difficulties that attend the working of representative government—and both England and America, having many times experienced these difficulties in the past, are still experiencing some of them even now—must be well aware that the passage from the close and rigid feudal system of Japan (which flourished down to 1867) to a parliamentary system can only with safety be made gradually, and those are enemies and not friends of Japan who would urge the country to rush with heedless impetuosity along the path of political progress. Mr. Mounsey correctly and judiciously states the case when he says: "As at present constituted, the government is an oligarchy, composed of a small body of the most enlightened and enterprising men in the country, ruling under the supreme authority of the Mikado; but, if Japan is to continue to assimilate European institutions, this form of government can only be transitional, and the provincial assemblies will, in all probability, be eventually developed into a national parliament."* Having had the best opportunities for ascertaining the opinions of the government, I can state with confidence that this is precisely the view which the ministers of Japan themselves take of the position, their great anxiety being to assist the emperor in carrying out his oath of 1868,† as he earnestly desires to do, and to move forward neither too swiftly for the peace and security of the country, nor too slowly for the rapid development of those representative institutions which, as they know, form the surest basis for internal tranquillity and external respect. Mr. Mounsey, to what I have already quoted, well adds: "The difficulties in the way of such a vast change must be self-evident to all who bear in mind the shortness of the interval which separates Japan from its first acquaintance with Europe, and the country will require the services of all its best men to surmount them. It is, therefore, to be hoped that the Satsuma rebellion, which deprived Japan of two of her most prominent public men . . . may have proved to the members of all political schools in Japan the uselessness of precipitation and violence, and

---

* 'The Satsuma Rebellion' (Murray).   † See page 280

the necessity of moderation ; and that thus any constitutional changes which may be considered advantageous to the country may be effected without civil war or bloodshed, and in a gradual and peaceable manner."

The form of the present government is as follows. There is first the supreme council, or cabinet, which is composed nearly as our own cabinet is composed. This body is designated the Dai-jo Kuwan (great governing council), taking that designation from a council constituted in the eighth century. At that ancient period the Dai-jo Kuwan was formed to relieve of part of its duties a still older and greater council, named Jin Gi Kuwan (council of the gods). In the modern supreme council are centred all the power and authority of the empire, so that the difficulties of a divided government is obviated. It is composed of a prime minister, two vice prime ministers, and several other ministers who preside over the departments of state * The following is a list of the present members of the Dai-jo Kuwan, or cabinet †:—

Sanjo Saneyoshi, Prime Minister.
Iwakura Tomomi, Vice   „
Terashima Munénori, Minister of Foreign Affairs.
Ito Hirobumi,   „   Home   „
Okuma Shigenobu,   „   Finance.
Saigo Tsukumichi,   „   War.
Kawamura Sumiyoshi,   „   Marine.
Enouyé Kawori,   „   Public Works.
Oki Takato,   „   Justice.
Kuroda Kiyotaka,   „   Colonies and Agriculture.

---

* The prime minister is designated Dai-jo-Dai-jin, or great minister of the great government, a title which, like those about to be mentioned, comes down from the ancient period named in the text. The vice prime ministers are designated Sa Dai-jin, great minister of the left, and U Dai-jin, great minister of the right. The remaining ministers are known as Sanghi, or Sangi, which means high councillors.

† The list of cabinet ministers given in the text was prepared at the time of our visit. Subsequently Mr. Terashima vacated the foreign office, in which he has been succeeded by Mr. Enouyé. The latter has been succeeded in the public works department by General Yamada, and Mr. Terashima has become minister of education.

These are all men distinguished in the country, and of several of them I have had occasion to make mention in former chapters. The prime minister, Sanjo, took a very leading part, as we have seen, in the changes that led to the imperial restoration; and although in his earlier years he shared, as was natural, the views and feelings of the Kioto court, in which he had been brought up, being himself a Kugé, or court noble, there has not of late years, I am informed, been a more loyal supporter of the new order of things than he, or one more devoted on the one hand to the emperor and on the other to his colleagues in the cabinet and to the people of the country. The holding by Sanjo of the office of prime minister has had a great effect in reconciling the antagonisms of the ancient and modern systems. His vice minister, Iwakura, a court noble like himself, also took an active part in the transition from feudalism to the present form of government. Brought up as Kugé at the court city, and becoming in early life a personal attendant upon the Mikado, he was one of the few whose energetic action in 1867–68 effected the abolition of the Shogunate and the restoration of the imperial power. When, early in the latter year, the dominant court party were overthrown, and the youthful emperor rescued, so to speak, from their hands, Prince Arisugawa was for the time entrusted with the supreme administration, and these two, Sanjo and Iwakura, became his assistants. They have ever since remained at the head of affairs. But while Iwakura probably did more than any other individual in those critical times to restore and secure the independence of the Mikado, he was not in those days by any means an advocate of unrestricted foreign interference with his country. At a later period he was nominated the head of a Japanese mission to Europe and America, which left Japan in December 1871, and which had for its primary object the relaxation of some of the stipulations pressed upon Japan by foreign governments. He has therefore had foreign as well as home experience to guide his recent policy.* That policy is entirely in accord with that of the chief minister, Sanjo, and of his other cabinet colleagues. This minister, in 1874, came very near forfeiting his life in the service of his country. On the night of the 14th of January of that year he was returning from an interview with the emperor, and was attacked just outside the Kuchigai gate of the castle of Tokio, by fourteen men from the province of Tosa. "In the twinkling of an eye, his *betto* was cut down, the driver wounded, and the sides of the carriage pierced and cut to ribbons with spear-points and sword-blades. Iwakura, wounded in two places, leaped out on the edge of the moat. He fell, and rolled into the water. The foiled assassins, in the pitch darkness, not daring to linger for search, and unable to see or find their victim, made off. In spite of wounds, cold, and immersion, the U Dai-jin recovered" (Griffis). The Tosa men were soon afterwards captured, tried, and executed.

Mr. Terashima, the minister for foreign affairs, is a gentleman of singular talents, whose long connection with the foreign office has made him closely acquainted with the relations existing between his own and other countries. He is a Satsuma man, with a considerable knowledge of our language, and has devoted most of his efforts for several years past to the recovery for the Mikado and his government of those imperial rights and that liberty of action within their own country that the foreign powers wrested from them in the days of their revolutionary troubles—a laudable and proper object, which England alone, or chiefly now, resists, but will doubtless not resist much longer.

Mr. Ito, the home minister, is an accomplished English

---

* "Mr. Iwakura was a man of much ability. He had belonged to the anti-foreign party, but lately had been converted to what was called the liberal cause. He left Japan accompanied by the brightest lights of the empire, Okubo, Kido, and many others. His object in visiting the United States and the several countries of Europe was: 1, to revise the treaties, and 2, to gather as much information as possible concerning the circumstances of foreign countries, their industries, their customs, systems of government, &c."—Le Gendre's 'Progressive Japan.'

scholar, speaking our language with perfect fluency. He also has travelled abroad, having formed one of the Iwakura mission to America and Europe, and has held other offices in the state, being much looked up to as one of the ablest men in the country, in every way well fitted to improve its administration and develop its resources.

Mr. Okuma, the finance minister, is an extraordinary example of the manner in which the Japanese character, especially in its intellectual functions, adapts itself to European systems. I have had the advantage of many conversations with this gentleman, and but for the fact of an interpreter being necessary—in consequence of his facility in the use of our language being limited, while my ignorance of Japanese is almost total—I might well have imagined on such occasions that I was conversing with one of those half-dozen eminent financiers whom the Liberal party at home have in reserve as future Chancellors of the Exchequer. The most characteristic feature of his financial administration is one which has worked with great advantage of late years under our own treasury. It consists in forcing the so-called spending departments—the army, navy, public works, etc., to conform their expenditure to their estimates, obtaining new credits for any outlays which prove indispensable, and paying into the treasury all the savings which are effected. Taking an example from our naval administration, I may say that before the adoption of this system it was possible for the admiralty to greatly exceed its expenditure upon repairs of old vessels, for example, and to recoup the extra outlay by selling vessels which could be spared. This is no longer possible, all receipts from the sale of old vessels being taken direct to the treasury credits. The same check has been adopted, by Mr. Okuma's advice, in the administration of the public departments in Japan; and I cannot better illustrate his character as a finance minister than by quoting the following from a translation of one of his submissions to the prime minister. He said: "It is my opinion that any fixed system of finance is difficult to establish, and easy to be destroyed; that it is difficult to preserve pure in its springs, and liable to be polluted in its course. Estimates are necessary in order to prevent irregular expenditure, and to strengthen habits of economy. If this object is not attended to and this evil repressed, the projects of officials will be allowed free scope, their minds will become relaxed, requests will be acceded to which ought not to be granted, and there will be an increase of expenditure which ought to have been curtailed. If this evil overflowing from above should find its way below, and the amount fixed here should be exceeded, these tables would be no better than books on a shelf, and in the end no good result would be attained by them. My apprehensions are no doubt excessive, but I have felt bound to state my honest opinion." This language might have come from the pen of Mr. Gladstone. The government issued a decree embodying the finance regulations thus advocated by this able minister.

General Saigo, the minister at war, is an officer of the highest repute in Japan. It is his melancholy distinction to be the brother of Marshal Saigo, whose name, notwithstanding his great and splendid personal qualities, will go down to future generations as that of the unsuccessful rebel of Satsuma, whose revolt inflicted terrible griefs, wrongs, and losses upon his country at a time when it most deserved the patient service of its sons. This revolt was a source of the greatest pain and trouble to his brother, the present minister, whose sympathy was throughout with the imperial government, though distracted by his regard for a brother whom he warmly loved and admired. The present general and minister, after greatly distinguishing himself in the wars of the restoration, and more especially in the hard fighting at Wooyeno in Tokio, brilliantly commanded, it will be remembered, the Japanese army in Formosa, and now wears upon his wrist a bracelet of silver placed there by the Formosan chieftains in token of their submission to him. When the recent Satsuma troubles began, General Saigo of course found himself in a very unhappy position, being one of the most highly placed of the loyal generals, and yet with war to be made upon his own beloved, though misguided, brother. He nevertheless performed his duty nobly.* Previously, General Saigo had been vice-president of a commission, of which the lamented minister Okubo was the president, and the object of which was to represent Japan at the American Centennial Exhibition. After the Satsuma war was over, and the brother slain, General Saigo was called upon to play an accidental but painful part, in May 1878, as the discoverer of the remains of his friend and comrade Okubo, whom half-a-dozen men from Kaga had assassinated and left by the wayside, as elsewhere related. As General Saigo is a relation of Admiral Kawamura by marriage, and a frequent visitor to his house, we had many opportunities of seeing and conversing with him, these opportunities being much increased in number by the repeated kindnesses and hospitalities shown to us by the general himself. The general is every inch a soldier, and well fitted to be the war minister of a wealthier and more powerful country than Japan—although I doubt not that he would make Japan powerful enough to satisfy any one if he had free command of the "sinews of war." The financial straits of Japan make it necessary for the emperor and his cabinet to keep the expenditure upon both the army and the navy down to the lowest possible point consistent with their maintenance in a state of efficiency at their present nominal strength, and to this necessity General Saigo and Admiral Kawamura both submit with the best grace; but it is impossible to meet and mix with these ministers without observing that their visits abroad have had the effect of inspiring them with the ambition of endowing Japan with as much as possible of that scientific fighting strength which has come, oddly

---

* "The execution of all these measures [for increasing the imperial army] fell to the lot of General Saigo, a younger brother of the rebel commander, who, in the absence of Yamagata and Oyama, the minister and vice-minister of war, had charge of the war office. His post was not an enviable one, for, putting aside the feelings induced by near relationship, fears of disturbances in Tokio were entertained by many people, and were increased by the occurrence of an unusually large number of fires, many of which were attributed to incendiarism."— *Mounsey.*

enough, to command far more respect than anything else at the present time among the great Christian and civilised states of Europe. In spite of the recent tragedies with which he has been associated, General Saigo is a man of excessive energy and buoyancy of spirit, and although having but a limited acquaintance with our language, contrived to add greatly to the enjoyment of our visit.

Of Admiral Kawamura I have had to speak already in the brief story of the Satsuma rebellion, in the suppression of which he took so leading a part. I first had the pleasure of making this officer's acquaintance on the occasion of his visiting England a few years ago, to obtain information respecting our navy and naval services. The brief hospitality which I was able to extend to him, and of which he has ever since been unduly mindful, gave me the opportunity of observing with how much directness of purpose and clearness of judgment the high officers of Japan were able to penetrate into the most novel and complicated subjects of inquiry, and I for one was not surprised to learn that Admiral Kawamura had soon afterwards succeeded to the ministry of marine, or later, that he had been entrusted, though a Satsuma man, to serve as the principal adviser of the imperial Prince Arisugawa during the late Satsuma war. Nor was I surprised, either, at the zealous friendship which he then displayed in his endeavours to allay the anger and avert the treason of the disaffected marshal, or at the firmness and ability with which, when all persuasions failed, he bent his whole energies to the subjugation of his rebellious relative.

Of his excellency Enouyé Kawori, the minister of public works, I have for some time enjoyed the personal friendship, as he recently resided for some years in London, acquiring a perfect command of our language, and diligently studying our political and municipal institutions, our modes of conducting public business, our public works' systems, and above all those great principles of national finance which have contributed more than anything else to the acknowledged eminence of this country in financial credit. Returning to

Japan with the results of such studies, and of the observations of a keen observer of men and things, Mr. Enouyé was almost immediately appointed to a place in the cabinet as minister of public works, which was vacated by Mr. Ito's transfer to the home office. The addition of such a man to the government of Japan must be of great advantage to the country at a time when finance on the one hand and foreign relations on the other form the most important subjects of cabinet deliberation. Mr. Enouyé once came even nearer than Mr. Iwakura to sacrificing his life for his country, his foreign associations and sympathy with the new order of things having led to his being cut down in the most dreadful manner in the days of the *samurai* discontents, and left, bleeding from head to foot, with many wounds, to an apparently certain death. It being winter time, and snow lying upon the ground, his wounds were stanched by the cold till help arrived, and thus his life was preserved. He was associated with General Kuroda in his mission to Korea in 1875, after which he made a long visit to England, as previously stated.*

In a preceding chapter we have made the acquaintance of his excellency Oki Takato, the minister of justice. His first office under the new government was, as we have seen, that of minister of education, which he became in June 1871. In October 1872 he was appointed minister of religion also. In the following year he was made minister of justice, with a seat in the cabinet. I had the advantage of frequently meeting this distinguished member of the government, and found him keenly alive to the importance of a prompt and efficient administration of justice, and minutely acquainted with the practice of the courts. No one whom I met seemed more sensible than he of the necessity for further reforms in the law, some of which he was good enough to sketch during our conversations. In fact nothing is more remarkable in the intercourse which one had with the ministers of Japan than

---

* Since the above was written Mr Enouyé has, as stated in a previous footnote, become minister of foreign affairs—a post for which his antecedents, no less than his remarkable abilities, eminently qualify him.

the total absence of that lethargy and indifference which we are accustomed to attribute to all Eastern peoples.

No doubt a good deal of time is sometimes lost in the transaction of business, and Europeans in Japan have had often to complain of uncertainty and variableness in official quarters. But I am persuaded that this has been due to the novelty of the business and of the business methods that have come suddenly into vogue, and not at all to Oriental idleness in the men who have undertaken to govern. We are apt to forget that in Japan we have to deal with men who have had to cast away every tradition, every habit, and every principle and mode of action with which even the youngest of them began official life. Old things have passed away, and *all* things have become new. But I can with confidence assert that whenever it has been my duty to discuss business matters with the ministers of Japan, either at home or abroad, I have had no cause whatever to complain of delay or indifference, or any dilatory tendency whatever.

The last of the ministers whom I have to name, but not the least, is General Kuroda Kiyotaka, the minister in charge of the agriculture of the country and of the colonial department, the chief duty of which latter is to administer the government of the great northern island of Yezo. We lately saw this officer employed on a mission to Korea, which was fulfilled with so much skill that war was avoided, although the relations between Korea and Japan remain far from satisfactory.* General Kuroda is a member of an ancient and distinguished princely house, and himself a brave and experienced officer, who rendered good service during the insurrections that followed the abolition of the Shogunate. In the administration of Yezo the general has an arduous and important duty to fulfil, and he wisely spends much of his

---

* "The Korean affair ended happily. . . . Kuroda Kiyotaka with men-of-war entered Korean waters. Patience, skill, and tact were crowned with success. On behalf of Japan, a treaty of peace, friendship, and commerce was made between the two countries, Feb. 27, 1876. Japan has thus peacefully opened this last of the hermit nations to the world."—*Griffis*.

time in the island. personally inspecting the many mining and other operations in progress there.

The above ministers compose the present Dai-jo Kuwan, or cabinet. The second of the governing bodies of the state is the Genro-In (house of seniors), or senate.* This body is composed of nobles, men who have served the country with recognised distinction (*sonin*), officers who have given signal proofs of ability in the administrative departments, and men eminent in politics throughout the country. In creating this body the emperor's decree intimated that it was to enlarge the law-creating power, and although in the rules framed for its guidance by the prime minister, Sanjo, its powers are more restricted, as was to be expected, than those of our House of Lords, and although the initiative of its business comes from above, even those who complain of its constitution and operation admit that very much is to be said in favour of this body, so far as it goes. The American general Le Gendre, for example (in the work just quoted in a footnote), who criticises the rules of the senate adversely, admits that "the rules of the Genro-In, although restrictive, were so worded that to convert it into a thoroughly legislative assembly only one of the articles had to be changed;" and explains that "this was the seventh, whereby the power of the Mikado regarding the enactment of laws was made exclusive and absolute." I am bound to say that his appears to me to be a somewhat far-fetched complaint, nor is it altogether reasonable to suppose that the Mikado and the cabinet could in any case concede full legislative powers to a single body composed as this senate is; still less is it to be supposed that the sovereign should surrender all control over the legislation of the country in its present condition. To expect this is to expect a greater surrender of power than any constitutional monarch that we know of has exercised, and greater than the president of the United States Republic even

---

* "*Gen* means root and *ro* old, and the two taken together mean old men. *In* means house; so that *Genro-In* means old men's house; and, inasmuch as age is supposed to give experience, and experience wisdom, wise men's house."—Le Gendre's 'Progressive Japan.'

has been called upon to make. It cannot be doubted that the creation of this senate was a remarkable evidence of the earnestness of the emperor in his expressed desire to gradually popularise the system of government; nor can it be doubted that this influential body has rendered, and is rendering, good service. As it gains experience and wisdom it will gain increased power, and will ultimately acquire the same kind and measure of power as our own House of Lords possesses; but before this can be brought about, the representative system has to be gradually developed, as it doubless will be. In these matters, however, "great haste" may prove "less speed," and prudent men will not urge Japan to attempt in a day what other nations have taken far longer to accomplish.

Last year (1878) another most remarkable step was made in furtherance of representative institutions, elective assemblies being established throughout the empire. They are to be local assemblies, sitting in March of each year for not more than a month, and, subject to the control of the home minister, are to deal with all questions of local taxation. They may also petition the central government on other matters of local interest. The qualifications for membership are an age of not less than twenty-five years, a three years' residence in the electoral district, and the payment of a land-tax within that district of not less than £2. The qualification for electors (males only) are an age of twenty years, inscription on the register, and payment of a land-tax of £1. The voting is by ballot, but the names of the voters are to be written by themselves on the voting papers. I cannot help thinking that by thus cautiously but steadily advancing along the approved path of political progress the emperor and the existing government of Japan are insuring a better future for their country than would be at all likely to result from a less gradual method of proceeding.

END OF VOL. I.

www.ingramcontent.com/pod-product-compliance
Lightning Source LLC
Chambersburg PA
CBHW051732300426
44115CB00007B/523